D0080582

Here are four good reasons why you should buy the new edition of *What If?*

1. **New Exercises.** The third edition features many new class-tested exercises that aim to improve your writing techniques and to enlarge your understanding of the art and craft of fiction.

2. **New Student Examples.** These examples provide you with models of work created by your peers. Many of these examples have gone on to become published stories.

3. **Over 25 percent of the stories in the book's mini-anthology are new.** Many stories have been replaced with new, highly teachable, contemporary selections. These include works by ZZ Packer, Richard Russo, Dagoberto Gilb, Sandra Cisneros, and Bruce Holland Rogers. One story, "Leave of Absence," by Jennifer Shaff went through several drafts in Pamela Painter's Revision Workshop at Emerson College (see Exercise 86), and went on to be selected by Jane Smiley, who edited *Best New American Voices of 2006.*

4. **New Quotations.** Writing-related quotations are included to inspire your writing and serve as signposts for your life as a fiction writer.

PEARSON
Longman

Other Books by the Authors

ANNE BERNAYS

Novels
Trophy House
Professor Romeo
The Address Book

The School Book
Growing up Rich

The First to Know
Prudence, Indeed
The New York Ride
Short Pleasures
Nonfiction
Back Then; Two Lives in 1950's New York (with Justin Kaplan)
The Language of Names (with Justin Kaplan)

PAMELA PAINTER

Getting to Know the Weather
The Long and Short of It

WHAT IF?

Writing Exercises for Fiction Writers

THIRD EDITION

COLLEGE EDITION

Anne Bernays

Nieman Foundation, Harvard University
Lesley University

Pamela Painter

Emerson College
Vermont College

Longman

Boston   Columbus   Indianapolis   New York   San Francisco   Upper Saddle River
Amsterdam   Cape Town   Dubai   London   Madrid   Milan   Munich   Paris   Montreal   Toronto
Delhi   Mexico City   São Paulo   Sydney   Hong Kong   Seoul   Singapore   Taipei   Tokyo

Senior Acquisitions Editor: Vivian Garcia
Senior Supplements Editor: Donna Campion
Executive Marketing Manager: Joyce Nilsen
Production Manager: Bob Ginsberg
Project Coordination, Text Design, and Electronic Page Makeup: Electronic Publishing
   Services Inc., NYC
Cover Design Manager/Cover Designer: Wendy Ann Fredericks
Cover Photo: © Cormac Hanley/Photonica/Getty Images
Senior Manufacturing Buyer: Alfred C. Dorsey
Printer and Binder: RR Donnelley & Sons Company/Harrisonburg
Cover Printer: Lehigh Phoenix

This college edition is published by Pearson Education, Inc., by arrangement with
HarperCollins.

For permission to use copyrighted material, grateful acknowledgment is made to the
copyright holders on pp. 433–434, which are hereby made part of this copyright page.

Library of Congress Cataloging-in-Publication Data
Bernays, Anne.
    What if? : Writing exercises for fiction writers / Anne Bernays and Pamela
Painter. — 3rd ed.
      p. cm.
    Includes bibliographical references.
    ISBN-13: 978-0-205-61688-6
    ISBN-10: 0-205-61688-7
  1. English language—Rhetoric—Problems, exercises, etc.   2. Fiction—Technique—
Problems, exercises, etc.   3. Fiction—Authorship—Problems, exercises, etc.
4. Fiction—Authorship—Textbooks. I. Painter, Pamela. II. Title.
PE1413.B47   2009
808.3—dc22   2009013048

16 DOH 16 15

Longman
is an imprint of

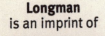

www.pearsonhighered.com

ISBN-13: 978-0-205-61688-6
ISBN-10:   0-205-61688-7

To Our Students

Contents

PART THREE
Point of View,
Perspective, Distance 55

PART FOUR
Dialogue 73

PART FIVE
The Interior Landscape
of Your Characters 89

PART SIX
Plot 111

PART SEVEN
The Elements of Style 133

PART EIGHT
A Writer's Toolbox 143

PART NINE
Invention and a
Bit of Inspiration   169

PART TEN
Revision: Rewriting Is Writing   197

PART ELEVEN
Sudden, Flash, Micro, Nano: Writing the Short Short Story 223

PART TWELVE
Learning from the Greats 247

PART THIRTEEN
Notebooks, Journals, and Memory 261

PART FOURTEEN
A Collection of Short Short Stories 273

PART FIFTEEN
A Collection of Short Stories 287

Preface

W*hat If?* was designed to help the beginning writer get started—and to continue until the short story or novel has been completed. Over the years, we have taught numerous workshops—using exercises—and at times deciding not to use exercises. We discovered that, by far, exercises are the more effective method for exploring the wonderful array of tools that every writer should have in their writer's toolbox. And we don't waste time on that pesky question "can writing be taught." We agree with John Barth, who said in the *New York Times* Book Review, "I'm not going to address whether it can be taught, it is."

The exercises in this book fall largely into one of three categories: those that stretch the imagination, those that refine the kind of sensibility writers of fiction must have, and those that focus on a specific skill or tool. Each one is intended to focus on a single aspect of the process of shaping an idea and extending it into a strong work of fiction. The exercises are short and as arbitrary as piano scales or athletic workouts. Very few people are "natural" writers in the sense that they know exactly what to do to tell a good, compelling story. Most of us need some guidance and this is what the exercises in this book are guaranteed to do.

What If? Writing Exercises for Fiction Writers was first published in 1990 in a shorter version, with no stories and many fewer exercises. Since then the book has received enthusiastic responses from teachers, students of writing, and others interested in learning the skills needed to write a compelling story or novel. More than any other consideration, this book puts the process and the practice of writing ahead of theoretical, abstract, or emotional approaches. Students learn to write not by thinking about writing or negotiating with their feelings but by sitting down and actually writing.

Approach and Organization

Conventional wisdom urges beginning writers to get in touch with their feelings. We're convinced that these feeling are like wild horses; it's our job as writers to round them up, tame them, and make them behave the way we want them to. Out of this conviction came a second one, namely that structure helps rather than hinders those who are just starting to explore a new discipline. Absolute freedom, as in "go home and write a story," leads the student to flounder and to make the same mistakes over and over again. By breaking down the elements of fiction, we give students the opportunity to master each of these—one at a time.

The format of this third edition remains essentially the same as the previous editions. The book is organized around the following topics: Beginnings; Characterization; Point of View, Perspective, Distance; Dialogue; The Interior Landscape of Your Characters; Plot; The Elements of Style; A Writer's Toolbox; Invention and a Bit of Inspiration; Revision: Rewriting Is Writing; Sudden, Flash, Micro, Nano: Writing the

Short Short Story; Learning from the Greats; and Notebooks, Journals, and Memory. There is also a selection of short-short and longer stories at the back of the book.

As before, each section starts with a short introduction and goes on to offer exercises that fall into the topic at hand, each one starting with an introductory paragraph, followed by instructions on how to do the exercise, a paragraph explaining its objective, and finally, in most cases, an example of how the particular exercise was done by one of our students—the student example. (We are pleased to note that many of the exercises that were included in earlier editions of *What If?* have now become full-fledged, published stories in *The Atlantic, GlimmerTrain,* and *North American Review,* among others.)

Enduring Features

As in the previous editions, this edition includes exercises by other fiction writers who are also teachers—Douglas Bauer, Ron Carlson, DeWitt Henry, Hester Kaplan, William Kittredge, Margot Livesey, David Ray, Frederick Reiken, and Melanie Rae Thon among others, and, sprinkled throughout are quotes about writing from well-known and wise authors, both living and dead.

New to This Edition

We haven't added new sections to this edition of *What If?* because the individual sections from the last edition have served our students well. Rather, we have added completely new exercises to most sections in order to put more tools in each sections' toolbox. For example, the new exercise "Second Sentences as Different Paths" opens up a world of possibilities, even probabilities, with just this one exercise. "The Morning After" asks your characters to confront a difficult situation—after they've had an entire night, perhaps a sleepless night, to reflect on what they've done. "Five Years From Now" illustrates how the statement can affect a story's structure—depending on whether this is said at the beginning of a story or at the end. Another exercise, "How to Keep Narrative Moving Forward," asks the student writer to pretend she has her foot on the gas pedal as she reads a story to determine how fast or how slowly, and how effectively, the narrative is moving forward. "Story Swap" from Jordan Dann of the Aspen Writers' Foundation asks the writer to walk in someone else's shoes. And we have also added exercises that experiment with form: Students are asked to write a story that is all questions, or explore subtext in the contrapuntal duet of "he said/she said," or write tiny stories we call "nano" fictions. We have deleted the section on humor because it is such a difficult and problematic subject to teach, especially in this format. We do urge, however, that beginning writers keep in mind that humor does not take away from the seriousness of a story—but instead, used judiciously, enhances it. So now our exercise on humor is more of a mini-essay titled "An Intact Frog."

Finally, in addition to retaining superb stories by Charles Baxter, Kate Wheeler, and Ron Carlson, we have added new stories by ZZ Packer, Richard Russo, Dagoberto Gilb, Sandra Cisneros, and Bruce Holland Rogers, stories that best illustrate the art and craft of fiction.

Since *What If?* was first published, this book has been used by undergraduates and extension school classes, graduate writing programs, writing conferences, and high school writing classes. People writing alone use it. References to *What If?* appear on hundreds of blogs. And our writing friends report that they continue to dip into it for inspiration and direction when they are beginning a new novel or have encountered a thorny issue in a story.

Suggestions on How to Use *What If?*

Many teachers we know create their own path through *What If?* And the class syllabi that are based on *What If?* are as different as igloos, tents, and triple-deckers. One teacher might begin with "Notebooks, Journals, and Memory," another might begin with "Characterization" or "Learning from the Greats." Using the structure of our exercises as a model, some teachers require their students to create their own exercises based on the work of a writer they admire. This assignment encourages students to read like a writer. Another teacher instructs her students to write five first sentences every week so that at semester's end each student will have fifty to seventy-five possible new stories to return to. This teacher, halfway through the semester, tells her students to begin to attach second sentences to the thirty new first sentences they have just finished. Other teachers have come up with ways to use the quotes. One asks her students to write a short paragraph each week in response to a quote from *What If?* that becomes a personal sign post for their own writing process. Another instructor tells her students to find quotes from interviews with writers, to bring copies for the class that are then taped into their copies of *What If?* Their textbooks are bristling with new wisdom by the end of the semester. But most of all, we encourage students and also writers working on their own to find their own path through *What If?* and then go back and take a few detours. And to truly take to heart and mind the words "what if?"

Acknowledgments

During our revisions, we have had help, encouragement, and advice from a lot of people. We want to thank all our students who have done the exercises and offered suggestions. We thank the students who contributed their examples—students from Arizona, California, Connecticut, Massachusetts, Michigan, Ohio, Tennessee, Utah, Vermont, Copenhagen, and Paris. They are too numerous to name here, but it has been gratifying to see many of these student examples enlarged to become published stories.

We want to thank the teachers of fiction who have used the trade edition of *What If?* and helped us to refine our work, and we particularly thank those who reviewed and made suggestions for this revised and expanded edition of *What If?*—Gail Galloway Adams, West Virginia University; Ann Kiernan Davis, Dalton College; Anne Greene, Wesleyan University; Karla Horner, Chattanooga State Technical Community College; Mona Houghton, California State University, Northridge; Jo-Ann Mapson,

Orange Coast College; Mary O'Connor, South Dakota State University; Karen Piconi, Iowa State University; John Repp, Edinboro University of Pennsylvania; Chris Roberts, Clark State Community College; Ronald Spatz, University of Alaska Anchorage; and David Wojahn, Indiana University.

We are also especially grateful to those teachers who have contributed their own exercises to this book: Thomas Fox Averill, Tony Ardizzone, Douglas Bauer, François Camoin, Ron Carlson, George Garrett, Katherine Haake, Christopher Keane, William Melvin Kelley, Rod Kessler, William Kittredge, Elizabeth Libbey, Margot Livesey, Alison Lurie, Robie Macauley, David Madden, Carol-Lynn Marrazzo, Christopher Noël, David Ray, Frederick Reiken, Ken Rivard, Lore Segal, Thalia Selz, James Thomas, and Melanie Rae Thon. We thank the students and former students who have granted us permission to print their entire stories in *What If?*: Derrick Ableman, Kathleen Blackburn, Annie Cardie, Antonia Clark, Chip Cheek, Kat Gonso, Lee Harrington, Brian Hinshaw, Hester Kaplan, Molly Lanzarotta, Sean Lannigan, Kim Leahy, Mariette Lippo, Matt Marinovich, Melissa McCracken, Sheehan McGuirk, Christine McDonnell, Tom McNeely, Josie Milliken, Judith Claire Mitchell, Terry Theumling, and Kate Wheeler.

We also thank the following people for their editorial and emotional support: Justin Kaplan, Robie Macauley, Hester Kaplan, Anne Brashler, Alice Hoffman, Alexandra Marshall, Mako Yoshikawa, Rick Kot, Lisa Moore, Barbara Santoro, Tom Maeglin, Gina Maccoby, Roberta Pryor, Colleen Mohyde, and our colleagues at the Nieman Foundation at Harvard University, Lesley University, Vermont College, and Emerson College.

ANNE BERNAYS

PAMELA PAINTER

Introduction

ANNE BERNAYS: Good writers know how to do two very different things equally well—write like a writer and think like one.

Writing like a writer is about craft, and means gaining absolute control over your material and your tools. It means, for instance, knowing when to use dialogue and when to summarize discourse, learning how to use adjectives and adverbs—that is, sparingly—and concentrating on the specific rather than the vague and abstract. It means anchoring your story in a particular time and place; beginning writers often neglect to supply basic and crucial information: Who are these characters? Where are they? When is this story taking place?

Thinking like a writer is more complex, because it involves the unconscious. You can rely just so much on your five senses; after that you must call on curiosity, imagination, and skepticism—an open attitude not to be confused with cynicism. Skepticism obliges you to look beneath the obvious to get at the true meaning of, say, a smile, a crying jag, or a burst of anger. Things, in other words, are rarely what they seem. The writer must "think" his or her way past *seems* to *is*.

We have included exercises that ask you to assume the voice of the opposite gender, to search for subtext, and to supply several scenarios leading up to the same event—in other words, to enhance that intuitive quality of mind possessed by all good fiction writers.

PAMELA PAINTER: The exercises in *What If?* are also meant to set something in motion. Each exercise is designed to help you to think in new ways, to discover your own material, to enrich the texture and language of your fiction, and to move steadily toward final meaning. And coming full circle, to help you begin again. No matter how widely published a writer is, there is always the need to begin again. The blank page.

We hope this book will be useful for people who have begun to publish and for those who have never written a word of fiction and are just now taking their first workshop. Our objectives for a workshop are that students will become familiar with the various techniques for writing fiction, the language used to talk about the creative writing process, and the tools to discuss and criticize each other's work in a supportive and constructive manner. When reading each other's work, it is important to make up your own mind about the effectiveness of a story's beginning, or whether there are missing scenes, or how clear the ending is, etc. The more you hone your critical skills in regard to the work of others, the more you will be able to revise your own work with a cool, discerning eye.

BERNAYS: "Can you *really* teach people how to write?" I have been asked this question more often than any other during almost three decades of teaching. Beneath the question is the implication that being able to write well is a divine gift—either

1

you have it or you don't, so no amount of schooling is going to make a difference. Obviously I disagree. Besides, if you alter the question slightly and make it, "Can you really demystify the process of inventing stories and writing them down?" my answer is, "Absolutely."

This book separates and isolates the many elements of fiction, making them a manageable size and shape. Thus broken down and examined one by one, the components of a story or novel are rendered easier to master. This book should help you solve specific writing problems, like finding a good title, deciding on a point of view, discovering where and how to enter a story. Once you feel confident in your ability to exploit these particular skills, it's time to move on and fuse and combine what you have been learning step by step from *What If?*

At the very least you will feel more at ease with written prose and will experience the joy of saying exactly what you want to say the way you want to say it.

PAINTER: To "demystify the process" was the precise intention of *What If?* We didn't set out to write a book about how to write a short story—a write-by-numbers manual—because it can't be done. One of my students, Robert Solomon, spoke to this issue: "The book's value lies in helping me to understand fiction's components and their significance. . . . The exercises serve a preparatory function for when I begin my own true work, when I must deal with various choices and issues in accordance with my own particular vision and the demands it makes."

Writing exercises have long been a part of the learning process for new and established writers. A good many entries in the published notebooks of writers such as Chekhov, Flaubert, Hemingway, Fitzgerald, and Maugham, among others, are unlabeled writing exercises—exercises that grew out of analyzing or talking about what these authors were reading at the time. And many entries are tributes to those writers who had shown them by written example how something worked in fiction. Fitzgerald speaks of a "trick" he and Hemingway learned from Conrad (page 248). John Gardner says of writing that it is a matter of "catching on." In *The Art of Fiction,* he says of exercises, "When the beginning writer deals with some particular, small problem, such as a description of a setting, description of a character, or a brief dialogue that has some definite purpose, the quality of the work approaches the professional." And eventually, for writers who are persistent, the exercises you do here will strengthen your writing as a whole.

BERNAYS: It's possible for one person to be a marvelous storyteller—so long as he or she doesn't have to write it down. Another can form adequate sentences, even whole pages, and yet her story will just lie there, dead on the page.

The exercises in this book should help you sharpen your skills, both in the use of various tools and in the play of your mind. After completing these exercises the raconteur will be able to translate his story into writing and the competent but reticent writer will have learned to exploit her imagination.

You will notice that we make a point of distinguishing and segregating the elements of fiction rather than focusing on the novel and the short story as discrete entities. This is because we believe that the tools and processes are similar for both, as is the emphasis on precision, clarity, and freshness.

PAINTER: We also believe in practice and more practice. Just as every singer, visual artist, dancer, and composer must constantly practice his craft, the writer too must practice. Even though we use language every day in talking and in writing letters, notes to "fill up the gas tank and leave the keys in the pantry," memos for our jobs, or ad copy or newspaper articles, new entries on MySpace, or your Web site or blog, this does not mean that we can forego the practice required in other arts. Practice and persistence are also crucial to a writer. Learn to throw away the flawed sentence, to recast a weak character without a sense of failure. You are growing by making these evaluations of your work. You are practicing the writer's craft. And when you give yourself wholly to your work, you will feel it giving something back to you as if it had a will and energy of its own.

BERNAYS: If the writer's engine is persistence, then the writer's fuel is the imagination; unlike real fuel, we have an endless supply of it and it costs nothing. Imagination is there in all of us, just waiting to be released.

PAINTER: I became a believer in exercises when I did one for the first time in a writing workshop taught by Tom Bracken, a cofounder of *StoryQuarterly.* Bracken gave us disparate elements to combine and weave into a story: banjo music, a penny, and an arresting photograph of two eyes peering through the grainy slats of a boarded-up window. Suddenly, for me, these things were transformed into a story about a lonely teenage girl sitting on an orange crate in a country store. She has a penny under her shoe—and knows that only the boy watching her through the boarded-up window has seen her slide it there. Even using the same details, we were amazed at how our stories were totally different from the others. Of course: because each individual imagination—and voice and vision—used these details in a unique, personal way. Remember—the writer weaves not only plot but also texture.

Since that time, I have worked with all kinds of exercises. Some are created as a result of reading the work of another writer—I think I will always ask of a particularly effective beginning: What has been set in motion, and how? Some exercises simply appeared out of thin air: "What if?" And others grew out of class discussion, as when my student Ben Slomoff asked a question that suddenly illuminated everything. "You mean it's as if every story has its own history—its own back story?" Yes, yes—that's it.

BERNAYS: A boring story is worse than one with rough edges. As a matter of course, I always start off the semester with: "I don't want to see any polite stories." In order to keep you from long-windedness, hot air, and the temptation to stray from the point, we have kept many of these exercises down to 550 words. When you don't have much space, you learn not to waste words. I've found that when a student goes much over the word limit, his or her work tends to sound fuzzy and padded. Each exercise is meant, like a well-designed container, to hold the material destined for it.

Either Ms. Painter or I have assigned every one of these exercises to our students (some undergoing revision along the way) at such places as Harvard, Emerson College, Vermont College, Holy Cross, the University of Massachusetts, and numerous summer writing conferences and workshops.

PAINTER: I should say a word here about our "contributors." We've included a number of exercises from friends who are writers who also teach and use exercises in their classrooms. These exercises include "Ways to Begin a Story," from Robie Macauley, who wrote one of the great books on writing fiction, *Technique in Fiction,* and other exercises from Richard Bausch, Ron Carlson, DeWitt Henry, William Kittredge, Margot Livesey, Alison Lurie, James Thomas, etc. We are all writers who believe in the power of exercises to demystify writing and at the same time to instill an appreciation for the joy and magic of writing something well.

BERNAYS: The trade edition of *What If?* came out in 1990. Since then our students have published stories in numerous magazines and journals, and many students who contributed the "Student Examples" in the original edition of *What If?* went on to use that beginning or excerpt for stories that were eventually published. Others have won competitions or awards. Still others have gone on to become teachers of writing, making up new exercises for their students. We hope you'll invent your own exercises for particular skills or techniques and paste them onto the white spaces in this book.

PAINTER: Yes, for example, Hemingway is known for his stripped-down dialogue, so you can imagine my delight when a student brought in a superb example of summarized dialogue from one of Hemingway's stories. I first pasted it into my book, and it is now printed in this edition.

BERNAYS: Unlike the trade edition, this textbook incorporates 28 stories by contemporary writers such as Ron Carlson, Raymond Carver, Sandra Cisneros, ZZ Packer, and Alice Munro, among others. They are here as examples of the art at its best and most powerful, and demonstrate a challenging diversity of subject matter, style, voice, and narrative technique.

The table of contents of this book is a more or less arbitrary arrangement of the elements and techniques of fiction. Some exercises are more difficult than others, but you won't find the easiest is the first in any one section, nor the hardest the last. Don't feel you have to do them in any particular order but complete those that seem to meet your immediate needs. We do suggest that you read the introductions to each section before starting to work.

PAINTER: We made several discoveries while shaping the table of contents. We found that both of us believed in "character-driven" stories as opposed to "plot-driven" stories when we realized that we'd left "plot" as a distinct category out of our first draft. And when asked to add a section on revision, we realized that many of the exercises scattered elsewhere in the book were actually exercises about revision.

We hope you will return again and again to various sections of *What If?*—combining and rearranging the exercises to lead you into your own limitless well of material, to explore that wonderful intersection of biography and fiction, and to realize your potential as a writer. We also hope that you will use the writers whose work we have cited in our examples as a sort of organic reading list. Buy or borrow their books and read them; highlight specific passages, write in the margins, type out their sentences. The work of the masters is for the writer the best education, the best inspiration of all.

PART ONE

Beginnings

First sentences are doors to worlds.
—URSULA K. LE GUIN

New writers often think they have to know where their story is going and how it will end—before they even begin. Not true. Flannery O'Connor says, "If you start with a real personality, a real character, then something is bound to happen; and you don't have to know what before you begin. In fact, it may be better if you don't know what before you begin. You ought to be able to discover something from your stories. If you don't, probably nobody else will."

Another stumbling block for new writers—whether they're starting a story or a novel—is that they take the word "beginning" too literally. They cast around for the "beginning" of a story, forgetting that the place where it all began probably showed no hint of the conflict, trouble, or complications to come.

But, you might ask, what about the "beginning" of the story itself? Well, a few years ago, during the discussion of a flashback, a student said, "You mean it's as if every story has its own memory, its own history." Yes, that is exactly right. Each story has a history; all characters have pasts; the plots of most stories or novels are affected by something that happened before sentence one on the first page. Yet this history is woven so skillfully into the narrative of the story that most times we don't realize we are actually reading about the past of the story—the back story. A story can begin with dialogue, narrative summary, description, or whatever, but it must begin *in medias res,* in the middle of things.

It might be helpful to think of the story as a straight line with the first sentence appearing somewhere beyond the start of the line—ideally near the middle. At some point, most stories or novels dip back into the past, to the beginning of the straight line and catch the reader up on the situation—how and why X has gotten himself into such a pickle with character Y. Tolstoy's novel *Anna Karenina* starts off with a household in a flutter over the husband's affair with the governess. Margaret Atwood's novel

5

Life Before Man starts *after* someone has committed suicide. Yet these events foreshadow and affect the stories to come.

The forward movement of Flannery O'Connor's "A Good Man Is Hard to Find" is so compelling that it is easy to overlook how the grandmother's past informs the action of the story. And the past of Amy Hempel's story "Today Will Be a Quiet Day" is filled with ominous events: children's fights that led the father to say he wanted "Today will be a quiet day" written on his tombstone; the parents' divorce; the boy's friend who told the boy, "Never play Ping-Pong with a mental patient because it's all we do and we'll kill you" and who later committed suicide; the kids learning the guillotine joke; the dog that had to be put to sleep—all this happens before page one. That's good writing.

So you must resist the temptation to give the reader too lengthy an explanation as to how things got to this point. Remember, you are trying to hook the reader's attention, to pull the reader into your story so that he won't wonder, *What's on television tonight?*

The following exercises are designed to encourage you to think about real characters who are involved in situations that are already under way—situations that are starting to unravel because of, or in spite of, the desires and actions of their beleaguered characters. Proceed sentence by sentence. Just give yourself over to setting stories in motion—you will soon know which stories capture your imagination and seem unstoppable, which stories demand to be finished. Until that time, begin and begin and begin.

PARIS REVIEW INTERVIEWER: *How do you describe the perfect state in which you can write from early morning into the afternoon?*

JOYCE CAROL OATES: *One must be pitiless about this matter of "mood." In a sense, the writing will create the mood. If art is, as I believe it to be, a genuinely transcendental function—a means by which we rise out of limited, parochial states of mind—then it should not matter very much what states of mind or emotion we are in. Generally I've found this to be true: I have forced myself to begin writing when I've been utterly exhausted, when I've felt my soul as thin as a playing card, when nothing has seemed worth enduring for another five minutes . . . . and somehow the activity of writing changes everything.*

EXERCISE 1

First Sentences:
Beginning in the Middle

In a *Paris Review* interview, Angus Wilson says, "Plays and short stories are similar in that both start when all but the action is finished." This echoes Horace's injunction to begin the story *in medias res*—in the middle of things.

Yet, beginners' stories often meander for three or four pages before the story begins to rear its head. One day, out of curiosity, we decided to examine the first lines of stories in big and little magazines, story collections, and anthologies. We discovered that many *first sentences* put the reader in the middle of things. Something unusual is already happening. That exploration became the basis for this first exercise.

All of the following examples are the first sentences of short stories. We suggest that you begin a list of first sentences from novels that also illustrate *in medias res*.

The Exercise

Consider how many of the opening lines below pull you into the center of the story. What do you know about the story—situation, characters, geography, setting, class, education, potential conflict, etc.—from reading the titles and the following opening lines? What decisions has the author already made about point of view, distance, setting, tone, etc.? Notice how many of the titles are directly related to the first line of the story.

"The Lady with the Dog"   ANTON CHEKHOV
They were saying a new face had been seen on the esplanade: a lady with a pet dog.

"Lost"   ROBIE MACAULEY
Morning was desolate, with a wet wind blowing from the northeast, off the ocean, and the sky like a dirty sheet, but Uncle Gavin rose at six and made a pitcher of bloody marys, which put all the other adults, as one by one they rose from bed and wandered into the kitchen, in a philosophical mood; not so the children.

"Love Is Not a Pie"   AMY BLOOM
In the middle of the eulogy at my mother's boring and heartbreaking funeral, I began to think about calling off the wedding.

7

"What You Pawn I Will Redeem" SHERMAN ALEXIE
One day you have a home and the next you don't, but I'm not going to tell you my particular reasons for being homeless, because it's my secret story, and Indians have to work hard to keep secrets from hungry white folks.

"Gesturing" JOHN UPDIKE
She told him with a little gesture he had never seen her use before.

"The Sunday following Mother's Day" EDWARD P. JONES
When Madeleine Williams was four years old and her brother Sam was ten, their father killed their mother one night in early April.

"Exchange Value" CHARLES JOHNSON
Me and my brother Loftis came in by the old lady's window.

"Buried Lives" BHARATI MUKHERJEE
One March midafternoon in Trincomalee, Sri Lanka, Mr. N.K.S. Venkatesan, a forty-nine-year-old schoolteacher who should have been inside a St. Joseph's Collegiate classroom explicating Arnold's "The Buried Life" found himself instead at a barricaded intersection, axe in hand and shouting rude slogans at a truckload of soldiers.

"Everywhere My Father" ANNE BRASHLER
Gramma said an eight-year-old girl shouldn't sleep with her own father, but my father said that a rolled-up rug down the middle made a double bed the same as two beds.

"The Remission" MAVIS GALLANT
When it became clear that Alec Webb was far more ill than anyone had cared to tell him, he tore up his English life and came down to die on the Riviera.

"Medley" TONI CADE BAMBARA
I could tell the minute I got in the door and dropped my bag, I wasn't staying.

"A White Horse" THOM JONES
Up and down the dull coastline of her desk, Amerylis ticked her fingernails, Minnie Mouse airbrushed onto each bismuth pink shield.

"A Girl Like Elsie" KIRAN KAUR SAINI
I tell Mama I waitress in the Village so she don't have to cut me out of her heart.

"Covering Home" JOSEPH MAIOLO
Coach discovered Danny's arm when Danny's parents were splitting up at the beginning of the season.

"Werewolves in Their Youth" MICHAEL CHABON
I had known him as a bulldozer, as a samurai, as an android programmed to kill, as Plastic Man and Titanium Man and Matter-Eater Lad, as a Buick Electra, as a Peterbilt truck, and even, for a week, as a Mackinac Bridge, but it was as a werewolf that Timothy Stokes finally went too far.

"The Ant of the Self"   Z. Z. PACKER
"Opportunities," my father says after I bail him out of jail.

"Judgment"   KATE WHEELER
When Mayland Thompson dies he wants to be buried with the body of a twelve-year-old girl.

"The Blue Men"   JOY WILLIAMS
Bomber Boyd, age thirteen, told his new acquaintances that summer that his father had been executed by the state of Florida for the murder of a Sheriff's deputy and his drug-sniffing German shepherd.

"Sonny's Blues"   JAMES BALDWIN
I read about it in the paper, in the subway, on my way to work, I read it, and I couldn't believe it, and I read it again.

"Nickel a Throw"   W. D. WETHERELL
These are the things Gooden sees from his perch eight feet above the dunking tub at the Dixford Congregational Church's Charity Bazaar.

"The Water-Faucet Vision"   GISH JEN
To protect my sister Mona and me from the pains—or, as they pronounced it, the "pins"—of life, my parents did their fighting in Shanghai dialect, which we didn't understand; and when my father one day pitched a brass vase through the kitchen window, my mother told us he had done it by accident.

"Freeze"   DAVID JAUSS
At first Freeze Harris thought Nam was a crazy nightmare, an upside-down place where you were supposed to do everything that was forbidden back in the world, but after a while it was the world that seemed unreal.

"Bigfoot Stole My Wife"   RON CARLSON
The problem is credibility.

"Demonology"   RICK MOODY
They came in twos and threes, dressed in the fashionable Disney costumes of the year, Lion King, Pocahontas, Beauty and the Beast, or in the costumes of televised superheroes, protean, shape-shifting, thus arrayed, in twos and threes, complaining it was too hot with the mask on, *Hey, I'm really hot!,* lugging those orange plastic buckets, bartering, haggling with one another, *Gimme your Smarties, please?* as their parents tarried behind, grownups following after, grownups bantering about the schools, or about movies, about local sports, about their marriages, about the difficulties of long marriages, kids sprinting up the next driveway, kids decked out as demons or superheroes or dinosaurs or as advertisements of our multinational entertainment-providers, beating back the restless souls of the dead, in search of sweets.

"Sinbad's Head"   PAUL WEST
In every library there is a book that kills.

"Rock Springs"   Richard Ford
Edna and I had started down from Kalispell, heading for Tampa-St. Pete where I still
had some friends from the old glory days who wouldn't turn me in to the police.

"Saturnino el Magnifico"   Alberto Alvaro Rios
The entire circus train fell in the manner of a child's toy into the ravine just outside
of town, its cars folding up in the fall so that from a distance they looked like the rough-
angled line of teeth on a saw.

"Woman Hollering Creek"   Sandra Cisneros
The day Don Serafin gave Juan Pedro Martinez Sanchez permission to take Cleofilas
Enriqueta DeLeon Hernandez as his bride, across her father's threshold, over several
miles of dirt road and several miles of paved, over one border and beyond to a town
en el otro lado—on the other side—already did he divine the morning his daughter
would raise her hand over her eyes, look south, and dream of returning to the chores
that never ended, six good-for-nothing brothers, and one old man's complaints.

"The Silver Bullet"   James Alan McPherson
When Willis Davis tried to join up with the Henry Street guys, they told him that first
he had to knock over Slick's Bar and Grill to show them what kind of stuff he had.

"Wickedness"   Ron Hansen
At the end of the nineteenth century a girl from Delaware got on a milk train to Omaha
and took a green wool seat in the second-class car.

"Jump-up Day"   Barbara Kingsolver
Jericha believed herself already an orphan—her mother was in the ground by the time
she could walk on it—so the loss of her father when it came was not an exceptional thing.

"The Handsomest Drowned Man in the World"   Gabriel García Márquez
The first children who saw the dark and slinky bulge approaching through the sea let
themselves think it was an enemy ship.

Now, write ten of your own opening lines for ten different stories. When you read,
look for opening lines that immediately pull you into the story. And if you keep a journal or notebook, consider starting a new section and adding one first sentence each
day—for the rest of your life.

The Objective

To cultivate the habit of beginning your stories in the middle of things. Because you
are not obligated to finish these stories, this exercise lowers the emotional stakes and
helps to shake up and surprise the imagination.

Student Examples

She was trying to tell the joke right but it was his joke and she had to keep checking
with him.

—Frances Lefkowitz

I don't know who found me, or why I was left in a dumpster, but there was one piece of lore about my rescue that was not forgotten and that they made sure to hand down to me: written on my chest in navy blue Magic Marker, my original owner had put the word "Gem," and that is my real and only name.

—Brigid Clark

Jason Dyvik's heart, like all bartenders' hearts, was a needy and gluttonous muscle.

—Eric Mecklenburg, "Yellow Silk"

Nothing more to say—the storm, son walking further along the cliff than dad, normal as you please, and the sea reached up and snicked him.

—Perry Onion

By the time I was ten I had concluded that death was just a matter of moving furniture.

—Amanda Claiborne, "Jemma"

My mother explained what sex was the day after I first had it.

—Christy Veladota

When the fog rolls into Portsmouth a peculiar, anonymous intimacy descends, taming difficult women and angry men.

—Jim Marsh

At Saint Boniface, on the first day of school, Mrs. Riordan found her fourth-grade class was nothing more than Sister Mary's third grade from the year before, with one exception: A quiet boy with eyes the color of water, who occupied the front row window seat the way a vacuum takes up space.

—Bridget Mazur

Anecdotes don't make good stories. Generally I dig down underneath them so far that the story that finally comes out is not what people thought their anecdotes were about.

—Alice Munro

EXERCISE 2

Second Sentences as Different Paths

Now that you have written a number of first sentences for "First Sentences: Beginning in the Middle" it is time for you to explore the power of adding one more line to see how just one line can take your story down a totally different path from another second line—a path that will lead to a very distinct story, with different characters and different plots and outcomes.

The Exercise

Use one of your first sentences from the first exercise and take it to entirely different stories by adding five or seven or ten second sentences. Consider how your story will change when you do the following: change the setting; add a line of dialogue; move to the future; make your main character think of someone else who matters to the story; add a loved/hated pet.

And here are some other possibilities for second sentences: make your main character think of a popular song that takes him/her back to an important memory; add an accident; bring the police to the scene; make someone arrive with a mysterious or alarming message. Think of some of your own paths for second sentences. Then choose the path you want to follow—a sentence at a time.

The Objective

To learn that you don't have to know where a story is going when you begin. All you need is a first sentence with possibilities. Then you can build stories one sentence at a time.

Student Example

Note how this student came up with her own second sentence directions.

Story 1: Change the setting.
Cynthia has made several plans for the summer, including: get a tan, don't burn while trying to tan, buy shoes that don't leave the bottoms of her feet different colors, cut down her consumption of ranch dressing (she has it on everything: French fries, macaroni and cheese, sour-cream crackers that leave crumbs all over her bed), and convince her little sister to stop crimping her hair. Halfway across the country, her summer boyfriend Brad is deciding whether or not a torn pair of swim trunks are still any good, shuffling around his bedroom to create static, a small thrill for the humdrum task of packing to go away.

Story 2: Add a line of dialogue.
Cynthia has made several plans for the summer, including: get a tan, don't burn while trying to tan, buy shoes that don't leave the bottoms of her feet different colors, cut down her consumption of ranch dressing (she has it on everything: French fries, macaroni and cheese, sour-cream crackers that leave crumbs all over her bed), and convince her little sister to stop crimping her hair.

She yells to her sister, "I swear to God, Leslie, if you put my birth control pills in the washer again, I will end you!"

Story 3: Add a loved/hated pet.
Cynthia has made several plans for the summer, including: get a tan, don't burn while trying to tan, buy shoes that don't leave the bottoms of her feet different colors, cut down her consumption of ranch dressing (she has it on everything: French fries, macaroni and cheese, sour-cream crackers that leave crumbs all over her bed), and convince her little sister to stop crimping her hair.

She's also determined to end the misery of her bunny, Rex, who is eight years old and suffering from what the vet called "bunny leukemia," the symptoms of which included an inability to eat and awful whimpering.

Story 4: Have the main character suffer a severe physical injury.
Cynthia has made several plans for the summer, including: get a tan, don't burn while trying to tan, buy shoes that don't leave the bottoms of her feet different colors, cut down her consumption of ranch dressing (she has it on everything: French fries, macaroni and cheese, sour-cream crackers that leave crumbs all over her bed), and convince her little sister to stop crimping her hair.

Instead of doing these things, Cynthia will be laid up in the hospital after a car accident in which she was the front passenger, and she will suffer through physical therapy and hate it until she gets a cute new therapist.

Story 5: The character discovers someone close to them is a criminal.
Cynthia has made several plans for the summer, including: get a tan, don't burn while trying to tan, buy shoes that don't leave the bottoms of her feet different colors, cut down her consumption of ranch dressing (she has it on everything: French fries, macaroni and cheese, sour cream crackers that leave crumbs all over her bed), and convince her little sister to stop crimping her hair.

What she has not planned for the summer is visiting her father in jail, but that is what she will be doing every Tuesday evening after he gets locked up following an embezzlement conviction.

—KATE MICHKO

This discovery of being bound to a particular society and a particular history, to particular sounds and a particular idiom, is for the writer the beginning of a recognition of himself as finite subject, limited, the beginning of a recognition that first puts his work in a real human perspective for him. It is a perspective which shows him his creaturehood.
—FLANNERY O'CONNOR

Ways to Begin a Story

from Robie Macauley

There are many different means a writer might use to begin a story, and the problem is to choose one that most appropriately raises the curtain on the narrative to follow. Ask yourself such questions as these: Do I want my story to open with the sound of voices as people discuss something about their lives? Or do I want to bring one important character forward into the descriptive spotlight and let the reader have a good, long look at her before action begins? Or do I want to begin with an activity—one person, or more than one, engaged in doing something that will be significant for the story to follow?

To judge these three possible openings, the writer might then ask questions of the unwritten story: Story, are you going to be about some involvement of people and their attitudes and opinions; are the ways they voice their thoughts going to be important? Or, Story, are you going to concern yourself with the traits, ideas, experiences, and emotions of one person who must seize the reader's imagination at once? Or are you going to be involved with an event—or events—in which the characters take part, and thus you want an opening that shows actions? Here are some of the possible ways of leading off.

With a Generalization

My mother believed you could be anything you wanted to be in America.

—AMY TAN, "TWO KINDS"

When people become characters, they cease to be regarded as human, they are something to be pointed out, like the orange tree that President Kruger planted, the statue in the park, or the filling station that once was the First Church hall.

—NADINE GORDIMER, "THE LAST KISS"

What really separates animal from man is the ability of one to accept the unexpected as the way things are, and the inability of the other to do anything but come up with theories.

—RITA DOUCETTE, "BULLET ADAGIO"

With a Description of a Person

He was lifting his knees high and putting his hand up, when I first saw him, as if crossing the road through that stinging rain, he were breaking through the bead curtain of a Pernambuco bar. I knew he was going to stop me.

—V. S. PRITCHETT, "THE SAILOR"

14

Besides the neutral expression that she wore when she was alone, Mrs. Freeman had two others, forward and reverse, that she used for all her human dealings.

—FLANNERY O'CONNOR, "GOOD COUNTRY PEOPLE"

With Narrative Summary

An unfortunate circumstance in my life has just recalled to mind a certain Dr. Crombie and the conversations I used to hold with him when I was young. He was the school doctor until the eccentricity of his ideas became generally known.

—GRAHAM GREENE, "DOCTOR CROMBIE"

The Jackman's marriage had been adulterous and violent, but in its last days they became a couple again, as they might have if one of them were slowly dying.

—ANDRE DUBUS, "THE WINTER FATHER"

Jim and Irene Westcott were the kind of people who seem to strike that satisfactory average of income, endeavor, and respectability that is reached by the statistical reports in college alumni bulletins.

—JOHN CHEEVER, "THE ENORMOUS RADIO"

With Dialogue

"Don't think about a cow," Matt Brinkley said.

—ANN BEATTIE, "IN THE WHITE NIGHT"

I'm afraid Walter Cronkite has had it, says Mom.

—JAYNE ANNE PHILLIPS, "HOME"

With Several Characters but No Dialogue

During the lunch hour, the male clerks usually went out, leaving myself and three girls behind. While they ate their sandwiches and drank their tea, they chattered away thirteen to the dozen. Half their conversation I didn't understand at all, and the other half bored me to tears.

—FRANK O'CONNOR, "MUSIC WHEN SOFT VOICES DIE"

With a Setting and Only One Character

After dinner, with its eight courses and endless conversation, Olga Mikhailovna, whose husband's birthday was being celebrated, went out into the garden. The obligation to smile and talk continuously, the stupidity of the servants, the clatter of dishes, the long intervals between courses, and the corset she had put on to conceal her pregnancy from her guests, had wearied her to the point of exhaustion.

—ANTON CHEKHOV, "THE BIRTHDAY PARTY"

With a Reminiscent Narrator

I was already formally engaged, as we used to say, to the girl I was going to marry.

—PETER TAYLOR, "THE OLD FOREST"

With a Child Narrator

Eugene Kessler was supposed to be my brother's best friend, but he and I actually had a lot more in common.

—ALICE HOFFMAN, "FLIGHT"

I don't have much work to do around the house like some girls.

—TONI CADE BAMBARA, "RAYMOND'S RUN"

When I was in the third grade I knew a boy who had to have fourteen shots in the stomach as the result of a squirrel bite.

—ELLEN GILCHRIST, "VICTORY OVER JAPAN"

By Establishing Point of View

First Person
Since Dr. Wayland was late and there were no recent newsmagazines in the waiting room, I turned to the other patient and said: "As a concerned person, and as your brother, I ask you, without meaning to offend, how did you get that scar on the side of your face?"

—JAMES ALAN MCPHERSON, "THE STORY OF A SCAR"

There was no exchange of body fluids on the first date, and that suited both of us just fine.

—T. CORAGHESSAN BOYLE, "MODERN LOVE"

I left India in 1964 with a certificate in commerce and the equivalent, in those days, of ten dollars to my name.

—JHUMPA LAHIRI, "THE THIRD AND FINAL CONTINENT"

I'm Push the bully, and what I hate are new kids and sissies, dumb kids and smart, rich kids, poor kids, kids who wear glasses, talk funny, show off, patrol boys and wise guys and kids who pass pencils and water the plants—and cripples, especially cripples.

—STANLEY ELKIN, "A POETICS FOR BULLIES"

Third Person
The August two-a-day practice sessions were sixty-seven days away, Coach calculated.

—MARY ROBISON, "COACH"

Climbing up with a handful of star decals to paste on the bathroom ceiling, Claire sees a suspect-looking shampoo bottle on the cluttered top shelf.

—FRANCINE PROSE, "OTHER LIVES"

The Exercise

This one is in two parts. First experiment with different types of openings for different stories until you feel comfortable with the technique of each. Then see how many ways there are to open one particular story you have in mind. How does the story change when the opening changes from a generalization to a line of dialogue?

The Objective

To see how experimenting with several ways of opening your story can lead you to a better understanding of whose story it is, and what the focus of the story will be.

> *For me writing—the only possible writing—is just simply the conversion of nervous force into phrases.*
> —JOSEPH CONRAD

EXERCISE 4

Begin a Story with a "Given" First Line
from William Kittredge

It can be challenging to begin a story with a "given" first line—especially one that starts in the middle. You can use a line from a poem, make one up, or use the one in this exercise. Or ask a friend or fellow writer to give you a first line—this is what Doris Lessing's characters do in her novel *The Golden Notebook*. When we come to the place in the novel where Saul gives Anna the first line "The two women were alone in the London flat," we realize that Anna did write her book, and that *The Golden Notebook*, which begins with that exact line, is Anna's novel.

The Exercise

Begin a story with this line: Where were you last night?

The Objective

The objective is to once more start the story *in medias res*—in the middle of things. Notice how this question begins in the middle of a situation. For example, "last night," the subject of the question, has already happened. If one character asks another this question there are already two people "on stage." And the question will probably produce a conflict. But don't get hung up on making it a line of dialogue—it can be used many different ways.

Student Examples

Where were you last night was the one thing she couldn't ask him anymore, so they talked about the death of Huey Newton. They were in the kitchen having breakfast, Marcy was eating Special K and Tom, Shredded Wheat. As usual, he had bought two copies of the *Times* and they each came upon the story at the same time. Twenty-three years had gone by since they had met and fallen in love during the height of the demonstrations at Berkeley and now Huey Newton was as dead as their marriage.

—LYNDA STURNER

"Where were you last night?" Tony asked, wiping down the bar in front of me with a gray towel. He doesn't look me in the eye.

"Vegas," I said, fingering an earring, noticing how bald he is, how short. "Where do you think?" Of course, I didn't really spend the night in Vegas or in any place worth mentioning, but when you're forty-one and planted on a bar stool, it's nice to think you still have possibilities, even if you can only reach them in your head.

—BRIDGET MAZUR

Where was I last night and how did I get here? I am lying on the sofa in my old apartment where my ex-boyfriend, Roy, still lives. The afghan I made for him a year earlier is draped over me. I pull it up to my chin. It smells like Roy: Old Spice and Camel filters.

Maria walks out of my old bedroom wearing Roy's blue and white striped Oxford. "You're awake," she says. "Roy says I have to let you stay here as long as you want."

I sit up. My head hurts and my teeth taste like vodka. From Chessy's Bar and Grill. I ran into Roy over by the pinball machines. He made me give him my car keys. They are on the coffee table now, next to my bag and earrings.

"Have a little too much, Janis?" Maria walks past me to the kitchen.

I stand up, holding the arm of the sofa. "Where's Roy?"

Maria puts enough water on for one cup of coffee. "He opens the 7-Eleven on Saturdays. Don't you remember?"

—CHRISTY VELADOTA

Here are several other "given" first lines:

- The neighbors were at it again.

- "One more thing before you go."

- This is a story I've been avoiding for a long time:

- If I went there a second time . . .

(This is the first line of Enid Shomer's poem "First Sunset at Outler's Ranch" from her book, *Stalking the Florida Panther*.)

Sharon Sheehe Stark gives her students the following prompts:

- I haven't been the same since . . .

- See that house over there? Let me tell you . . .

I remember a sentence I opened one story with, to show you how bad I was: "Monsieur Boule inserted a delicate dagger in Mademoiselle's left side and departed with a poised immediacy." I like to think I didn't take myself seriously then, but I did.

—EUDORA WELTY

EXERCISE 5

Free Associating from
Random Sentences

from DeWitt Henry

First sentences need to be laden with story, not just to capture the reader, but to "ride on their own melting," as Robert Frost said of poems. In reading other writers, watch for sentences that have this potential.

Some of my favorite sentences include:

I was ashamed of my conscience. —TIM O'BRIEN

Inside, where it matters, the quietness is like snow falling in a forest, where Santa has never visited with his terrible sack of presents. —CHARLES BAXTER

She rolled her eyes and screwed up her mouth and stuck her leathery thin face into his smooth bland one. —FLANNERY O'CONNOR

Worms shot like subway trains through the dirt of gardens, among the writhing roots of roses. —URSULA K. LE GUIN

They were burning beef in their backyards, brown burly men with beer cans. —DONALD BARTHELME

The hall was clogged with bodies; none of them hers, but who could be sure? —LEONARD MICHAELS

The Exercise

Take your stolen sentence and use it as the beginning of a story, free-associating. Try writing all in one rush, under pressure, for twenty minutes or so. Then go back and revise with art.

The Objective

The objective(s): to surprise the mind with the no-mind, the way a quick sketch frees up an instinctive sense of form for painters; also to summon a sense of meaning and form without premeditation; and to discover the importance of opening sentences.

Below is a riff on O'Brien's sentence.

One Day

I was ashamed of my conscience. Ashamed for worrying because this wasn't a riot. That I was not with otherwise respectable and law abiding friends, who, when the mobs of heat driven protestors broke wild suddenly, when shop windows burst from anonymous bricks, when burglar alarms sounded futilely in a melee of emergency sirens; one and all, without second thought, joined with looters on all sides, climbed through display windows in a holiday of theft and lust. There was no Bernice, star law student at Boston University, child of Scarsdale, impressive feminist and environmentalist, suddenly rushing and climbing, pushing with faceless others into Orlando's on Newbury Street, madly grabbing lingerie and cocktail dresses, coats, slacks, scarves, sweaters, and more and more, arms full to spilling. There was no Stan, fitness buff, computer engineer, breaking loose in the darkened liquor mart, brazen with a shopping cart.

There were no strangers, no wild-eyed hoards. Just me, alone.

And a story from a first line by Leo Tolstoy:

Happy Families Are All the Same

Happy families are all alike; every unhappy family is unhappy in its own way. Happy families all share similar features; every unhappy family, however, is alien to every other, at least in terms of its unhappiness. Given any set of happy families, Family X will always be equal to Family Y, whereas in any given set of unhappy families, the unhappiness of any two families will never be equal. Happy families tend toward increasing homogeneity, while unhappy families, via the irrational ordering presence of the human mind, reverse this trend by giving rise to distinct, isolated systems of unhappiness. Though widespread variations exist among cultures and across time, stable and cohesive—that is to say, *happy*—families exhibit similar forms and behaviors within any given society (the nature of these forms and behaviors depending on the organization of the society in question, such as, for example, the patriarchal and class-based structure of wealthy Nineteenth Century Russian households), while fractured, inconstant—or, to put it simply, *unhappy*—families exhibit their unhappiness in widely diverse and mutually inimitable forms and behaviors (this diversity owing itself to the family members' irrational *deviations* from the norms of the society in question— for example, throwing oneself under the wheels of a passing railroad car). Happy families are all the same, but the Oblonsky family, with which this great novel you are presently reading begins, stands apart, distinct and individual, because it is unhappy. If it weren't for unhappiness, all families would be the same. Thankfully not all families are happy, because happy families are all identical and that would make an exceedingly monotonous book—and, as you will see, the families in this book are refreshingly dissimilar. The Oblonsky family is not like other families: the Oblonsky family is very unhappy (but in a way that is different from other unhappy families). Happy families are all alike, which may comfort some people and bore others, but whatever one's feelings about happy families, surely everyone can agree that, at the very least, each and every unhappy family offers a new and exciting experience of unhappiness, which surely must be worth something, at least for great novels like this one, which will include such unhappy distinctions as deceptive French governesses; drunken siblings who date prostitutes; cuckolded Russian aristocrats who attempt to mask their philistinism with an interest in Beethoven; full-grown women named Kitty; stuffy, itchy, red-velvety dinner parties and balls; and, of course, innovative methods of suicide. Happiness in families is always general and abstract, while unhappiness is specific and concrete. Unhappy families bear no precedents and yet they are everywhere, while happy families seem to copy themselves over and over again and at the same time exist in no tangible place, the reason for this being clear on closer inspection, namely, that there are really no such things as happy families.

—CHIP CHEEK, FROM *BREVITY AND ECHO*

Literature was not born the day when a boy crying "wolf, wolf" came running out of the Neanderthal valley with a big gray wolf at his heels: literature was born on the day when a boy came crying "wolf, wolf" and there was no wolf behind him.
—VLADIMIR NABOKOV

EXERCISE 6

Person, Place, and Song

from Ron Carlson

At the outset of any writing class I always give an assignment. I don't want to see the stories that these writers have in their files—yet. I also don't want to start a class with them talking; they are without exception excellent talkers. They are experts. I want to use that expertise later. Right off, I want them to write. No fears, tears, theory, or clashing agendas. Just a little writing. I want them to take the risk of writing something new—*all of them on an equal footing*.

The assignments I've been making have changed several times, but they're all essentially *prompts*, specific ways of starting. The most recent I simply call Person, Place, and Song. It comes from the second paragraph of Leonard Michaels' story "Viva La Tropicana," which appeared in *The Best American Short Stories 1991*. The paragraph starts:

> The first time I heard mambo, I was in a Chevy Bel Aire, driving from Manhattan to Brooklyn with Zev's son, my cousin Chester. We'd just graduated from high school and were going to a party. To save me the subway ride, Chester came to pick me up. He wore alligator shoes, like Zeb's dancing shoes, and a chain bracelet of heavy silver, with a name tag, on his left wrist. It was a high school fashion, like penny loafers and bobby socks. Chester had spent time in Cuba, but mainly he lived with his mother in Brooklyn and hardly ever saw his father. Uncle Zev, I believe, didn't love Chester too much, or not enough. This accounts for an eccentric showy element in his personality, which distinguished him in high school as a charming ass, irresponsible to girls, obnoxious to boys. As we drove, he flicked on the radio. The DJ, Symphony Sid, began talking to us, his voice full of knowing, in the manner of New York. He said we could catch Tito Puente this Wednesday at the Palladium, home of Latin music, 53rd and Broadway. Then Symphony Sid played a tune by Puente called "Ran Kan Kan."

This paragraph is rich with the specific data that offers clues and sets the tone for the rest of the piece. I could talk about it—all the work it does—for half an hour.

The Exercise

Write a short piece of fiction—about a thousand words. It may be a complete short story and it may be the beginning of a longer piece. But it starts as follows:

The first time I (or Name) heard SPECIFIC SONG TITLE by SPECIFIC ARTIST OR GROUP, I (or Name) was down/up/over at PLACE and we were doing ACTION.

The Objective

To begin a story simply and specifically. Nothing grand, just close evidence that may lead somewhere. As I have said somewhere else, at greater length: solve your problems through physical detail.

Student Examples

The first time I heard the song, "Let it Be," was on Route 80 near Wheaton, Pennsylvania, three days after my divorce. I was coming cross country in a Pinto wagon with my ex-husband. It was hour number five.

I was leaving New York to be poet-in-residence at Grailville, a women's retreat in Loveland, Ohio. James was moving back to our old hometown in Findlay, to take over his father's medical practice. Pretty separate paths, huh? They should have been separate journeys too, but God must have been bored one day and needed to see a good show, because 48 hours after I said a final goodbye to James, I was saying hello to him on the phone.

He called in a panic. His car had been stolen, his job started in two days, he didn't have any money for a plane ticket because he'd spent it on legal fees for the divorce I had wanted, and he was desperate. Would I please take him with me to Ohio.

I liked the desperate part, so I said yes.

—KRISTINA M. ONDER

The first time Benny heard "Two of Us" by the Beatles, he'd been driving down I-44 toward Tulsa, where he'd been born and where he hoped he'd be able to find something about his twin. He listened to the lyrics and thought, yes, we're on our way back home. He thought maybe the song was a sign from God, or maybe his twin was a local radio DJ. He probably played this song because he knew, through some psychic twin connection, that Benny was on his way and that this song would guide him. Benny's parents had tried to tell him he didn't have a twin. They even showed him his birth certificate. "Says right there: single birth," his dad said. But Benny knew that wasn't right.

—REBECCA FLANAGAN

EXERCISE 7

Stirring Up a Fiction Stew

We urge you to write plots that are character-driven. That is, where the action grows out of who the characters are rather than through accident or coincidence. Still, it's important, in plotting, to see and make use of seemingly unrelated incidents, elements, and characters. The fiction writer should be able to perceive patterns where others see only randomness. The ability to discern patterns is a skill that improves with practice—it's not magic or ESP. Thanks to Sharon Sheehe Stark for contributing to this exercise.

The Exercise

Select for yourself three objects such as a tape measure, a bible, and a ham sandwich. These are examples; you can choose anything, so long as they appear to be random. Weave these disparate objects into a plausible, coherent story. They should be essential to the story, integrated into the plot, not incidental or mere props.

The Objective

To underscore that you are in charge of the material and not the other way around. You should be able to manipulate the elements of a story or novel, using your imagination to invent alternate action and dialogue, alternate incidents and even characters in order to make the story proceed smoothly and plausibly. It's all about perceiving and articulating relationships inherent in characters, elements, and incidents.

Student Example

Below are the words students chose in a workshop and one student's story written from this list.

pyromaniac	skycap
all-night diner	tuna fish
bowling pin	gardenia
polyester	infinity

Next to the airport: Dante's Diner, open 24 hours, red neon sign blinking on and off. Red's a cheerful color.

I been night cook here at Dante's for twenty years. Dante, he died last March. House burned down; some pyromaniac lit it. Hell of a thing. Dante's kid owns the place now. Never seen her. But her lawyer came by yesterday—skinny guy, in one of those crummy polyester suits. Asking a lot of questions, sticking his pointy nose into everything. Told me she wanted to sell.

What does she care? So I'm out of a job—so what's it to her? They'll turn the goddamn place into a Lum's or a Hardee's or something. Progress. Premade frozen burgers—premeasured milk shake mix—packaged pie. Progress? Hey, this is a diner—a *diner*, with diner food: hot beef sandwiches, real mashed potatoes, rice pudding, tuna on rye with potato chips and a pickle, and my lemon meringue pie.

I like the people who come in here: skycaps, tourists, kids on dates, hippies, businessmen. Last night a bowling league came in from a tournament over at Airport Lanes. All of them in satin jackets with big bowling pins embroidered on the backs, eating and talking and looking at a couple of pretty girls in the back booth, girls with long hair, shiny pink lips and perfume like gardenias.

I like night work. It's my time. The nights stretch on forever—what's that word? Infinity. The dark outside, all blue, the red neon blinking. Jukebox going. The way I slap my spatula down on the grill, the way I flip eggs over. The way people look when they come in—hungry, tired, and when they leave, they look fed. I get so I'm almost sorry when it's morning. Especially now with that lawyer ruining my day.

—Gina Logan

One of the most difficult things is the first paragraph. I have spent many months on a first paragraph and once I get it, the rest just comes out very easily. In the first paragraph you solve most of the problems with your book. The theme is defined, the style, the tone. At least in my case, the first paragraph is a kind of sample of what the rest of the book is going to be. That's why writing a book of short stories is much more difficult than writing a novel. Every time you write a short story, you have to begin all over again.

—Gabriel García Márquez

EXERCISE 8

The Newspaper Muse:
Ann Landers and the
National Enquirer

In her essay, "The Nature of Short Fiction; or, the Nature of My Short Fiction," Joyce Carol Oates says that she is "greatly interested in the newspapers and in Ann Landers' columns and in *True Confessions* and in the anecdotes told under the guise of 'gossip.' Amazing revelations!" She says she has written a great number of stories based on "the barest newspaper accounts . . . it is the very skeletal nature of the newspaper, I think, that attracts me to it, the need it inspires in me to give flesh to such neatly and thinly-told tales, to resurrect this event which has already become history and will never be understood unless it is re-lived, re-dramatized." One student, Tom McNeely, brought in a newspaper clipping and a very strong story beginning, and I said, "Keep going." His complete story "Sheep," which was eventually printed in *The Atlantic Monthly,* appears on page 363.

The Exercise

Collect Ann Landers columns, gossip columns, and stories from *Weekly World News* or *True Confessions* that seem to you to form—either partially or wholly—the basis for a story. Often, these newspaper accounts will be the "end" of the story and you will have to fill in the events leading up to the more dramatic event that made the news that day. Or perhaps the story leads you to ask what is going to happen to that person now.

Clip and save four or five items. Outline a story based on one of them, indicating where the story begins, who the main characters are, what the general tone (that is, the emotional timbre of the work) will be, and from whose point of view you elect to tell the story. These articles can be used for shorter, more focused exercises. For example, describe the car of the person in the article, or the contents of his wallet. Or have the person from the article write three letters.

The Objective

The objective is threefold. One is to look for an article that triggers your imagination and to understand how, when you dramatize the events, the story then becomes *your* story.

The second is to increase the beginning writer's awareness of the stories all around us. And third, to practice deciding how and where to enter a story and where to leave off.

Student Example

One writer used an article from *Weekly World News* about a Japanese moving company that specializes in moving people at "odd times of the day." The service was popular with debtors avoiding creditors and with girlfriends leaving boyfriends. In one case, a woman took her boyfriend to dinner so that the moving company could remove her possessions from their apartment without his knowledge.

When I went for the job interview, I found the owner in a garage-office, seated at his desk, which wobbled on three legs and a stack of cinder blocks. He was writing in a ledger and stuffing a jelly doughnut into his mouth between calculations.

I cleared my throat and he turned to boom a "Hi there, kid" at me, then wiped his fingers on his shirt and shook my hand. We sat down on the ripped red vinyl of an old car seat and Jake lit up a Marlboro. In between drags, he tried to explain how he'd founded the business, but he kept getting interrupted by calls from potential customers. He'd put each caller on hold, telling them he'd have to check with the personnel department or ask the mechanics about the truck fleet. When I asked what all that was about, he said he wanted people to think his company was some kind of big deal outfit.

"Impresses the hell out of most of them." He glanced out the door at the company truck—the "fleet" that he'd mentioned on the phone—parked by the curb. "There's another gag I pull. Y'know what people always ask me?" When I shrugged he said, "They ask, 'Where's Darkness Falls?'"

I wanted the job so I humored him. "So what do you say?"

I tell them it's just south of Northboro. Sometimes I say just east of Westboro. I want them to think that we're a really mysterious outfit."

"What's so mysterious about moving stuff?"

His cigarette ashes fluttered down on my jeans as he leaned toward me. "It's not that simple, Kerry. Let's say you want to be moved with no questions asked, any time of night. Maybe your business wasn't cutting the mustard, so you figure you better move your equipment before the bank moves it out for you. Who do you call? The Darkness Falls Moving Company," he said, grinning. "When you want to make a sudden move, we're the move to make."

Everyone else who interviewed me had given me the look of death when I said I had to quit in September, but Jake just shrugged and said he could use me about four nights a week. "Be prepared to work anytime between dusk and dawn," he said. "I'm the Robin Hood of the moving business."

—SCOTT WEIGHART, "THE DARKNESS FALLS MOVING COMPANY"

EXERCISE 9

Taking Risks

One of the great pleasures of writing fiction is letting your imagination and fantasies take off anywhere they want to go. Most people feel guilty when they think of doing something awful to someone they dislike; writers can invent a story and in it fling a hated character from a moving car or have him go blind. Another fantasy you can play out is doing something the very idea of which terrifies you—like parachuting from a plane or sailing across the ocean solo. As a fiction writer you're at a serious disadvantage if you can't write about an experience you're unlikely ever to know firsthand. This is not as easy as it seems, because you must sound not only plausible when you describe diving to the depths of the Aegean, you've also got to know what you're talking about—all those details about the scuba gear have to sound absolutely authentic. This is why a lot of novelists spend so much time in libraries—they're making sure they get it right.

The Exercise

Using the first person, describe an event or action you are fairly sure you will never experience firsthand. Be very specific—the more details you incorporate the more likely it is that your reader will believe you. Include your feelings and reactions.

The Objective

"Write what you know" is all very well but it restricts most of us within narrow confines. You must also be able to write what you don't know, but can imagine. This is what your imagination is for. Let it fly.

Student Example

I've been a missing person for ten days and the novelty is starting to wear off. My wife is on the eleven o'clock news and my girlfriend's losing her patience.

"How can you just lie there and watch her cry like that?" Maura says.

"I left a note for Chrissakes. She's trying to humiliate me," I say. Every day, all over America, guys leave their wives and nothing happens. Mine calls the FBI and reports me as missing.

Joe Shortsleeve, WBZ-TV's intrepid reporter, is asking my wife if I was involved in any illegal activities.

"No," she says gloomily. Her eyes are puffy. "He's the most normal person in the world."

"You can have him back," Maura shouts at the television. She's lying next to me like a big white corpse. Naked. I wish she'd cover herself after sex. I already feel like I know her too well. She's furious that I'm getting all this attention. The camera is following a helicopter as it circles above some wooded area. I can't figure out why they're searching for me there. I hate forests.

Tomorrow I'll go home and become the biggest joke in Massachusetts.

I tell Maura I'm going to take a walk, and I put on my Celtics cap. It's one of the items I was wearing when my wife last saw me. I might as well be conspicuous, now that things have been decided.

My first stop is the Store 24, where I buy the *Boston Herald* and a scratch ticket. I let the little Pakistani guy behind the counter get a real good look at me. He points to something on the front page and smiles. That's it, I say to myself, it's all over.

"Beel Clin-Ton," he says and shakes his head in mock disgust.

I wind up at Mister Donut. There's a cute girl there who works the late shift. It's starting to snow and we're talking about skiing. She tells me she gets homesick every time it snows because she grew up in Vermont. I sip my coffee but save my jelly stick for later. I don't like eating donuts in front of good-looking women because crumbs get stuck in my moustache. I watch her as she mops between the tables. I can't be sure if she likes me or she's just a nice person, but I have the secret that might tip the scales. I want to confess.

"I'm a missing person," I say as she squeezes the water into a grimy yellow bucket on wheels.

"Listen," she says. "I know the feeling."

—MATT MARINOVICH

PART TWO

Characterization

I live with the people I create and it has made my essential loneliness less keen.

—Carson McCullers

Whenever we meet someone for the first time, we unconsciously, instinctively size them up. Our senses register the look on their face, their clothes, their general attitude, the way they talk to you and to other people. We pick up and process scores of clues to their identity in an instant or two, without even thinking about what we're doing—or why we're doing it.

Fictional characters don't come equipped with clues; you, as writer, must supply them. The more specific you make these clues, the more immediate your characters will be. "Beautiful" is not enough. You must describe her eyes, her expression, her skin, her self-confidence, etc. Thus, characterization means fleshing out the people who inhabit your story or fictional world by providing them with physical characteristics, habits and mannerisms, speech patterns, beliefs and motives, loves and hatreds, desires, a past and a present and, finally, actions. This last—how your characters behave in a given situation—will determine their future and shape and give pace to the forward motion and final resolution of the story or novel. In this sense, as Heracleitus said, "character is destiny."

The writer must know more about her character—we'll call him Brad—than she puts into her story. For example, she should know what kind of toothpaste Brad uses, whether or not his father was a forgiving person, what extracurricular things he did in high school, how many pairs of running shoes he owns, etc. The more you know of Brad's biography, habits, and tastes, the more real he will be to the reader.

The names you give to your characters tell us a great deal about how we are meant to feel about him. Naming your baby is much easier than naming a character, largely because when you name a baby you're taking a chance that the name will suit the person he or she eventually becomes. When you name a character, you must pack it full

31

of suggestive stuff, indicating certain traits, social and ethnic background, and even how things are going to eventually work out for your character. Names such as Nabokov's Humbert Humbert, Dickens' Uriah Heep and Ebeneezer Scrooge, Arthur Conan Doyle's Sherlock Holmes, sound so right, work so well, you can't imagine these characters having any other name. The names you choose have a strong, and often subtle, influence on how the reader will respond to your characters.

Now, where fully realized characters come from is another story. Perhaps it is best summed up by Graham Greene when he says, "One never knows enough about characters in real life to put them into novels. One gets started and then, suddenly, one can not remember what toothpaste they use; what are their views on interior decoration, and one is stuck utterly. No, major characters emerge; minor ones may be photographed." One place that characters can emerge from is your notebooks. For example, read F. Scott Fitzgerald's notebooks to see how a writer's mind works. He even had classifications for notes such as *C—Conversation and Things Overheard, P—Proper Names, H—Descriptions of Humanity,* etc. Notebooks are a good place to collect names, lines of dialogue, and those details you just couldn't make up—like the guy we saw on the subway who, just before he got off, carefully tucked his wet chewing gum *into* his ear.

Fiction gives us a second chance that life denies us.
—PAUL THEROUX

EXERCISE 10

Oh! . . . That Sort of Person

Carefully chosen details can reveal character in fascinating and different ways. Writer and teacher Ron Carlson calls such details "evidence"—as if you were creating/gathering evidence for/against your character to bring his case (his story) to the reader. Sometimes details tell something about the character described as well as something about the character making the observation.

This is true of Anna Karenina's reaction on seeing her husband, Alexey Alexandrovitch, after a trip to Moscow, during which she patched up her brother's marriage and also met her future lover, Vronsky. Anna returns to St. Petersburg and is met at the train station by Alexey: "'Oh, mercy! Why do his ears look like that?' she thought, looking at his frigid and imposing figure, and especially the ear that struck her at that moment as propping up the brim of his round hat." We see him as stern and ludicrous and we also feel her dismay as she becomes aware of her feelings toward him for the first time.

In other cases a character reveals more about himself than he suspects. For example, there is a vivid character in *The Great Gatsby* called Meyer Wolfsheim who calls Nick Carraway's attention to his cuff buttons and then boasts, "Finest specimens of human molars." Clearly, Wolfsheim means to impress his listener, but instead of charming Nick (or the reader), this detail has the opposite effect.

In *Rabbit, Run*, John Updike uses physical characteristics to account for Rabbit's nickname. "Rabbit Angstrom, coming up the alley in a business suit, stops and watches, though he's twenty-six and six-three. So tall, he seems an unlikely rabbit, but the breadth of white face, the pallor of his blue irises, and a nervous flutter under his brief nose as he stabs a cigarette into his mouth partially explain the nickname, which was given to him when he too was a boy." And clearly, Rabbit is still appropriately called Rabbit, even though he's dressed in a suit and is no longer a boy.

In Pam Houston's story "Highwater," two women tell each other about the men in their lives. Houston writes:

> Besides drawing me a picture of Chuck's fingers, Casey told me these things: Chuck used to be a junkie but now he's clean, he had a one-bedroom basement apartment and one hundred and twenty-seven compact disks, and he used moleskin condoms which don't work as well but feel much better. This is what I told her about Richard: He put marinated asparagus into the salad, he used the expression "laissez-faire capitalist" three times, once in a description of himself, he played a tape called "The Best of One Hundred and One Strings," and as far as I could tell, he'd never had oral sex.

The women's early descriptions of apparently dissimilar men are important because by the end of the story, they have each been abandoned by their lover, and Millie says,

"I wondered how two men who at one time seemed so different could have turned out, in the end, to be exactly the same."

The first lines of Bobbie Ann Mason's "Shiloh" also bring a character immediately to life. "Leroy Moffitt's wife, Norma Jean, is working on her pectorals. She lifts three-pound dumbbells to warm up, then progresses to a twenty-pound barbell. Standing with her legs apart, she reminds Leroy of Wonder Woman." By the end of the story, Norma Jean is working just as hard at improving her mind—and at not being Leroy's wife.

The Exercise

First work with a story that you've already written, one whose characters need fleshing out. Write the character's name at the top of the page. Then fill in this sentence five or ten times:

He (or she) is the sort of person who _____.

For example: Meyer Wolfsheim is the sort of person who boasts of wearing human molars for cuff links.

Then determine which details add flesh and blood and heart to your characters. After you have selected the "telling" detail, work it into your story more felicitously than merely saying, "She is the sort of person who. . . ." Put it in dialogue, or weave it into narrative summary. But use it.

The Objective

To learn to select revealing concrete details, details that sometimes tell us more than the character would want us to know. Evidence.

Student Examples

Phillip is the sort of person for whom every transaction in life can be enacted with a Post-it Note.

—DINA JOHNSON

Mary is the sort of person who gets cast as a tree with two lines, and becomes the most interesting part of the play.

—JAMES FERGUSON

Emily was the sort of person who was practical in situations where most people were sentimental: When someone died she arrived with toilet paper, paper cups, and a three-pound can of coffee.

—BETSY CUSSLER

Will Greene is the sort of person who always has to be the better-looking one in a relationship.

—ABBY ELLIN

At fifteen, Tony was the sort of person whose heart rejected premarital sex, but whose body was already down at the corner drug store buying condoms.

—JOANNE AVALLON

She is the sort of person whose bookshelf is lined with Penguin classics but she has hundreds of Harlequins stacked behind the dresses in her closet.

—TED WEESNER, JR.

He's the kind of guy who borrows your car and brings it back empty with an I.O.U. taped to the steering wheel.

—MIKE QUINN

He was the kind of man who vacuumed for his wife after a fight because it was cheaper than buying her flowers.

—EMILY MOECK

He is the sort of person people came to with their problems because they knew his answer would always be to share a joint.

—KEITH DRISCOLL

Shelly Kim was the sort of girl who buttoned all her buttons.

—MACKENZIE SCHMIDT

She was the kind of person who never sat down to eat a meal, preferring instead to graze throughout the day like the large land mammal that she was.

—KATHERINE SIMS

He's the kind of kid who'd make fun of your lunch.

—ERIC MAIERSON

I always write from my own experiences whether I've had them or not.
—RON CARLSON

EXERCISE 11

What Do You Know about Your Characters?

*I could take a battery of MMPI and Wonderlic
personality tests for each of my people and answer
hundreds of questions with as much intimate
knowledge as if they were taking the test.*

—RICHARD PRICE

In *Death in the Afternoon,* Hemingway said, "People in a novel, not skillfully constructed characters, must be projected from the writer's assimilated experience, from his knowledge, from his head, from his heart and from all there is of him. . . . A good writer should know as near everything as possible." Yet students frequently write stories about a major event in a character's life, although they don't know some of the most elementary things about that character—evidence, information that, if known, most certainly would affect the character's motives and actions.

Hemingway again speaks to this issue of being familiar with characters:

> If a writer of prose knows enough about what he is writing about he may omit things that he knows and the reader, if the writer is writing truly enough, will have a feeling of those things as strongly as though the writer had stated them. The dignity of movement of an iceberg is due to only one-eighth of it being above water. A writer who omits things because he does not know them only makes hollow places in his writing.

The Exercise

Work with one of your completed stories that has a character who needs fleshing out. Take out a sheet of paper and number from one to fifty-three. At the top of the page, write in the title of your story and the main character's name—and start filling in the blanks.

Character's name: _____

Character's nickname: _____

Sex: _____

36

Age: _____

Looks: _____

Right- or left-handed: _____

Education: _____

Vocation/occupation: _____

Salary: _____

Status and money: _____

Marital status: _____

Family, ethnicity: _____

Diction, accent, etc.: _____

Relationships: _____

Places (home, office, car, etc.): _____

Primary mode of transportation: _____

Halloween costumes: _____

Tricks: _____

E-mail address, blog, and/or Web site: _____

Passwords: _____

Possessions: _____

Recreation, hobbies: _____

Obsessions: _____

Addictions _____

Beliefs: _____

Attitudes: _____

Superstitions: _____

Prejudices: _____

Politics: _____

Sexual history: _____

Medical history, allergies, etc.: _____

Ambitions: _____

Religion: _____

Fears: _____

Character flaws: _____

Character strengths: _____

Secrets: _____

Pets: _____

Taste in books, music, etc.: _____

Journal entries: _____

Correspondence: _____

Food preferences: _____

Handwriting: _____

Astrological sign: _____

Talents: _____

Friends: _____

Relatives: _____

Enemies: _____

As seen by others: _____

As seen by self: _____

Scars: _____

Tattoos, piercings, etc.: _____

What is kept in purse, wallet, fridge, glove compartment, medicine cabinet, junk drawer (calendar, appointment book, rolodex, etc.): _____

No doubt you will be able to add to this list.

Note: This exercise should be done *after* you have written your story. It is not a way to conceive a character, but rather a way to reconceive a character. It is designed to discover what you know about your characters *after* you have written your story—and what you don't know. For example, one writer, Samuel R. Delany, tells his students to know exactly how much money their characters make and how they make it. And why not apply this list to some of your favorite stories? Note how much is known about the unforgettable grandmother in Flannery O'Connor's story "A Good Man Is Hard to Find" or about the compelling, bewildered narrator in Peter Taylor's story "The Old Forest."

The Objective

To understand how much there is to know about a character you have created. Of course, it is possible to write a successful story about a character without knowing everything on this list—or perhaps only knowing two or three things. On the other hand, beginning writers often don't know more than a character's age or gender—and frequently neglect an essential piece of information that would have greatly informed or shaped their story. You needn't include these details in the story, but their presence in your mind will be "felt" by the reader.

> *All really satisfying stories, I believe, can generally be described as spendthrift. . . . A spendthrift story has strange way of seeming bigger that the sum of its parts; it is stuffed full; it gives a sense of possessing further information that could be divulged if called for. Even the sparest in style implies a torrent of additional details barely suppressed, bursting thought the seams.*
> —ANNE TYLER, INTRODUCTION TO *BASS 1983*

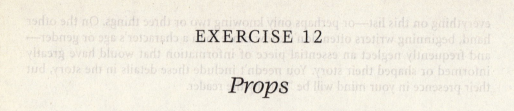

EXERCISE 12

Props

A lot of beginning fiction writers fail to understand how important it is to tell the reader where a scene is taking place and just what "props" are present to indicate a character's personality and economic and/or marital status. No one exists in blank space; people live and work in rooms or offices or barns or factories. The particular clothes, furniture, food, pictures, computers, etc., with which you surround your characters tell the reader a good deal about the characters' inner and outer lives, their tastes, backgrounds, and health, both mental and physical.

The Exercise

Invent a character. Then list most—but not necessarily all—of the items in his/her clothes closet, medicine cabinet, and refrigerator/freezer. Each object should inform your reader's understanding of who your characters are and how they live—or want to live. Think of yourself as the set designer or wardrobe person of a movie or play. What kind of lamp would you put on the side table? How would you dress the grandmother? Each item has to perform what words articulate.

The Objective

To understand the subliminal power of the objects surrounding and on the body of a character. An author who was hyper-aware of this power was Edith Wharton. Read her novel *The Age of Innocence* to see her close attention to what we call "props."

Student Example

Taylor Wombat
Bathroom: a foldout convex/concave mirror over the sink, an electric toothbrush, expensive eau de cologne, a tube of Rogaine, and a pair of hairbrushes. Medicine cabinet: Ambien, Anacin, mouthwash, condoms, and personal lubricant. Bedroom: electric shoe polisher, electric pants presser, battery-driven revolving rack of neckties. Framed photo of self and mother, framed photo of self with Dartmouth crew. On the wall a Dartmouth 1986 class banner. Double bed. Refrigerator: champagne, vodka, paté, tonic, soda, canned juice. On a desk in living room: a combined telephone/answering machine/fax, a pile of telephone books, and a street map of greater Boston.

Marcia Mendell
NordicTrack machine in bedroom. Single bed. Pile of *NY Review of Books* at foot of bed. One pair of sweats on bed, a second drying in shower. Scale in bathroom. Refrigerator: Organic apple juice, Poland Springs water. Vegetable juicer. Menorah. Running shoes in foyer. Pile of manuscripts on desk; glasses, laptop.

Marcia Mendell's sister
Stuffed animals on bed. Magazines strewn: *Vanity Fair, Vogue, People, US.* Posters of Elton John, David Bowie, The Police. Humongous TV in bedroom. Lots of pocketbooks in closet—maybe fourteen pairs of shoes. Man's rugby shirt & shorts balled up on closet floor; also the guy's shoes.

—MARK TOBIAS

What makes me feel as though I belong here, out in this world, is not the teacher, not the mother, not the love but what goes on in my mind when I am writing. Then I belong here, and then all of the things that are disparate and irreconcilable can be useful. I can do the traditional things that writers always say they do, which is to make order out of chaos. Even if you are reproducing the disorder, you are sovereign at that point. Struggling thought the work is extremely important—more important to me than publishing it.
    If I didn't do this, then I would be part of the chaos.
—TONI MORRISON

EXERCISE 13

What Do Your Characters Want?

In her superb book *Writing Fiction,* Janet Burroway stresses the importance of knowing what characters *want:*

> It is true that in fiction, in order to engage our attention and sympathy, the central character must *want* and want intensely. The thing that character wants need not be violent or spectacular; it is the intensity of the wanting that counts. She may want only to survive, but if so she must want enormously to survive, and there must be distinct cause to doubt she will succeed.

Sometimes *want* is expressed in terms of *need, wish, hope,* etc.—and it is amazing how many times these words appear in the first two pages of stories.

In the Gabriel García Márquez story "No One Writes to the Colonel," a colonel has been waiting for a certain letter for almost sixty years. As a young man, he had taken part in a successful revolution and, afterward, the government had promised him and other officers travel reimbursement and indemnities. The colonel's whole life has been a matter of marching in place and waiting ever since. Even though he has hired a lawyer, filed papers, written endlessly, and seen laws passed, nothing has happened. The lawyer notes that no official has ever taken responsibility. "In the last fifteen years, there have been seven Presidents, and each President changed his Cabinet at least ten times, and each Minister changed his staff at least a hundred times." The colonel says, "All my comrades died waiting for the mail"—but he refuses to give up, even though his life has been wasted and he has grown older, sicker, and crankier in the course of time.

The *want* that gives dynamic force to the story can take the form of a strong emotion, or an obsession, such as the colonel's determination to have his place in history recognized (probably his real motive); or it can be expressed in some specific plan or scheme.

Henry James's novel *The Wings of the Dove* is a good example of an elaborate scheme. Kate Croy, a London woman, knows that her one-time acquaintance Milly Theale, a rich and charming American, is dying of a mysterious disease. The doctors think that Milly's only chance for recovery lies in finding happiness—such as that of falling in love. Kate's scheme is to have her lover, Merton Densher, woo and marry Milly, inherit her money when she dies, and then marry Kate.

In Fitzgerald's *The Great Gatsby,* Jay Gatsby's whole ambition is to recover the past—specifically the idyllic time of his love affair with Daisy Buchanan years before.

Sometimes an ostensible *want* hides or overlays a greater one. Robert Jordan in Hemingway's *For Whom the Bell Tolls* intends to blow up a bridge to halt the advance of Franco's fascist troops. But as he waits for the strategic moment, an underlying desire to experience the life of Spain and identify with the Spanish people emerges as his real *want*.

Leslie Epstein's *King of the Jews* offers the reader an enigmatic mixture of purposes. I. C. Trumpelman, the Jewish puppet-leader whom the Nazis install as head of the ghetto, wishes to preserve his people from the Holocaust—but he also has a drive to rule, dictate to, and punish them.

Wants in fiction aren't always simple and straightforward things, just as people's motives are seldom unmixed. The more complicated and unsuspected—both to her and to us—are a protagonist's aims, the more interesting that character will be and the more interesting will be the unfolding of her story.

The Exercise

Look at the stories you've already written and ask

- What does the central character want?
- What are her motives for wanting this?
- Where in the story is this made clear to the reader?
- How do we learn what the central character wants? Dialogue? Actions? Interior thinking?
- What or who stands in the way of her achieving it?
- What does that desire set in motion?

If you don't know the answers to these questions, you don't know your character and her desires as well as you should. Aristotle said, "Man is his desire." What your central characters desire will inform the situations and ultimately the elements of the plots in which they are involved.

The Objective

To understand how your central character's desires shape her life. To see characterization as more than description and voice and mannerisms.

It's not wise to violate the rules until you know how to observe them.
—T. S. Eliot

EXERCISE 14

Making Heroes Flawed

from Douglas Bauer

In *Aspects of the Novel*, E. M. Forster wrote that "all actors in a story are, or pretend to be, human beings. Since the fiction writer is also a human being, there is an affinity between him and his subject matter which is absent in many other forms of art." If we think of this natural affinity as a tool to employ—one human being (the writer) identifying with another human being (his or her character)—then we can begin to understand the responsibility a writer has to create characters with complex personalities and contradictory make-ups. This complexity is especially important in creating protagonists, the heroes of the story, the character we want our readers to root for. While it's true that the most richly rewarding stories are populated with protagonists, or heroes, whose efforts and intentions are admirable, no credible fictional character is entirely admirable, purely heroic. This becomes obvious when, remembering Forster, we think of our fictional creations as human. The most virtuous of human beings is flawed. That's what it means to *be* human. So, too, with our protagonist heroes.

The Exercise

Here's one way to consider creating heroic characters, employing that affinity Forster described, which helps to guard against making them impossibly good. Think of this exercise as a credit-and-debit sheet.

First, write a brief synopsis of your hero's personality, highlighting his or her best qualities. Then make a list of those highlighted qualities: for example, fairness, integrity, charitable impulses, modesty, etc.

Next, imagine a not so admirable, offsetting personality trait that your hero has to struggle to control, and match it with the admirable trait. He may or may not be conscious of that struggle. If you listed "fairness," for instance, you might place next to it something like, "pride." If you listed "integrity," you might list, on the debit side, "intolerance." And so on.

Finally, mix the good and the bad, so that, in the first case, you have a hero who is fair in the end, but who occasionally self-servingly makes clear to one and all that he is one who has to suppress the impulse to do so. Perhaps he boasts, if only to himself, about some objectively scrupulous action he's taken. He's fair, but he's sometimes a bit pleased with himself.

Or, if your hero resists the temptation to cheat and thereby profit in the process, perhaps she harbors a suspicion that her business partner isn't behaving quite so honorably, interpreting her actions as suspect, even if there's no clear evidence. She's honest as the day is long, but is apt to define that quality too strictly.

The Objective

The key is to make the admirable aspect the dominant of the two, but also to remember, as you set your protagonist heroes free to determine the outcome of the story, that they have that negative component lurking in their personalities as well. Maybe the hero is aware of his flaws and consciously fights back their emergence. Maybe someone else in the story perceives the hero's flaws. In any case, by mixing the two ingredients, one from the credit and one from the debit side of the ledger, you'll be helped to resist creating the unconvincing and—equally damning—uninteresting saintly hero.

I never travel without my diary. One should always have something sensational to read on the train.
—OSCAR WILDE

EXERCISE 15

Creating a Character's Background, Place, Setting, and Milieu

from Robie Macauley

You are what you buy, own, eat, wear, collect, read, and create; and you are what you do for a living and how you live. If somebody broke into your home or apartment while you were away, chances are he could construct a good profile of who you are. You should be able to do exactly that for your characters even when they are "offstage." This exercise is the reverse of Exercise 12, "Props."

The Exercise

Create a setting for one or more of the following and furnish a place with his character—you create the character through observation of the setting. The place can be any kind of locale—house, a specific room in a house, outdoor grounds, an office, a cell, even a bed. The description must incorporate enough characteristic things so that the reader can visualize the absent dweller accurately. Try to avoid stereotypes.

An unsuccessful painter
A member of a lunatic fringe political group
A former movie star who still thinks she's famous
A foster child
A high school senior about to flunk out
A fugitive from the law
A social climber
A cocktail waitress down on her luck
A blind person
A paraplegic
A paranoid person
A supermarket checkout woman who just won the state lottery

The Objective

To be able to select details that will create a character and furnish the world of that character. Note which details indicate the circumstances of the subject—such things as success or lack of success, social status and habits. Which details indicate emotions, personality, intelligence, character, and outlook on life?

Student Example

Jeremy told me that after the accident his mother set up his room like the face of a clock. As I stand in the doorway, at what must be six o'clock, I see what he means.

Straight ahead, against the far wall is Jeremy's bed—twelve o'clock. His mom made the bed with tight hospital corners and his pajamas, black and white striped like a prisoner's uniform, are laid out for him.

His desk is at three o'clock. Braille copies of *A Tale of Two Cities* and *Wuthering Heights* sit next to small cassette recordings of our Psych textbook. Tapes for American History, Econ., and Chemistry are stacked alongside.

I move to five o'clock and touch his empty bookcase. On the third shelf up, his initials, J. M.—Jeremy Malone—are etched deep in the wood. I close my eyes and run my fingers over them. Jeremy made this bookcase a year ago—about two months before his motorcycle accident on Route 9. Jeremy told his parents to take his books away.

The closet door, at nine o'clock, has been scrubbed with Murphy's Oil Soap. His stereo sits at ten o'clock, power off, but the volume turned nearly to its maximum. His posters of *Easy Rider* and the Budweiser girl are gone.

—CHRISTY VELADOTA

I have always regarded fiction as an essentially rhetorical art—that is to say, the novelist or short-story writer persuades us to share a certain view of the world for the duration of the reading experience, effecting, when successful, that rapt immersion in an imagined reality that Van Gogh caught so well in his painting "The Novel Reader." Even novelists who, for their own artistic purposes, deliberately break that spell have to cast it first.

—DAVID LODGE

EXERCISE 16

Put Your Characters to Work

Have you ever worked as a carpenter, cabdriver, bouncer, dentist, bar pianist, actor, film critic, drummer, teacher, domestic, waiter, coach, stockbroker, plumber, therapist, minister, police officer, or mail carrier? If not any of these, you have probably worked at one or several jobs and have a job now. Have you ever used a job as background for a story? Better yet: Have you ever put a character to work in a job you've never had?

Work seldom finds its way into the stories of beginning writers, although this is fertile ground for harvesting the details of language, setting, socioeconomics, and "machinery." In an interview in *StoryQuarterly,* Grace Paley is asked about her statement that "the slightest story ought to contain the facts of money and blood." Paley replies:

> It really means family, or the blood of ordinary life. . . . As for money, it's just that everybody makes a living. And that's one of the things that students forget entirely. . . . [I]t's just that they never go to work. The story takes place between eight in the morning and eight the next morning with nobody ever leaving the room! And those are the things that our life in this world and in this society and in every other society is really made up of. . . . Our family relationships are of the utmost importance, and when they don't exist they're equally important—and how we live, how we make a living. The money in our lives: how we either have it or we don't. . . . If people live without working, that is very important. It's called "Class." And that really is another way of saying that you really DO write about classes, whether you know it or not.

Ethan Canin's first collection of stories, *Emperor of the Air,* is a good example of work as foreground and background. His characters teach astronomy, biology, and English, coach basketball and baseball, sell movie tickets and run the projector, make prints, or play the horn. Other characters are a hospital orderly, a medical student, a grocery store owner, and a retired auto upholstery salesman. Some of these jobs are central to their stories and others are simply what his characters do for a living, but each job is given the respect of particularity.

Every writer should have on his bookshelf Studs Terkel's *Working.* It is a gold mine of people talking, explaining, and complaining about their respective jobs. Listen to their talk:

A DOORMAN: "If tenants came by, you had to stand up. If you were sitting down, you'd stand up. As a doorman then, you couldn't sit like this. When I was first hired,

I sat down with my legs crossed. The manager came over and he said, 'No, sit down like this'—arms folded, legs stiff. If tenants came in, you had to stand up quick, stand there like a soldier."

A NURSERY ATTENDANT: "I now work in a greenhouse, where we grow nothing but roses. You can walk in there and the peace and quiet engulfs you. Privacy is such that you don't even see people you work with for hours on end. It is not always pretty. Roses have to have manure put around their roots. So I get my rubber gloves and there I go."

A PHARMACIST: "All we do is count pills. Count out twelve on the counter, put 'em in here, count out twelve more. . . . Today was a little out of the ordinary. I made an ointment. Most of the ointments come already made up. This doctor was an old-timer. He wanted something with sulphur and two other elements mixed together. So I have to weigh it out on the scale. Ordinarily I would just have one tube of cream for that."

JOCKEY: "You go to the barn and start as a hot walker. He's the one that walks the horse a half-hour, after he's been on the track for his training, while he drinks water. About every five minutes, you gotta do about two or three swallows. Then you keep with him until he's completely cooled down, until he's not sweating any more. You do this every day. You might walk six, seven horses, which starts building your legs up. We all started this way. There's no short cuts. . . . Willie Shoemaker's the greatest. He has the old style of the long hold. He has a gift with his hands to translate messages to the horse. He has the gift of feeling a horse's mouth. But it's a different style from ninety percent of us. We've gone to the trend of the South American riders. They ride a horse's shoulder, instead of a horse's back."

DENTIST: "Teeth can change a person's appearance completely. It gives me a sense of satisfaction that I can play a role. The thing that bugs me is that you work hard to create, let's say, a good gold bridge. It requires time, effort, and precision. Before I put them in place, I make the patient look at them. An artist can hang his work on the wall and everybody sees it. No one sees mine except me." (Read Jane Smiley's *The Age of Grief*.)

AN INTERSTATE TRUCKER: "Troopers prey on truck drivers for possible violations— mostly regarding weight and overload. It's extremely difficult to load a steel truck legally to capacity. . . . You have to get around the scales. At regular pull-offs, they'll say: Trucks Must Cross Scales. You pull in there and you find, lo and behold, you're five hundred or a thousand pounds over. You've got to pay a ticket, maybe twenty-five dollars, and you have to move it off. This is a great big piece of steel. You're supposed to unload it. You have to find some guy that's light and break the bands on the bundle and transfer the sheets or bars over on the other truck. Occasionally it's something that can't be broke down, a continuous coil that weighs ten thousand pounds. . . . You wish for the scale to close and you close your eyes and you go like hell to try to get out of the state. You have a feeling of running a blockade in the twenties with a load of booze."

Books on work make fascinating reading; one example is *Seven Days a Week: Women and Domestic Service in Industrializing America* by David Katzman. Do research for your stories; talk to people about their jobs. Judith Rossner must have spent weeks reading for her novel *Evangeline.* John Updike sent away for manuals on how to run a car dealership when he was writing *Rabbit Is Rich.* Work is at the heart of everyone's day. Faulkner said, "You can't eat for eight hours a day nor drink for eight hours a day nor make love for eight hours a day—all you can do for eight hours a day is work. Which is the reason why man makes himself and everybody else so miserable and unhappy."

The Exercise

Read twenty or thirty pages of *Working*—just enough to whet your appetite for writing fiction about the workplace. Then write a story in which a character is having a personal problem that is being played out where he or she works. You might want to choose a job that you haven't had so you can bring a fresh eye to its language, its details.

The Objective

To put your characters back to work so we meet them at work—and play.

Student Example

The whole thing started when Sparky came unglued in the trunk of my car. That's the number one thing a ventriloquist never does—leave his dummy in ninety-six degree heat in a parking lot. And that's the first thing Lester ever told me. Lester's my older brother and he's a professional ventriloquist. He works the Carmen Miranda room at the Chelsea Hotel on Monday nights. It's the kind of place that keeps its Christmas lights strung up year round. I like to go there and order something ritzy, like a Manhattan, and watch him. Lester's a wizard.

His lips are never more than a quarter inch apart. He can drink a whole glass of water and the Colonel keeps jabbering away. The Colonel's the name of his dummy. The rack of medals above the Colonel's pocket—those are Dad's medals from WWII, and Dad would be proud to have them on display in such a classy place as the Carmen Miranda room. Lester says ventriloquism is going to make a comeback, just like everything.

Lester and I live together. When he saw Sparky was falling apart, he really blew his top. He asked me to repeat the most important rule a ventriloquist must remember.

"Keep your buddy clean," I said. "Sparky is my life-time partner."

Lester's scrunched-up face went back to normal.

We worked on Sparky in silence, gluing the bottom half of his mouth again.

—MATT MARINOVICH, FROM "SPOKEN FOR," PUBLISHED IN *THE QUARTERLY*

I give characters more moral latitude than I give myself. And when I create characters who transgress on moral codes I possess—they startle me.
—EVE SHELNUTT

EXERCISE 17

The Morning After

Nothing and nobody exists in a vacuum. We all have histories that impinge on our present lives. Wouldn't you want to know if the man you're seeing spent the last five years behind bars? So too do fictional characters drag their histories into relationships. It's important for the fiction writer to know his characters' biographies before starting out to write a story or a novel about them. This is like having a flashlight in a dark room rather than feeling your way around. The exercise combines making sure you know your characters' back stories and making appropriate use of dialogue to underscore that knowledge.

The Exercise

This is based on a true story. A man, getting ready to drive to a friend's house with his baby daughter, puts the car seat with the baby in it on top of the car while he packs some things in the trunk. He gets into the car, drives off, forgetting the baby on top of the car. The car seat flies off the roof, does a somersault, and lands on the street, upside down. The baby is unhurt. The scene you're asked to write is what takes place between the man and his wife at breakfast the next morning: how they behave toward each other, what they say to each other. The critical decision you're asked to make is how strong the marriage was before yesterday's incident. If the marriage is okay, they will act and talk one way; if it was shaky to begin with, they will talk in an entirely different way. Remember that what is not said is often more effective than what is said.

The Objective

The reason this scene takes place on the morning after is to let the characters "sleep on it," instead of starting to shout at each other or cry. They will have examined their life together before they start breakfast. Will the wife use her husband's potentially tragic lapse to get out of a bad marriage or will she support him and try to make him feel better? Is the husband defensive or abject? This exercise allows you to pull together a lot of what you know, both about human psychology and about the uses and the possibilities of language.

Student Example

"I'm sorry to be late. My electric shaver is on the fritz, I had to use a grown-up razor, and, as usual, cut myself. Hell of a way to get started!" Dwayne sat at the kitchen counter.

51

Alison had set his place with a bowl of melon chunks, a plate of scrambled eggs and sausages, a buttered English muffin with marmalade, and coffee with hot chocolate mixed in. "What a spread! Beats corn flakes and banana."

"No problem," she said. "It gave me time to do some reflecting about us. I still feel shook up after yesterday—and our talk last night didn't help. And by the way, don't you want to kiss Amelia before you start? She is your daughter, you know."

"Sorry, I guess I'm a little distracted this morning. I really do appreciate this breakfast. The eggs are delicious—just the right texture, soft, not lumpy. I'm glad you used the blue cheese even though it's a bit overpowering. How did you sleep?"

"Not terribly well, to tell you the truth. Come to think of it, why are you asking this in the first place? As for breakfast: You say—'I really do appreciate . . . delicious . . . etc., etc.' That doesn't sound like you at all! You sound as if you were reading from a script. Besides, how do you think I slept?"

Dwayne put his fork down and refolded his napkin. "Alison, I think we ought to slow down. I feel one of your moods coming on. I know you're upset and are being extra nice to me, but I'm not sure I know why you'd want to do this, and, to be honest, it's having the opposite effect. You're making me feel awful. Is that what you want? OK, I made a terrible mistake. I wish you'd sit down and talk straight to me instead of fussing over Amelia."

"Fussing—is that what you think I'm doing? She's needs me to give her more cereal, pick up her bottle from the floor, wipe her chin. She probably needs changing too. And a hundred other things I take care of while you're eating fancy expense-account lunches with your clients or playing squash at the club. Sometimes I wonder if you ever gave a thought almost two years ago—when I got pregnant and you said I had to give up my job at the agency to be a full-time mother—to what it would mean to us as a couple to have a baby in the first place, much less what you have to do to help take care of her. You certainly weren't thinking of her yesterday when you 'nipped in,' as you like to say, to pick up a case of wine and rearrange your clubs in the back seat. You forgot all about Amelia. You don't take responsibility—your mother once told me this, and I was loyal and dumb enough to argue with her—and you think you can joke reality away. It isn't going to work this time. Do you remember what you said to me last night when we knocked off the merlot you said was such great stuff? That maybe Amelia ought to put in for frequent-flier miles. Along with something about glide angle and airfoil integrity. Even though we were both a little fuzzy by then with that plonk of yours, what you said was so totally heartless and depraved—I still can't believe you thought it was funny. Anyhow, while I was cooking your 'delicious' breakfast and 'fussing' over Amelia, I decided your lame joke about her being airborne may have changed for good the way I think about you."

—Mark Tobias

No man consciously chooses evil because it is evil; he only mistakes it for the happiness that he seeks.
—Mary Wollstonecraft Shelly

EXERCISE 18

He/She: Switching Gender

As a writer of fiction you're seriously handicapped if you can't write convincingly about people unlike yourself. You should be able to assume the voice (or, at least, the point of view) of a child, an old person, a member of the opposite gender, or someone of another race. An accomplished writer assumes as many shapes, sizes, colors, etc., as the fictional occasion demands. This requires you to do what actors do when taking on a role: They not only imagine what it's like to be another person, they transform themselves, they get inside their character's skin.

In a *Paris Review* interview, Nadine Gordimer says, "Look at Molly Bloom's soliloquy. To me, that's the ultimate proof of the ability of either sex to understand and convey the inner workings of the other. No woman was ever 'written' better by a woman writer. How did Joyce know? God knows how and it doesn't matter." Here is an excerpt from *Ulysses:*

> . . . I smelt it off her dress when I was biting off the thread of the button I sewed on
> to the bottom of her jacket she couldn't hide much from me I tell you only I oughtnt
> to have stitched it and it on her it brings a parting and the last plumpudding too split
> in 2 halves see it comes out no matter what they say her tongue is a bit too long for
> my taste your blouse is open too low she says to me the pan calling the kettle black-
> bottom and I had to tell her not to cock her legs up like that on show on the win-
> dowsill before all the people passing they all look at her like me when I was her age of
> course any old rag looks well on you then. . . .

Sue Miller in "Inventing the Abbotts" establishes early in the story that she is writing in the first person from the point of view of a teenage boy when she writes, ". . . at least twice a year, passing by the Abbotts' house on the way to school, we boys would see the striped fabric of a tent. . . ." And here is Doug coming upon his older brother Jacey:

> When I got home that night, I saw the light on in my brother's room. I went in and
> stood awkwardly in his doorway. He was reading in bed, the lower part of his body
> covered with a sheet, the upper part naked. I remember looking at the filled-in, grown-
> up shape of his upper body and momentarily hating him.

In "Gemcrack," Jayne Anne Phillips uses the first person to create a serial killer who was abused by his uncle as a boy. Here is one of his early school memories:

> The girls twirled, seeing how big their skirts became. I lay on the floor inside the circle
> of chairs. Above me the skirts volumined like umbrellas. I saw the girls' legs, thin and

coltish. Pale. The ankle socks chopped their calves above the ankle and gave the illusion of hooves. I saw their odd white pants and their flatness. They were clean like dolls. They smelled of powder. They flashed and moved. I turned my face to the hard blond legs of the chairs.

In *Professor Romeo*, Anne Bernays uses the third person to write from the point of view of a man accused of sexual harassment:

> "Why do all you girls think you're fat? [Barker asks] Even you skinny ones?"
>   "You really think I'm skinny?"
>   Barker saw Kathy's teeth for the first time as she grinned at him. He had almost forgotten that bit of magic: Tell a female she's thin and she's yours for life.

The Exercise

Write a page in the first person, assuming the voice of someone of the opposite gender. This can be a description, a narrative, or a segment of autobiography. The main point is to completely lose yourself and become another.

The Objective

To learn how to draw convincing verbal portraits of characters different from yourself and to make them sympathetic, rounded, and complex even though you don't especially "like" them or admire what they represent.

Student Example

Since I broke my hip I haven't been out of the apartment in three months. A young lady—couldn't be more than seventeen or eighteen—brings in my breakfast and supper. She comes in carrying a tray covered with foil. Her name is Debby and she works for the state.

It must have been a shock for Debby first time she saw me naked. It was end of July and hot as blazes. I tried to cover my parts but I wasn't quick enough. She looked away and said, "I've brought you some waffles, Mr. Pirjo, I hope you like them." Then she busied herself getting my knife and fork. They should have told me she was coming at seven in the morning. Every time Debby comes by I ask her to sit down and have a cup of coffee with me but she says she has five more people on her list, then she's in and out of her so fast, she's like a rabbit you only see the tail of.

—Judith Hope

Hate the sin but love the sinner.
—St. Augustine

PART THREE

Point of View, Perspective, Distance

Henry James called point of view the "central intelligence" of a story or novel. By this, he meant that the point of view operates as the eyes, ears, memory, and revelation through which a narrative is sifted and makes its progress. This central intelligence is, of course, the writer's singular take on her material. If you keep that in mind, you'll discover that you have more control over your narrative than if you just let it "write itself" (a very risky idea).

Three concepts seem to baffle beginning writers: How do I tell this story? Shall I use the first person, or the third? Should I contribute authorial comments or leave myself out of it entirely? Occasionally, with luck, you will hit it right the first time. But getting it right is more often a matter of trial and error, doing a chapter or a story one way, then deciding that the point of view and/or perspective isn't really working and starting over from scratch, using another point of view. Don't be discouraged if you don't get it right the first or even the second time.

There are various forms of points of view (often referred to as POV): the first person "I" as in *Moby Dick* and Eudora Welty's story, "Why I Live at the P.O."; Salinger's *The Catcher in the Rye;* the rarely used "we" as in Joan Chase's *During the Reign of the Queen of Persia;* the even more rarely used "you" employed by Jay McInerny's *Bright Lights, Big City.* Finally, the third person—"he," "she," "they." The third person can be used to convey the thoughts, emotions, and actions of one character only, as in Rachel Ingall's *Mrs. Caliban.* This POV can't move outside the character through whom you're telling your story. That is, this character can't accurately describe what he looks like from behind; he can only surmise.

Finally, there is the omniscient POV, in which the author moves from distant description and scene-setting to getting inside the heads of his characters. Tolstoy's *War and Peace* is a classic example of the use of the omniscient POV, as are Alice Hoffman's novels *White Horses* and *Turtle Moon.* The omniscient POV is not used today nearly as much as it once was; novelists and short-story writers seem to want to use one character through whom to render the action.

When trying to decide which POV to tell the story from, ask yourself whose vision and insights are the most dramatic and effective. Sometimes it can be a seemingly minor character—such as Nick Carroway in *The Great Gatsby*—through whose perspective we view the panorama of Gatsby's story or Ishmael in *Moby Dick,* telling Captain Ahab's story. More often, however, a story is told from the major player's POV.

Another consideration when determining POV concerns psychic distance, defined by John Gardner as "the distance the reader feels between himself and the events in the story." In Exercise 20, psychic distance is further explored and explained.

Suggested reading on POV: Wayne C. Booth's *The Rhetoric of Fiction,* John Gardner's *The Art of Fiction,* and Macauley and Lanning's *Technique in Fiction.*

It's astonishing how accurate intuition and imagination can be when given their heads.

—SYDNEY LEA

EXERCISE 19

First Person or Third

When you begin a story, you are faced with the immediate decision of point of view, and more often than not you will choose either the first or third person. For some writers, this decision is a conscious choice involving questions and answers about the most effective "central intelligence." For other writers, point of view is a given—it seems to come with the story they are about to tell.

The first-person point of view has the advantage of immediacy and a clear, singular voice—think of John Dowell in Ford Madox Ford's *The Good Soldier;* Captain Charles Ryder in Evelyn Waugh's *Brideshead Revisited;* Benjy, Quentin, and Jason in William Faulkner's *The Sound and the Fury;* Grendel in John Gardner's *Grendel;* Ruthie in Marilynne Robinson's *Housekeeping;* Antonio in Rudolfo Anaya's *Bless Me, Ultima;* Philip Carver in Peter Taylor's *Summons to Memphis;* Anne August in Mona Simpson's *Anywhere But Here;* and Jing-Mei Woo in Amy Tan's *The Joy Luck Club.* Each of these first-person narrators has a special voice that draws us in to his or her world. The limitation of this point of view is that the "I" should be present when most of the action takes place and is the only interpreter, aside from the reader, of what happened.

The third-person point of view is a familiar and reliable kind of central intelligence, one that allows the writer greater latitude in terms of distance and the authority to shift point of view. Several novels using third person are Joseph Heller's *Catch-22,* Christina Stead's *The Man Who Loved Children,* Leslie Epstein's *King of the Jews,* and Charles Baxter's *First Light,* whose chapters alternate between a brother and sister's point of view.

The decision whether to use first person or third is often a difficult one. Anne Bernays wrote her novel *Growing Up Rich* using the third-person point of view, then realized it belonged in the first person and rewrote it, starting on page one; it took a year. Changing point of view like this involves a great deal more than simply turning all the "she's" into "I's"; the author must step completely away from the story and let I's voice speak for itself. Too often, writers begin a story in the first person because it makes them feel closer to the story, yet the voice isn't unique enough to warrant first person. In general, if you can substitute "he" or "she" for "I," then your story should be in third person.

The Exercise

Begin a story with a third-person point of view, making a conscious decision about distance. Write two or three pages. Then begin this same story again using a first-person point of view, rewriting the same two or three pages. Do the same in reverse—changing a first-person narrative into third.

The Objective

To understand the limitations and powers inherent in both the first- and third-person points of view. To make you more aware of the choices available to you as author and storyteller.

Fiction is nothing less than the subtlest instruments for self-examination and self-display that mankind has invented yet.
—JOHN UPDIKE

EXERCISE 20

John Gardner on Psychic Distance

In the introduction to this section, we said that understanding and controlling "psychic distance" was as important to fiction as choosing a point of view. John Gardner's superb chapter "Common Errors," from *The Art of Fiction,* illustrates the range of psychic distance in five possible openings for a story:

1. It was winter of the year 1853. A large man stepped out of a doorway.

2. Henry J. Warburton had never much cared for snowstorms.

3. Henry hated snowstorms.

4. God how he hated these damn snowstorms.

5. Snow. Under your collar, down inside your shoes, freezing and plugging up your miserable soul.

Note how the first opening begins at a great distance from the reader in terms of time and space as it places the year of the story and introduces its character as "a large man." Isaac Bashevis Singer often begins his stories at this distance:

It was during the summer of 1946, in the living room of Mrs. Kopitzky on Central Park West.

—"THE SEANCE"

In the town of Shidlovtse, which lies between Radom and Kielce, not far from the Mountains of the Holy Cross, there lived a man by the name of Reb Sheftel Vengrover.

—"THE DEAD FIDDLER"

Then, like a camera zooming in on a scene, in each of the above stories Singer draws the reader closer to his characters and into their thoughts. At other times Singer begins stories closer in:

Harry Bendiner awoke at five with the feeling that as far as he was concerned the night was finished and he wouldn't get any more sleep.

—"OLD LOVE"

I never learned his name.

—"TWO MARKETS"

> I often hear people say, "This cannot happen, that cannot be, nobody has ever heard of such a thing, impossible." Nonsense!
>
> —"ZEITL AND RICKEL"

As you can see, there is enormous elasticity available in distance but it must be carefully controlled—especially since you can change the distance within a story. In general, the distance at which you begin a story or novel is the outer boundary beyond which you cannot go within that story. For example, if you begin a story at distance 3, as Singer did with Henry Bendiner in "Old Love," you cannot then draw back to the more formal stance of distance 1 by saying "The large man had never slept well." But if you begin at distance I, as Singer does with ". . . there lived a man by the name of Reb Sheftel Vengrover," you can "zoom in" like a camera within the story, even into a character's thoughts, to say "Reb Sheftel was almost speechless with terror, but he remembered God and recovered." Then, you can pan back out to "Reb Sheftel was the first to die" and "More years went by, but the dead fiddler was not forgotten."

A careless shift in psychic distance would be to begin with "It was winter of the year 1853. A large man stepped out of a doorway" and move to "God how he hated these damn snowstorms." Although both employ the third-person point of view, the psychic shift from one to the other is jarring. Gardner's example of a shift in psychic distance that doesn't work is this: "Mary Borden hated woodpeckers. Lord, she thought, they'll drive me crazy! The young woman had never known any personally, but Mary knew what she liked."

The Exercise

First, go back to the list of beginning sentences on pages 7–10, and read each sentence to determine its psychic distance from the reader—from 1, the greatest distance, to 5, where the psychic distance almost disappears.

Next, begin a new story five times using as your guide Gardner's five beginnings.

Finally, begin a new story at distance 1 or 2 and within 200 words gracefully decrease the psychic distance until you have reached distance 4.

The Objective

To understand how psychic distance works so that you can make conscious decisions about the range of psychic distance to use in each story or novel you write.

Successful characters are not merely invented, but should emerge from a writer's latent, even secret anxieties, hungers, and obsessions.
—MARIA FLOOK

EXERCISE 21

Shifts in Point of View

New writers are often told to use one point of view when telling a story—and for good reason. Shifts in point of view are difficult to do and depend on the writer's absolute control of language, detail, and observation. Four writers who shift point of view are Flaubert in *Madame Bovary,* Shirley Hazzard in *The Transit of Venus,* Alice Hoffman in *White Horses,* and Alice Adams in many of her short stories. Also, shifts in point of view must be warranted. The reader has to learn something from each character's viewpoint that he cannot learn from the perspective and interpretation of one character alone. Note in Kate Wheeler's story "Under the Roof" on page 414 how each character has information and perceptions the other characters couldn't possibly know.

Some writers indicate a shift in viewpoint by putting the narrator's name at the beginning of their sections, as Faulkner does in *As I Lay Dying,* Anne Tyler in *Celestial Navigation,* and Rosellen Brown in *The Autobiography of My Mother.*

Other writers, such as Sharon Sheehe Stark in *A Wrestling Season,* depend on indications in the narrative for us to know that we are now in a different character's point of view. Chapter 28 ends with Louise: "No wonder she hadn't heard the usual ferocious kabooms of some engine racing before takeoff. He had gone, yes, but not so far. As usual he was camping just outside the thumping, ridiculous mystery of her wifely heart." Chapter 29 begins with Michael: "And Michael woke early to dread. Sometimes that stalled-heart dream of his left him heavy like this, dejected. Yet he was quite certain the night had passed without fatality, dreamlessly indeed."

In Pamela Painter's story "Intruders of Sleepless Nights," the point of view shifts among three characters: a husband and wife pretending to be asleep in their bedroom and a burglar on his way there to steal the wife's jewelry. Each section begins with an observation that tells the reader whose point of view we are in. The burglar is first: "They own no dogs; the maid sleeps out. The catches on the windows are those old-fashioned brass ones, butterfly locks. No alarm system or fancy security." A few sentences later, the wife is next: "Her husband is asleep—finally. His back is to her, his right shoulder high, and now his breathing has slowed to a steady pace like some temporarily regulated clock." After more of the wife's observations, the husband's section is next: "His wife thinks he is sleeping. He knows this by the way she begins to move, adjusting the sheets, almost gaily like a puppet released to live." The story then returns to the original order: the burglar, the wife, and the husband throughout.

Shifts in point of view from paragraph to paragraph, or within the same paragraph, are more difficult to do and few writers attempt this. One writer who does is Alice Adams. For example, her story "The Party-Givers" opens with three people sitting around at the end of a party. In the space of the first two pages, the point of view shifts from Josiah, to his wife, Hope, to Clover, a former lover of Josiah's. Adams writes:

> Josiah liked the party; he smiles to himself at each recounted incident.
>
> Hope, Josiah's small, blond and very rich newlywed wife, during the noisy hours of the party has been wondering if she should kill herself. . . . This is Hope's question: if she killed herself, jumped off one of the bridges, maybe, would Josiah fall in love with Clover all over again? marry her? or would her death keep them guiltily apart?
>
> Clover, a former lover of Josiah's, of some years back, is a large, dark, carelessly beautiful woman, with heavy dark hair, a successfully eccentric taste in clothes. In the intervals between her major love affairs, or marriages, she has minor loves, and spends time with friends, a course that was recommended by Colette, she thinks. This is such an interval, since Josiah who was once a major love is now a friend, and maybe Hope is too; she can't tell yet.

Adams accomplishes her many point-of-view shifts by skillfully weaving attributions for thought into her narrative: "smiles to himself at each recounted incident," "has been wondering," "this is Hope's question [thought]," "she thinks," and "she can't tell yet." Graceful transitions are worth all the time and energy you invest in them.

The Exercise

Write a scene involving two or three characters who have secrets from each other—or possess different perspectives on what they are doing or have just done. Or write a story using several points of view. Remember that the point of view shifts must be warranted by the information and perspective each brings to the story.

The Objective

To experience how a shift in point of view works and what conditions of the situation make it necessary.

One must avoid ambition in order to write. Otherwise something else is the goal: some kind of power beyond the power of language. And the power of language, it seems to me, is the only kind of power a writer is entitled to.

—CYNTHIA OZICK

EXERCISE 22

An Early Memory,
Part One: The Child
as Narrator

"Write what you know" is by now such a cliché that people tend to ignore it. For the beginning writer it's pretty good advice. Your own life—and your memories of it—have an intensity and immediacy useful in creating fiction. It's not just what you know, however, but how you see it, shape it, and enhance it with your imagination. This is the crucial difference between fiction and fact. Fiction is always sifted through a singular set of perceptions, feelings, and wishes, while fact can be recorded by a machine designed for that purpose—a tape recorder or camera. Furthermore, the fiction writer often supplies an implicit rather than an explicit moral attitude.

Keep in mind when doing this exercise that even though you are writing from the point of view of a child or a young adult your audience is still an adult audience. Christine McDonnell, author of the young adult book *Friends First,* which has a fourteen-year-old narrator, makes this distinction:

> In adult fiction, when a story has a child's point of view, usually the child is scrutinizing the adult world, trying to make sense of adult behavior or adult society, as in J. D. Salinger's *Catcher in the Rye,* the childhood chapters in Anne Tyler's *Dinner at the Homesick Restaurant,* the children in Dickens's novels or Susan Minot's *Monkeys.* Children's points of view can add humor—O'Henry—or moral commentary—Mark Twain's Huck Finn. Sometimes, from a child's point of view, the situation seems more frightening or dangerous, as in Robb Forman Dew's *The Time of Her Life,* when the child is caught in her parents' ugly, boozy separation, and in Suzanna Moore's *My Old Sweetheart,* about a mentally unstable mother and philandering father. In all of these, the scope of the story is larger than childhood. Children are windows onto a larger picture, and that larger picture is of interest to adults.

The young narrators in Sharon Sheehe Stark's "Leo" and Charles Baxter's "Gryphon" are child narrators trying to make sense of the larger adult world at the point it intersects with their own.

The Exercise

Using the present tense, write an early memory in the first person. Choose something that happened before you were ten. Use only those words and perceptions appropriate to a young child. The memory should be encapsulated in a short period of time—no more than an hour or so—and should happen in one place. Don't interpret or analyze; simply report it as you would a dream. When you can't remember details, make them up; you may heighten the narrative so long as you remain faithful to the "meaning" of the memory—the reason you recalled it in the first place. Limit: 550 words.

The Objective

A fiction writer should be able to present a narrative without nudging the reader or in any way explaining what she has written. The narrative should speak for itself. In using a child's voice you are forced not to analyze but merely to tell the story, unembellished.

Student Example

The doorbell rings and I know it's Aunt Judith, the old lady I've been hearing about. She's come to visit us from where she lives, San Francisco, which is very far away. It takes almost a whole day to fly to my house from there in an airplane. She's very old, probably around eighty. I'm peeking through the stair railings when my father answers the door. All I can see is a gray coat and some white hair. She must be deaf because my father's voice is loud when he says hello.

My mother calls, "Come down and meet your Aunt Judith." She's holding her aunt's hand and smiling. I come down and stand behind my mother when I say hello. I don't want her to kiss me. She has more wrinkles on her face than I ever saw. She pats my head and says, "So big for five."

My father says he's going to make some tea. My mother and Aunt Judith and I go into the living room and sit down.

"Come here, Emily, and sit by your old aunt," she says, patting the couch next to her. I feel funny but I go and sit where she says. She smells like bread in the oven.

"Tell Aunt Judith about school," my mother says.

"I'll be in first grade next September," I say.

My father comes in with the teapot on a tray and some cups. I'm too young to drink tea. I tried it once and it tasted like dirt.

My mother and Aunt Judith are talking about people I don't know. My father looks like he doesn't know them either. I'm staring, but Aunt Judith doesn't mind. She has a mouth that sticks out like a fish with hairs over her top lip. Then I say, "You know what Aunt Judith? You have a mustache." I don't make it up; she does have a mustache; it's just like my grandfather's only not quite so bushy. Aunt Judith gets a funny look on her face. She stands up and says, "Where's the bathroom?"

My mother shows her where the bathroom is and when she comes back she tells me that I shouldn't have said that about Aunt Judith's mustache. "But it's true!" I say.

My mother tells me that just because something's true doesn't mean I have to say it out loud. She looks angry.

Aunt Judith stays in the bathroom a very long time. I want to tell Aunt Judith I'm sorry but I don't know how to. Finally, my mother knocks on the bathroom door. "Are you all right, Judith?" Maybe she thinks she's dead or something.

I can hear Aunt Judith's voice but not what she says. My mother says, "She's okay." My father says, "Big-mouth Emily."

I'm not staying around any more. I go upstairs but not to my room. I sit at the top where I can hear Aunt Judith when she finally comes out of the bathroom.

—Emily Honig

> [Do] not suspend the rest of the world while dialogue takes place. "Let the sounds of the world continue," I tell them, "almost like method acting. If you don't, you'll end up with those amputated-seeming, isolated exchanges in which the rest of the world has withdrawn out of deference. Much of the conversation that takes place has a background of assorted noises, and actions too. O for peace and quiet, but not in fiction."
> —Paul West

I can hear Aunt Judith's voice but not what she says. My mother says, "She's okay." My father says, "Big-mom..." I'm not staying around any more. I go upstairs but not to my room. I sit at the top where I can hear Aunt Judith when she finally comes out of the bathroom. —Emily Hoxie.

EXERCISE 23

An Early Memory, Part Two: The Reminiscent Narrator

Something crucial to remember: The story doesn't exist until you tell it, and the same holds true for when and how your narrator chooses to tell her story. Eudora Welty in *One Writer's Beginnings* speaks of this ordering of time:

> The events in our lives happen in a sequence of time, but in their significance to ourselves they find their own order, a timetable not necessarily, perhaps not possibly, chronological. The time as we know it subjectively is often the chronology that stories and novels follow: it is the continuous thread of revelation.

This is especially true of the reminiscent narrator who is looking back and reinterpreting or confronting the past because it has a special pointed meaning for her—a meaning that has often eluded the narrator until this particular telling of the story.

The reminiscent narrator of Peter Taylor's story "The Old Forest" is telling his story from a vantage point of forty-plus years. The tone and distance from past events are established immediately with the first line, "I was already formally engaged, as we used to say, to the girl I was going to marry." The narrator goes on to recount events that occurred when he was in an accident with another young woman a week before his wedding. At one point he wonders why these events and the images of Lee Ann's footprints in the snow and of his own bloody hand have stayed with him. "In a way it is strange that I remember all these impressions so vividly after forty years, because it is not as though I have lived an uneventful life during the years since." He goes on to list his World War II experiences, the deaths of his two younger brothers in Korea, the deaths of his parents in a terrible fire, and also the deaths of his two teenage children. As he continues the story, he learns perhaps for the first time to speak of his failures—the most important perhaps was the failure to follow his own heart. He has had a good, long life with the girl he was engaged to. He learned to follow his heart when he left the Memphis social and business community to become an English professor, but it was a lesson he learned through the events of this particular story—and with the help of Caroline his wife.

Alice Munro is another writer who brilliantly employs the reminiscent narrator to tell her story in such stories as "Friend of My Youth," "Wigtime," "Hold Me Fast, Don't Let Me Pass," and "Differently"—stories in which the present is informed by the past.

The Exercise

In no more than two pages, use the incident of "An Early Memory, Part One" and tell it from the vantage point of who you are today, that is, inject it with adult vocabulary, insight, subtlety, and comprehension. For example, "My father was obviously confused" replaces "funny look." Change the way the incident is told without altering its content. Use the past tense but keep it a first-person narrative. As in the first part of this exercise, try to let the material speak for itself. We draw up out of the well of our unconscious those things that have emotional significance. In contrast to the previous exercise, this one will force you to search—with an adult sensibility—for the underlying "meaning" of the event you simply reported in "An Early Memory, Part One" (page 63). What have you learned in the interim? What can be gained—or lost—by hindsight?

The Objective

As in many of these exercises, the idea is to empower the writer with the knowledge that he controls the material, and not the other way around. There are countless ways to tell the same story and each way says something and reveals something a little different, not only about what happened but also about how the teller feels about it.

Student Example

At the age of five I learned how easy it is to wound someone simply by pointing out to them something obvious to everyone else. I think that I forgot this from time to time as I got older but I certainly learned it in a dramatic way.

My mother's Aunt Judith was then in her late eighties—an old but vigorous childless widow who had helped translate the books of Thomas Mann and lived alone in Berkeley, California. She had come East to visit her brother, my mother's father, and was paying a call at our house. I had never met her and was a timid child anyway, so I hung back until she patted the couch beside her and told me to come sit next to her. I could tell by the expression on my mother's face that she was anxious to have Aunt Judith like and approve of me. I think my mother and she had had an unusually close relationship when my mother was young and lived in New York—where Aunt Judith also lived before she moved to the West Coast.

My father offered to make tea and disappeared into the kitchen. I mainly listened while my mother and Aunt Judith reminisced about people whose names I didn't recognize. But I didn't really mind because I was having such a good time staring at her face. It was a mass of veins and wrinkles—far more than my grandfather had. And she had a black mustache. If you hadn't seen her clothes or heard her speak you might have thought she was a man.

My father came back with the tea and they all drank, Aunt Judith making slurping noises and seeming to enjoy herself except that she really didn't have any idea how to talk to a child as young as I was. She asked me one question—I think it was about school—and then seemed to forget I was there.

But, as I said before, I didn't mind at all; I was a watcher.

Did I know, at some depth, that I should not say what I then said? To this day I'm not certain. But, with no windup, I suddenly said, "You know what, Aunt Judith? You have a mustache."

Her hand flew to her mouth: she looked as if someone had just pierced her lung with a sharp knife. She stared at me, got up, and said, very quietly, "Anne, will you please tell me where the bathroom is?"

My mother was obviously flustered and led her to the downstairs bathroom.

When she came back my mother tried to explain to me that just because something was true did not mean that you had to say it out loud. On my part, I tried to argue but soon gave up because I felt so bad. My father told me I was a bigmouth.

Aunt Judith stayed in the bathroom for fully fifteen minutes. I think my mother was worried that she had fainted. I knew what she was doing: She was studying herself in the mirror, perhaps seeing this horrible mustache for the first time; it must have been a shock.

They were annoyed at me and embarrassed by what I had done (and I can't say I really blame them. A big child but a tactless one). They were nice enough to let me go upstairs. The truth doesn't carry with it its own protection against pain.

—EMILY HONIG

Recently, I was engaged in a profoundly meaningful conversation in one corner of a large common room. In the corner opposite somebody was trying to conduct some silly group discussion. Presently, a young man strode briskly across the floor and tapped me on the shoulder. "Can you try and keep it down?" he said. "You can't imagine how your voice carries." . . . It carries. Yes, that's the idea, isn't it? You say what you have to say the way you have to say it and hope to hell you're bothering somebody.

—SHARON SHEEHE STARK, *OTHER VOICES*

EXERCISE 24

The Unreliable Narrator

You may find that you want to create a character who says one thing and unwittingly reveals another—for example, a teacher who claims to love all her students, even those with "funny, hard-to-pronounce names and weird haircuts." The unreliable narrator—between whose lines the author invites you to read—is a classic fixture in works of fiction. Eudora Welty's narrator in "Why I Live at the P.O." is a wonderful example of unreliability. So is the narrator of Ford Madox Ford's *The Good Soldier*. And more recently, Stevens, the butler of Kazuo Ishiguro's *The Remains of the Day*, totally deludes himself about the pre–World War II politics of his employer, Lord Darlington, and about his own feelings for another servant, Miss Kenton. And consider the voice of the narrator in Jenefer Shute's acclaimed first novel *Life Size*. Josie has been hospitalized for starving herself and is told that she cannot yet begin psychotherapy because she is "a starving organism" whose brain is "not working the way it should." She thinks to herself, "On the contrary, it's never been purer and less cluttered, concentrated on essentials instead of distracted by a body clamoring for attention, demanding that its endless appetites be appeased. . . . One day I will be pure consciousness, traveling unmuffled through the world; one day I will refine myself to the bare wiring, the irreducible circuitry that keeps mind alive." Were Josie allowed to have her way, she would surely die.

The Exercise

Using the first person, write a self-deceiving portrait in which the narrator is not the person she thinks she is—either more or less admirable. You must give your readers clues that your narrator is skewing the truth.

The Objective

To create a narrator who unwittingly reveals—through subtle signals of language, details, contradictions, and biases—that his or her judgment of events and people is too subjective to be trusted. The reader must thus discount the version of the story offered by the narrator and try to re-create a more objective one for himself.

Student Example

A young girl should stand up straight, that's what I told my daughter-in-law, Ruthie. "Don't slouch," is what I really said, "look proud to be with my son." I must say I've never seen anyone take such offense at a harmless comment.

"You're always criticizing me," Ruthie said. "First you tell me I don't keep the house clean enough, and then you tell me I'm not feeding your son."

I have to defend myself, don't I? To begin with, I said, "These things you call criticisms—they aren't. They are helpful suggestions, something one woman can say to another. I never said the house wasn't clean enough, it's just that with two small children, sometimes you get too busy to keep house the way you'd like to." The only reason I mentioned the dust balls under the couch was for the children's sake. And, I certainly didn't say that my son wasn't being fed. I only remarked that he was so skinny, that maybe he didn't have time to eat a good meal because of all the work he has to do, being such a nice man to help his wife the way he does. Really, my daughter-in-law is a good girl. She learns fast. I know her mother—she can't help it that she has some bad habits.

And then my son, Geoff, he feels he should protect his wife, so he says, "Ma, quit ragging on Ruthie. Mind your own business, Ma." I understand how he has to take his wife's side so she doesn't get angry at him. But me and Geoff, we have an understanding. I know he agrees with me, so I'm just helping him out a little by mentioning these things, right? He could have had any girl. He's a nice boy to stay with Ruthie and the kids and I just want her to appreciate what she's got.

—HESTER KAPLAN

In conversation you can use timing, a look, inflection, pauses. But on the page all you have is commas, dashes, the amount of syllables in a word. When I write I read everything out loud to get the right rhythm.

—FRAN LEBOWITZ

EXERCISE 25

Family Stories, Family Myths

from Katherine Haake

What I sometimes describe as the "private enduring instinct behind the narrative
impulse" is the habit of making things up as you go along. And sometimes I think that
"who" I am is just a combination of all the stories I have told about myself, or those
others have told about me. And "my" stories are only a fraction of the larger family
stories, this enormous mythology about our history and something else as well, something like our fate, that determines who we all are in the intricate interconnectedness
of our lives.

All four of my grandparents met and married in a small mining town in northern California that was subsequently flooded behind Shasta Dam, which my uncle
designed and helped to build. My grandmother decorously lit the wicks of candles before
she put them out, while her daughter, my mother, chased neighbors with a pitchfork.
My father never speaks of his own father, who died when he was very young. I have a
therapist sister who makes up her own stories about my father's silence, my mother's
early violence, what went on in the town under the lake, and of course I have my own
version of things.

To live in a family, any family, is to participate in the making of myths, and the
myths are all different, depending on who is constructing them. Writing, in large part,
is a process of translating those myths into language.

The Exercise

Part One

Select a family story, any family story but especially the kind that gets told over and over
again—about, say, Aunt Ethyl's one true love, or why the Brewer twins refused to dress
alike anymore in high school—and assume the persona of one of the central players.
Become Aunt Ethyl herself, or one of the twins, and explain in a letter to another family member (again, not yourself) the "truth" of exactly what happened. That's it. Don't
think too much. Just write the way you'd write any letter to someone about whom you
care a great deal and whom you suspect won't entirely believe you.

71

Part Two

Select a writing partner and exchange letters. Read your partner's letter, and respond by writing a letter in the persona of the addressee in your partner's original letter.

The Objective

To understand the story-making elements of family life and their relation to writing fiction. To gain some distance on our own mythologies by reading them as other people read them. To discover the unexpected character that lives in the space between letter and response. To be aware of how all written narratives contain, in addition to the narrator, who speaks, a narratee, who listens, and of how each profoundly affects both writing and reading. To see how our families, our pasts, and we ourselves are made and perpetually transformed in language.

A true work of fiction does all of the following things, and does them elegantly, efficiently: it creates a vivid and continuous dream in a reader's mind; it is implicitly philosophical; it fulfills or at least deals with all of the expectations it sets up; and it strikes us, in the end, not simply as a thing done but as a shining performance.
—JOHN GARDNER, "WHAT WRITERS DO"

PART FOUR

Dialogue

Dialogue is what people do to each other.

—Elizabeth Bowen

Like all good writers, Elizabeth Bowen understands that dialogue should be used to demonstrate attitude rather than to supply information. Dialogue used for exposition sounds stagey, unreal, stilted—"Aren't you the kid who helped my wife and me move into our new house after Hurricane Mabel, the storm that blew up the East Coast and left most of it in shambles?"

Dialogue used to convey attitude is a powerful tool, revealing who your characters are and what they're up to, and moving your story forward by suggestion and implication. Furthermore, dialogue is an economical way of defining a character through her speech, accent, vocabulary, idiom, inflection, etc.

The writer should be aware that dialogue in fiction is never a faithful rendering of the way we speak in real life. At its most poetic it's the iambic pentameter of Shakespeare's plays; at the other end of the spectrum is the vernacular of Mark Twain's Huckleberry Finn, using the Mississippi Valley vernacular of the 1840s. Both Shakespeare and Twain omit the hesitations, repetitions, false starts, meanderings, and aborted phrases that make human talk so much less dramatic than the dialogue made up by writers. Read a transcript of court testimony or a taped telephone conversation, or listen attentively to a person with whom you're having a conversation, and you'll realize that fictional dialogue is only an approximation of human speech; it has been focused, shaped, and concentrated to deliver a particular message.

Paradoxically, dialogue is often used to imply what is not being said. This is what we call the *subtext,* or the meaning beneath spoken language. For example, if you want to indicate that a wife wants to avoid talking to her husband at breakfast with their children, about his affair with the nanny, she will talk around the subject, ask him whether he would like another cup of coffee, tell him about her mother's health, then switch to the weather, and so on. They both know what's on both their minds—and the reader's—but they want to avoid talking about it. In using dialogue this way, you're asking the reader to read between the lines.

Most of us cover the nakedness of our true intentions with camouflaged clothing. The smile may disguise a grimace, the laugh stifles a sob. The text is right out there; the subtext is what's really going on. The two states don't necessarily have to contradict each other, but it's important for the writer to be aware of the subtext and to make sure the reader is also aware of it by skillfully inviting the reader to interpret what's obvious on the surface.

In John Updike's story "Still of Some Use," Foster and his former wife are cleaning out the attic of the house where they once lived together.

> "How can you bear it?" [Foster] asked of the emptiness.
> "Oh, it's fun," she said, "once you get into it. Off with the old, on with the new. The new people seem nice. They have little children."

Nothing but pain lies beneath the wife's flippancy.

In Anne Tyler's novel *The Accidental Tourist,* a couple, Sarah and Macon, whose son has recently been killed by a deranged gunman, are riding together in a car when the following conversation takes place.

> "Did you notice that boy with the motorcycle?" Sarah asked. She had to raise her
> voice; a steady, insistent roaring sound engulfed them.
> "What boy?"
> "He was parked beneath the underpass."
> "It's crazy to ride a motorcycle on a day like today," Macon said. "Crazy to ride any
> day. You're so exposed to the elements."

Exposed, just as their son was exposed, as we all are. Remember that dialogue is about attitude, not information.

Finally, it's important to learn when to use direct discourse (he said, they said) and when to summarize in indirect discourse (summarized dialogue). This is partly a matter of what feels right and partly a matter of our first point, namely, "attitude." For example, Al, the narrator, has to answer a phone that's ringing. You don't want to make him say "hello," and listen for Buddy's hello. This is flat and boring and a waste of words. Far better to cut to the chase—what the phone call is all about and how that moves your story forward. "The phone rang. It was Buddy, wanting to borrow my pickup. I said, 'Okay, but this time don't bring it back without a full tank of gas.'" Dialogue generally goes for the heart of the story—the exchange that matters or the confrontation.

Read, read, read. And write every day. Never compare yourself to anyone
but yourself. The question you ask of yourself each evening is: Did I write,
did I spend time? Show up for work every day, like any good citizen.
—RICHARD BAUSCH

EXERCISE 26

Speech Flavor, or Sounding Real

from Thalia Selz

Here comes your character. She's Irish, Hispanic, Vietnamese, a Maine congresswoman, a shrimp boatman from Louisiana, or a black professor of English in an Ivy League college who retains traces of her Chicago slum childhood in her speech. Your character is eager to have the conversation that the structure of the story demands. Or maybe she wants to tell the story herself, as in a first-person narrative. Either way, you want that speech to have its own flavor, to suggest the character and background of the person uttering it, without using much phonetic spelling because it can be hard to read. Characters in fiction, like real people, have to come out of a context to be convincing and intriguing—even when that context is imaginary, like post–atomic holocaust England in Russell Hoban's *Riddley Walker*.

The Exercise

Observe how the following speech fragments convey a sense of accent or national, regional, race, class, or cultural distinctions mainly through word choice and arrangement. Easily understood foreign words or names can help, too. What do these fragments suggest about the individual speakers by conveying the flavor of their speech?

> My mama dead. She die screaming and cussing.
> —ALICE WALKER, *THE COLOR PURPLE*

> "'I won't keep you,' I says. 'You must get a job for yourself.' But, sure, it's worse whenever he gets a job; he drinks it all."
> —JAMES JOYCE, "IVY DAY IN THE COMMITTEE ROOM"

> "*Muy buenos*," I said. "Is there an Englishwoman here? I would like to see this English lady."
> "*Muy buenos.* Yes, there is a female English."
> —ERNEST HEMINGWAY, *THE SUN ALSO RISES*

> ". . . the working mens one Sunday afternoon taking they only time off. They laying around drinking some moonshine, smoking the hemp, having a cock fight."
> —PETER LEACH, "THE CONVICT'S TALE"

"My own wife is seven years older than me. So what did I suffer?—Nothing. If Rothschild's daughter wants to marry you, would you say on account her age, no?"
—BERNARD MALAMUD, "THE MAGIC BARREL"

"Why me?" she rumbled. "It's no trash around here, black or white, that I haven't given to. And break my back to the bone every day working. And do for the church."
—FLANNERY O'CONNOR, "REVELATION"

"Father says for you to come on and get breakfast," Caddy said. "Father says it's over a half an hour now, and you've got to come this minute."
"I ain't studying no breakfast," Nancy said. "I going to get my sleep out."
—WILLIAM FAULKNER, "THAT EVENING SUN"

"Copy our sister-in-law," Brave Orchid instructed. "Make life unbearable for the second wife, and she'll leave. He'll have to build her a second house."
"I wouldn't mind if she stays," said Moon Orchid. "She can comb my hair and keep house. She can wash dishes and serve our meals. . . ."
—MAXINE HONG KINGSTON, *THE WOMAN WARRIOR*

Now write five of your own speech fragments.

The Objective

In this case, it is threefold: to help reveal character, to convince your reader by making your dialogue sound credible, and to add variety. Differences in speech aren't just realistic; they're interesting and provocative, and they can give vitality to your story. Speech without flavor is like food without savor.

The difference between the right word and the nearly right word is the same as that between lightning and the lightning bug.
—MARK TWAIN

EXERCISE 27

Telling Talk: When to Use Dialogue or Summarized Dialogue

One of the most important decisions a writer must make is whether to use dialogue or to summarize what is said. Too often dialogue is incorrectly used to provide information that could have been artfully done in summarized dialogue. Or else the reader is given pages of an entire scene—for example, the full escalation of an argument—when in fact only the closing lines are important to hear verbatim.

Summarized dialogue allows the writer to condense speech, set the pace of the scene, reveal attitudes, use understatement, make judgments, describe the talk, avoid sentimentality, and emphasize crucial lines of actual dialogue.

Study the following passages to learn what summarized dialogue accomplishes. If writing summarized dialogue eludes you, type out some of the following examples to *feel* how it works. Then transform the summarized dialogue into dialogue to understand why the author chose to condense it.

So this ordinary patrolman drove me home. He kept his eye on the road, but his thoughts were all on me. He said that I would have to think about Mrs. Metzger, lying cold in the ground, for the rest of my life, and that, if he were me, he would probably commit suicide. He said that he expected some relative of Mrs. Metzger would get me sooner or later, when I least expected it—maybe the very next day, or maybe when I was a man, full of hopes and good prospects, and with a family of my own. Whoever did it, he said, would probably want me to suffer some.

I would have been too addled, too close to death, to get his name, if he hadn't insisted that I learn it. It was Anthony Squires, and he said it was important that I commit it to memory, since I would undoubtedly want to make a complaint about him, since policemen were expected to speak politely at all times, and that, before he got me home, he was going to call me a little Nazi cocksucker and a dab of catshit and he hadn't decided what all yet.

—Kurt Vonnegut Jr., *Deadeye Dick*

She sits in the visitor's chair beside the raised bed, while Auntie Muriel, wearing an ice-blue bed-jacket, cranked up and propped up, complains. They put extra chlorine in the water here, she can taste it. She can remember when water was water but she doesn't suppose Elizabeth can tell the difference. At first she could not get a private room. Can Elizabeth imagine? She had to share a room, share one, with a terrible old woman who wheezed at night. Auntie Muriel is convinced the woman was dying.

She could hardly get any sleep. And now that she's finally here in her private room, no one pays any attention to her. She has to ring and ring, three times even, before the nurse will come. They all read detective novels, she's seen them. . . . She will speak to Doctor MacFadden, tomorrow. If she has to stay here for a little rest and some tests, which is what he says, the least he can do is make sure she's comfortable. She's never been sick a day in her life, there's nothing really wrong with her now, she isn't used to hospitals. Elizabeth thinks this may be true.

—MARGARET ATWOOD, *LIFE BEFORE MAN*

That afternoon, Dr. Fish sent a psychiatrist to my bed. He spoke to me kindly in a low voice, and he had a white beard that I found reassuring. He didn't ask about Mrs. O. until the very end. Instead, he inquired about my studies, my parents, my friends. He wanted to know when my headache started and what my other symptoms were. He touched on the subject of my love life with great delicacy and registered my response that it was nonexistent with half a nod. I tried to speak in good sentences and to enunciate clearly. My head hurt, but my breathing was much improved, and I think I convinced him that I was sane. When he finally asked me why I had been screaming at Mrs. O., I told him very honestly that I didn't know, but that at the time it had seemed important to do so, and that I hadn't been screaming but calling. He didn't seem at all shocked by this answer, and before he left he patted my hand. I think I would have enjoyed my talk with him had I not worried about what the conversation was going to cost. He looked expensive to me, and I kept wondering if his sympathy was covered by my insurance.

—SIRI HUSTVEDT, "HOUDINI"

Papa-Daddy woke up with this horrible yell and right there without moving an inch he tried to turn Uncle Rondo against me. I heard every word he said. Oh, he told Uncle Rondo I didn't learn to read till I was eight years old and he didn't see how in the world I ever got the mail put up at the P.O., much less read it all, and he said if Uncle Rondo could only fathom the lengths he had gone to to get me that job! And he said on the other hand he thought Stella-Rondo had a brilliant mind and deserved credit for getting out of town. All the time he was just lying there swinging as pretty as you please and looping out his beard, and poor Uncle Rondo was pleading with him to slow down the hammock, it was making him as dizzy as a witch to watch it.

—EUDORA WELTY, "WHY I LIVE AT THE P.O."

At half-past two in the morning Jerry called. He was sorry about the mix-up, but he could explain everything. It turned out that while Father Leo was upstairs that first night Jerry had met a fellow on his way to a poker game outside town. It was a private game. The players were rich and there was no limit. They'd had to leave right away, so Jerry wasn't able to tell Father Leo. And after he got there he'd had no chance to call. The game was that intense. Incredible amounts of money had changed hands. It was still going on; he'd just broken off to catch a few winks and let Father Leo know that he wouldn't be going back to Seattle the next morning. He couldn't, not now. Jerry had lost every penny of his own savings, the seven thousand from the man at Boeing, and some other cash he had held back. "I feel bad," he said. "I know this is going to put you in an awkward position."

—TOBIAS WOLFF, "THE MISSING PERSON"

They poured me more wine and I told the story about the English private soldier who was placed under the shower bath. Then the major told the story of the eleven

Czechoslovaks and the Hungarian corporal. After some more wine I told the story of the jockey who found the penny. The major said there was an Italian story something like that about the duchess who could not sleep at night. At this point the priest left and I told the story about the travelling salesman who arrived at five o'clock in the morning at Marseilles when the mistral was blowing. The major said he had heard a report that I could drink. I denied this. He said it was true and by the corpse of Bacchus we would test whether it was true or not. Not Bacchus. Yes, Bacchus, he said.

—Ernest Hemingway, *A Farewell to Arms*

One evening, Cole and I lay side-by-side on our big brass bed after dinner. Our bellies were full, and the swelter of the day still stuck to us. We lay with our heads toward the foot of the bed, our legs in the air, as we rubbed our feet against the cool white surface of the wall, leaving black smears from the dirt on our soles. We could hear our parents fighting through the heating vent. Muted obscenities. You pompous prick. You fat white mammy. We were trying to block them out with talk of Elemeno. Cole was explaining to me that it wasn't just a language, but a place and a people as well. I had heard this before, but it never failed to entertain me, her description of the land I hope to visit some day. We whispered questions and answers to each other like calls to prayer. *Shimbala matamba caressi. Nicolta fo mo capsala.* The Elemenos, she said, could turn not just from black to white, but from brown to yellow to purple to green and back again. She said they were a shifting people, constantly changing their form, color, pattern, in quest for invisibility. According to her, their changing routine was a serious matter—less a game of make-believe than a fight for survival of their species. The Elemenos could turn deep green in the bushes, beige in the sand, or blank white in the snow, and their power lay precisely in their ability to disappear into any surrounding. As she spoke, a new question—a doubt—flashed through my mind. Something didn't make sense. What was the point of surviving if you had to disappear? I said it aloud—*peta marika vadersa?* But just then the door to our room flew open.

—Danzy Senna, *Caucasia*

Note how telling stories lends itself to summarized dialogue in the Hemingway and Senna passages.

When I went to the school in S for the first time the following morning, the snow lay so thick that I felt a kind of exhilaration at the sight of it. The class I joined was the third grade, which was taught by Paul Bereyter. There I stood, in my dark green pullover with the leaping stag on it, in front of fifty-one fellow pupils, all staring at me with the greatest possible curiosity, and, as if from a great distance, I heard Paul say that I had arrived at precisely the right moment, since he had been telling the story of the stag's leap only the day before, and now the image of the leaping stag worked into the fabric of my pullover, could be copied onto the blackboard. He asked me to take off the pullover and take a seat in the back row beside Fritz Binswanger for the time being, while he, using my picture of a leaping stag, would show us how an image could be broken down into numerous tiny pieces—small crosses, squares or dots—or else assembled from these.

—W. G. Sebald, *The Emigrants*

There is *only* summarized dialogue in Sebald's extraordinary book, yet its varied voices are as distinct as any we might hear in literature.

Not all summarized dialogue occurs in blocks. In the following passage, from "Saul and Patsy Are Getting Comfortable," Charles Baxter summarizes a number of phone calls from Saul's mother before he comes to a particular conversation that he puts into actual dialogue:

> Saul's mother, Delia, a boisterous widow who swam a mile a day, played bridge on Tuesdays, tennis on Fridays, called her son every other weekend. When Patsy answered, Saul's mother talked about recipes or the weather; when Saul answered, she discussed life and the nature of fate. In February, after Saul and Patsy had been in Five Oaks for nine months, she said that she had heard from a friend that wonderful teaching jobs were opening up outside Boston, and even closer, right here, outside Baltimore. I heard this, she said, from Mrs. Rauscher. Saul listened to his mother go on for five minutes, and then he stopped her.
>
> "Ma," he said. "We're staying."
>
> "Staying? Staying for what? For how long?"
>
> "For as long as it takes."
>
> "As long as what takes? Honey, you'll never have a normal life as long as you stay there."
>
> "What's normal?"

Alice Munro often intersperses dialogue with summarized dialogue. In her story "Differently," two friends meet at a "hippie restaurant" where they wear "cheap, pretty Indian cotton dresses and pretended to be refugees from a commune...." Munro writes:

> When they weren't playing these games, they talked in a headlong fashion about their lives, childhoods, problems, husbands.
>
> "That was a horrible place," Maya said. "That school."
>
> Georgia agreed.
>
> "They were poor boys at a rich kids' school," Maya said. "So they had to try hard. They had to be a credit to their families."
>
> Georgia would not have thought Ben's family poor, but she knew that there were different ways of looking at such things.
>
> Maya said that whenever they had people in for dinner or the evening, Raymond would pick out beforehand all the records he thought suitable and put them in a suitable order. "I think sometime he'll hand out conversational topics at the door," Maya said.
>
> Georgia revealed that Ben wrote a letter every week to the great-aunt who had sent him to school.
>
> "Is it a nice letter?" said Maya.
>
> "Yes. Oh, yes. It's very nice."
>
> They looked at each other bleakly, and laughed. Then they announced—they admitted—what weighed on them. It was the innocence of these husbands—the hearty, decent, firm, contented innocence. That is a wearying and finally discouraging thing. It makes intimacy a chore.
>
> "But do you feel badly," Georgia said, "talking like this?"

Note how the summarized dialogue summarizes what the women usually talk about before it gives way to specifics in dialogue. It also describes the pace of their talk as "headlong." Also note how words like "agreed," "revealed," "insisted," "wailed," "announced," "squealed," "accused," and "admitted" go well with summarized dialogue but are almost never used with actual dialogue.

The Exercise

Highlight the dialogue in a story by a writer you admire. Then determine how much dialogue is summarized rather than presented in quotation marks.

Next, set up a situation in which one character is going on and on about something—complaining about grades, arguing with a spouse about the children, or recounting an accident to a friend. Summarize the dialogue, occasionally interspersing it with comments and stage directions.

The Objective

To understand what summarized dialogue accomplishes and how it affects tone, pace, and the shaping of a scene.

Student Example

No one could be certain whether Kadi had died by accident or by her own design, yet it was much debated over smoky fires far into the humid West African night, in the manner peculiar to the Fula people. Adulai Embalo, speaker for the village elders, cited the evidence indicating an accident: that Kadi had often slipped at the muddy, sloping edge of the well as she drew water; that she had been up that morning before first light and could not have seen clearly where the bucket-ropes of other women had worn a new incline at the lip of the well; and that her sandals were found nearby, but not her enormous tin washbasin, suggesting that she had been mounting the heavy load on her head when her wet bare feet lost their hold on the slick clay.

The others listened respectfully to this, and paused in silence to consider it in the glow of the dying coals. Mamadu then proposed the facts that suggested Kadi had taken her own life: that she had quarreled with her husband Demba the night before; that she had been ashamed not to have conceived since her third miscarriage the previous rainy season; and that her rice plot had been damaged by wandering cattle so that her harvest would be less than half of what she and Demba needed toward the purchase of medicine to fertilize her womb, or toward the purchase of a second wife for Demba. But little could be done about Kadi now, except to discuss and turn over each point cited by the speakers, which is what the other village elders did as the fire slowly died, savoring the joy of conversation in the arcane Fulani of older men.

—CAMERON MACAULEY, "THE WOMAN AT THE WELL,"
PUBLISHED IN *PRISM INTERNATIONAL*

The short story apologizes for nothing. It exults in its shortness. It wants to be shorter still. It wants to be a single word. If it could find that word, if it could utter that syllable, the entire universe would blaze up out of it with a roar.

—STEVEN MILLHAUSER

EXERCISE 28

Who Said That?

Well, often we're not quite sure because the dialogue is not attributed to a particular character. Yet, it is crucial to know who is saying what to whom because dialogue is central to a scene's drama and forward movement. We need to know whether the wife or the husband says, "I've decided to leave—and no further discussion is necessary." Whether the teenager or the parent says, "You're always taking something the wrong way." Whether the mugger or the victim says, "Don't let things get out of hand here."

There are various ways of attributing speech to make it clear to the reader who is talking. The easiest way is to use *he said* or *she said* or the person's name as in the following example:

"I've decided to leave," George said. "No further discussion necessary."

"So, no discussion," Mary said. "I'll just list all the reasons I'll be glad to see you gone."

"Tell it to the dog," he said.

"That's reason number one. The dog goes too," she said.

"Said" works most of the time and does not draw attention to itself. Occasionally use "asked" and "replied," but avoid words like "hissed," "trumpeted," "rejoined," "growled," etc. Trust the growl to be inherent in what is said and how the person is described.

Other ways to attribute dialogue to a character are:

■ Use the name of the person being spoken to:

"Jesus, Benjy, my job's more important than your marathon Monopoly game."

"Aw Mom, you're always taking something the wrong way."

■ Use emotional clues:

His head was fizzing and he had trouble keeping the gun pointed at the man's tie. Didn't know who was scareder. "Don't let things get out of hand here."

The man nodded and nodded. "Take it all, you can have it all."

■ Use action:

She filled a grocery bag with dog food and topped it off with a can of draino. "You getting the picture."

■ Use physical description:

Benjy's T-shirt said "Death by Doughnuts" and his hair rode his shoulders, Christ-like. "Monopoly is teaching me real estate, banking, investment."

"Just don't get too attached to those dice." Her T-shirts never said anything and her hair had been shorter than his for the past five years.

■ Use thinking by the point-of-view character:
He should have stuck up some woman first. "Just turn around and start walking."

Attribution doesn't only tell you who is speaking. It also provides a way for pacing a scene, for juxtaposing speech with thought, for slowing the action so the reader can absorb what is going on, for including physical details of the scene, for providing emotional clues, and for adding to the rhythm of the sentences.

Finally, most dialogue important to the drama and forward movement of a story is set off by itself, with its method of attribution. When the speaker changes, you begin a new paragraph as in the above examples. However, sometimes exchanges of dialogue are woven into a paragraph, as in the following passage from Anne Tyler's *Celestial Navigation*:

He held out his hand and said, "Well, goodbye for now, Mrs.—Mary," and she said, "Goodbye, Jeremy." Her hand was harder than his, and surprisingly broad across the knuckles. While he was still holding it he said, "Um, may I come back sometime?"—the final hurdle of the visit. "Well, of course," she said, and smiled again as she closed the door.

When dialogue or what is said is not central to a scene's forward movement, but you still want to include the characters' voices, place the dialogue inside a paragraph. Be sure that we know who is saying what. This alternative way of presenting dialogue is an important tool for controlling the pace and shaping the drama of a scene.

The Exercise

Highlight all the dialogue in one of your own stories. Next, find out how many methods of attribution you have used. Remember that attribution contributes a lot more to a scene than just telling us who said what. Then, examine how you have presented your dialogue. Would some lines of dialogue serve your story better inside a paragraph? Are the important lines presented in a dramatic way? Now, rewrite the scene using the tools you have acquired in this exercise.

The Objective

To learn to shape a scene with the tools of dialogue placement and attribution.

Style and structure are the essence of a book; great ideas are hogwash.
—VLADIMIR NABOKOV

The Invisible Scene:
Interspersing Dialogue
with Action

Flannery O'Connor, in her essay "Writing Short Stories," says that in beginning stories,

> dialogue frequently proceeds without the assistance of any characters that you can actu-
> ally see, and uncontained thought leaks out of every corner of the story. The reason
> is usually that the student is wholly interested in his thoughts and his emotions and not
> in his dramatic action, and that is he is too lazy or highfalutin to descend to the con-
> crete where fiction operates.

When you are writing a scene in a story, it might help to think of your characters
as being onstage. Your reader will want to know what they look like and what the stage
setting looks like. Next, your reader will want to have a sense of how your characters
move around and interact with the furniture of their stage world—in other words the
stage business, body language, or choreography. Characters live in a concrete world and
it is your job as a fiction writer to keep them there.

The Exercise

Write a scene in which a character's body, as well as his mind, is engaged in doing
something—stage business. Here are some possibilities:

Repairing something
Playing solitaire or a game involving other players
Doing exercises
Painting a canvas or a wall
Cutting down a tree
Giving someone a haircut

Come up with your own suggestions.

Explore how various activities and settings can change what happens within a scene.
For example, what happens when characters are planning their honeymoon while they
are painting an apartment or while one of them is cutting the other's hair? Or what happens when characters are having a confrontation in public—say in a fancy restaurant—
rather than in the privacy of their home?

It is also instructive to analyze how a writer you admire handles the interweaving of dialogue and body language. Go through one of your favorite stories and highlight all the body language and choreography. We guarantee this will teach you something.

The Objective

To give concrete life to the scenes our characters inhabit. To understand how action and choreography relate to the objects in the scene and how all of these relate to and help shape dialogue and the engagement of the characters.

Student Example

The church was condemned last week, so my sister Marion decided to have the wedding in Mom and Ivan's backyard, in front of the herb garden. I drove by the church yesterday to see the steeple that was sitting on a trailer in the parking lot. Luckily they found that it was rotting and took it down before it fell on people. Marion should take the hint.

An hour ago Mom put me in charge of weeding the old patch of dirt. "It's the least you can do for your sister's special day," Mom said. It had rained last night, so the garden was thick mud. The knees of my new red sweat pants would be stained and I'd need a hairbrush to get it out from under my fingernails.

"Colleen! Where are the car keys?" Marion called, her face pressed against the window screen.

"I put them on the counter," I said.

"They aren't there. Come in here and find them."

I threw another weed on the weed pile and slammed the screen door into the kitchen. Marion's face was pink and her hands shook. "Don't do this to me, Colleen. Mom and I need to leave now." The wedding was two days away and Marion had the whole house preparing. Ivan was at Woolworth's getting new lawn furniture and Mom was at the sink drowning a pot of peeled potatoes.

I wiped my hands on my jeans and pulled the keys from the Union Trust mug next to the sugar bowl. I threw them at her left hand. "Where's Gabe?" Her fiancé lived in the apartment buildings across town. He was nearly thirty, but he still mowed lawns and delivered papers for a living. Instead of a bike, he drove a red Mustang. I figured he should be here weeding the parsley too.

"Shut up, Colleen," Marion said. She bent down to look at her reflection in the microwave door.

"Girls," Mom said, turning off the water hard. She gave me a look and left to get her coat.

—KIM LEAHY

Every writer is a reader moved to emulation.
—SAUL BELLOW

THE INVISIBLE SCENE: INTERWEAVING DIALOGUE WITH ACTION • 85

It is also instructive to analyze how a writer you admire handles the interweaving of dialogue and body language ... favorite stories and highlight all the body language and choreography. We guarantee this will teach you something.

The Objective

To give concrete life to the scene our characters inhabit. To understand how action and choreography relate to the objects in the scene and how all of these relate to and help shape dialogue and the engagement of the characters.

Students ...

EXERCISE 30

A Verbal Dance: Not Quite a Fight

Good dialogue is not at all the way human beings speak to each other—it's an approximation. Dialogue takes human speech and renders it condensed, highlighted, and pointed. Dialogue is extremely useful when you want to show what a character is thinking and want to avoid the leaden "she thought" formulation. Simply bring on another character and have the two of them hold a conversation. Dialogue reveals character—as anyone who has ever seen a decent play knows. It is also good for breaking up long paragraphs and provides an opportunity to use common idioms. The way a character talks—vocabulary, tone, style, and sense of humor—can tell your readers exactly what you want them to know in a "showing" way that narrative can only "tell."

The Exercise

Write a dialogue between two people who know each other, each taking the opposite side of an issue or problem. This should be a verbal dance, not a shouting match. The issue you choose should be something immediate and particular (like whether to spend money on a vacation or put it in the savings account) rather than abstract (terrorism will be with us for a long time). The speakers should be equally convincing. That is, you, the author, can't load the argument on one side or the other. Make each person distinctive in her oral style, for example, in vocabulary and tone. Keep in mind that the subtext—what the conversation reveals about the speakers' relationship to each other—is as important as the manifest text. For example, in the what-shall-we-do-with-the-money conversation the subtext is about which of the two speakers has more power—and is willing to exploit it. Limit: 550 words.

The Objective

To learn to use dialogue to reveal character and human dynamics and to understand that speaking style says as much about a person as her behavior does. Incidentally, you should also recognize that dialogue should not be used for the following: for lengthy exposition, to furnish your stage, as a substitute for action, and as a vehicle for showing off your own vocabulary and education. A false line of dialogue can ruin an entire scene.

Student Example

"I'm giving up, Jim," Maria said to her husband. "I'm done, finished. No more doctors, no more tests. The end." She pulled the Sunday crossword toward her and looked around the kitchen table for a pencil.

"Maria," Jim said patiently, handing her a red pencil. "I think we should keep trying. You know the doctors say there's still a chance."

"They might say that," Maria said, "but I know there isn't." My body just doesn't want to have a baby. You know how there are some places in the city that just can't make a go of it? A restaurant moves in, people line up, and in six months it's gone. Or a new store moves in, and business is great at first, but then customers stop coming and the business folds? Think of it that way, Jim. My body is a low-rent district for good reason."

"God, Maria," Jim covered his face. "You know I hate it when you talk like this, when you put yourself down. It's beneath you."

Maria tapped the pencil on the table. "I'm not putting myself down. I'm simply stating the fact that I'm not going to get pregnant. And the sooner you admit it, the sooner we can start looking for a baby to adopt."

"No, Maria. We can't adopt. It's not right."

"What do you mean, 'right'?"

He was looking at her now. "You know what I mean. Right. Who is the baby's family? Is it healthy? Things like that."

"You mean a baby's parents had to go to Yale?"

He put his hand out to still her tapping pencil. "You know that's not what I mean, Maria. But here we are—well educated, smart—we could end up with—"

"With what, Jim. A stupid, ugly baby? Someone who wouldn't look too good at your twenty-fifth reunion?" Maria said. She pulled her pencil free.

"You're twisting my words around, and you know it," he said, putting his hand on the partially filled-in puzzle. "You always pretend not to understand what I'm saying. You never give me what I want."

"What you want?" Maria pushed the crossword away from her and stood up. "Is that it, Jim? I knew there was a reason I wasn't getting pregnant. I guess I just don't want it enough."

"Your sarcasm isn't very productive, Maria." He looked up at her.

"Neither are we, Jim. That's what we're talking about here, isn't it?"

—HESTER KAPLAN

Fiction extends our sympathy.
        —SUSAN SONTAG

PART FIVE

The Interior Landscape of Your Characters

Hate is a failure of Imagination.

—GRAHAM GREENE

Characters reveal themselves through what they say, through their actions and body language, and also through the shape of their mental landscape. In story after story, novel after novel, a character's interior landscape is one of the most powerful resources in the art of fiction. Anything is possible when you allow your characters, through the use of their imaginations, to explore their worlds, their relationships, occasionally to transcend the confines of their point of view, and experience the full range of how they lead their inner lives.

We all lead inner lives that run parallel to what we are actually doing or saying. For example, while you are driving west to start a new job, you might recall the disaster of the last job, regret past mistakes, make plans for your first day at work, entertain fears and hopes—all this while also listening to Miles Davis, mentally revising the last story you wrote, obsessing about the welfare of the cat in his cage in the backseat, and traveling at seventy miles per hour. You might also be carrying on a lively conversation with an amiable hitchhiker, while divulging none of your misgivings about this move. In dialogue much goes unsaid, but it needn't go unthought. The same is true for your characters. Every point-of-view character has an interior landscape, and you as author must respect this landscape (as distinct from your own) and allow her full access to its terror, mystery, and beauty.

Your characters can explore or chart their interior landscapes in many ways—they might examine their own motives for doing something, or wonder what might happen in the future, or remember the past, or follow an obsession to the point of folly, or project what is happening in the life of someone important to them *at that very moment,* or even imagine the life of another character. Below are other ways in which your characters might engage with their interior landscapes and lead their inner lives. They will:

imagine	fear	wonder	yearn
dread	suspect	project	grieve
plan	judge	plot	envy
lie	repress	pray	relive
regret	dream	fantasize	compose
associate	brood	doubt	feel guilt
speculate	worry	wish	analyze
glorify	romanticize	scheme	hate
interpret	obsess	compare	extrapolate
hallucinate	recreate	guess	hope
feel anything	realize	fret	interpret
misinterpret	decide	envision	posit

Literature thrives on characters who imagine, brood, fantasize, remember, and regret. The following examples of characters exploring their interior landscapes, using their imagination to enlarge their understanding of the world, or even falling victim to their imaginings should serve as the beginning of your own exploration of this powerful and useful tool in the art of fiction.

In *Beloved,* Toni Morrison's Sethe is haunted by the past and laments that her mind just won't stop:

> She shook her head from side to side, resigned to her rebellious brain. Why was there nothing it refused? No misery, no regret, no hateful picture too rotten to accept. Like a greedy child it snatched up everything. Just once, could it say, No thank you. . . . I don't want to know or have to remember that. I have other things to do: worry, for example, about tomorrow, about Denver, about Beloved, about age and sickness not to speak of love.
>
> But her brain was not interested in the future. Loaded with the past and hungry for more, it left her no room to imagine, let alone plan for the next day. . . . Other people went crazy, why couldn't she?

And in this wondrous way, Morrison leaves it to the reader to decide just how far Sethe travels into her interior landscape.

Margaret Atwood's novel *Bodily Harm* ends entirely in the mind of her character Rennie, who says, "This is what will happen." She goes on to imagine being saved in passages that alternate with the terrible reality of her situation. Rennie knows there is no real hope—but still she keeps imagining salvation in spite of herself.

Charles Baxter's story "Gryphon," which appears on page 287, is told by a young boy fascinated with a substitute teacher's lessons, lessons both true and false—such as her claim that Beethoven only pretended to be deaf to make himself famous. Her lessons grow more and more fantastic, and finally she makes a dire prophecy about one of the protagonist's classmates. To behold this teacher's interior landscape as she calmly predicts his death is to witness a dramatic and terrible event.

A story can end with a character imagining the future. Ray Carver's story "Where I'm Calling From" ends in the story's future. The first-person narrator imagines calling first his wife and then his girlfriend. He pulls change from his pocket. He imagines his conversation with his wife. It is enough to make him think that he might call his girlfriend first: "'Hello, sugar,' I'll say when she answers. 'It's me.'"

The young narrator in Don Lee's story "Casual Water" imagines what he'll do with an old seaplane that belongs to his profligate father, who has abandoned his teenage sons just as his wife did. "He would take it out to sea, far off the coast. He would remove the drain plugs from the pontoons, pour gasoline over the cabin, and throw in a book of lit matches. Then he would run the boat some distance away and drift with the swell, watch the fire accumulate, the gas cans erupt. He would wait until the seaplane began to crumple into the water, and then he would move the boat a little closer and watch it sink." And with it, all of his father's things—because he knows that his father is never coming home.

Marilynne Robinson's novel *Housekeeping* also ends in the imagination of Ruthie, its first-person narrator. Ruthie, together with her Aunt Sylvie, is a drifter now, moving from one town to the next, working occasionally as a waitress. Ruthie's sister Lucille has opted for respectability and stayed behind. Ruthie imagines the house they tried to burn down, but says she knows that Lucille no longer lives there. A few sentences later Ruthie ends the book still thinking of Lucille and imagines her in a restaurant in Boston, waiting for a friend. "No one watching this woman smear her initials in the steam on her water glass with her first finger, or slip cellophane packets of oyster crackers into her handbag for the sea gulls, could know how her thoughts are thronged by our absence, or know how she does not watch, does not listen, does not wait, does not hope, and always for me and Sylvie." Ruthie and Sylvie are separated from Lucille forever, yet Ruthie's mind renders them together in the only way she knows how: in her imagination.

The character's capacity to imagine anything is again at work in William Gass's novella "The Pedersen Kid" when the narrator, a teenager, goes down to the crib to see where they found a half-frozen, but still living boy. "Who knows, I thought, the way it's been snowing, we mightn't have found him till spring. . . . I could see myself coming out of the house some morning with the sun high up and strong and the eaves dripping, the snow speckled with drops and the ice on the creek slushing up . . . and I could see myself . . . breaking through the big drift that was always sleeping up against the crib and running a foot right through into him, right into the Pedersen kid curled up, getting soft. . . ." Notice how even though the narrator speculates in his imagination, he uses concrete, sensory language.

On your own, look for examples of a character's interior landscape in stories and novels you admire. Look for characters having dreams or nightmares, awaiting an event with anticipation or apprehension, imagining what another character is doing, or telling the reader how they feel about what is happening at a crucial point in the story—often in the moment of realization, of epiphany. For example, in Theodore Weesner's story "Playing for Money," we see how narrating a character's feelings at a moment of epiphany can employ wondering and speculation about another character's feelings. Glenn has finally won money at pool, but his feelings surprise us and him. "He has never won big before, and the feeling within him now, to his surprise is closer to disappointment than satisfaction. He feels unclean picking up the nickel. Why is it he wonders, that his pride seems shaky and Jim Carr's pride seemed okay?" We would not have known this from only seeing Glenn's actions; we needed access to his interior landscape. The story ends as ". . . Glen sits hearing the music, looking away, and can see that he is on the wrong side of something, maybe of everything." For further discussion of how the art of "telling" is connected to a character's interior landscape in a story, turn to "Show and Tell," on page 205.

Characters can also be tragically wrong in what they think—they can misinterpret the actions of others, misjudge the world in which they live, as Othello tragically does in *Othello*, and Stevens, the perfect butler and unreliable narrator, does in Ishiguro's *The Remains of the Day*.

Sometimes entire novels are the figment of a character's imagination or dreams—such is the case in Elizabeth Jolley's *Foxy Baby*, whose narrator imagines the entire action of the novel after there is an accident and she has a bump on her head. The same is true for Tim O'Brien's *Going After Cacciato*, in which the narrator wakes at the novel's end and realizes the entire story has been a dream.

And sometimes, one character feels compelled to try to understand another character by imagining the life and point of view of that other character. Russell Banks' novel *Affliction* is narrated by Rolfe Whitehouse, whose older brother has gone on a killing spree. In the first chapter, Rolfe begins the novel by saying, "This is the story of my older brother's strange criminal behavior and his disappearance. No one urged me to reveal these things; no one asked me not to." He says he feels separated from their family, from all who loved Wade. "They want through the telling to regain him; I want only to be rid of him. His story is my ghost life, and I want to exorcise it." Soon the narrator asks the reader to "Imagine with me that on this Halloween Eve up along the ridge east of the settlement it was still and silent and very dark." He describes the movements of a group of boys who are stealing jack-o'-lanterns, then he begins Chapter 2 with the same instructions to the reader. "Let us imagine that around eight o'clock on this Halloween Eve, speeding west past Toby's and headed toward town on Route 29 from the interstate turnoff . . ." is Wade Whitehouse, his brother, with his daughter Jill in the car. The novel continues with Wade's story up to the last sentences before the Epilogue, when Wade kills for the second time. The shifts in point of view are Rolfe's way of reminding us from time to time ("Picture, if you will . . .") that he is telling the story and imagining Wade's interior landscape in order to understand both of their stories, and to rid himself of Wade's ghost.

Imagination can almost kill, too. The narrator of Tim O'Brien's story "The Man I Killed" is paralyzed by imagining the life of the young man lying dead before him. "His jaw was in his throat, his upper lip and teeth were gone, his one eye was shut, his other eye was a star-shaped hole. . . ." The narrator says, "He had been born, maybe, in 1946," and goes on to imagine his early years in the village, listening to heroic stories of war. He imagines the young man wanted to be a teacher of mathematics, he imagines the seventeen-year-old girl he fell in love with. "One evening, perhaps, they exchanged gold rings." He goes on to imagine that the young man hoped the Americans would go away, that he hoped he would never be tested because he was not a fighter. Finally, the narrator imagines that this soldier—a soldier for a single day—had returned from university to his village "where he enlisted as a common rifleman with the 48th Vietcong Battalion. He knew he would die quickly. He knew he would see a flash of light. He knew he would fall dead and wake up in the stories of his village and people." "Talk," Kiowa says, desperately, to the narrator. And he did, and now we have his story, this collection, *The Things They Carried*.

Another of the most astonishing examples of a character's use of his imagination is the imagined dialogue that the narrator carries on with God at the end of Andre Dubus's story, "A Father's Story." Early on in the story the protagonist tells the reader he talks to God every morning, and then he goes out to the stable with an apple or a carrot for his horses. When his daughter causes a car accident, he proceeds to cover up for her and is himself possibly responsible for the young man's death. He soon sends his daughter to Florida and now lives with the terrible secret of what he has done—a secret he must keep from his best friend, Father Paul. Again, he tells us that he talks to God in the mornings. "Of course He has never spoken to me, but that is not something I require. Nor does He need to. I know Him, and I know the part of myself that knows Him, that felt Him watching from the wind and the night as I knelt over the dying boy. Lately, I have taken to arguing with him." Indeed, such an exchange ends this marvelous story as the father tells God, "I would do it again," not for his sons, but for his daughter. Then he tells God:

> But you never had a daughter and, if You had, You could not have borne her passion.
> So, He says, you love her more than you love Me.
> I love her more than truth.
> Then you love in weakness, He says.
> As You love me, I say, and I go out with an apple or carrot out to the barn.

In this imagined exchange—fully a rendering of the narrator's interior landscape—is the narrator's understanding that he and God love in the same flawed, abiding way.

A work of art is first of all work.
—PAUL ENGLE

EXERCISE 31

The Interior Landscape of Vision and Obsession

Have you ever been captivated by a story or an idea and subsequently had this story take over your life—to the extent that your imagination is running your life? Alice Hoffman's novel *White Horses* is about such a character, Dina, who, as a child, was fascinated by her father's tales of Arias. Arias were outlaws, "men who appeared out of nowhere, who rode white horses across the mesas with no particular destination other than red deserts, the cool waterholes. . . ." Men who weren't lost but "never turned back, never went home, they were always traveling west, always moving toward the sun." Dina runs away with King Connors, a man she thinks is an Aria—even though her father belatedly tells her, "I don't even know if there is such a thing. I may have invented Arias." No matter that Arias were an invention of her father's imagination, Dina believes in Arias even when her husband turns out not to be one. "When Dina discovered that she was wrong about King, that he was as far from an Aria as a man can be, it was too late, she could never have admitted her error to her father. But these days, Dina felt it had not all been in vain; these days, she was certain her father had been describing someone not yet born." This someone is her son, Silver, whom she describes as "the perfect stranger she had known forever."

Literature is rich with characters who get carried away by their imaginations. Such characters are useful to writers because their journeys are so compelling.

Remember the grandmother in Flannery O'Connor's story "A Good Man is Hard to Find," who brings her family to doom through her obsession with finding a plantation she incorrectly remembers from her past. "It's not much further," the grandmother said and just as she said it, a horrible thought came to her. An accident ensues that precipitates the climax of the story. Then we are once more in the grandmother's mind as she thinks, "The horrible thought she had had before the accident was that the house she had remembered so vividly was not in Georgia but in Tennessee." Think of Nabokov's novel *Pale Fire.* Charles Kinbote, the narrator, is obsessed with his neighbor, John Shade, and this obsession has led him to murder Shade. Subsequently, Kinbote tries both to confess to the murder and also cover it up in his commentary of Shade's poem, "Pale Fire."

The Exercise

Write a story about a character whose imagination is taken over with an obsession—an obsession with an idea, a tale, a vision—that determines the way in which your character lives his or her life, and acts out the forward movement of your story.

The Objective

To understand how longing and obsession can drive a story. To explore, through our characters, the mind's capacity to believe in the unbelievable, to long for something glimpsed but not seen, to imagine anything.

> *When you are writing you are not conscious of the reader, so that you don't feel embarrassed. I'm sure Joyce had a most heady and wonderful time writing the last fifty pages of* Ulysses—*glorious Molly Bloom. He must have written it in one bout, thinking: I'll show the women of the world that I am omniscient.*
>
> —EDNA O'BRIEN

EXERCISE 32

What Mayhem or Scene Is Happening Elsewhere?

Point of view can be as narrow or as all-encompassing as you want it to be because your characters can imagine anything. They can imagine scenes that are *simultaneously* happening elsewhere. This works best when a character knows or suspects how other characters would react in a given situation.

Early in John Irving's novel *Hotel New Hampshire,* John, the young narrator, goes off to bed while his parents leave for a walk. The novel is in the first person, so John, who is in bed, is not there when his parents talk to Howard Tuck, a policeman, and walk past the old Thompson Female Seminary, which they decide to buy and turn into a hotel. But John can imagine this crucial scene and proceeds to do so—he delivers this passage to the reader in the conditional tense:

> "Wutcha *doin'* here?" old Howard Tuck must have asked them.
> And my father, without a doubt, must have said, "Well, Howard, between you and me, we're going to buy this place."
> "You *are?*"
> "You betcha," Father would have said. "We're going to turn this place into a hotel."

A little further along in the scene, Irving reminds us that his young narrator is imagining this conversation, with clues such as "anyway" and "remember." The narrator says:

> Anyway, it was the night duty town patrolman, Howard Tuck, who asked my father, "Wutcha gonna call it?"
> Remember: it was night, and the night inspired my father. . . . There in Elliot Park, with the patrol car's spotlight on him, my father looked at the four-story brick school that indeed resembled a county jail—the rust-iron fire escapes crawled all over it, like scaffolding on a building trying to become something else. No doubt he took my mother's hand. In the darkness, where the imagination [his own young imagination] is never impeded, my father felt the name of his future hotel, and our future coming to him. "Wutcha gonna call it?" asked the old cop.
> "The Hotel New Hampshire," my father said.
> "Holy Cow," said Howard Tuck.
> "Holy Cow" might have been a better name for it, but the matter was decided: the Hotel New Hampshire it would be.

After this, there is a space break and we are back with the young boy who says, "I was still awake when Mother and Father came home. . . ." Note that his imagination takes us

96

into this scene so convincingly that toward the end he drops the conditional. Also note that the young narrator says, "In the dark where the imagination is never impeded . . . ," which should serve as instruction to all writers: Allow your characters to imagine scenes that inform their own lives, just as they inform the reader's knowledge of their story.

The Exercise

From the point of view of your main character, have him or her imagine a scene that is happening elsewhere—a scene that *is* happening without your narrator being there, except in his or her imagination. For example, a father might be driving home after a hard day's work and imagining that his son is stealing money from his top drawer, something he has suspected for a long time. Then he gets home and the money is gone—and the reader realizes that the imagined scene was most probably true. Or a roommate might be watching TV and feeling abandoned by the other two room-mates who urged him or her to go to a party. He or she might then imagine the party where they do outrageous things before the police are called in. And sure enough when he is called to post bail he says "their account of the party is just what he imagined." Keep in mind that the crucial word is "simultaneously"—the scene *is happening*, but elsewhere, and your character is imagining it happening.

The Objective

To transcend the traditional confines of point of view. To allow your characters' imag-inations to take them and you into scenes that are simultaneously happening elsewhere, into scenes that matter to our enjoyment and understanding of the story.

Student Examples

Italics indicate what the character is imagining.

In this passage, a young man is thinking about his girlfriend (the "you") and what she is doing:

> I've been on this train for seven hours and the only interesting thing I've seen is seven drowned, bloated cows. Some guy in the back thought he was having a heart attack near Tuscaloosa, but it was a false alarm and now he's sending his wife back to the club car for more beer. It's seven o'clock in Boston. Antennas blink on the horizon. *Voices are trying to get to you. Through your television. Through your radio. Even your answering machine is turned off. The cat prowls between your legs. You are reading love poems, pointing to words you love though no one is reading over your shoulder. The crazy lady who lives next door to you is singing in the hallway again, but her own opera is beyond her tonight. The air conditioner clicks on and your lamp dims for a split second.*
>
> *You turn another page.*
>
> *A bag of groceries sits on your kitchen counter. The frozen yogurt is melting and the snow peas are defrosting, but it will be hours before you notice.* I want to speak to you. Tell

you about the baby in front who is finally asleep, about my damp socks, about the slight delay in Birmingham, and all the other minor details I wish you lived for.

—MATT MARINOVICH

In this example, a man has returned home for his father's funeral and imagines what it will be like. After imagining the scene (for himself and for the reader) he decides not to go, but because he has imagined the scene so vividly we feel as if we have been there—and indeed it is important for the reader to know what Leonard is missing by not going.

Yet Leonard did not feel pressed for time. He had been deliberately vague with his sisters regarding his return home and knew he was not expected at any specific hour. He imagined the scene awaiting him: *his older sister Carla standing at the door in a business suit would direct the mourners along the receiving line. She would submerge her contempt for her father in a display of sober piety while adjusting her skirt every minute or so. Sandy would resent her sister's command of the situation and sit by their mother, sighing more in frustration than in loss, yet gratified by Carla's increasing weight—stock ammo at family gatherings. Their mother, handkerchief in hand, would sob and shake her head at the flower-encircled casket. Her hair would be up in a bun held in place with a silver pin. Between sobs she would say that her husband had been allergic to flowers and would never allow them in the house, meaning: he never brought any home for her. On her left, Dennis, the youngest, would clasp and unclasp his mother's hands, attempting to console her, though she'd shrug off his hands and ask for Leonard, the very image of his father. Then the siblings would have their moment of solidarity, eyes meeting like lifted glasses, for Leonard would certainly receive the lion's share of the inheritance, and would surely be there soon to take it.*

—JONATHAN KRANZ FROM "WAKE" PUBLISHED IN *ASCENT*

I remember standing on a street corner with the black painter Beauford Delaney down in the Village waiting for the light to change, and he pointed down and said, "Look." I looked and all I saw was water. And he said, "Look again," which I did, and I saw oil on the water and the city reflected in the puddle. It was a greater revelation to me. I can't explain it. He taught me how to see, and how to trust what I saw. Painters have often taught writers how to see. And once you've had that experience, you see differently.

—JAMES BALDWIN

EXERCISE 33

"I Know Just What She'll Say"

And you probably know just what he'll say, too. Often, we imagine a conversation with someone we know really well—well enough to be able to imagine just what they will say about a given subject or situation. Your point of view characters do too, and they are capable of imagining what another character would say, and of delivering this imagined conversation to the reader, without the need to bring this character on stage or to shift the point of view.

In Philip Roth's novel *Zuckerman Unbound,* Nathan Zuckerman is reaping the rewards of the success of his novel *Carnovsky* at the same time that he is regretting his hasty departure from his marriage on the eve of *Carnovsky*'s publication. Early in the novel, Zuckerman says, "How could you not love generous, devoted, thoughtful, kindhearted Laura? How could he not? Yet during their last months together in the Bank Street floor-through, virtually all they had left in common was the rented Xerox machine at the foot of their tub in the big tiled bathroom." Their estrangement was made even more final because Zuckerman used so much from their marriage in his novel.

Toward the end of the book, Zuckerman decides he wants her back and imagines an entire conversation with Laura on the way to see her. He jumps in a cab and heads for the village with "Time enough, however, for Zuckerman to gauge what he'd be up against with Laura. *I don't want to be beaten over the head with how boring I was for three years.* You weren't boring for three years. *I don't please you anymore, Nathan. It's as simple as that.* Are we talking about sex? Let's then. *There's nothing to say about it. I can do it and you can do it. I'm sure there are people both of us could call in to verify that. The rest I refuse to hear. Your present state has made you forget just how much I bored you. My affectless manner, as it is called, bored you . . . The way I make love bored you. Not making love bored you.* The way you make love did not bore me. Far from it. *But then it did. Something did, Nathan. You have a way of making things like that very clear.*"

This imagined conversation goes on for several pages until finally Nathan says, "He could only hope that she wouldn't be able to make the case against him as well as he himself could. But knowing her, there wasn't much chance of that." And Zuckerman has presented her part of the case so well, that Roth doesn't even bring her on stage. Nathan's wife is not home and she never appears in the book, although we feel as if we know her because Nathan has imagined what she might have said in such a compelling way.

The Exercise

Add an imagined conversation to one of your own stories from the point of view of your main character. This imagined conversation should be one that will never happen, but it should tell us something important about a character whose point of view we are not privy to, and about a situation that is enlarged by our "hearing" what is "said." It can also cause the character imagining the conversation to act or not act, depending on what they know the other person will say. Note how the names "Nathan" and "Laura" are used to remind us who is being addressed. Note also, how an imagined conversation doesn't need setting or body language, just italics to keep it all straight.

The Objective

To use the imagination of your characters to deliver scenes and conversations that are important for the reader to see and hear, but which may never happen.

In probing my childhood (which is the next best to probing one's eternity) I see the awakening of consciousness as a series of spaced flashes, with the intervals between them gradually diminishing until bright blocks of perception are formed, affording memory a slippery hold.
—VLADIMIR NABOKOV

EXERCISE 34

Mixed Motives and Maybes

Art is writing clearly about mixed emotions.

—W. H. Auden

Have you ever been asked: Why did you do that? And you couldn't honestly answer the question. You don't know why you acted in such a way or why you did such a dastardly thing. You just did it. You might be able to come up with several possible reasons for your behavior—yet still not know precisely which one is the truth. Allow your own characters the same latitude you allow yourself.

The narrator in Pam Houston's story "Selway" uses the word "maybe" to explore her motives for making a dangerous highwater trip down the Selway River. She says, "And I knew it was crazy to take a boat through that rapid and I knew I'd do it anyway but I didn't any longer know why. Jack said I had to do it for myself to make it worth anything, and at first I thought I was there because I loved danger, but sitting on the rock I knew I was there because I loved Jack. And maybe I went because his old girlfriends wouldn't, and maybe I went because I wanted him for mine, and maybe it didn't matter at all why I went because doing it for me and doing it for him amounted, finally, to exactly the same thing. And even though I knew in my head there's nothing a man can do that a woman can't, I also knew in my heart we can't help doing it for different reasons." Later in the same story, the narrator wonders if the trip's danger would make Jack propose to her. She says, "Maybe he was the kind of man who needed to see death first, maybe we would build a fire to dry ourselves and then he would ask me and I would say yes because by the time you get to be thirty, freedom has circled back on itself to mean something totally different from what it did at twenty-one." Examining one's motives leads to insight and self-knowledge, and often determines how a character acts or reacts to a situation.

In Richard Ford's story "Privacy," the narrator questions his motives when he begins to watch, through opera glasses, a woman disrobe night after night in a window across from his bedroom. "I don't know all that I thought. Undoubtedly I was aroused. Undoubtedly I was thrilled by the secrecy of watching out of the dark. Undoubtedly I loved the very illicitness of it, of my wife sleeping nearby and knowing nothing of what I was doing. It is also possible I even liked the cold as it surrounded me, as complete as the night itself, may even have felt that the sight of the woman—whom I took to be young and lacking caution or discretion—held me somehow, insulated me and made the world stop and be perfectly expressible as two poles connected by my line of vision. I am sure now that all of this had to do with my impending failures." What a place for this soul-searching to bring him: it had to do with his "impending failures."

A character in Rosellen Brown's novel *Before and After* imagines what her father is thinking about her mother as the family sits together in front of the TV replaying their recent, unbelievably painful ordeal—her brother's trial for murder, with his parents on opposite sides of the question. "Somewhere along the way I saw that my father, there on the couch beside her, had turned to my mother and was staring at her, not at her flat image out there in front of him. . . . She looked totally different and yet wasn't— and was—and I thought how we had all dragged through so much together and I still couldn't dare guess what he was thinking about her. If deep down he respected her or hated her for what she was saying, or if he could even understand it. Was he, like, trying to lay one image on the other and see if they really matched? Or guess what she felt when he looked at her that way, he seemed so astonished and hurt and familiar and far away, right there at her side?"

Note that both Ford's and Brown's characters profess to not know what they thought or to be incapable of guessing, but they in fact go right on to do just that.

The Exercise

Return to one of your stories in which your character's behavior has puzzled you or your classmates. Then come up with four or five reasons your character might have acted in such an abominable or deceptive or ingratiating or (you choose the adjective) way— from your character's POV. Next, in another story, have your point-of-view character wonder why another character did what she did. Often, the reasons are varied and some- times wrong, but it is also easy to tuck in to this list what might be an unpleasant truth on its own.

The Objective

To understand that people rarely have only one motive for an action—hence the term "mixed motives." And to allow our characters to explore their own motives as well as those of other characters important to their story world.

Planning to write is not writing. Outlining . . . researching . . . talking to people about what you're doing, none of that is writing. Writing is writing.

—E. L. DOCTOROW

EXERCISE 35

The Need to Know:
The Solace of Imagination

Our characters are often haunted by dramatic events that have happened to someone else, and the only way they can come to terms with them is to imagine how those events unfolded for that other character. In the Introduction to this section, we referred to Russell Banks' novel *Affliction,* in which one brother is compelled to imagine the life of his violent and doomed brother. In *The Great Gatsby,* Nick Carroway imagines Gatsby and Daisy's first kiss:

> Now it was a cool night with that mysterious excitement in it which comes at the two changes of the year. The quiet lights in the houses were humming out into the darkness and there was a stir and bustle among the stars. . . . His heart beat faster and faster as Daisy's white face came up to his own. He knew that when he kissed this girl, and forever wed his unutterable visions to her perishable breath, his mind would never romp again like the mind of God. So he waited, listening for a moment longer to the tuning-fork that had been struck upon a star. Then he kissed her. At his lips' touch she blossomed for him like a flower and the incarnation was complete.

Nick pretends to have summarized what Gatsby told him, but this scene is clearly Nick's own imagined version of it.

In Margaret Atwood's novel, *Cat's Eye,* her point-of-view character is haunted by a tragic event and so she must imagine it. This novel is told from the first-person point of view of Elaine, an artist, whose beloved brother was killed in an airplane hijacking. His death haunts Elaine, as it haunts the novel, and finally toward the novel's end, she imagines the precise details of his death. This chapter begins: "My brother Stephen died five years ago. I shouldn't say died: was killed. . . . He was sitting on a plane. He had a window seat. This much is known. In the nylon webbing in front of him was an inflight magazine with an article in it about camels, which he'd read, and another about upgrading your business wardrobe, which he hadn't."

It is with that sentence that Elaine begins to imagine his ordeal. He's traveling to a conference to deliver a paper on the "probable composition of the universe" and is "having doubts" about his theories. Note that Elaine is now imagining what her brother is thinking—she has slipped into his point of view. The plane has been hijacked by men wearing pillowcases over their heads and Elaine imagines her brother thinking: "They're like those characters in old comic books, the ones with two identities. These men have been caught halfway through their transformation: ordinary bodies but with powerful, supernatural heads, deformed in the direction of heroism, or villainy." Then she reminds us that she is the one imagining this by immediately saying: "I don't know whether or not this is what my brother thought. But it's what I think for him, now." She continues to imagine the scene, the other passengers, her brother's curiosity about what country they are in, and finally the appearance from the cockpit of a new hijacker. The next paragraphs read:

> The new man starts to walk down the aisle of the plane, his oblong, three-holed head turning from side to side. A second man walks behind him. Eerily, the taped music comes on over the intercom, saccharine, soporific. The man pauses; his oversized head moves ponderously left, like the head of some shortsighted, dull-witted monster. He extends an arm, gestures, with the hand: *Up*. It's my brother he points to.
>
> Here I stop inventing. I've spoken with the witnesses, the survivors, so I know that my brother stands up, eases himself past the man in the aisle seat saying "Excuse me." . . . Perhaps they have mistaken him for someone else. Or they may want him to help negotiate, because they're walking toward the front of the plane, where another pillowhead stands waiting.
>
> It's this one who swings open the door for him, like a polite hotel doorman, letting in the full glare of day. After the semidarkness it's ferociously bright, and my brother stands blinking as the image clears to sand and sea, a happy vacation postcard. Then he is falling, faster than the speed of light.
>
> This is how my brother enters the past.

And this is how Elaine renders her brother's death for herself and for the reader. Atwood is a genius in her use of her characters' interior landscapes and her books should be read for immense pleasure and for their brilliant instruction in the art of fiction.

The Exercise

Return to a draft of a story or begin a new story in which your point-of-view character needs to understand events that have happened to someone they care deeply about. Then have that character imagine those events from the point of view of the character who experienced them.

The Objective

To explore how a character can be drawn to imagine the life of someone important to his or her life—someone who will or can no longer speak for herself.

EXERCISE 36

The Inside/Outside Story

This exercise owes its origin to Ron Carlson, who has his students ask of all their stories: "Into what life has this trouble come?" and goes on to say that "trouble"—the outside story—is the engine that drives the story. It might even be helpful to think of the trouble as often not having anything to do with the character's life—until it appears in the story. But before that trouble begins, your character has a past, a present life filled with texture and relationships—a life apart from the trouble. Keep in mind what Carlson was quoted as saying in our introduction to Part Six, "Plot": "No one is a blank tablet waiting for trouble; everyone has an agenda, even children and dogs."

The Exercise

First, think of something that might be the trouble in a story—a holdup in a store where your character is shopping, a salesperson who comes to your character's door and refuses to leave, an unexpected and unwelcome guest arrives to spend the night, or the week, and so on. Second, create a character to whom this might happen. Give that character a life before they went shopping, before the unwelcome guest appeared, and also give your character an agenda. What is going on in your character's life that will be affected by the story's trouble—soon to appear on the horizon? What are your character's concerns and issues—her agenda, the inside story—and how will it affect how she acts or reacts when the trouble appears? Then bring on the trouble. It can be as "small" as the splinter in Sheehan McGuirk's story "Pricks" below—or as large and "troublesome" as the blind visitor in Ray Carver's story "Cathedral" on page 306.

The Objective

To be able to imbue your characters with life and your stories with trouble. And to understand the interaction between the two—how the outside story is the engine that drives the story while the inside story is the heart of what really happens.

Student Example

Pricks
After I slammed my pointer finger in the car door last week, I waited for the swelling to go down. At the tip, it is a small but perfect plum. I ask Mickey if he will take me to the emergency room.

"When? Now?" He hangs his jump rope around his neck and checks his heart rate with the gadget I bought for him last Christmas, when we moved in together.

"Today or tomorrow," I say and lean back against the garage door.

"You know," he says, "they're going to charge you for sticking a stupid pin in it."

He looks at my finger from across the room, I put my hands behind my back.

"It's giving me headaches," I say. He puts down the jump rope and lies back on the mat with his Abflex.

"Did you take the B-12 I left out for you?" he asks.

"I forgot."

He rolls his eyes in mid-ab-contraction, when his chin is tucked into his upper chest.

"Can you?" I ask.

"What, now?"

That night I try sleeping with my arm extended above my head. I prop it up with couch cushions and other pillows from around the house. I am fine for a while and then my arm begins to ache. I lie there staring at the ceiling and rubbing my finger against my lips. With my left arm, I reach over to Mickey and slip my hand beneath his pajamas, then his boxers.

"Now?" He looks over his shoulder at the pile of cushions. I tell him I can't sleep, it hurts too much.

"It's late," he says. It's a little after midnight.

"I know, I'm sorry." I move my hand down. He rolls over and tells me to get some sleep.

I am up at 5:30. After six Aspirin and a shot of Tequila I hide behind the microwave, my finger is no better. At 7:30, I call in sick to work and get Debra.

"You still haven't gone to the hospital?" she says.

"I was waiting, I thought it would go down."

"Do you need a ride?" She sounds annoyed.

"No, of course not." I have to hang up because I'm in too much pain. I lie back on the couch and raise my arm over my head. I try to read magazines, but there are only *Men's Health* and *Health and Fitness*. When I wake up Mickey is squatting beside me, inspecting my finger.

"Did you take your B-12?" he asks.

"What?" I'm still coming out of sleep. "No, I forgot I guess." He is talking funny. I lower my arm slowly so it won't throb too much. Something shines from between his lips. I sit up fast.

"I think," he says standing up, "I should go in through the nail." A sewing needle sparkles on his tongue.

"Mickey," I say, "I want to go to the emergency room." He tips my head down and looks me in the eyes.

"You don't smell like liquor," he says, "do you?"

"What?" I say. He makes a show of looking me up and down, stopping at my feet in his new socks then at the mess of magazines on the floor.

"Are you drunk?"

"Jesus, I am not drunk." I push myself up out of the couch and slip on a magazine. "I'm going to the hospital," I say, walking past him to the bedroom. He grabs my shoulder and turns me around.

"You are not driving drunk." I realize my T-shirt is wet and clinging to my back. My forehead is damp. I could faint.

"Fine," I say. "I don't care, whatever, do it."

"Go sit, I'll get something for the blood." I follow him back into the kitchen and sit down at the table. He's beside me with a rag and a lighter. Under the lamplight, he holds the needle above the flame while the tip turns black. I am watching him for signs of pleasure as I remember it is my only needle.

"Is it going to feel better though?" I ask. He doesn't answer and he doesn't look up from the flame.

—SHEEHAN MCGUIRK

> If the work weren't difficult I'd die of boredom. After The Recognitions, where there is a great deal of authorial intrusion and little essays along the way, on alchemy or what have you, I found it was too easy and I didn't want to do it again. I wanted to write something different. I wanted to do something which was challenging, to create other problems, to force this discipline on myself.
> —WILLIAM GADDIS

EXERCISE 37

Five Years from Now . . .

Characters often muse about their future—with anticipation or perhaps with regret. We have noticed that when characters announce what they think their futures will hold at the beginning of the story, then the story often moves forward to produce the opposite outcome. On the other hand, when a character muses about the future near the end of the story, then what the character suspects and dreads will happen is probably the actual fate of that character.

The Exercise

Go to the beginning pages of one of your stories that is in a first-draft stage. Then, have your point-of-view character finish this sentence: "Five years from now, I'll probably be _____." It should be about 150 words. Then, demonstrate how the story works against this prediction. The expected becomes the unexpected.

    Next, in the same story, pretend that you did not write the above paragraph, and instead, using the same point-of-view character, go to the *end* pages of the story and have the character finish the same sentence: Five years from now, I'll probably be _____. Again write about 150 words. At this point, what the character expects will happen should reveal to the reader the actual truth of this character's life.

Objective

To learn how to write against a prediction when it appears at the beginning of a story, and how to accept a prediction when it appears at the story's end.

I never desire to converse with a man who has written more than he has read.

—SAMUEL JOHNSON

EXERCISE 38

The Power of "Seemed" and "Probably"

Beginning writers often think they have to go into the heads of all their characters in order for the reader to know what they are thinking. They forget that people can reveal themselves in a myriad of ways: dialogue, body language, and so forth. They also forget that in reality no one has access to another person's thoughts and that, in addition to listening to what those close to us say and observing how they act, we are constantly assuming, suspecting, projecting, and imagining what they think.

Learn to give your characters (especially the point-of-view character) the same imagination that you have. An example of this occurs in a Bartholomew Gill mystery novel, *McGarr and the Politician's Wife*. The entire plot turns on the word *seemed*. A man, Ovens, has a head injury and is lying in a coma. The detective goes to see him and needs to know if he might have just fallen or if there was foul play. He asks the doctor if Ovens can speak and the doctor says not for another forty-eight hours.

The author writes, "Ovens' eyes, however, seemed to contradict the assessment of the insouciant young doctor. Dark brown, almost black, they told McGarr that Ovens knew the score: that his was not merely a medical problem that a favorable prognosis could eliminate, that whoever had done this to him had a very good reason, and those eyes, suddenly seeming very old, realized his troubles weren't over." So McGarr doesn't have to wait forty-eight hours. He starts his investigation immediately.

Ann Beattie's use of the word *probably* in her story "Afloat" indicates that the story is not third person from the point of view of the sixteen-year-old child who is introduced at the beginning of the story. Beattie writes, "When she was a little girl she would stand on the metal table pushed to the front of the deck and read the letters aloud to her father. If he sat, she sat. Later, she read them over his shoulder. Now she is sixteen, and she gives him the letter and stares at the trees or the water or the boat bobbing at the end of the dock. It has probably never occurred to her that she does not have to be there when he reads them." The "probably" is a clue that someone else is making this conjecture. Sentences later, after the letter is presented, the first-person narrator comes in with "he hands the letter to me, and then pours club soda and Chablis into a tall glass for Annie and fills his own glass with wine alone."

The Exercise

Write a scene that involves two characters. Now, allow the point-of-view character to suspect or imagine what the other character might be thinking. Or, have your point-of-view character imagine something that is probably true.

The Objective

To show how your characters can use their imaginations to interpret the behavior and dialogue of other characters.

Student Examples

His son was *probably* with the girl down the street, learning what his father had been too afraid to talk to him about.

—KEITH DRISCOLL

Eleanor *seemed* like she knew what the doctor was going to say, and the way she didn't quite look him in the eye suggested that she had already been planning the next step without me, *probably* never once taking into consideration whether I might want to keep the baby.

—KAVI WILLIAMS

She *probably* expects me to keep on mowing her lawn and trimming her hedge all summer even though I told her there was no way that dog and me were going to be friends. She *probably* thinks it's something we can work out, me and the dog, like I got time for throw and fetch.

—JACK NEISSEN

Jennifer was *probably* getting high in the bathroom, but Shaun had grown tired of listening at the door years ago; if she didn't want help, he wouldn't give it.

—STEVEN LaFOND

She looked at me with an expression of forgiveness, but *probably* wasn't going to let me forget last night.

—THOM PLASSE

The answer is never the answer. What's really interesting is the mystery.
If you seek the mystery instead of the answer, you'll always be seeking. I've
never really seen anybody find the answer—they think they have, so they
stop thinking. But the job is to seek mystery, evoke mystery, plant a
garden in which strange plants grow and mysteries bloom.

—KEN KESEY

PART SIX

Plot

In this book, we have emphasized character-driven stories more than those that are heavily plotted. In fact, it wasn't until we finished the manuscript and had started on a table of contents, that we realized we had left out *plot* as a distinct category. Virginia Woolf in her watershed essay, "Mr. Bennett and Mrs. Brown," writes about how a twentieth-century sensibility—that is, the interior life taking a direct role in motivation without conscious prompting—changed fiction from plot- to character-driven stories and novels. No more Dickensian coincidences, no more life-changing accidental meetings or vile kidnappings. Things happened because characters/people made them happen, partly from who they were and what they wanted and partly because the author has supplied them with what writer/teacher Ron Carlson calls "trouble." Carlson asks his students to answer this question: "Into what life has this trouble come?" and goes on to say that the "trouble is the engine that drives the story. The plot of many short stories is triggered by "trouble" before the story actually begins. A man comes home to find that his house has been stripped of furniture and his wife and children are gone. The story takes off from that point and there are as many versions of the story as there are people to write them. But before the trouble begins, your character has a life apart from the trouble. As Carlson says, "No one is a blank tablet waiting for trouble. Everyone has an agenda, even children and dogs."

In a *Paris Review* interview, William Kennedy speaks to this issue. He says:

> Hemingway's line was that everything changes as it moves; and that is what makes the movement that makes the story. Once you let a character speak or act you now know that he acts this way and no other. You dwell on why this is so and you move forward to the next page. This is my method. I'm not interested in formulating a plot to which characters are added like ribbons on a prize cow. The character is the key and when he does something which is new, something you didn't know about or expect, then the story percolates. If I knew, at the beginning, how the book was going to end, I would probably never finish.

Thus the forward movement of a story or novel derives from how a character observes—acts or reacts—and the more surprising the better.

111

In their book *Technique in Fiction,* Robie Macauley and George Lanning suggest that Heraclitus's observation that "character is destiny" should be "written on the wall of every novelist's study." They go on to say that character is only half the dynamics of plot, that a given situation is the other half. How a particular character observes and deals with the circumstances of that situation and chooses to act or not act moves the story forward into plot.

Macauley and Lanning discuss plot in these terms: In the beginning you present a particular character in a situation. The situation should have opposing forces and alternatives, and your central character should have choices—ways of acting or not acting. The situation should grow more complicated, more grave, and finally reach a point of crisis. Thereafter follows the resolution of the crisis—or at the least "something happens." Almost always things will have changed.

Doug Glover, another writer/teacher, uses the term "unstable situation" when discussing plot. Consider how writers have placed certain characters in an unstable situation and set them in motion, from which point they move forward, driven by the force of their own personalities: Isabella Archer in Henry James's *Portrait of a Lady,* Humbert Humbert in Vladimir Nabokov's *Lolita,* Hester Prynne in Hawthorne's *The Scarlet Letter,* and Yossarian in Joseph Heller's *Catch-22.*

Janet Burroway, in *Writing Fiction,* makes the distinction between story and plot. She says, "A story is a series of events recorded in their chronological order. A plot is a series of events deliberately arranged so as to reveal their dramatic, thematic, and emotional significance." She notes that E. M. Forster makes the same distinction in *Aspects of the Novel,* in elaborating on the difference between "and then" and "why." Burroway says:

> The human desire to know why is as powerful as the desire to know what happened next, and it is a desire of the highest order. . . . When "nothing happens" in a story, it is because we fail to sense the causal relation between what happens first and what happens next. When something does "happen," it is because the resolution of a short story or a novel describes a change in the character's life, an effect of the events that have gone before. This is why Aristotle insisted with such apparent simplicity on "a beginning, a middle, and an end." A story is capable of many meanings, and it is first of all in the choice of structure—which portion of the story forms the plot—that you offer us the gratifying sense that we "understand."

It is in this discussion that Burroway also speaks to the difference between the short story and the novel. She says:

> Many editors and writers insist on an essential disjunction between the form of the short story and that of the novel. It is my belief, however that, like the distinction between story and plot, the distinction between the two forms is very simple, and the many and profound possibilities of difference proceed from that simple source: A short story is short, and a novel is long.

In our minds, Burroway has the final word on the matter.

Most discussions of plot recognize the importance of conflict and here we defer to Rust Hills' discussion of "mystery," "conflict," and "tension," in his book titled *Writing in General and the Short Story in Particular.* (This is another book that should be on every writer's shelf.) He argues that tension is the most effective technique for creating suspense and derives from the Latin verb *tendere,* meaning stretch. He says, "Tension in fiction has that effect: of something that is being stretched taut until it must snap. It has the quality of force under pressure, as for instance when it is achieved through characterization in a 'coiled motive'—tightly wound motivation in a character that we know must spring loose on the action. The most obvious way to create it is by simply saying something is going to happen, and then putting it off." Tension, he says, "both foreshadows and creates suspense." The beginning of Andrea Barrett's story "Servants of the Map" is a brilliant example of tension at its most effective and artful.

Once you have placed a character in an unstable situation, our exercise "What If?" is designed to provide you with several organic ways to move your story forward toward complication and resolution. Always, always, with character in motion. In her wonderful book *Mystery and Manners,* Flannery O'Connor recalls lending some stories to a neighbor who, when she gave them back, said, "Well them stories just gone and shown you how some folks would do." And O'Connor comments, "I thought to myself that that was right; when you write stories, you have to be content to start exactly there—showing how some specific folks will do, will do in spite of everything." And that doing becomes your plot.

> *My early life was very strange. I was a solitary; radio fashioned my*
> *imaginaton. Radio narrative always has to embody a full account of both*
> *action and scene. I began to do that myself. When I was seven or eight,*
> *I'd walk through Central Park like Sam Spade, describing aloud what I*
> *was doing, becoming both the actor and the writer setting him into the*
> *scene. That was where I developed an inner ear.*
> —ROBERT STONE

EXERCISE 39

The Skeleton

The simplest stories are fairy tales and myths in which a central character—who is on some sort of quest or journey—is continually on stage and secondary characters only appear to assist or thwart her. This is what we call a "skeleton" story—you can see its bones. There are no subtleties, motivation is a given, emotions are unanalyzed, and the narrative proceeds in a linear way. In the skeleton the world and its people are viewed in morally black-and-white terms. The temptation to stray will be almost irresistible, but if you do, you will drag your reader into thickets of subplots and gangs of minor characters. (The following exercise is based on a suggestion by folklorist Lawrence Millman.)

The Exercise

Write a linear story, in which a strong main character is on a quest for something important and specific (e.g., a shelter for the baby, medicine for a sick mother, or the key to the storehouse where a tyrant has locked away all the grain from a starving populace). The object is a given—don't explain its importance. The main character starts acting immediately. She then meets a (specific) obstacle; finally she triumphs over the obstacle by means of a magic or supernatural element that comes from the outside (like Dorothy's red shoes in *The Wizard of Oz*). You may introduce minor characters but the narrative should never abandon your main character. This story should be told through action and dialogue. Limit: 550 words.

The Objective

Like a medical student who must learn the names and location of human bones before going on to more complex systems, a beginning writer must be able to handle and control basic plot before moving on to more subtle elements like motivation, subtext, and ambiguity. Many of the greatest novels incorporate a quest (*Moby Dick*), a journey (*David Copperfield*), and triumph over an obstacle (*The Old Man and the Sea*). These works also concentrate on one protagonist and end, if not happily, at least on an emotionally satisfying note of resolution.

Student Story

The Nanny—A Fairy Tale
There once was a young woman who wanted a baby. The urge to produce another life in her own body hit suddenly, like a squall or a virus.

"A baby," said her husband. "You don't know a diaper from a linen handkerchief. Babies are loud, they're smelly, and they cramp your sex life. We're fine as we are."

She worked on him. Walking through the park, she'd point out babies sleeping like sacks in strollers, crowing and waving from backpacks, or toddling on creased legs. "Let's eat Chinese tonight," he said. If only she could find the secret crack in his heart, the place where the gates would swing open when the magic words were said, letting the idea of their own baby enter like the children of Hamlin.

She took to sitting on playground benches, thinking. She could leave him and find a man who shared her longing. But she loved the fullness of his laugh, the way he sang as he cooked, the curls behind his ears when his haircut was overdue.

One day as the young woman sat on a bench near a wading pool, a gray-haired nanny sat down beside her, starched uniform gleaming in the sun. "Have any children?" she asked, starting to knit.

The young woman smiled and shook her head.

"Too bad. You'd like a child, wouldn't you? Not married? Men are hard to find these days, they say."

Though partly put off by the nanny's presumptuousness, the young woman shared her problem. "My husband doesn't want children. At least not yet."

"Stalled adolescence," the nanny said. "See it more and more. Want a solution?" Without waiting for an answer, she pulled a pomegranate out of her knitting bag. "Serve him this for dessert tonight and for the next two nights and have some for yourself, too. Be sure he sucks the sweet red part, and doesn't eat the seeds. If he balks, tell him it's better than kiwi."

The young woman did as she was told, carefully watching her husband savor the sweet sharp taste and spit the seeds on his plate. At first she noticed no change in her husband. But on the third day, while sipping cappuccino in an intimate Italian restaurant, he said "What the hell. You want a baby? What are we waiting for?" And he took her home to bed.

Months later, her stomach full as a spinnaker, the young woman sat again on the bench near the wading pool, resting her legs. The nanny sat down next to her as she had before, uniform crisp, oxfords firmly tied. Eyeing the young woman's belly with a smile, she pulled out her knitting and said, "Looking for a nanny?"

—CHRISTINE MCDONNELL

Fiction has traditionally and characteristically borrowed its form from letters, journals, diaries, autobiographies, histories, travelogues, news stories, backyard gossip, etc. It has simply pretended to be one or the other of them.

—WILLIAM GASS

EXERCISE 40

From Situation to Plot

If you haven't read our introduction to the section on plot, please go back and read it now before doing this exercise. It is important that you understand our preference for character-driven—not plot-driven—stories.

This exercise is designed to illustrate how easy it is to come up with characters in particular situations from only a few given details.

The Exercise

Begin a story using one of the following as your main character:

- A young boy whose father is in jail
- A waitress who likes her menus to rhyme
- A policeman with ten cats
- The driver of a hit-and-run accident

(Do you see how a policeman with ten cats is a situation in itself just waiting for a little opposition?)

Now, complicate your character's life with opposing forces, with tension and conflict, and offer your character alternatives within that situation. Ask: What does my character want? What would my character do? How will he act or react? How will those actions propel the story forward?

Then experiment with creating your own sets of details involving character and situation. Do ten or fifteen as fast as you can.

The Objective

To understand how the most effective plots are those driven by character. To see how a character within a given of any situation creates his own destiny.

Student Example

Intelligence
I'm eight years old. But I have the mind of a nineteen-year-old. Mom says it's making up for all the wrong Dad did. Today there's going to be a whole camera crew here.

They're going to film different angles of me beating myself at chess. Then they want me to walk around the neighborhood in my Eagle Scout uniform. Dad doesn't want to talk to them. So I guess they'll do an exterior of the penitentiary.

Dad called a few hours ago. Mom handed me the phone. She never wants to talk to him. I end up answering all the questions he wants to ask her. He asked me when was the last time Mom talked about him. I told him she said something at the bowling alley because we were having trouble keeping score. Mom doesn't care how much I lie to him because she says he's going to rot in jail. I miss him. But I can't tell him that. Mom would hit the roof and call me a traitor and start that whole thing about who's bringing me up and who's the slob behind bars. With Mom, eventually everything comes down to physical appearances. "It was a choice between your Dad and Henry Lee," she says when she reminisces about marrying Dad. "And Henry Lee had hair on his back."

On the phone, I asked Dad what he made in woodshop, and he asked me if I was eating lots of peas and carrots because the brain is just another muscle and you can't feed it junk. Dad thinks he's grooming me for the Nobel Prize. I made a few reading suggestions. I send him books and tell him to highlight the difficult parts. He's not very easy to explain things to. If he doesn't get it the first time, he gets angry—and when he gets angry, he automatically thinks of Mom and says, "Don't sign anything. Not even your homework. I own the rights to you. Every single cent you make, you freak of fucking nature."

I never hang up on him, no matter what he says.

I wait until he calms down, and then give him an update on how many sparrows have moved into the birdhouse we built.

But it's really sitting in the basement.

The camera crew is here. Taping down cable and knocking over chairs. Mom's on the phone right now because the producer wants a shot of me playing with my friends. I told him I could punch up some people on my computer. But he wants the real thing. So Mom's on the phone, asking Mrs. Milgram if she can borrow her son for the afternoon. That's the same kid who smashed up my invention for the Science Fair last year. The key grip is showing me how to throw a frisbee. The producer is suggesting a shot of me bicycling down Quarry Lane with my dog running after me. But Einstein has arthritis and bleeding gums. He can barely stand up.

The whole neighborhood's watching us. Kids on mountain bikes and skateboards are casing our house, making circles in the road. When Dad was taken away, Mom ran out and aimed the sprinkler at them. Now she's too busy. She's even got a pencil behind her ear.

I tell the producer I know what people want to see. They want to see me in my tiny apron making a white sauce. Or me playing the piano. A little Vivaldi and maybe the camera panning to my sneakers dangling a foot from the floor while my mother turns the pages and presses the pedal. I love it when she steps on the pedal, when the notes run together and take too long to end.

I lower my head and pretend that this is sadness.

—MATT MARINOVICH, PUBLISHED IN *THE QUARTERLY*

Writer's block is only a failure of the ego.
—NORMAN MAILER

EXERCISE 41

Peter Rabbit and Adam and Eve: The Elements of Plot

from Thomas Fox Averill

For the fiction writer, telling a whole story—and not just writing dialogue, or setting scene, or creating character—is crucial. Yet, plotting is often difficult for beginning writers. One way to practice plotting is to work with story elements, putting them in patterns, and writing a story to their specifications. By "story elements" I mean basic plot moves—those things that have nothing to do with specific character, setting, or even conflict.

For example, the Peter Rabbit and the Genesis garden stories share plot elements. In both, an authority figure tells the character what not to do (eat fruit from the tree of knowledge of good and evil, or go into Farmer McGregor's garden). In each story, the protagonist "does" the "don't." Anything else and the story would be over, of course. "Doing the don't" has two levels of consequence in each story—the personal consequences and the consequences with the authority/prohibitor.

In Peter's case, he enjoys the garden, but, once spotted, he is chased, he gets wet, he loses his clothes and he finally escapes, sick and tired and naked; his mother puts him to bed with a cup of tea. His sisters eat bread, milk, and blackberries.

Adam and Eve, on the other hand, are immediately ashamed of their nakedness, and try to hide from God; they are punished with work, pain, and death and made to leave the garden.

The Exercise

Write a story that uses these four elements as a basic plot line:

- A prohibition
- Doing the prohibited
- Personal/immediate consequences
- Long-term/authority consequences

Note that the first and the final elements have to do with the prohibitor/authority, the middle two with the character who is doing the don't.

Note that simple variations are possible, by beginning the story with advice, warning, or prediction.

The Objective

To help you understand basic elements that underlie plots. You should become familiar with the stories collected by the Grimm Brothers, with *The Canterbury Tales,* with the *1001 Arabian Nights,* with the *Decameron,* and with books of myths, legends, and religious stories. The purpose is not to get you write to formula, but to make you aware of elements of structure and patterns that commonly appear together. Think of how many stories begin with either "lack" or "desire." Think of the role of luck and coincidence in stories. Think of how many stories turn on a lie. Think of how many stories reveal hypocrisy. Of how many require an arduous journey. All of these, used over and over by fiction writers, show us how few plot elements we have to work with, and yet they allow us infinite possibilities to tell our stories. The more we know them, the more we're in control of what and how we write.

Student Example

My father does not talk about Vietnam.

As a child, I would sometimes wonder what he had done there, or why he was there. He was married before my mother, but he doesn't talk about that, either. Sometimes, I made up stories about my father. I'd flop down in my dad's favorite chair, watch John Wayne annihilate masses of Northern Vietnamese, and dream about my father. He wasn't a big man, but he was stern. My family boasts many generations of warriors, and I wanted to be one.

One day, I picked open my dad's special suitcase. He had hidden it from us boys. We all thought he was hiding his nudie magazines, whatever we thought those were. Letters tumbled out, along with medals and pictures. After reading the letters, I realized that my father very much loved my mother. I also realized that my father had been a cold-blooded killer.

A picture caught my eye. My father and a black man had their arms around a sickly looking Vietnamese man. It was an odd picture; I had never seen my father smile before. For an instant I was proud of my father, until I noticed the Vietnamese man's left ear. It was missing. The man was dead.

I looked up from the picture to see my father staring blankly at me from the doorway. My father does not talk about Vietnam.

—JASON PUFF

I guarantee you that no modern story scheme, even plotlessness, will give a reader genuine satisfaction, unless one of those old-fashioned plots is smuggled in somewhere. I don't praise plots as accurate representations of life, but as ways to keep readers reading.
—KURT VONNEGUT JR.

EXERCISE 42

What If? How to Develop and Finish Stories

Writers sometimes have story blocks—they begin a story easily enough, but run into trouble when they try to finish it. Well, one possible reason is that some stories don't have enough forward motion to become a successful story—and these should be abandoned. On the other hand, many story beginnings just need to be examined and explored for their inherent possibilities. As François Camoin says, "A story needs to take a narrative fork."

The Exercise

Look in your files for a story that seems stuck, a story that has a story block. Next, write at the top of a separate sheet of paper the two words *What If*. Now write five ways of continuing the story, not ending the story, but continuing the story to the next event, scene, etc. Let your imagination go wild. Loosen up your thinking about the events in the story. Your what if's can be as diverse as your imagination can make them. More than likely, and this has proved true through years of teaching and writing, one of the what if's will feel right, organic, to your story and that is the direction in which you should go. Sometimes you will have to do several groups of what if's per story, but that's okay as long as they keep you moving forward.

The Objective

To illustrate that most story beginnings and situations have within them the seeds of the middle and end—seeds that spark not only your creativity but also your curiosity. You just have to allow your imagination enough range to discover what works.

Student Example

One writer began a story about a young boy, Paul, who shoplifts with a cousin. The story opens when they take something more expensive than they have ever taken before. This raises the stakes immediately. After writing a superb opening scene of two-and-a-half pages, the writer didn't know where to go with the story. Below are her five what if's for this beginning.

1. Paul decides to admit to shoplifting, but hopes not to implicate his cousin.
2. Paul is excited by shoplifting something more expensive, and talks his cousin into going back again soon.
3. The store security guard notices their theft and decides to set a trap. (Involves some point-of-view issues.)
4. Paul feels brave now and steals something from his stepfather—something Paul has wanted for a long time.
5. There is a time shift to five years later when Paul commits a major burglary.

The writer continued the story with the fourth idea because she felt it was a more complex development of Paul's situation. If she hadn't explored several alternatives, she might not have arrived at this story line.

A story isn't about a moment in time, a story is about the moment in time.
—W. D. WETHERELL

EXERCISE 43

There's a Party
and You're Invited
from Margot Livesey

We all know the standard workshop questions—Whose story is this? What do they want? What prevents them from getting what they want?—questions designed to help bring the story into focus, for both reader and writer, and to heighten both the forward movement and the conflict. These questions are genuinely helpful and they work particularly well for certain kinds of stories, especially plot-driven ones. Sometimes, though, I find it more useful to think in terms of the occasion of the story. Why are these characters showing up here, now, for these events? Why are we, as readers, being invited today rather than yesterday or tomorrow?

In the best fiction the occasion nearly always turns out to be more complicated than we expect. Katherine Mansfield's "The Garden Party" declares its occasion in the title; there's a party and we're invited. But other people, the poor people who live down the lane, are not and this painful juxtaposition between luxury and poverty becomes the true occasion of the story.

Sometimes a story turns out to have two distinct occasions—the one that we discover in the opening pages and the other that gradually surfaces. In Charles D'Ambrosio's "The Point," the first occasion of the story is yet another party given by the teenage narrator's mother after which he ends up escorting yet another drunken adult home. But as we continue to read, we realize that behind the difficulties of maneuvering the very drunk Mrs. Gurney back to her home, lies another much darker occasion: the morning when the narrator discovered his father dead in his car by his own hand.

The Exercise

Re-read the opening scene or section of your story and answer the question: What is the occasion of this story? Now read the remainder of the story and answer the question again.

The Objective

Readers are our guests and we need to make them feel as soon as possible in a story that this is an occasion, somber or joyful, worth attending. And we need to reward that attendance by the end of the story.

EXERCISE 44

So, What Happened?

In his introduction to a stellar group of stories, *American Stories: Fiction from the Atlantic Monthly,* C. Michael Curtis says, "Each achieves the sort of transforming moment one looks for in the short story form, a shift in understanding, a glimpse of unexpected wisdom, the discovery of unimagined strength. . . . You will find no minimalism here, no sketches or portraits, no glimpses, merely, of 'things as they are'; these are honest-to-God stories, in which Something Happens." We also feel that *something has to happen* in a story once the original situation has been presented—something in terms of the consequences of situation and action.

In Janet Burroway's discussion of conflict and resolution, she says, "Still another way of seeing the shape of the story is in terms of situation-action-situation. The story begins by presenting us with a situation. It then recounts an action, and when that action is over, we are left with a situation that is the opposite of the opening situation. This formula seems oversimplified, but it is very difficult to find a story it does not describe."

Keep in mind that "opposite" can mean that the narrator at the beginning of the story does not understand her situation, but after one scene or several scenes (action), and by the end of the story, she does. Or she might understand something about another person, an event, or a relationship. Note that Curtis talks about the "transforming moment" in terms of "a shift in understanding," a "glimpse of wisdom," and the "discovery of unimagined strength"—all internal changes, cerebral transformations. James Joyce calls such a moment the "epiphany."

Burroway goes on to say that the "moment of recognition" must be manifested or externalized in an action, in the concrete world of the story: the prince recognizes Cinderella, and the shoe fits. (See page 205, "Show and Tell.")

And what of those stories in which "nothing happens"? Rust Hills, in *Writing in General and the Short Story in Particular,* discusses the "kind of story that seems at first to be a character sketch." The character seems unaltered at the end of the story—more firmly entrenched in his situation than ever. Yet, what has happened is that his "capacity for change" has been removed. There is no longer any hope for him: that is the change. Janet Burroway uses the metaphor of war to explain this type of story—a story that began with two sides hopeful about victory ends with two survivors, one from each side, grasping the border fence with bloodied fists. "The 'resolution' of this battle is that neither side will ever give up and that no one will ever win; there will never be a resolution." In both instances, possibility and hope are gone. What happens, happens for the reader who has witnessed this failure.

The Exercise

One by one, review five or six of your stories and look for "what happened" in each story. Mark the moment of transformation, the moment of recognition, the epiphany in each—and then look for the corresponding action that makes these moments manifest.

The Objective

To write stories in which something happens.

Student Example

(In "Matrimony," the first-person narrator finally realizes that she and her ex-husband should stay parted. This is made manifest by the last lines of the story.)

> That night Phillip went back to his own apartment, and I played the videotape of our wedding. I watched the whole thing through, and then again as it rewound. I watched as our lips disengaged from our first kiss as husband and wife, as we made frenzied, backward steps down the aisle, and finally walked out of the church at different times, alone.
>
> —DINA JOHNSON

I write in longhand. My Baltimore neighbor Anne Tyler and I are maybe the only two writers left who actually write with a fountain pen. She made the remark that there's something about the muscular movement of putting down script on that paper that gets her imagination back in the track where it was. I feel that too, very much so. My sentences in print, as in conversation, tend to go on a while before they stop: I trace that to the cursiveness of the pen. The idea of typing out first drafts, where each letter is physically separated by a little space from the next letter, I find a paralyzing notion. Good old script, which connects this letter to that, and this line to that—well, that's how good plots work, right? When this loops around and connects to that . . .

—JOHN BARTH

EXERCISE 45

Flash Forward:
or "Little did I know . . . ."

Students have long been cautioned against using the cliché "little did I know" to reveal to readers something that will happen in the future—something the character did not know at the time. Many writers, such as Frank Conroy, Lorrie Moore, Edward P. Jones, and Salman Rushdie, however, have used this technique to great advantage and the writing student should also add it to their toolbox. The flash forward allows the narrator to tell the reader something that was not available to him or her at the time of the story. Such a revelation adds tension to the story as the reader sees the narrator acting and reacting to events without this knowledge.

In her story "Paper Losses," Lorrie Moore uses flash forwards to tell the reader what her narrator, Kit, doesn't yet know about her husband's strange behavior which began with his making model rockets in the basement. Kit thinks, "What had happened to the handsome hippie she married? He was prickly and remote, empty with fury. A blankness had entered his blue-green eyes." A few sentences further on Moore writes, "Of course, later she would understand that all this meant that he was involved with another woman, but at the time, protecting her own vanity and sanity, she was working with two hypotheses only: brain tumor or space alien." So now there is a gap between what the reader knows and what Kit knows. This gap creates anticipation on the part of the reader to see how the dissolution of the marriage plays out. When the divorce papers arrive, Moore again adds a flash forward to the narrative. "Rafe [her husband] was still living in the house and had not yet told her that he'd bought a new one." And though Rafe tries to talk her out of going on the Carribean vacation that they have already booked because it will give the children false hope, she insists on going saying "Hope is never false. Or it's always false. Whatever. It's just hope." And again, the reader knows something she does not: that her own hope is in vain. And later she unpacks the "condoms and candles, her little love sack" that was part of her hope for a reconciliation or a "final lovemaking scene of sentimental vengeance." Moore uses two more flash forwards in the course of the story, and in the last one writes, "What bimbo had he wanted to give her ticket to? (Only later would she find out. 'As a feminist, you mustn't blame the other woman,' a neighbor would tell her. 'As a feminist, I request that you no longer speak to me,' Kit would reply.)" Her anger at finally knowing is at last given voice in the story. And part of the story's drama stems from the reader knowing more than Kit does—and waiting for her reaction when she discovers the truth. This technique is somewhat similar to the use of an unreliable narrator—but similar only because the narrator doesn't have all the facts—yet, as opposed to the unreliable narrator who distorts the truth.

Edward P. Jones uses "flash forwards" to great effect—often employing the word "later" to indicate the reference to future time. In Jones' O'Henry Prize story, "Old Boys, Old Girls," his character Caesar receives letters from his brother and sister when he is close to getting out of jail for two murders. He tears the letters up because he doesn't ever want to see his family again. Then Jones writes, "He would be glad he had done this as he stumbled, hurt and confused, out of his sister's car less than half a year later." So the reader anticipates the meeting with his sister that Caesar, in current story time, swears will never happen. Jones again uses a flash forward to tell us that Caesar will eventually encounter Yvonne Miller, the woman he'd once loved—a woman who disappeared years ago. Caesar has moved into a rooming house and Jones writes, "He would not know until his third week there that along the other hall was Yvonne Miller."

Several of Jones's stories use a flash forward in the opening sentences. The first sentence of "The Girl Who Raised Pigeons" is: "Her father would say years later that she had dreamed that part of it, that she had never gone out through the kitchen window at two or three in the morning to visit the birds." And here is the first sentence of "The First Day": "On an otherwise unremarkable September morning, long before I learned to be ashamed of my mother, she takes my hand and we set off down New Jersey avenue to begin my very first day of school." Note how he makes us anticipate a time when he is ashamed of his mother. And here is a sentence that appears toward the end of the first paragraph in "A New Man." "He would be in that same position some thirteen years later, when death happened upon him as he bent down over a hotel bathroom sink, about to do a job a younger engineer claimed he could not handle." Meanwhile, he is very much alive and has come "home early and found his daughter with two boys."

Salman Rushdie uses flash forward over and over again in *Midnight's Children* to alert the reader to what is coming in the future. "Years later, when Uncle Puffs tried to sell me his daughter by offering to have her teeth drawn and replaced with gold, I thought of Tai's forgotten treasure . . . and, as a child, Aadam Aziz had loved him." Do return to this novel just to learn the many ways Rushdie uses this technique.

The Exercise

Find a story in which you can insert a sentence that refers to something that is going to happen "later" in the life of the story or the character—something the character doesn't yet know. It also should not be the ending, as in "The End Foretold," but rather a detail that will make the reader anticipate what is to come. Do it as economically as possible with only one or two sentences.

The Objective

To be aware that you are the storyteller and can decide what to reveal and when. To learn how to add drama, anticipation and apprehension to a story by revealing something that gives the reader more information than the narrator has at that particular time in the story.

EXERCISE 46

Plot Potential

The main thing to keep in mind as you're doing plot is that *you're the boss* and not the other way around. It's your story, and you have an infinite number of choices. As a creator of fiction, you should feel supremely at ease in the role of storyteller.

The Exercise

Write five mini-stories (limit: 200 words each) to account for a single event or set of circumstances, such as a man and woman standing on a city sidewalk, hailing a cab. Each story should be different—in characters, plot, and theme—from the others.

The Objective

To loosen the bonds that shackle you to a single, immutable version; to underscore the fact that plot is not preordained but something you can control and manipulate at will, like the strings of a marionette; and to demonstrate once more that there are many ways to skin a cat.

Student Example

1. At 2:00 in the afternoon, John, a forty-four-year-old man in a business suit, and Dawn, a twenty-two-year-old woman in a tight skirt and high heels, came out of the Hancock Building. While John stood in the street trying to hail a cab, Dawn stayed on the sidewalk, sobbing. John is Dawn's boss and she is his secretary. At 1:45 she'd gotten a call from the hospital; her mother had a heart attack and was in intensive care. When Dawn told John why she had to leave so suddenly, he looked as though it was his mother who was in the hospital. Dawn could not understand why he was so concerned, and why he was going with her to the hospital. John held Dawn's hand in the cab and said, "Oh God, oh God." And he wondered how he was going to tell Dawn that he was her mother's lover, that they'd fallen in love the night Dawn brought her mother to the company Christmas party.

2. As usual, Pauline had been totally humiliated by her father, and now he was making a fool of himself trying to hail a cab. He'd insisted on coming to her interview with her. He insisted on sitting in the waiting room while she was in with the personnel director, and he pestered the receptionist with stories about how cute

127

Pauline had been as a child and how smart she was as an adult. Pauline knew he did it with good intentions—he wanted her to be safe in the city, but it was driving her crazy.

3. Maggie hated the city, the people in it, the noise, the dirt, and especially that man who had stepped out in front of her and was trying to flag down the cab she had been waiting for. When a cab finally pulled up and he put his hand on the door, she banged him so hard with her hip that he fell to the street. "Get your own cab, buster."

   "Maggie?" he said, still on the ground. "Maggie Pillbox? Is that you?"

   "Wow," she said. "It's you, Doctor Pantry. Gosh, if I'd known it was you, I never would have hit you so hard."

   "Still hostile, eh?" he said. Doctor Pantry had been Maggie's psychiatrist. She helped him up, and for the next fifty minutes, they stood on the sidewalk, Doctor Pantry listening carefully and taking notes as Maggie told him all her life's woes.

4. The man and woman trying to hail down a cab, the ones dressed like insurance sales people, had just pulled off their greatest crime to date. It wasn't the big time, but eleven wallets, a watch, and a solar calculator weren't bad for five minutes' work. Once in the cab, they started going through the loot, unaware that the cabdriver was watching in his rearview mirror. The woman talked about how they could finally afford Cindy's braces. The man said he could now pay the rent, and the cabdriver took them on a circuitous route to the police station.

5. Joe had been driving a cab for only two weeks and still found the job intoxicating. He liked trying to figure out what each person was like before they got into his cab, though he was usually wrong about people. His last fare had turned out to be a transvestite so convincing that he'd almost asked him/her out on a date. Now this couple, the man in the three-piece suit waving him down and the much younger woman on the sidewalk, worked together and were lovers dying to get away for an afternoon of hot passion. Why else the unlikely pair? "Forest Lawn Mortuary," the man said as he got into the car. "And step on it. We don't want to be late."

   —TERRY FRENCH

A work of art has no importance whatever to society. It is only important to the individual.

—VLADIMIR NABOKOV

EXERCISE 47

Back Story as Narrative Summary: Who's Coming to Stay the Night!

Students often avoid narrative summary, even though a story might have a fascinating back story, or an important period of time that should be summarized. We sometimes suggest that our students type out a passage of narrative summary by a writer they admire to experience just how long a passage of narrative summary can be. One student chose to turn the beginning of Ray Carver's story "Cathedral" (page 306) into manuscript pages. Carver's narrator tells us in the first line, that "This blind man, an old friend of my wife's, he was on his way to spend the night." Then the narrator tells us about the blind man's life, his wife's friendship with the blind man, his own courtship of his wife—all in a detailed passage of narrative summary that goes on for three-and-a-half pages! Look for passages of narrative summary in the work of Tobias Wolff, Alice Munro, Junot Diaz, Antonya Nelson, Alice Hoffman, James Baldwin, and Richard Ford to see just how expansive and informative these passages are.

The Exercise

Using "Cathedral" as a model for your story, begin a story with one line that says who is coming to stay the night. It should be someone who is not considered a welcome guest by your narrator. So, introduce the impending visit with one line, then create a lengthy and detailed back story that tells who the guest is, why the narrator is not looking forward to the visit, and at the same time tell us something about the narrator's life. The guest can be someone the narrator knows—or does not know, in the case of "Cathedral." The unwelcome guest can be an old roommate, your spouse's inlaws or your spouse's ex-boyfriend or ex-girlfriend, an estranged sibling. Tell the reader they are due to arrive any minute. Then while the narrator and the reader are awaiting their arrival, allow the narrator to tell us the back story of the tensions in their lives.

The Objective

To be able to write passages of narrative summary that are informative and provide the back story to how the story is going to play out, passages that keep the reader engaged and wanting to know more.

EXERCISE 48

The End Foretold

Few readers are tempted to turn to the end of a novel to find out "what happens," because the journey to the end is one of the pleasures of being inside that particular story. However, some writers tell future events at the beginning of their story or novel, trusting their storytelling abilities to keep the reader reading. Early on in his story "White Angel," Michael Cunningham writes about two brothers, the younger of whom adores his older brother, Carlton. "I was, thanks to Carlton, the most criminally advanced nine-year-old in my fourth-grade class. I was going places. I made no move without his counsel." The next sentence begins, "Here is Carlton several months before his death, in an hour so alive with snow that earth and sky are identically white." And we continue reading on for that "hour so alive"—alive even more so in the face of Carlton's impending death.

Rudolfo Anaya also foretells events in his novel *Bless Me, Ultima*. In the first pages his narrator tells us, "The attic of our home was partitioned into two small rooms. My sisters, Deborah and Theresa, slept in one and I slept in the small cubicle by the door. The wooden steps creaked down into a small hallway that led into the kitchen. From the top of the stairs I had the vantage point into the heart of our home, my mother's kitchen. From there I was to see the terrified face of Chavez when he brought the terrible news of the murder of the sheriff; I was to see the rebellion of my brothers against my father; and many times late at night I was to see Ultima returning from the Llano where she gathered the herbs that can be harvested only in the light of the full moon by the careful hands of a curandera." Note how murder and his brothers' rebellion are woven into a sentence that brings us through to his adored Ultima.

In the beginning of *Stones for Ibarra*, Harriet Doerr writes, "Here they are, a man and a woman just over and just under forty, come to spend their lives in Mexico City and are already lost as they travel cross-country over the central plateau. The driver of the station wagon is Richard Everton, a blue-eyed, black-haired stubborn man who will die thirty years sooner than he now imagines. On the seat beside him is his wife, Sara, who imagines neither his death nor her own, imminent or remote as they may be."

In the first paragraph of Howard Norman's novel *The Bird Artist*, Fabian Vas makes a startling revelation. It begins: "My name is Fabian Vas. I live in Witless Bay, New Foundland. You would not have heard of me. Obscurity is not necessarily failure, though; I am a bird artist, and have more or less made a living at it. Yet I murdered the lighthouse keeper, Botho August, and that is an equal part of how I think of myself." The murder doesn't occur till almost the end of the novel.

Other works of fiction that foretell their endings are Elizabeth Jane Howard's "The Long View" and Gabriel García Márquez's *Chronicle of a Death Foretold*.

The Exercise

Select one of your own stories that has an ending that is final—a story in which someone leaves a place or person forever, someone dies, or something irrevocable and irreparable takes place. Now move this "news" to the beginning of your story. Be brief. Then read your story again to see if the journey through the story is rewarding in itself.

The Objective

To put pressure on the story—sentence by sentence—by "giving away" the ending. To understand that chronology is fluid and sometimes irrelevant to the experience of the story.

The Exercise

Select one of your own stories that has an ending that is final—a story in which some-one leaves a place or person forever, someone dies, or something irrevocable and irreparable takes place. Now move this "news" to the beginning of your story. Be brief. Then read your story again to see if the journey through the story is rewarding in itself.

The Objective

To put pressure on the story—sentence by sentence—by "giving away" the ending. To understand that chronology is fluid and sometimes irrelevant to the experience of the story.

PART SEVEN

The Elements of Style

Style is the feather in the arrow, not the feather in the cap.

—George Sampson

We have borrowed the title of this section from E. B. White and William Strunk's writing bible of the same name. White said during an interview, "I don't think style can be taught. Style results more from what a person is than from what he knows." He went on to say that there are a "few hints that can be thrown out to advantage. They would be the twenty-one hints I threw out in Chapter V of *The Elements of Style*. There was nothing new or original about them, but there they are, for all to read." Everybody should have a copy of this book on his shelf, but as a reminder we have listed the section headings of Chapter V below:

> 1. Place yourself in the background; 2. Write in a way that comes naturally; 3. Work from a suitable design; 4. Write with nouns and verbs; 5. Revise and rewrite; 6. Do not overwrite; 7. Do not overstate; 8. Avoid the use of qualifiers; 9. Do not affect a breezy manner; 10. Use orthodox spelling; 11. Do not explain too much; 12. Do not construct awkward adverbs; 13. Make sure the reader knows who is speaking; 14. Avoid fancy words; 15. Do not use dialect unless your ear is good; 16. Be clear; 17. Do not inject opinion; 18. Use figures of speech sparingly; 19. Do not take shortcuts at the cost of clarity; 20. Avoid foreign languages; 21. Prefer the standard to the offbeat.

Strunk and White is a good place to begin, but it isn't the whole story of style in fiction. What would John Barth be without his instructional presence; Didion without Didion; Vladimir Nabokov without his complicated, high style; Alice Adams without her qualifiers; Laurie Colwin without her breezy manner; Russell Hoban without his unorthodox spelling; Nicholson Baker without his explanations; Flannery O'Connor without her inventions in dialect; Joseph Conrad without his opinions; John Updike without his figures of speech; Thomas Mann and Sandra Cisneros without their foreign languages; and Donald Barthelme without the offbeat?

Begin with Strunk and White, but as you grow more experienced in writing and life, you will grow into a more individual style. Style is a kind of personal signature, made up of the writer's particular vocabulary, sentence structure, subject matter, inflection, attitude, tone, and vision.

Cyril Connolly, the English critic, said, "Style is manifest in language. The vocabulary of a writer is his currency, but it is a paper currency and its value depends on the reserves of mind and heart which back it. The perfect use of language is that in which every word carries the meaning that it is intended to, no less and no more."

Jazz great Miles Davis said, "You have to play a long time to play like yourself." The same is true of writing fiction. The exercises in this section are designed to make you more aware of the elements of style, style in language—sentence structure, word choice, diction, tone, etc.—in your own work and the work of writers you admire. Surprisingly, John Updike once grumbled to an interviewer that his prose always sounded like John Updike no matter how hard he tried to sound like someone else. He also says that the best way to get the kinks out of your prose is to read it aloud. The eye and ear are connected and what the reader sees will somehow be transmitted to his inner ear. Too many sentences with a similar construction will make your reader yawn. Too many unintended repetitions of words of phrases will also displease the reader's ear. Know which words you use too often, such as "and," "just," "look," "even," and so on. Always read your work aloud before showing it to anyone. Doing this will help you avoid monotony, repetition, flatness, unintentional alliteration, and other impediments to smooth, fluid prose. Your teachers, fellow students, and future editors will know when you have not read your work out loud.

> I have lost too much by losing, or rather by not having acquired, the note-taking habit. It might be of great profit to me; and now that I am older, that I have more time, that the labor of writing is less onerous to me, and I can work more at my leisure, I ought to endeavor to keep, to a certain extent, a record of passing impressions, of all that comes, that goes, that I see, and feel, and observe. To catch and keep something of life—that's what I mean.
>
> —HENRY JAMES, NOTEBOOKS, NOVEMBER 25, 1881

EXERCISE 49

A Style of Your Own

from Rod Kessler

Students are often surprised to discover patterns within their own writing styles. Sometimes the patterns reveal strengths of style, but sometimes the patterns uncover easy-to-fix problems, such as "having the as's"—using too many "as he was walking" constructions.

The Exercise

Make a photocopy of a page from a story you've already put into final form. This can be the opening of the story or a page from the middle, it doesn't matter—but be sure the page is typed neatly. Also bring in a copy of a page from a fiction writer you admire. Analyze your page for:

1. Sentence length. From the top of your page count down ten sentences. Make a list indicating the word length of each sentence. How varied in length are your sentences? Do you have a mix of short and long, or are your sentences around the same length?

   Next, add up all the words in your ten sentences and divide by ten—which gives you your average sentence length.

   Now, perform the same counts on the page from the writer whose work you admire—writer X. How varied are these sentences compared with your own? What is the writer's average length?

2. Modifier density. On your own writing sample, mark all of the adjectives and adverbs you've used in the first 100 words and add them up. This gives an approximate percentage of modifiers. (If you counted 5, that's 5 out of 100 or 5 percent).

   Perform the same count on the page from writer X. How do your styles compare?

3. Sentence structure. Does each of your paragraphs contain a mixture of simple, complex, and compound sentences? Or are they all of the same structure? How many times do you begin, say, with participial phrases (Running to the station, Jack. . . . Looking up at the sky, Joan. . . .)? How many times do you use "subject-verb" constructions? How many times do you use "as" as a conjunction (Jerry turned to go as the bell chimed.)? (Read John Gardner's discussion of "The Sentence" in *The Art of Fiction*, in which he teaches the lesson of the sentence by example.)

4. Diction. How many of the first 100 words exceed two syllables? Three syllables? More than three? (Again, read Gardner's section "Vocabulary," same book.)

5. Verbs. What percentage of your verbs are forms of the boring verb "to be"? How often do you use the passive voice?

The Objective

To enable you to regard your own prose style objectively and decide if you need to make changes—perhaps vary your sentences or cut out an obvious mannerism. Some students might want to go beyond ten sentences and one hundred words to do a closer study of their "natural" prose.

> *I got the idea of Loving from a manservant in the Fire Service during the war. He was serving with me in the ranks, and he told me he had once asked the elderly butler who was over him what the old boy most liked in the world. The reply was: "Lying in bed on a summer morning, with the window open, listening to the church bells, eating buttered toast with cunty fingers." I saw the book in a flash.*
>
> —HENRY GREEN

EXERCISE 50

Taboos: Weak Adverbs and Adjectives

Voltaire said the adjective is the enemy of the noun and the adverb is the enemy of the verb. Thus war ensues on both—with the object of banishing adjectives and adverbs forever. Banishing them precipitously and unfairly. John Gardner said, "Adverbs are either the dullest tools or the sharpest tools in the novelist's toolbox." Adverbs are not meant to augment a verb—as in walked *slowly*—but to create friction with the verb or alter its meaning. For example, pair the following adverbs with different verbs to see how they change those verbs: relentlessly, conscientiously, chastely, uncharacteristically, reluctantly, gratuitously, erroneously, furtively, and inadequately. This is what Mark Twain wrote to a young admirer: "I notice that you use plain simple language, short words [brief sentences. That is the way to write English. . . . Stick to it] don't let fluff and flowers creep in. When you catch an adjective, kill it. No, I don't mean that, utterly, but kill most of them—then the rest will be valuable. They weaken when they are close together, they give strength when they are wide apart."

Adjectives may seem to bolster nouns when in fact they often weaken them. Yet some adjectives have everything to do with style and meaning. Whenever you use an adjective, try to make it unexpected; it should pull away from the noun, giving the two words a sort of delicious tension. The same goes for the adverb.

The following are examples of adverbs and adjectives that are used well:

She had been to Germany, Italy, everywhere that one visits *acquisitively.*
　　　　　　　　　—ELIZABETH BOWEN, *THE LAST SEPTEMBER*

Within the parson's house death was *zealously* kept in view and lectured on.
　　　　　　　　　—ISAK DINESEN, "PETER AND ROSA"

She jammed the pedal to the floor, and like something huge and prehistoric and pea-brained, the Jeep leapt *stupidly* out of its stall.
　　　　　　　　　—SHARON SHEEHE STARK, *A WRESTLING SEASON*

I have always enjoyed gestures—never failing to bow, for example, when I finished dancing with a woman—but one attribute I have acquired with age is the ability to predict when I am about to act *foolishly.*
　　　　　　　　　—ETHAN CANIN, *EMPEROR OF THE AIR*

137

She reached again for the door and kept her eyes on him, like a captive who edges *watchfully* towards escape.

—Shirley Hazzard, *The Transit of Venus*

So closely had we become tied to the river that we could sense where it lay and make for it *instinctively* like cattle.

—W. D. Wetherell, *Chekhov's Sister*

When Sula first visited the Wright house, Helene's *curdled* scorn turned to butter.

—Toni Morrison, *Sula*

With a *bladdery* whack it [the boat] slapped apart and sprang away.

—Sharon Sheehe Stark, *A Wrestling Season*

Charmian sat with her eyes closed, attempting to put her thoughts into *alphabetical* order.

—Muriel Spark, *Memento Mori*

Hank was not accepted at Harvard Law School; but *goodhearted* Yale took him.

—John Updike, "The Other"

On the far side of the room, under the *moiling* dogs the twins are playing.

—François Camoin, "Baby, Baby, Baby"

"Perhaps the Beauforts don't know her," Janey suggested, with her *artless* malice.

—Edith Wharton, *The Age of Innocence*

And he contemplated her absorbed young face with a thrill of possessorship in which pride of his own masculinity was mingled with a tender reverence for her *abysmal* purity.

—Edith Wharton, *The Age of Innocence*

The Exercise

Circle all the adverbs and adjectives in a published story and decide which ones work. Then, exchange all weak adverbs and adjectives for strong ones of your own. Consider omitting them altogether. Now, do the same exercise with one of your own stories.

The Objective

To be alert to the power—and the weakness—of these verbal spices. To avoid them except when they can add something you really need.

To underscore the fact that verbs and nouns are stronger alone than when coupled with modifiers that add nothing to nuance or meaning and are about as useful as a pair of broken crutches.

Student Examples

Hunched over, scissors clasped in her hands, the old woman passed like a shadow behind a screen of young birch and stepped *possessively* into her neighbor's garden.

—COLLEEN GILLARD

I clatter Sparkey's mouth and make him laugh *demonically,* or have him insult the guy who is sitting too near the stage.

—MATT MARINOVICH

I want stories to startle and engage me within the first few sentences, and in their middle to widen or deepen or sharpen my knowledge of human activity, and to end by giving me a sensation of completed state-ment. The ending is where the reader discovers whether he has been reading the same story the writer thought he was writing.
—JOHN UPDIKE, INTRODUCTION TO *BASS 1984*

EXERCISE 51

Word Packages
Are Not Gifts

A word package is a group of neutral words strung together into a hackneyed phrase. Word packages are used by lazy writers searching for an easy way out of a difficult or slippery thought. (Frequently they are found at the beginnings of sentences.)

The Exercise

Stay away from the following word packages. They signal to the smart reader that you lack freshness and are an uninteresting writer.

Better than ever
For some curious reason
A number of . . .
As everybody knows
She didn't know where she was
Things were getting out of hand
It came as no surprise
It was beyond him
Needless to say
Without thinking
He lived in the moment
Well in advance
An emotional roller coaster
Little did I know
To no avail
The only sound was

The Objective

To learn to write without word packages until your use of them is absolutely deliberate and to some purpose.

EXERCISE 52

Practice Writing Good,
Clean Prose
from Christopher Keane

Too often new writers think in terms of story, rather than in terms of words—of building a story with words. As a result, their early efforts are often overwritten and flowery. The following exercise will challenge your use of language—and it might change the way you write.

The Exercise

Write a short story using words of only one syllable.

The Objective

To make you conscious of word choice.

Example

Fire

I see her in a red dress, a red bow in her hair. She would have on black shoes and white socks. The socks would be up to her knees. She would have been, say, five years old at the time the fire broke out. It would have still been dark; it would have been cold.

She would be in her room at the time.

She would have waked from a deep sleep as if pushed or shoved. She would have known what to do. She was that way, they tell me. She was that kind of child.

I see her leave her room, stand at the top of the stairs in the front hall, smell the smoke. She would be dressed; she put on her clothes when she climbed out of bed. When she smelled smoke she would scream a fire scream that would start at the base of her throat, pass through her lips in a howl. The howl would wake those in the rest of the house. It would curl through the rooms, ride the smoke that climbed the stairs, seep through doors, cloud the glass.

The man got up first and woke his wife. They heard the child's howl filled with smoke, and they raced to the cribs of the twins, they raced to their room. Flames licked the closed doors, climbed the walls.

The man and his wife crept down the back stairs. They heard the girl's scream but there was no way to reach her. There was no time. They did not want to leave the house, but they had to. While there was still time. They must save at all cost what they had in their arms. Each held one of the twins that they took from the cribs. The twins slept on. They slept a dead sleep, safe in the arms that held them.

I see her red dress. I see a red bow in her hair. She would be told she saved them all, and she would be glad. She would have scars on her face and arms. The scars would hurt. The fire would be with her through life.

She would see the red dress and the red bow in her dreams, the white socks up to her knees. In her dreams, she would stand at the top of the stairs in the front hall. She would smell smoke and start to howl. The scars would not have come yet, nor the pain.

—ANNE BRASHLER, EDITOR, *StoryQuarterly*

PART EIGHT

A Writer's Toolbox

As we said in our introduction—and we think it's worth repeating—a writer must think like a writer and also master the tools needed to write smoothly, with feeling, and control. Thinking like a writer means being open, skeptical, curious, passionate, forgiving, and truthful. Writing like a writer involves learning specific techniques of the craft and, not incidentally, shedding bad habits such as using stale or approximate language, wasting words, and working in haste.

What we call "tools" includes solving the problems presented by time and space, bringing abstract ideas to life, learning to show more and tell less, handling transitions, and naming everything from diners to dogs.

A few blessed people seem able to sit down and immediately turn out polished and exciting prose. Most of us, however, must go through a long apprenticeship, trying one way after another until our fiction falls into the right place; there is no substitute for trial and error. And as you revise you will find yourself being a ruthless self-editor, cutting and shaping until you get it the way you want it. The following exercises were designed to provide you with company along the way. They should help take you from the uncertainty and disarray of a first draft to a finished piece of work you have every right to be proud of.

EXERCISE 53

Handling the Problems of Time and Pace

from Robie Macauley

The traditional rule is that episodes meant to show important behavior in the characters, to make events dramatic as in theater, or to bring news that changes the situation, should be dealt with in the scenic, or eyewitness, manner. Stretches of time or occurrences that are secondary to the story's development are handled by means of what is called a narrative bridge. Dialogue is the direct report of speech; indirect discourse is the summary of what was said. Some examples:

Scenic
Now they were at the ford, the rain was still falling, and the river was in flood. John got out of the jeep and stared at the white violence of the water they must cross to reach the place where the muddy road picked up again.

Narrative Summary
The journey to Punta Gorda took two days by near-impossible road. At one point, they had to cross a raging river and follow a muddy track that only a jeep could manage.

Dialogue
"Now how are we going to get across this monster?" Lisa asked.
   "Easy," said John. "We take the rope over, get it around that big tree and use the winch to pull the jeep across."
   "But who swims the flood with the rope?"
   "Well, I can't swim," he said, "but you're supposed to be so good at it."

Indirect Discourse
When they came to the swollen river, John suggested that they put a rope across and then use the jeep's winch to pull the vehicle to the farther bank. Because Lisa had talked so often about her swimming ability, he suggested ironically that she be the one to take the rope over.

The Exercise

As a class, come up with a plot or a series of events that might make a long short story. Next, write a scenario in which you indicate

- Where you would place a full scene or incidental scene.

- Where you would use summaries, either narrative summaries or summarized scenes.

The Objective

To learn to identify which parts of a story should be presented in a scene and which parts of a story should be summarized. To develop an understanding of pace.

A writer is someone for whom writing is more difficult than it is for other people.
—THOMAS MANN

EXERCISE 54

Exposition: The Pet Store Story

from Ron Carlson

A fair beginning of the discussion of any story would be to determine the percentage of exposition; this sounds clinical, but it is a useful way to offer an exact description of the story's components, and identify where further evidence is required. We're defining exposition as anything that happens before the first moment of the current story; it also could be anything that happens after the current story—sometimes offered in conditional or future tenses (look for would). Some stories have almost no stated exposition (it is implied—as in Hemingway's "Hills Like White Elephants") and some stories are dominated by exposition. Many stories have multiple layers of exposition, that is many time periods that are being brought to bear on the current story. (See Alice Munro's story, "Save the Reaper.") While the plot (the current story) remains the motor of any story, the characters are the freight.

This assignment will result in a short short story, 600 to 1,000 words in length. If it is less than 600 words, you will need your instructor's permission. If it is more than 1,000 words, you will need your instructor's permission. If it goes onto the fifth page—oh, just make it short.

The story will feature two people (opposite sex, any relationship) who go to a pet store on a mission.

The Exercise

It is a three-part story; it starts in the middle, goes back to the beginning, and jumps to the ending. In the story (1) two people approach the pet store; (2) we find out their recent and not-so-recent history; (3) they go into the pet store.

1. Write one page in which two people approach a pet store, any pet store except Mammals and More, because that's been used. It can be freestanding or in a mall. The duty of this page is to convince us that two actual people are in an actual place. There can be dialogue, but this section should be at least 90 percent outer story: the day, the sounds, the imagery through which two people approach the pet store.

2. Write one page in which we discover from where they've come most recently (today) and what their larger history is.

3. Write one to two pages in which they enter the store and pursue their objective. This section will include current story and flashback as necessary. There probably will be another character introduced. The two people either will or will not fulfill their mission.

The Objective

The value of the current story is established/determined/colored by the exposition. The dynamic between current action and the past is a key operating feature of every story.

Student Example

Jenkins Pet & Supply

We're on our way to Jenkins Pet & Supply, a huge converted airplane hangar full of all things pet. Part of the ritual is I always come along. A punishment. A penance. I come because I can give my wife these things.

Judy drives through traffic like a stock car racer, changing lanes without signaling, riding people's tails. Her hands shift the gear violently, like it's done her a disservice. Every time I try to turn the radio on, she slaps my hand, so we ride in silence. I roll the window down and let the stiff breeze whoosh against my face. Then I turn to her and stare, waiting to see if she'll say anything. She looks good for her age, forty-one, taking a large amount of pride in never having color-treated her hair, which is so brown it looks black. "It proves I still have my youth," she always says, like it's a threat, like it might last forever.

The Jenkins lot is crowded; it's a Saturday. We walk in behind a father and his two young children. The pigtailed girl says she wants goldfish. The boy says guppies. The father says he thinks the two can live together, in the same tank. But the boy wants his own tank. So does his sister.

"Any ideas?" I ask Judy. "More goldfish?" She ignores me.

I would love Judy to choose more goldfish, but she won't. She's here to prove a point. Whenever I do something she considers "wrong," a breach of trust, an ill-chosen phrase, and now, the latest, my failure to "properly grieve" her mother—she takes me to Jenkins and picks out a new pet. This has gone on too long. Living alongside us in our four-bedroom Meridian Township Colonial are: three dogs, a cat, a hamster, a ferret (illegally), a trio of bunnies, a turtle, a pair of canaries, an iguana, and too many fish to keep track of. Our home is never without barking, chirping, purring, squawking, and the hum of tank filtration systems. Judy has given each pet a name, and takes care of the feedings and cage cleanings. This all began four years ago, when we left Dr. Alistair's office with news that it would never happen naturally for us, a problem Judy blamed on me. The doctor's results were inconclusive, a mystery, but I still felt guilty, somehow inadequate, so I silently shouldered the responsibility. Pulling out of the office parking lot that day, she blurted out "I want a dog." Roxanne, an amiable Collie named for the first child we wouldn't have, came home with us that afternoon.

Ted's the salesperson wondering if he can be of any assistance. He's in his twenties, but adolescent uncertainty tinges his speech as he tells us the Sun Conure is the clown of the parrot world. "A regular Bozo," he says, like it's something he's rehearsed. "But smart, very smart." He fidgets, scratches his arm. "You people have other birds in the house?"

"Canaries," I tell him. Looking in at the bird, the only thing that seems clownish is its multitude of colors—like a bird made for tropical weather. Wings the color of lemon, a hint of lime at the tips. A wash of orange over its head and down its breast. The bird sizes me up with beady black eyes.

Ted mulls this over, and says it should be okay, but perhaps keep the birds in separate rooms. The Conure can intimidate and impose their will on other domestic birds.

"Does he speak?" Judy asks.

"With training," Ted explains. "One method is to hold a mirror up to the bird. Keep your own face behind it and speak. He'll think it's a fellow bird talking, and will imitate."

"I like him," Judy says, without turning to me for consultation.

"One thing," Ted says, his tone taking on a note of seriousness, "the Conure will live up to thirty-five years. With proper care." He twists his fingers together, seeming uncertain as to our intentions. "It's a lifetime commitment," he concludes.

"We'll take the bird," Judy tells him, waving into the cage with a crooked index finger.

We exit Jenkins Pet & Supply with our new parrot. I carry bags with bird play-toys, food pellets, different apparatus to make his living space resemble a children's jungle gym. Early evening dusk has settled over the parking lot, and for a moment, things are silent. I stare in the direction of where the sun has set and the sky is the dynamic color of our new pet.

"Ronald," Judy says. "We'll call him Ronald." She always gives our pets human names. Beth, Christopher, Tim. Jack, Katherine, Paul.

"Honey," I say.

She holds the large cage at face level. "Here Ronnie, Ronnie. Here, birdie."

—SEAN LANIGAN, PUBLISHED IN LOST

A story is a way to say something that can't be said any other way, and it takes every word in the story to say what the meaning is.
—FLANNERY O'CONNOR

EXERCISE 55

Bringing Abstract Ideas to Life

One of the principal problems in writing stories is to make abstract ideas come to life. It is not enough to talk of poverty or ambition or evil, you must render these ideas in a concrete way with descriptive sensory details, similes, and metaphors. Examine how growing old is handled in Muriel Spark's *Memento Mori,* poverty in Charles Dickens's *Bleak House* and Carolyn Chute's *The Beans of Egypt, Maine,* racism in Ralph Ellison's *Invisible Man,* growing up in Frank Conroy's *Stop-Time,* ambition in Theodore Dreiser's *An American Tragedy,* the immigrant experience in Zadie Smith's *White Teeth,* and evil in William Golding's *Lord of the Flies.*

The Exercise

Make several of the following abstractions come to life by rendering them in concrete specific details or images.

racism	poverty
injustice	growing up
ambition	sexual deceit
growing old	wealth
salvation	evil

The Objective

To learn to think, always, in concrete terms. To realize that the concrete is more persuasive than any high-flown rhetoric full of fancy words and abstractions.

Student Examples

Racism
referring to others as "you people"

—FRED PELKA

Poverty
eating Thanksgiving dinner in a church basement

—ANNE KAPLAN

Sexual Deceit
splashing on Brut to cover the smell of a woman's perfume

—SANFORD GOLDEN

Evil
purposely running down animals on the road

—SANDY YANNONE

Prejudice
Victoria slipped the camphor between her skin and her undershirt before opening the library door. Her mother made her wear it from Rosh Hashanah to Passover, a guard against winter colds. "In Poland it was colder," she always said, "yet we never got sick in the winter." It was useless for Victoria to point out that one aunt and uncle had died in Polish winters despite their health charms.

She placed her bag of books on the library's high stone counter where "Returns" was written in beautiful penmanship. "I hope you didn't tear any of these," Mrs. Holmes said, pausing in her friendly chat with a woman who looked like Betty Crocker. One by one she checked in the ragged copies of kids' classics saying that sometimes it looked as if Victoria had eaten her dinner on these books. She smiled to the woman. "Everything turns into rags in their hands, you know."

Victoria went to sit in the children's section of the library. Three new books were displayed on the table. She might get through them by closing time. She knew Mrs. Holmes wouldn't let her take out these books 'til yellow tape obscured some of the words. She wondered if it might make a difference if Mrs. Holmes knew that she was the best reader in the whole fifth grade.

—BARBARA SOFER

Life knows us not and we do not know life—we don't even know our own thoughts. Half the words we use have no meaning whatever and of the other half each man understands each word after the fashion of his own folly and conceit. Faith is a myth and beliefs shift like mist on the shore; thoughts vanish; words, once pronounced, die; and the memory of yesterday is as shadowy as the hope of to-morrow—only the string of my platitudes seems to have no end.

—JOSEPH CONRAD

EXERCISE 56

Transportation: Getting
There Isn't Half the Fun—
It's Boring

This isn't strictly an exercise: It's more of a reminder. When moving characters from one place to another, write about how they got there only if it's crucial. Think of the movies—rarely do we see a character on a bus or in a train *unless the trip itself tells us something we absolutely need to know about the story or the character*. The lovers are in bed; next thing we see they're in a bistro, smooching over a glass of Pernod. Who cares how they got from bed to bistro? Avoid stairs, sidewalks, subways, planes, trains, and automobiles if you can tell your story as richly without them.

Writing about what you know does not usually mean writing about your own life. Writing about what you know means writing about the girl whose fierce-looking father picked her up from school on his Harley-Davidson motorcycle, about the Rhode Island red hens on your aunt Beulah's farm, or the way a carburetor works on a 1950 Plymouth. Writers are meant to peer outward at others with an inward passion and sympathy.

—RON HANSEN

Naming the Diner, Naming the Diet, Naming the Dog

During the course of writing stories set in counties and towns with restaurants and mortuaries, stories in which characters play in rock bands, buy race horses, play on football teams, or found new religions, you are going to have to name them all. Think of William Faulkner's Yoknapatawpha County, Thomas Hardy's Wessex, Willa Cather's Red Cloud, Marilynne Robinson's Fingerbone Lake, Anne Tyler's Homesick Restaurant and travel-guide series, *The Accidental Tourist,* and Oscar Hijuelos's Mambo Kings. Names matter.

The Exercise

In your notebook, keep a list of unusual names for potential characters. In fact, every writer should have a collection of old yearbooks, benefit programs, phone books, and so forth to browse through when he needs to name a character. And don't stop there. Keep lists for things you might need to name in a story.

Name the following things. Imagine stories they might go in. Remember that tone is important, so choose both an earnest name and a farcical one.

a desert town	a football team
a race horse	a diner
a literary magazine	a new religion
a new disease	a new planet
a rock band	a polluted river
a summer cottage	a poetry collection
triplets	a chihuahua
a liqueur	a burglar
a beauty salon	a bar
a new diet	a lipstick color
a soap opera	a yacht

The Objective

To loosen up your imagination by naming things you wouldn't ordinarily have to name—never mind "own."

Student Examples

Clearly, the students had more fun with the farcical names.

Desert Town
Drymouth   NOREN CACERES

Racehorse
Windpasser   SAM HALPERT
Race Elements   JAY GREENBERG

Summer Cottage
Bric-a-Brac   KARLA HORNER

Triplets
Farrar, Straus
and Giroux   ROBERT WERNER

Beauty Salon
Tressed for Success   E. J. GRAFF

Diner
Crisco   DAVID ZIMMERMAN

New Religion
People of the Tree   KARLA HORNER

Planet
Pica   DAWN BAKER

Polluted River
Floop River   DANIEL BIGMAN

Chihuahua
Bruno's Lunch   KAREN BROCK

Burglar
Nick Spieze   GREG DUYCK

Diet
Body Carpenter   DAVID ZIMMERMAN

Soap Opera
The Rammed
and the Damned
(on cable TV)   SANFORD GOLDEN

Yacht
Waves Goodbye   MOLLY LANZAROTTA

> *The whole secret of a living style and the difference between it and a dead style, lies in not having too much style—being, in fact, a little careless, or rather seeming to be, here and there. It brings wonderful life into the writing . . .*
> —THOMAS HARDY

EXERCISE 58

Transitions: Or, White Space Does Not a Transition Make

Often in the course of a story or novel you need a transition to indicate a movement in time, a movement in space, or a movement from scene to narrative summary. Many writers have trouble with transitions. They either treat them too elaborately so that they jar the reader out of what Gardner calls "the vivid and continuous fictional dream," or they ignore them altogether and rely on white space to indicate that some shift has occurred. In each case, writers neglect the very medium they are using—language—to do it for them, and do it gracefully.

In the examples below, each writer has used white space to indicate visually that a shift has occurred, but they do not rely entirely on white space to make the shift for them. In each example, the language and/or details in the text above the white space is connected to the language and/or details in the space directly below.

Here's Ray Carver, in "Where I'm Calling From," moving from the present to the past:

". . . If, if you ask for it and if you listen. End of Sermon. But don't forget. If," he says again. Then he hitches his pants and tugs his sweater down. "I'm going inside," he says. "See you at lunch." "I feel like a bug when he's around," J. P. says. "He makes me feel like a bug. Something you could step on." J. P. shakes his head. Then he says, "Jack London. What a name. I wish I had me a name like that. Instead of the name I got."

WHITE SPACE

Frank Martin talked about that "if" the first time I was here.

Notice how Carver not only uses "first time I was here" to indicate that there has been a shift, but he also reuses the "if" to make it graceful.

In Alice Munro's "Differently," there is a time shift after a woman lies to her babysitter:

"My car wouldn't start," she told the babysitter, a grandmother from down the street. "I walked all the way home. It was lovely, walking. Lovely. I enjoyed it so much."
Her hair was wild, her lips were swollen, her clothes were full of sand.

WHITE SPACE

Her life filled up with such lies.

Sometimes it is more efficient to use phrases to indicate a shift in time or place. Here are several phrases that Carver uses in his story "Fever": "all summer, since early June," "In the beginning," "in the living room," "That evening, after he'd put the children to bed," "After he'd hung up," "After Eileen had left," "This was the period when," "Just before the incident with Debbie," "Over the summer," "But a few hours later," "Once, earlier in the summer," "The next morning," "In a little while," "For the first time in months," "During first-period art history," "In his next class," "As he moved down the lunch line in the faculty dining room," "That afternoon," "That evening," "It was the middle of the fall term," and "The next time he awoke." All of these phrases are used to move the story along in space and time. Note how the school day is gracefully moved along from "first-period art history" to "next class" to "the lunch line."

The Exercise

Turn to a third or fourth draft of a story and examine your transitions. Is what is happening clear? Do your transitions employ language or are you depending on white space and your reader's imagination? Do your transitions gracefully connect the sections being bridged? Now rewrite your transitions, using language as a bridge to lead the reader from here to there to there.

The Objective

To be able to lead the reader gracefully over and around unnecessary parts of the story and to bridge with skill the shifts in time, memory, and space.

The best training is to read and write, no matter what. Don't live with a lover or roommate who doesn't respect your work. Don't lie, buy time, borrow to buy time. Write what will stop your breath if you don't write.
—GRACE PALEY

EXERCISE 59

How to Keep a Narrative Moving Forward

Narrative composition encompasses a number of various techniques. These are action, dialogue, interior monologue, description, exposition, flashback, and the author's own voice instructing the reader (this should be used sparingly, as the reader should figure out for him/herself what's happening). One way to construct a narrative that keeps moving forward is to think of the author as having her foot on the gas pedal of a car. When the author wants to move the story forward, she puts her foot on the pedal and the story goes into "drive." When she wants to supply description, exposition, dialogue, etc., the foot comes up and the car idles, as at a red light. The light turns green, the foot comes down and more action ensues.

The Exercise

Look at a short story—"White Angel" is an excellent example—and actually move your foot up and down as the action (down) in the story gives way to other techniques (up). Don't be put off by what might seem a mechanical approach. Our students have found this exercise extremely useful in writing their own stories.

The Objective

To illustrate the many modes available to the writer in moving her story along, at what pace, and with what "interruptions."

Nothing is less real than realism. Details are confusing. It is only by selection, by elimination, by emphasis that we get the real meaning of things.
—GEORGIA O'KEEFFE

EXERCISE 60

Noises Off: The Beauty
of Extraneous Sound

from Laurence Davies

In our lives, background noise may be annoying, sometimes maddening, but in our fiction it can work for us. A single interruption from a creaking stair, a song, a blast of radio, a whining fan belt, sharpens the most intense encounter. When cunningly paced, a whole sequence of extraneous sounds can make a stretch of dialogue resonate. Rather than distracting from it, patterns of noises, words, or music from outside the immediate scene create a sense of depth, giving the speakers in the foreground context and urgency. Noises off, as actors call them, may contradict your reader's first impressions or may reinforce them. Perhaps they will seem more menacing, or more vulnerable, even perhaps more ridiculous, but in any case your characters will spring to life.

In Part Two, Chapter Eight, of Gustave Flaubert's *Madame Bovary*, Rodolphe is in the town hall wooing Emma Bovary with romantic cadences, while bombastic speeches in the square mark the opening of an agricultural show. "Why castigate the passions?" asks Rodolphe. "Are they not the only beautiful thing there is on earth, the source of heroism, enthusiasm, poetry, music, art, of everything?" As Emma's would-be lover celebrates the passions, a local dignitary honors rustic produce: "Here the vine; there, the cider-apple trees; there, the rape-seed; further afield, cheese; and flax; gentlemen, let us not forget flax! Which has in recent years made great headway and to which I would most particularly draw your attention" (translation by Geoffrey Wall). From every field of expression, Flaubert collected clichés; here he gambles with his trophies, letting two kinds of banality create a scene that is anything but banal. At its climax, Rodolphe seizes Emma's hand just when the judges announce the winners of contests for best pig, best merino ram, and best manure heap. Does this episode of small-town claustrophobia make Emma seem foolish, pitiable, or both? Everything depends on Flaubert's exquisite sense of timing and his delight in counterpointed voices. We often talk about a writer's vision; perhaps we need a word for how an author *hears* the world.

Another outrageous juxtaposition occurs in Chapter Four of Joseph Conrad's *The Secret Agent*. Two anarchists meet in a basement restaurant, the Silenus. As they discuss police surveillance, the shortcomings of conventional morality, explosive chemistry, and a bomber's accidental death, a player-piano hammers out mazurkas. Then the Professor, who always keeps his hand around a detonator, leaves; Ossipon, an ineffectual terrorist but an energetic womanizer, lingers: "The lonely piano, without as much as a music stool to help it, struck a few chords courageously, and beginning a selection of national airs, played him out at last to the tune of 'The Bluebells of Scotland.'" Ossipon's visions of "horrible fumes . . . and mutilated corpses," ethical and pyrotechnic speculations, the plinking of a piano with a mind of its own: the whole sequence mingles irony and melodrama, horror and absurdity.

The background of the last example is seen as well as heard. The title character in James Baldwin's "Sonny's Blues" is a jazz pianist and heroin user. Sonny's fecklessness troubles the narrator, his hard-working schoolteacher brother. In this scene, Sonny has just been arrested for possession. The teacher walks through Harlem with one of Sonny's street acquaintances, a down-and-out young man. Just in front of a bar, they stop:

> The juke box was blasting away with something black and bouncy and I half watched the barmaid as she danced her way from the juke box to her place behind the bar. And I watched her face as she laughingly responded to something someone said to her, still keeping time to the music. When she smiled one saw the little girl, one sensed the doomed, still-struggling woman beneath the battered face of the semi-whore.
>
> "I never *give* Sonny nothing," the boy said finally, "but a long time ago I come to school high and Sonny asked me how it felt." He paused, I couldn't bear to watch him, I watched the barmaid, and I listened to the music which seemed to be causing the pavement to shake. "I told him it felt great." The music stopped, the barmaid paused and watched the juke box until the music began again. "It did."
>
> All this was carrying me some place I didn't want to go. I certainly didn't want to know how it felt. It filled everything, the people, the houses, the music, the dark, quicksilver barmaid, with menace; and this menace was their reality.
>
> "What's going to happen to him now?" I asked again.
>
> "They'll send him away some place and they'll try to cure him." He shook his head. "Maybe he'll even think he's kicked the habit. Then they'll let him loose"—he gestured, throwing his cigarette into the gutter. "That's all."
>
> "What do you mean, that's *all*?"
>
> But I knew what he meant. . . .
>
> . . . I felt that ice in my guts again, the dread I'd felt all afternoon; and again I watched the barmaid moving about the bar, washing glasses, and singing. "Listen. They'll let him out and then it'll just start all over again. That's what I mean."

Although his brother "didn't want to know how it felt," Sonny will later tell him that heroin feels like hearing gospel music. By the story's end, the unnamed teacher will recognize that the power of Sonny's music, as of other kinds of African-American music, grows from centuries of insult and abuse, and that music is a way of keeping going. In the background figure of the woman dancing to "black and bouncy music," Baldwin anticipates these insights, even as the brother sees her as both an equivalent to Sonny and as a representative of a whole community caught between experience and innocence.

The Exercise

Take a page or two of dialogue between two intensely engaged characters—preferably an entire scene. Work in some noises off. Experiment with different placings in your scene, and listen hard. Whatever their nature, the sounds should help control the pace, postponing the scene's resolution without losing momentum. They should also relate to something in the dialogue, strengthening or undercutting a theme, making a speaker sound more passionate, more pompous, or more poignant, adding oil to vinegar or vinegar to oil.

You might try: an auction; a television fundraiser; an ice-cream truck (playing what tune?); the passing of a very long and rumbly freight train; a trumpet lesson in the next apartment; the organ at a baseball game; a wedding reception (in the tradition of your choice); a grade-school arithmetic class; a political rally; doormen on duty at a club; a squabble over a parking space.

The Objective

To hear the difference between incidental noise and cunning discord. To vary the pacing of your dialogue. To put your characters in the buzz of life around them. Although this exercise has you playing with sound, think what you could do with smell (fish fried in garlic, honeysuckle, rain-drenched earth, hot metal), touch (satin, canvas, blistered hands), or sight.

EXERCISE 61

Separating Author, Narrator, and Character

from Frederick Reiken

Many students have experienced the problem of a short story or novel that feels flat because the protagonist is really nothing more than a passive observer of the action, and hence winds up being not so much a character as either a once-removed narrator (in the case of first-person POV) or the so-called "brain in a room" (in the case of third-person POV) in which the character sees and ruminates but never becomes the focus of the action. Often this is because the student is unconsciously "merged" with the protagonist in his or her imagination, whether the story is autobiographical or not.

When you are writing a conventionally character-driven story or novel, it is crucial to understand that the function of a narrator is to present and somehow to translate the action of the story, such that the reader can understand objectively what's happening, even if the protagonist does not. For example, in *Emma* by Jane Austen, Emma Woodhouse is quite sure that Mr. Knightly is wooing her friend Harriet, and over a sequence of scenes, urges Harriet, who has not interpreted Mr. Knightly's actions toward her as such, to believe that Knightly is indeed building up to a marriage proposal. If read carefully, however, all the scenes involving Emma, Harriet, and Mr. Knightly demonstrate objectively—and to comic and ironic effect—that Knightly is actually interested in Emma and that Emma has drastically misread the situation. Without overtly stating anything, the third-person omniscient narrator presents the drama in such a way that we, as readers, can see exactly what's happening, even as the protagonist Emma remains blind.

The same separation holds true for successful first-person narratives, even in the case of the most voice-driven and unreliable of narrator/protagonists. Holden Caulfield, for instance, narrates J. D. Salinger's *The Catcher in the Rye* from a vantage point beyond the time line of the story, alternately dramatizing himself as a character and then effortlessly moving back to the mode of narrator, in which he makes expository commentary about himself and the little odyssey he is unfurling. But even if Holden is absolutely sure of every last thing he asserts, author Salinger, who exists outside of Holden and the novel, has envisioned the narrative so that we see Holden objectively as a boy who is quite lost. The rift between Holden's perceptions and our objective perception—which has been built into the narrative through Salinger's ability to separate himself from Holden in his imagination—creates pathos as well as narrative tension.

162

The Exercise

Part One

Write the words "Once upon a time there was a(n)" on a sheet of paper and then continue, letting yourself write whatever story automatically ensues. Take five to ten minutes and then restart using the same "Once upon a time" prompt.

Part Two

Choose one of your two favorite fairy tales. Remove the "Once upon a time" from the beginning of the story and rewrite at least the first paragraph in a realistic manner, adding character details, realistic setting, modern syntax, etc.

The Objective

The phrase "Once upon a time" is a storytelling convention that we've all internalized. The words "Once upon a time" also prompt us to envision whatever character we choose to invent with an implicit separation between the time of story and the future vantage from which it is told. As a result, three things tend to happen automatically:

1. We do not mix ourselves up with the narrator

2. We do not mix the scene up with our present-day lives

3. We are oriented outward and hence cued to invent some character and/or place that is distinctly envisioned in our imagination.

Whether the story starts out with "Once upon a time there was a very sad turtle who lived in a dying lake," or with something more realistic such as "Once upon a time there was a woman who was dying of leukemia," or even something self-reflexive such as "Once upon a time I was walking down the street in Brooklyn," the separation will, in almost all cases, be apparent.

Of course, the separation is not always going to be this obvious in a realistic literary narrative, and while many authors will at times intentionally merge narrator and character for various rhetorical effects (one example of this is the free indirect discourse employed by writers such as Virginia Woolf and Alice Munro), a successful separation of author, narrator, and character is still the key to a work's texture, depth, and dimensionality. By translating your "Once upon a time" fairy tale to a more realistic narrative, which generally entails providing the characters with more specific and singular details as well as going deeper into a character's point of view, you should be able to see how the separation is structured into any good piece of fiction. Keep in mind that the separation begins in your head, and that no amount of tinkering with sentences is going to fix the problem unless you are able to envision your character, autobiographical or not, on the screen of your imagination. As John Berger writes in his essay "Lost Off Cape Wrath," the moment a writer "simply repeats facts instead of imagining the experience of them, his writing will be reduced to a document."

EXERCISE 62

Time Travel

When a writer is using narrative summary to provide the story's back story, he or she might want to cover a long period of time in only a few sentences. In "Sonny's Blues," Baldwin actually has six time changes in the span of only nine lines. The narrator is having a discussion with his mother about Sonny, his younger brother, who has been a problem for the family, then the narrator ships off to war, and comes back for the mother's funeral. (Our student, Tom Brady, wrote an essay that was the inspiration for this exercise.) This is the passage:

> "I won't forget," I said. "Don't you worry. I won't forget. I won't let nothing happen to Sonny."
> My mother smiled as though she were amused at something she saw in my face. Then, "You may not be able to stop nothing from happening to him but you got to let him know you's there." (TIME A)
> Two days later I was married (TIME B), and then I was gone. (TIME C). And I had a lot of things on my mind and pretty well forgot my promise to Mama (TIME D) until I got shipped home on a special furlough for her funeral. (TIME E)
> And, after the funeral (TIME F), with just Sonny and me alone in the empty kitchen, I tried to find out something about him.
> "What do you want to do?" I asked him.
> "I'm going to be a musician," he said.

The narrator's verbal assurance in TIME A becomes a "promise" in TIME D. Key transitional words such as "then," "until," and several "ands" and "after" denote time changes and allow Baldwin to make these shifts smoothly. Finally, Sonny, the subject of the conversation in TIME A speaks himself in TIME F, tying the beginning and end of this short passage together. Baldwin has covered an enormous amount of territory and moved the story forward in just nine lines.

The Exercise

Look at several of your own longer stories and determine where you might condense a long period of time into just a few sentences. *Or,* create a situation that needs a very condensed presentation of back story.

The Objective

To learn to travel over time with the grace of James Baldwin.

EXERCISE 63

Stairs: Setting and Place

Sometimes you will want to use a specific place or site as the central focus of a story. Fiction writers, such as William Faulkner and William Kennedy, are often identified with place, setting their work in a city, town, or countryside that seems like another character in the story. In this exercise we're asking you to use a staircase as the setting for your story. Stairs go up as well as down; while they don't move, they suggest motion and action. They are neither here nor there—but both.

The Exercise

Take the first sentence "I met him/her on the stairs" and build a story from it. The stairs should figure as importantly in the story as the two characters in this first-person narrative.

Here, character A may be climbing up, while B is going down—or vice versa. They may both be going in the same direction. They may know one another well, just by sight, or be strangers. Decide, before you start writing, who they are and what they're doing on this particular staircase.

The Objective

To remind the writer of fiction that anchors—time and place—are critical tools in developing plot, characterization, and theme. A meeting on a staircase, whether it's the entrance to a courthouse, the back stairs in an apartment house, or the way down to the subway, can suggest almost anything, functioning as the forward impulse of a narrative.

EXERCISE 64

Titles and Keys

A title is the first thing a reader encounters, and the first clue to both the initial meaning and the final meaning of the story. Look back to the sentences in the exercise "First Sentences." Notice how many first lines play off the title of the story.

Titles can also be a way of finding stories. Blaise Cendrars once said in an interview, "I first find a title. I generally find pretty good titles, people envy me for them and not only envy me but quite a few writers come to see me to ask for a title."

And until your book is in galleys, you can still change the title. Below are the titles of some famous novels, along with their original titles.

War and Peace—All's Well That Ends Well, by Leo Tolstoy
Lady Chatterley's Lover—Tenderness, by D. H. Lawrence
The Sound and the Fury—Twilight, by William Faulkner
The Great Gatsby—Hurrah for the Red, White and Blue, by F. Scott Fitzgerald
The Sun Also Rises—Fiesta, by Ernest Hemingway

New York Magazine has published a competition for many years. One example is a game in which you were asked to change some famous (and successful) title just enough to make it a loser rather than a winner. The difference between the true ring of the real title and the false note of the parody suggests how good titles are the ultimate test of the exact word, *le mot juste.* Here are some examples.

A Walk on the Wild Side, by Nelson Algren: *A Hike Through Some Dangerous Areas*
One Hundred Years of Solitude, by Gabriel Garcia Márquez: *A Very Long Time Alone*
Girls of Slender Means, by Muriel Spark: *Minimal-Income Young Women*
The Naked and the Dead, by Norman Mailer: *The Nude and the Deceased*
A Farewell to Arms, by Ernest Hemingway: *A Good-bye to War*

The best titles convey some immediate picture or concept to the reader and they do it with an exciting, tantalizing juxtaposition of words.

Finding the ideal title might take time—and effort. Ernest Hemingway says, "I make a list of titles after I've finished the story or the book—sometimes as many as a hundred. Then I start eliminating them, sometimes all of them."

The Exercise

Part One

Have a place in your writer's notebook where you play around with titles and start a list of possibilities for future stories.

Part Two

When you need a title for a new story or novel, make a list of possible titles from inside the story and from just thinking about the story. (Try for a hundred.) Then start eliminating titles you know you won't use and see what is left. Chances are that the title you choose will not be the first one that occurred to you or the "working" title of the story.

The Objective

To learn how titles can lead you to stories and to sharpen your instincts for a good title.

Student Examples

Company Time

—ANNE SPALEK

Sunday Funnies

—ELLEN TARLIN

Silence Between Songs

—FRANK BACH, FROM "CURES," A POEM BY DAVID RIVARD

Nights Take Care of Themselves

—LAINA JAMES, FROM "THE SATISFACTION COAL COMPANY,"
A POEM BY RITA DOVE

The Exercise

Part One

Have a place in your writer's notebook where you play around with titles and start a list of possibilities for future stories.

Part Two

When you need a title for a new story or novel, make a list of possible titles from inside the story and from just thinking about the story. (Try for a hundred.) Then start eliminating titles you know you won't use and see what is left. Chances are that the title you choose will not be the first one that occurred to you or the "working" title of the story.

The Objective

To learn how titles can lead you to stories and to sharpen your instincts for a good title.

Student Examples

Company Time

—ANNE SPALEK

Sunday Funnies

—ELLEN TARLIN

Silence Between Songs

—FRANK BACH, FROM "CURLS," A POEM BY DAVID JEVARD

Nights Take Care of Themselves

—LAURA JAMES, FROM "THE SATISFACTION COAL COMPANY," A POEM BY RITA DOVE

PART NINE

Invention and a Bit of Inspiration

We titled this section "Invention and a Bit of Inspiration" because we wanted to get as far away as possible from the notion that strong fiction depends on how and why the writer is "inspired," as if you can't write anything until the spirit outside hits you. We didn't want to imply that the writer should sit around waiting for inspiration to strike. It doesn't happen that way. You may not be aware of exactly how or why the germ of a story hits you, but that germ is only the beginning. The rest requires the careful, steady working out—and revising—the plan and strategy needed to compose a fresh, compelling story.

We're convinced that anyone can improve their inventive skills. As in music, say, or any athletic activity that requires intensive training, the more you practice fiction, the better you get. One of our classroom exercises—we call it "stretching"—is to present the class with a situation that seems ambiguous and ask them to provide various paths leading up to the situation, clarifying it. For example, the true event of the young female zookeeper who went into the puma cage after being told that this cage and its inhabitant were off limits. The puma killed her. The exercise for the students was to supply four reasons—of their own invention—to explain why she entered the cage. Each turns out to be a different story. In a class of seven we got thirty separate mini-plots, for example, she had done it on a bet; she thought the puma was hurt; she was on drugs and believed herself invincible; she wanted to commit suicide. And so on. Everyone doing similar stretching exercises reported that it was only difficult at first.

Where do our stories originate? From a pool so wide it has no boundaries; there are as many stories as there are people to write them down. Writers get their ideas from memory or from tales they have heard (Henry James carried a notebook in which he recorded bits and pieces of gossip he heard daily). They get their ideas from the newspapers, radio, television, and the Internet; from the tragedy down the street, the overheard conversation, the glimpse of a couple quarreling. You can train yourself to make up instant stories; this is a habit of mind, just as a photographer might look at a group of people sitting on the beach and say to herself, "That would make a terrific picture." You can train yourself to pick up triggers that set a story or novel in motion. Joan Didion began *Play It As It Lays* after seeing a young actress being paged in a Las Vegas casino. Didion says, "A young woman with long hair and a short white halter dress walks through the casino at the Riviera in Las Vegas at one in the morning. She crosses the casino alone and picks up a house telephone. . . . I know nothing about her. Who is paging her? Why is she here to be paged? How exactly did she come to this? It was precisely this moment in Las Vegas that made *Play It As It Lays* begin to tell itself to me."

The exercises in this section are designed to help the beginning writer recognize just such fictional triggers. While some of the triggers are general (e.g., "Sunday") others are specific, asking for different versions or accounts of particular events. Another exercise asks you to be the childhood bully you were once afraid of; as Rosellen Brown says "fiction always has an obligation to the other side whatever it is." Then there's the exercise on writing a compelling sex scene. Is being "explicit" necessary? To answer this, read John Fowles' *The Ebony Tower*. A final point: You will find that guidelines like the ones in this section are liberating. Doing a particular task (like actually being the bully) is not as hard as writing about something abstract, such as "meanness" or "childhood." The most important thing to remember in creating your fictional world is that you have a lifetime of experience to call on; all of it is potentially useful.

Memo from Atlantic *editors*
SUBJECT: *Articles and stories we do not want to read or edit*
Short stories which ask the reader to blame society for misfortunes
inflicted on the characters by the author.

EXERCISE 65

Illustrations

from Margot Livesey

I was talking to a poet friend about the difficulty of judging my work. "I have the same problem," he said. "If you ask me flat out which is my best poem, I'll shilly-shally and complain that it's like asking me to choose between my children. But if you ask me which poems I'm sending to the *New Yorker* and which to the *Ontario Nugget,* I can answer you in a flash."

We do know about our own work, its flaws and virtues, but it can be hard to gain access to this knowledge. One strategy that I use with myself and my students is to illustrate a story. Instead of beginning a workshop with a critique or a description of the work, we each draw a picture. When I suggest this, people always complain that they can't draw. But everyone does draw something and the pictures are wonderfully revealing. Some people sketch the climactic scene: Sonny playing the piano in the bar at the end of "Sonny's Blues." Some people draw something more metaphorical: a hearse and a cat for "A Good Man Is Hard to Find." Some people put together several scenes or draw crucial images—a hypodermic, say, for Dennis Johnson's "Emergency"; a beaten up Cadillac for Louise Erdrich's *Love Medicine.*

The Exercise

Drawing pictures can be useful at various stages. You might start by drawing pictures to illustrate your own work over the last couple of years. (If you're part of a writers' group, you might also do this for the work of your colleagues, and vice versa.) Then turn to your work in progress and draw an illustration for each scene or section of narration.

The Objective

Whatever the results in aesthetic terms (and usually they're much better than the artist expects), the pictures provide a highly useful map of the energy of a story and what has stayed with you as both author and reader. More importantly, I think, they provide information that might not come up if you'd simply plunged into verbal discussion.

EXERCISE 66

Bully

One of the most demanding challenges facing a fiction writer is to inhabit the mind and heart of a threatening, brutal, or seemingly loathsome character. While most of us dismiss or avoid their of real-life counterparts, writers of fiction avoid the unpleasant and/or brutal at the risk of leaving out the emotional high points of their story. Readers are drawn to and are fascinated by "villains." Beginning writers are reluctant to take on this sort of character because some of the "bad" might rub off on them or because they're afraid their readers might just believe they are capable of cruelty. You have to delete your reluctance and dive in. The trick is to render that character, if not exactly sympathetic, at least emotionally accessible.

The Exercise

Think of someone who, when you were a child, bullied you. This could be a teacher, a relative, neighbor, or schoolmate. Then, write a scene in which that person becomes the first-person narrator who bullies you—the other character in the story. Use your own name. You may embroider as much as you wish but the incident should be basically factual.

The Objective

To take over, as an actor doing a tyrannical role in a play or movie, the persona of someone capable of brutality; to be that person and to make him or her three-dimensional, capable of human feelings, and perhaps themselves a victim of cruelty.

Student Example

Bully

The first time I noticed Mark Tobias was in the fifth grade at the Center School.

Miss Cushman was out in the hall talking to another teacher, and while she was gone some of the kids pushed Mark onto the floor, piled on top of him, smeared chalk on his sweater, and threw his sissy glasses in the wastebasket. I watched for a minute and then I joined in. It looked like a lot of fun. I punched his nose and it began to bleed. He didn't howl or anything, which made me really mad because it must have hurt like crazy.

Then Miss Cushman came back into the room and yelled at us to go to our seats. Mark got up from the floor, tried to get off some of the chalk dust, grabbed his glasses out of the wastebasket and sat down at his desk. He never said a word. What kind of kid does that?

I wanted him to be angry or cry or something, but he just looked as if he hadn't got his glasses—a sort of "where am I?" look that really ticked me off. I hate kids who think they're better than us. Well, I didn't really hate Mark, but he was an orphan and all the mothers—we all had mothers, Mark didn't—made a big fuss over him. My old lady said we all should be nice to Mark 'cause his mother died. A lot I care. I wish I didn't have a mother sometimes; mine's always giving it to me 'cause she likes my little brother Stew better and is always asking me why I can't be more like Stew and makes me go to my room without supper—for no reason! I'd go to bed and cry myself to sleep and think what it would be like if my mom died suddenly and I'd be an orphan like Mark. I don't know.

Anyway, that same day at lunch Mark asked if he could sit with me and Bernie and Josh and then he sat down with us and gave me one of his Oreos cause he saw me looking at it. "Here," he said, "you take it. I've got plenty." What a jerk. He couldn't play ball, he was always dropping it, and he only had one friend, that kid, Stevie, who was as bad as he was except Stevie had a great left hook he learned somewhere. Mark couldn't climb a rope, and when we went out to the playground he read a stupid book instead of playing dodge ball. After that day, before they made me leave the Center School I forced him to carry my books, and once I talked him into putting a half-eaten egg salad sandwich in Miss Cushman's purse.

—MARK TOBIAS

A short story is like a flare sent into the sky. Suddenly and startlingly, it illuminates one portion of the world and the lives of a few people who are caught in its glare. The light is brief, intense, and contrasts are likely to be dramatic. Then it fades quickly and is gone. But, if it is worth its moment of brilliance, it will leave an afterimage in the mind's eye of the beholder.
—ROBIE MACAULEY

EXERCISE 67

Faraway Places

Many writers have written about places they have never been—Franz Kafka about America in *Amerika,* Saul Bellow about Africa in *Henderson the Rain King,* Thomas Pynchon about postwar Germany in *Gravity's Rainbow,* W. D. Wetherell about the Crimea in *Chekhov's Sister,* Oscar Hijuelos about Cuba in *Mambo Kings Play Songs of Love,* and Hilding Johnson about India in her BASS story "Victoria"—yet their descriptions of these places persuasively transport the reader there. Below are passages from a novel and a short story.

> Finally one morning we found ourselves in the bed of a good-sized river, the Arnewi, and we walked downstream in it, for it was dry. The mud had turned to clay, and the boulders sat like lumps of gold in the dusty glitter. Then we sighted the Arnewi village and saw the circular roofs which rose to a point. I knew they were just thatch and must be brittle, porous, and light; they seemed like feathers, and yet heavy—like heavy feathers. From these coverings smoke went up into the silent radiance.
> —SAUL BELLOW, *HENDERSON THE RAIN KING*

> Flowers stayed tight in the bud, drying in crisp pods and rattling to the ground one by one in the still night.
>
> The bearers brought half as much water, then still less. The children on the wards slid from whining into torpor.
>
> A sacred cow wandered into the hospital courtyard and could go no further. It was chalky, white, fleshless, its loose dry hide scarred in random constellations, a desiccated wreath of twisted flowers digging into its neck. It stood, eyes closed and head nearly to the ground, for a day and night. Early the next morning I came upon Richard holding a bucket of water beneath the animal's nose.
>
> I said, "We don't have much of that."
>
> "It's what I was allotted for shaving."
>
> I shrugged. "Suit yourself."
>
> In the afternoon the cow knelt, shuddered and died. The sweepers came with great hooks and dragged it out of the courtyard, leaving thin trails of scarlet in the pale dust.
>
> At supper, Richard said, "If they think so much of the beasts, how can they let them suffer?"
>
> "To them they're gods. In general, people don't care much about the suffering of a god. You should know that by now."
> —HILDING JOHNSON, "VICTORIA"

The Exercise

Choose a country where you have always longed to go but haven't yet been and set a story there. Read old and new Fodor's guides as well as other recent travel guides and *National Geographic;* buy a map; study the country's politics, religion, government, and social issues; read cookbooks—always, always looking for the persuasive detail, something you would almost have to be there to know.

The Objective

To write with authority and conviction about a place to which you have never been.

Student Example

One of the reasons Tess had come to Japan was to visit the fish auction by the Sumidagawa River, where her father probably went during his business trips when he wanted to feel at home. He'd run an auction in the back parking lot of St. Leonard's Church till Tess was ten. Near the marketplace, she knelt on the slick pavement and pulled heavy trash bags around each of her yellow sneakers. The auctioneers had already begun and the wholesalers were placing their bids. She spotted another tourist with plastic bags up to his knees. A brochure had advised wearing the bags because hoses would continually be pumping water over the pavement, washing away stray bits of raw seafood. Tess wove in and around the people and crates of tuna and crab. She took in small breaths through her mouth. Jake should have come with her to see this.

Jake was the first stranger Tess spoke with on her vacation. Her friend, Marlene, had worked late last night, so Tess had made her way to a sushi bar with a large fish tank at its center. She was wondering if the tank was in place of a printed menu. That was when Jake came up and asked if she'd like to join him. He was in Tokyo for three days on business.

The fish they ordered that night was sliced ribbon-thin, and shaped like roses. Jake used one chopstick to push some raw tuna into the green smudge of wasabi. He choked and rubbed his tongue on his sleeve. "That's a nasty little paste," he said. He coughed and took a long drink of beer. She looked at the paper lanterns over the bar. Her father used to attach one yellow balloon to a wooden sign that read "The Everything Auction." "It's horseradish," Tess said.

—KIM LEAHY

> I don't invent characters because the Almighty has already invented millions. . . . Just like experts at fingerprints do not create fingerprints but learn how to read them.
> —ISAAC BASHEVIS SINGER

EXERCISE 68

Story Swap

from Jordan Dann and The Aspen Writers' Foundation

_____

For this exercise, people in a group pair up with someone different from themselves in age, gender, race, or family background, etc. Each participant is asked to tell her partner an important story from her life that represents who she is. The partner is then asked to recreate the storyteller's narrative and write the story as though it were his own. The Story Swap program is an innovative project that uses storytelling and creative writing to generate understanding between various groups of diverse individuals. You can find out more about Story Swap at www.aspenwriters.org.

The Exercise

1. Select your partner.

2. Tell your story, then listen to your partner's story.

3. Swap stories.

4. Write your partner's story.

Instructions for the Storyteller During the "Swap"

Tell your partner a story from your life that has deep meaning to you. Choose a story that has emotional content that reveals the person that you are. This story should be one that you would put in a time capsule if the world were going to end tomorrow. Think of something that feels dangerous or exciting, and you will know you are on the right track. Be as specific and detailed as you can when telling the story to your partner.

Instructions for the Listener During the "Swap"

Listen attentively and openly to your partner's story. Notice whether you have preconceived notions as to who your partner is, or how the story might end; if so, try to put these feelings aside and listen to your partner without any preconceptions. At the end of the story you may ask questions to flesh out details or clarify any confusion you might have. Feel free to take notes.

Writing Instructions

Now, it is your turn to tell your partner's story as though it were your own. The objective is to take ownership of your partner's story and, relying on what you have heard as well as your imagination, tell the story in your own voice. Use the first-person point of view to get as close to the story as possible. Don't concern yourself with exact dates, times, or names. Imagination is at the heart of this project.

Objective

By swapping stories, participants walk in one another's shoes, therefore enhancing compassion through authentic engagement with one another. It is important for writers to open our minds to difficulties, hardships, joys, and successes that are not our own, and to share stories of family, landscape, and psychological and emotional differences that challenge our perception of the world.

Writing is a hard way to make a living but a good way to make a life.
—DORIS BETTS

EXERCISE 69

Humor: An Intact Frog

Humor is emotional chaos remembered in tranquility.

—JAMES THURBER

Styles of humor seem to change shape and kind more quickly than any other form of writing. From Ring Larder through James Thurber, S. J. Perelman, Ogden Nash, Nathanael West, Joseph Heller, John Kennedy O'Toole, and Woody Allen, we have American humor that ranges from gentle reminiscence to the grimmest shade of black. It may be true partly because one man's meat is another man's poison (or, as Ogden Nash said, "One man's Mede is another man's Persian"), and it's hard to get any large number of people to agree on what's a laugh. So, the writer of humor has to depend largely on her own sense of what is funny about life. As E. B. White said, "Humor can be dissected as a frog can, but the thing dies in the process and the innards are discouraging to any but the pure scientific mind."

Just as humor defies analysis, it seems to defy any rules—rules of tolerance or good taste. One of the classics of English satire is Jonathan Swift's cruel "A Modest Proposal"; W. C. Fields made fun of marriage, sobriety, and family values; Lenny Bruce relied heavily on racial slurs and intolerance to amuse his audiences. Some writers and comedians even risk scatology—traditionally the most despised form of humor.

All of which is to say that if you take a sardonic view of the world ("the world is a comedy to those who think, a tragedy to those who feel") and can express it with humor and wit, you should do your own thing. Read Lawrence Sterne, Kingsley Amis, Dave Barry, P. G. Wodehouse, Nicolai Gogol, Kurt Vonnegut, Lorrie Moore, Ilf and Petrov, Mark Twain, Michael Frayn, Evelyn Waugh, Somerville and Ross, Molly Keane, Oscar Wilde, George Saunders.

The main thing a writer should remember is that written humor is quite a different thing from comedy on the stage or that delivered by a stand-up comedian. Oral humor largely depends on timing, tone of voice, body language, and the infection of laughter in an audience. Written humor depends on language alone—words create the joke. Thus, the writer of fiction should not imitate—in fiction—what came off so uproariously or wittily on the stage, in a movie, or on TV. His nuances, allusions, surprises, and parodies all come from verbal skill and shrewdness. Good narrative, fresh language, succinct expression, the juxtaposition of incongruities—these are the heart of written humor. Or, as Shakespeare said it better, "Brevity is the soul of wit."

EXERCISE 70

Sunday: Discovering Emotional Triggers

Most of the time it doesn't matter on what day of the week you set your action—unless it's a Sunday (remember the movie *Sunday Bloody Sunday*?). Most people feel at loose ends on this day, even those who spend the morning in church. Instead of using the freedom wisely, a lot of us tend to overdo it—overeat, oversleep, overreact. Sundays bring out the worst in people. Children grow anxious as the weekend draws to a close and they realize they haven't done their homework. During football season, another possible area of tension opens up. Then there is the obligatory trip to grandma and grandpa's house for a large heavy meal and some equally heavy recriminations. Things happen on Sundays that wouldn't happen on weekdays. So if you want to examine domestic dynamics close up, set some action on a Sunday and let her rip.

The Exercise

Title it "Sunday." Write 550 words.

The Objective

Certain words and ideas, such as *retirement, in-laws, boss, vacation, pneumonia,* and *fraud,* serve as triggers for stories or scenes in fiction. *Sunday* is one of these. Try to think of others.

Student Example

On Sunday mornings, walking to the bathroom, I'd be treated to the sight of my roommate, Abby, in bed with a man, yet another man I didn't recognize. Every Sunday, I'd tell myself I needed to get my own apartment, or at least install some doors in this one. I used to love Sundays before Abby moved in. I'd sit in the sunny spot in the kitchen and drink cup after cup of coffee. I'd read the newspaper—first travel, then arts, weddings, the news—and then my mother would call. We'd talk about Sundays that we'd spent together—going to the planetarium, buying bras, cooking barley. Sundays, I didn't touch my students' papers I'd brought home. I didn't get dressed until 11:00 A.M. I didn't mind feeling lonely.

Now, when I was halfway through the arts section, a shirtless man came into the kitchen. I pulled my robe tighter.

"Geez, I hate Sundays," he said. "They're endless. Give me a Saturday night any day. Hi, I'm Stan," he said, putting out a hand. I shook it. Abby trailed in after him.

"Hi gorgeous," she said to me. "Met Stan?"

"Sure did," I said, smiling and turning back to the paper. Go away, I thought. Go back to bed. Leave me to my Sunday. The phone rang, and shirtless Stan twisted to pick it up.

"Good morning," he said. "Oh . . . It's for you," he said, handing me the phone.

"Her mother," Abby said. "Every Sunday. Kind of like church, I guess."

"No, Mom," I whispered into the phone that I'd dragged out into the hall. "No, Mom. That was not my boyfriend. . . . No, he's not a burglar . . . . No, I don't know who he is. . . . No, I don't let strange men into my apartment at all hours." And on it went. My head throbbed.

When I got off the phone I went back into the kitchen. Stan was sitting in my chair. Abby was sitting in Stan's lap twirling his chest hairs.

"Hey gorgeous," Abby said. "We're going to grab a bagel and then go to the planetarium. Half-price on Sundays. Want to come?"

"Better than sitting around here moping," Stan said. "Ouch. Stop pulling my hairs." He slapped Abby's hand away.

—HESTER KAPLAN

While short stories often tell us things we don't know anything about— and this is good of course—they should also, and maybe more importantly, tell us what everybody knows but what nobody is talking about. At least not publicly.
—RAYMOND CARVER, INTRODUCTION TO *BASS 1986*

EXERCISE 71

Kill the Dog

If you want to write serious fiction you have to kill the neighbor's dog. In fiction there's no avoiding the malevolent. In fact, there are very few states of mind or motivations that lie beyond your reach. You should be able to describe a tree, cooking a gourmet meal, and slaughtering an animal who, for one reason or another, you want to get rid of. Just as an actor assumes the role of a killer and makes him plausible and immediate (Anthony Hopkins doing Hannibal Lecter or Tony Perkins as the Bates boy), you should dispatch the animal convincingly and without flinching. Reread Tim O'Brien's "How to Tell a War Story" for the powerful scene, set in Vietnam, in which desperately angry soldiers slowly kill a baby water buffalo.

The Exercise

Take some time to imagine a situation where your neighbor's dog has become so threatening that it warrants being killed. It has bitten your child on the face; it had eaten all your chickens; it has come into your yard repeatedly and in spite of pleas to its owner, torn up all your flowerbeds. Or maybe you are angry at something totally different—and take your anger out on that unsuspecting animal. It is probably a given that you have a very short fuse. You decide to kill the dog. Figure out how you're going to do it—poison, a weapon, an "accident" of some kind—and go through the actions of carrying out your plan in a first-person narrative. Don't skip the grim details; get up close, let the reader be right there with you all along the way.

The Objective

We want you to be comfortable with the uncomfortable, and to document life's cruelest acts. Good fiction is not "polite"; it's raw.

Student Example

It began on a quiet Sunday morning in late August in Wellfleet, Massachusetts, on the outer end of Cape Cod. I woke up much earlier than usual and at first I was disoriented. I sensed that something had disturbed my sleep, but lying there groggy and still half-inhabiting my fading dream, I couldn't put my finger on a reason. I gradually became aware of a high-pitched yipping sound. Not a bird or a child. It was probably the nasty dog who had killed our kitten the year before.

I love animals. Perhaps cats more than dogs—but I really like dogs a lot.

The next morning I woke to the same sound, but earlier, around 7:30 A.M. My wife rolled over to face me. "I want to sleep. Somebody please shut it up—or shoot it!"

"It'll stop in a while" I said. The yapping went on for over an hour and then abruptly stopped. "See? That's it."

The next morning I woke up to the same sound, but earlier, around 6:30 A.M.

I got up and put on yesterday's clothes and stumbled out into what for me was an unfamiliar scene—early morning outside. The dog sounds were coming from our neighbor's house. As I approached the house, the barking got louder and more insistent. It knew I was there, but I was the only one. The people were out. A small dog was running back and forth on a screened porch. Actually, it seemed unfair to call it a dog. It had dog parts—a head, tail, legs—but they were mismatched, as though it had been assembled by someone who didn't know what a dog should look like. I thought to leave a note, but then I realized that people who would own a dog like this and unleash its incessant noise on their neighbors weren't likely to respond to a note. Like owner, like dog. Or like dog, like owner.

I looked out at the marsh and an idea formed—a way to do it that would technically absolve me of the crime and which had the added perk of irony.

Later that day when the yipping started again, I put on dark clothes and a hat I'd selected for the venture. I gathered up a rope, a knife and a stake I had crafted. I was careful not to be seen as I approached the doghouse. It was late enough that the sun was just hanging above the horizon. When I got to the screen porch, I opened the door and produced a biscuit for the yapping mutt. In the time it took for him to snatch it from me, I had him by the collar and stuffed him in a sack. He struggled at first as I quickly set off across the marsh, but soon settled down. Perhaps he sensed what was to come.

Far out on the marsh I stopped and knelt down. I drove the stake into the ground and attached the rope. Then I produced the dog from the bag and tied him to the other end. That was all I needed to do. I retreated to the edge of the marsh near my house and waited.

Just before dark they appeared, one by one, from further down the marsh. Attracted to the whining of the dog no doubt, which was now too far away to be heard by its owners, the coyotes approached cautiously. At first, they stayed back, yipping and signaling each other that they'd found something worth eating, but weren't sure how to proceed because it didn't (and couldn't) run away. And it was too late for me to change my mind. As the sun set I saw them converge. The barking stopped.

I sat there for an hour, until the coyote sounds had receded into the background noise of the night. Then, I went to bed knowing that my family would get an uninterrupted night's sleep, but for me this night could be the stuff of nightmares to come.

—FRED MAGEE

EXERCISE 72

Five Different Versions:
And Not One Is a Lie

We tell stories every day of our lives. But *how* we tell the story is often determined by who we are telling the story to. Think of the range of people in one's life—parents, spouse, children, friends, lovers, priests, in-laws, social workers, parole officers (come on—use your imagination), doctors, claims adjusters, lawyers, judges, juries, therapists, talk-show hosts, astrologers—the list goes on and on. And as we tell these people our story, we add or subtract, exaggerate or play down, tolerate or condemn, depending on the identity of the person to whom we are telling our tale.

The Exercise

Here is the situation: You have just come out of a movie theater at around seven in the evening and you are mugged—a person asks for your money, then knocks you to the ground before running away. Or make up your own situation.

Next, pretend you are telling the account of this event to five different people:

Your mother
Your best friend
Your girlfriend or boyfriend (or wife or husband)
A therapist
A police officer

The Objective

To become conscious of how we shape and shade the stories that we tell to each other according to the listener. Your characters also tell stories to each other and make selections about content according to whom they are telling the story, the effect they want the story to have, and the response they want to elicit from the listener. A lot of dialogue in fiction, in real life, is story telling—and there is always the story listener who is as important to the tale as the tale itself.

Student Example

Telling My Mother

No, I wasn't wearing my black mini. Anyway, I'd asked this guy—some kid from school—what time it was and he told me 7:10. Don't worry. He wasn't the mugger. It was Johnny Something from my morning Lit. 121. So I'm just walking down the sidewalk, heading for the car and it happened. Johnny Whozit must have heard it. He's a big kid, probably a football player or something, and that's all I could think about there, sprawled all over the ground. That kid could've helped me out.

Telling My Boyfriend

Listen, I have never, not once, taken anything so hard. They found me sprawled on the sidewalk in front of the Tivoli, my dress up around my bottom, crying, just out of my head. The policeman told me I was going to have to calm down, tell him some facts. But I couldn't even remember what film I'd been to. (I'd gone to *Hairspray* for the third time. I've got this thing about John Waters.)

Telling a Police Officer

I was just minding my business, leaving a little early. School tomorrow. I teach, you know, and he must have come out from one of those cars over there because I didn't see him in the building. He was real big, lots of muscles. I didn't get a good look at his face, but he was dressed like a street person and smelled like one. Strong, you know, in more ways than one.

—KARLA HORNER

When I used to teach creative writing, I would tell students to make their characters want something right away even if it's only a glass of water. Characters paralyzed by the meaninglessness of modern life still have to drink water from time to time. One of my students wrote a story about a nun who got a piece of dental floss stuck between her lower left molars, and who couldn't get it out all day long. I thought that was wonderful. The story dealt with issues a lot more important than dental floss, but what kept readers going was anxiety about when the dental floss would finally be removed. Nobody could read that story without fishing around in his mouth with a finger.

—KURT VONNEGUT, PARIS REVIEW INTERVIEW

He claimed he didn't have anything. When asked what was in his pocket, he produced a key ring with one key on it. It was _____, which he said he rode between his mother's house and his father's. He was only aware of the key ring's poignant sig-nificance when it was pointed out to him.

EXERCISE 73

Things You Carry

We all carry an assortment of objects in our pockets, on our wrists, around our necks and fingers, on our feet, over our heads, over our shoulders, etc. Some of these objects, such as a handkerchief or plastic comb, are generic and dispensable and have little or no significance in our lives. Others, like a wedding ring, a set of keys, or even a pen, have value because of what they represent to us and our personal histories. For the writer of fiction, carried objects—we think of them as props—tell the reader about his characters' traits in the same way a portraitist would paint a wrinkle of a face to suggest the age of the sitter. No one writing today supplies props better than Tim O'Brien. In his story "The Things They Carried," from the book of the same name, he writes "Henry Dobbins, who was a big man, carried extra rations; he was especially fond of canned peaches in heavy syrup over pound cake. Dave Jensen, who practiced field hygiene, carried a toothbrush, dental floss and several hotel-sized bars of soap he'd stolen on R&R in Sydney, Australia. Ted Lavender, who was scared, carried tranquilizers. . . ."

The Exercise

Choose an object on your person or in your bag that you're fond of. Describe it in no more than 100 words as if you were writing a missing-object description for the police. This means it should be clear, impersonal, and concise. A blind person should be able to "see" it from this description.

Next, in 200 or more words, give this object a "life." That is, tell the reader how and when you got it. What emotions connect you to it? Is there another person involved? (A grandfather who gave you the watch, a daughter who made you the ring, etc.) How would you feel if you lost it? This prop should give your character both density and singularity.

The Objective

To learn how to use everyday objects in a way that gives them emotional resonance and meaning. To understand how powerfully we invest our emotions in small things. One student was asked in class to show us something that he could write about in this way.

He claimed he didn't have anything. When asked what was in his pocket, he produced a key ring with one key on it. It was the key to his bicycle, which he said he rode between his mother's house and his father's. He was only aware of the key ring's poignant significance when it was pointed out to him.

EXERCISE 74

Psycho: Creating Terror

Beginning writers tend to shy away from doing scenes in which actual violence occurs. It's not clear whether this is because of inherent squeamishness—which most of us admit to having—or the feeling that they aren't up to creating it in words because they've never experienced it or anything like it themselves. In any case, violence and terror make for excellent drama; it's the tense situations and moments that give fiction its excitement. You should be able to handle violence and fear as capably as you might two people having a conversation over a couple of beers. One important thing for the writer to be aware of in creating a harrowing scene: the flatter your language and the fewer adjectives, the more immediate the scene will become. It's the action and dialogue that do the work for you in scenes where violence predominates.

The Exercise

You're taking a shower in your house or apartment. You are not expecting anyone and the front door is locked (the bathroom door is not). You hear a strange noise in a room beyond the bathroom. Now, take it from there for no more than two pages. This can be in either the third or the first person. Don't spend any time getting into the shower; you're there when the action begins.

The Objective

To tell a convincing story centered on speculation and terror.

Student Example

Ajax, my cat, must have crawled on top of the refrigerator again and knocked over the basket of onions. And now he's playing with the onions—that's the scraping noise—and when I get out of the shower they're going to be all over the floor. Sometimes when Ajax sees another cat he starts to moan and howl, like he's doing now—but he sounds strange. Maybe he's hurt himself.

I pull back the shower curtain and stick my head out to listen. The noise has stopped, but I think I just saw something move in the hall. I can't see much from here, but I'm sure a shadow darted past the door. I let the water run over my head again and shut my eyes as the soap runs by, and all of a sudden I feel a draft of cold air. I open my eyes through the soap and hold my breath; the soap stings my eyes. Everything is quiet. All I can hear is the sound of the water, but again I think I see a shadow change. I turn off the water and now I'm breathing fast. I'm standing on the bath mat and Ajax comes in and rubs against my wet legs and then the moaning starts again but it's not the cat, who jumps in fright. I clutch a towel to my chest. I don't know whether to look out into the hall or shut the door. I freeze. Things are crashing in the kitchen, glass breaks; a chair is moved. I slam the bathroom door and manage to lock it even though my fingers are trembling. I'm whimpering. Ajax is hunched in the corner, behind the toilet. The moans grow louder; they're coming closer.

What can I use as a weapon? A disposable razor? A tube of shampoo, a toilet brush, a bottle of Fantastik? I hold this bottle like a gun, my finger on its trigger. I've dropped the towel and I get into the other corner, making small sobbing noises. The moans stop abruptly; then the pounding on the door begins.

—HESTER KAPLAN

A good title should be like a good metaphor: It should intrigue without being too baffling or too obvious.

—WALKER PERCY

190 WHAT IF? WRITING EXERCISES FOR FICTION WRITERS

EXERCISE 75

One in the Hand

How and why are proverbs born? Most of us say them without giving them a second's thought. But if we look at them carefully we see that they contain a human drama, condensed. "A rolling stone gathers no moss." "A stitch in time saves nine." "A bird in the hand is worth two in the bush." Each of these suggests choices, conflict, and resolution. Narrative is everywhere; training yourself to see and catch it is one way of refining your craft.

The Exercise

Take one of the proverbs above (or another one you like) and outline a short story that uses it as both plot and theme.

The Objective

There are two here. The first is to make yourself super-sensitive to ordinary things that contain the essence of drama. The second is to transform what at first seems just another piece of old-fashioned wisdom into a shapely narrative.

Student Example

A Rolling Stone Gathers No Moss
While my two sisters and two brothers and I were growing up, we were nearly smothered by activities that never seemed to stop, not even on Sundays. There was baseball for Dave and Michael, soccer for me and Susan, violin for Rebecca, Hebrew lessons for all of us and—I can hardly believe it myself—etiquette for all of us; mom insisted. By the end of a typical day I was so tired I would fall asleep on top of the covers with my clothes on.

As a troubleshooter for the gas and electric company, Dad was on call twenty-four seven. Mom was one of those women who thought that if you didn't start every meal from scratch it wasn't worth eating. Maybe I'm exaggerating a little, but not that much. We tried to talk her into shortcuts in the kitchen. "What's wrong with using canned broth instead of boiling an entire fowl?" Dad would ask. "It's just not the same," she told him.

One day, after soccer practice, I walked into the kitchen for a snack and there was Mom, frozen in a pose that summed up our overprogrammed lives. Mom had her hand on the door of the toaster oven, about to pop in a homemade leftover Belgian waffle.

She had been zapped by some loose current and couldn't move. She looked at me, opened her mouth, and tried to say something. Her eyes pleaded for help; I called 911.

After the EMT guys loosened her grip on the toaster oven, they loaded her in an ambulance to be treated for second-degree burns and a mild state of shock.

Dad kissed her ashen face and then told us to get ready for Hebrew school. He herded us into the SUV and as we drove away he said, "I hope your mother won't have to stay there very long. We need her." Then he said that after class we probably still had time to rake some leaves and feed the compost heap before it got dark. "What do you guys say to a trip to Burger King after we're finished?" Just then his beeper went off.

—POLLY KAPLAN

EXERCISE 76

Notes and Letters

The first novels in the English language were in the form of letters—so-called "epistolary novels", such as Samuel Richardson's *Pamela* and *Clarissa*. Recent epistolary novels are Hal Dresner's *The Man Who Wrote Dirty Books,* Lee Smith's *Fair and Tender Ladies,* and Alice Walker's *The Color Purple.* And then there are the novels that employ letters. Herzog in Saul Bellow's novel by that name writes letters to Spinoza; to Willie Sutton, the famous bank robber; and to presidents. In Ann Beattie's novel *Love Always,* Lucy Spenser receives and replies to letters as Cindi Coeur, the Miss Lonelyhearts of a magazine called *Country Daze.* Sam Hughes, a feisty seventeen-year-old girl in Bobbie Ann Mason's *In Country,* meets the father, who died before she was born, in the diary he kept in Vietnam and his letters home. Tucked into the narrative of a work of fiction, a letter allows the author an especially intimate tone—somewhat like talking into the reader's ear. It's also useful at crucial moments in a plot—in it things get told economically and with a sense of urgency. A letter is often a quick way of delivering exposition, characterization, and voice.

The Exercise

Here are several situations and the letters they might engender. You're a senior in college writing home to tell your parent(s) that you're dropping out of school. You want them to understand, if not exactly approve of, your reason(s) for leaving. Make these reasons specific and persuasive. Then, write the answer, either from one or both of the parents. Or, you're writing a letter to your landlord to tell him you are withholding the rent until he addresses problems in your apartment. Or, you are leaving behind a note for your spouse explaining why you are leaving him or her. Or, you are writing literary graffiti on the walls of a toilet stall in the Library of Congress. Limit: 500 words.

The Objective

To get inside the head of another person, someone you've invented, and assume her voice to vary your narrative conveyance.

Student Example

Cher Mom and Dad,

    I hope you two know how to speak a little French, because I have some news for you that's going to knock your berets right off. Remember I told you that I was taking French this semester? Well, I didn't tell you that my teacher's name was Mademoiselle Pipette and I didn't tell you that I had a crush on her. It turns out that she had a crush on me too, and now we are madly in love. We want to get married so little Pierre or little Gigi will have a dad when he or she arrives at the end of May. I'm going to be a *pére*! (That's "father" in French.)

Jeannette can't support us on her teaching salary, so I'm dropping out of college. You've always taught me to be responsible for my actions and this seems like the correct thing to do. I'm going to get a job to support my family and make a home for us. Someday I'll go back to school. The dean assured me I can reapply later and finish my degree.

You two are going to be grandparents! I'm sure you're as excited by all this as I am. College seems unimportant at the moment in the face of these great changes. I know you'll love Jeannette and she sends a *bonjour* to you.

Avec amour (that's "with love"),

Teddy

Dear Teddy,

Forget it. No son of mine is going to drop out of college and get married just because a schoolboy crush on his French teacher went a little too far. I think I know better than you when I say that a twenty-one-year-old boy has no conception of what it means to be a responsible father and husband. And what kind of job do you imagine yourself getting? Who's going to hire a boy whose only work experience was mowing his parents' lawn?

I, too, talked to the dean. At the end of the semester, your Mademoiselle Pipette will say good-bye to teaching and to you. I have arranged for her go back to France and have the baby there. I have also gotten her assurance that she and you will have no more contact.

I've spared your mother the news of this mess. It would only make her sicker. Though you don't think so now, you will thank me in years to come for getting you out of this situation. In the meantime I suggest you get back to your studies and work hard toward that all-important degree.

Fondly,

Dad

—BRIAN FOSTER

EXERCISE 77

The Chain Story

This exercise is based on the story "Pumpkins" by Francine Prose, which appears in *Flash Fiction,* and can be found online at www.pifmagazine.com/vol3. Note how the story begins at a particular point in time and moves forward as a chain, with each forward movement establishing a link with what has gone immediately before, and what comes after. The story begins with the accidental death of a young woman whose severed head lands in a pile of pumpkins and moves on to the fact that her husband does not hear of this disturbing detail until he reads it in a newspaper, which is then read by a woman who passes the distressing news item on to her husband, whose guilty reaction causes the woman to realize that an affair he'd been having is not, in fact, over, which realization sends her to a therapist, who . . . etc., etc. The forward movement of the story depends on the author's "linking" or "overlapping" various events and details. Note also how the "accident" of the beginning sentence is repeated, in spirit, by the psychiatrist a bit later in the story when he makes a slip of the tongue. (The original exercise was suggested by a student, Cecelia Tan.)

Exercise

Write a 3+ page story that is a chain story. Your original "event" should be as dramatic as the accident in "Pumpkins." Be concrete. Bring several of the characters to life in the way that Francine Prose brings the betrayed wife and her psychiatrist to life. Use at least five "links." Be subtle: note how the last line of the story—in which the psychiatrist considers turning and going back, making a U-turn, but does not—echoes the U-turn made by the young woman killed at the beginning of the story.

Objective

To understand how linking details from the lives of various unrelated characters can move a story forward. This is perhaps one of the few times that coincidence works well.

Student Example

Where We Go When We Disappear
Eight-year-old Scooter goes missing for seven days. He returns just as mysteriously as he left, enters through the back door, kicks off his sneakers, and trots past his mother. She

193

is sitting at the kitchen table with her back to the door and she is crying loud and hard; delirious with exhaustion, she doesn't hear the shuffle of little boy feet or the latch click. Scooter knows to leave his mother alone when she's sad. She's been crying for years.

Scooter digs through pillows and piles of magazines and takeout containers gone soft with age. So intent is Scooter on locating the missing remote, that he doesn't notice his lopsided smile on the cover of *The News Herald*. He is unaware that he has been gone for seven days. He believes no time has passed. All Scooter knows is that he is hungry and would like to be fed before eight so he can watch the premiere of *X-Men: The Last Stand* on NBC.

When his mother hears the din, she runs toward it, and when she sees Scooter he smiles up at her with such innocence—not a scratch on him—that she faints from the shock of it all.

Scooter's father, Thomas, rushes home. His wife dabs a delicate kiss on his lips though they have not kissed for weeks, not even goodnight. Thomas examines Scooter—his cheeks, knees, and earlobes. When Scooter asks why everyone is in such a tizzy over him—tizzy, a word he plucked from his mother's vocabulary—Thomas realizes that his son has no recollection of the disappearance. Thomas shakes his son and weeps, hesitant to believe.

Detective Joseph Cain can't comprehend Scooter's vanishing act either. He unfolds paperclips with his teeth and gnaws on pen caps, a habit his wife detests. She grows worried after discovering a frazzled clump of his gray hair resting on the arm of the couch. Detective Cain tells his teenage daughter, Dee, she's not to leave the house until the case is solved. His wife disagrees, though she would never say anything. Dee prowls the halls, glaring, and later that night attempts to pierce her eyebrow. She uses a needle, rubbing alcohol, and ice dipped in Absolut.

Dee has taken up religion. Her parents are atheists and she knows this will drive them mad. After school she claims to be serving detention, but actually visits her friend The Nun, seeking advice. The Nun is dressed casually today, in jeans and an oversized purple sweatshirt to hide her from the chill that has covered the city for days. Dee wonders if it is a sin to wear tight jeans.

When The Nun asks Dee what happened to her eyebrow, she shrugs and looks to the young boy coasting his skateboard up and over a curb. He makes it look so easy. Dee tells The Nun that her parents are driving her crazy. Ever since the Scooter Hardy case her father has become overbearing, intolerable. She wishes she could disappear. When The Nun asks her where she would go, Dee doesn't have an answer.

The Nun refers her to an acupuncturist, claiming it will relieve stress. Dee is surprised and although she thinks it might be a good idea, she tells The Nun that acupuncturists, chiropractors, and shrinks are for pussies. The Nun doesn't appear as shocked as Dee would have hoped. She closes her eyes and chants "Away. Away. Away," because if you wish for something hard enough, it just might happen.

The Nun thinks back to the days before she became The Nun and how she visited Rome and Prague and Bruges. She could have stayed in Bruges, taken a lover, gorged on milk chocolates shaped like petite madeleines. But she didn't stay. She returned. During her next appointment with the acupuncturist—she goes to him every Friday—he chats while smoothing the skin of her back. She asks him what he thinks of the Scooter Hardy case, of time just standing still for seven days. Nothing seems to have happened to the boy. The doctors and police officers are relieved, yet puzzled. *What does it mean?* Like the others she has asked, he looks away, fidgeting, not knowing what to say to a nun who asks you to define a miracle.

That night the acupuncturist waits for his wife. She works at a meat-packaging plant. The acupuncturist hates how the number of buns in a pack never matches the number of hotdogs in a pack. He settles into his armchair, wishing someone would take the time to work out the kinks of his stress. Perhaps he will go to a chiropractor. Or a shrink. Or both. He reaches for the remote, only to find it missing—lost once again.

—KAT GONSO

That night the acupuncturist waits for his wife. She works at a meat-packaging plant. The acupuncturist hates how the number of buns in a pack never matches the number of hotdogs in a pack. He settles into his armchair wishing someone would take the time to work out the kinks of his stress. Perhaps he will go to a chiropractor. Or a shrink. Or both. He reaches for the remote, only to find it missing—lost once again.

—KAY GONSO

PART TEN

Revision: Rewriting Is Writing

Revision is just that: a chance to reenvision your work, to revise your story or chapter until it feels finished. By revision, we mean building on that first draft, revising it with various strategies until it becomes a second draft, and continuing to revise your story or chapter or novel until it is finished. It is important to note that when you finish a draft and move on to the next one, you put the previous draft(s) aside. You do not want six different versions of the same story; you want one draft—although it may be your sixth draft. Although there might be writers who start over again and again, we don't advise this. There is almost always something wonderful in what Robert Frost calls "that first melting" that must be saved, and revised around. Often the difference between a good story and a publishable story is revision. Ted Solotaroff, in his essay "Writing in the Cold," says:

> Writing a first draft is like groping one's way into a pitch-dark room, or overhearing a faint conversation, or telling a joke whose punchline you've forgotten. As someone said, one writes mainly to rewrite, for rewriting and revising are how one's mind comes to inhabit the material fully. In its benign form, rewriting is a second, third, and nth chance to make something come right, to "fall graciously into place," in Lewis Hyde's phrase. But it is also a test: one has to learn to respect the misgiving that says, This still doesn't ring true, still hasn't touched bottom. And this means to go back down into the mine again and poke around for the missing ore and find a place for it and let it work its will.

We didn't understand the reluctance of beginning writers to rewrite—and in fact ascribed it to a lack of commitment—until one student wrote in her class evaluation: "The most important thing I learned this semester was that rewriting is writing. Although I understood in theory the importance of revising work, somehow I felt guilty unless I produced something new—and preferably something good—the first time. Rewriting felt like cheating." When we brought this up in subsequent classes, most

197

students admitted that they mistrusted the degree to which established writers say they revise. "Surely Saul Bellow doesn't have to rewrite!" Yet Bellow rewrote *Herzog* twenty times. "The first chapters of Gish Jen's novel flow so smoothly that they must have come right the first time." Yet Jen rewrote her opening chapters forty times. Since that class, we have made it a point to show students that *rewriting is writing* and that revising a story or novel—two, ten, or forty times—is part of the pleasure of writing. We also encourage our students to see rewriting as a continuum. One must write the next draft in order to get to the point in the process to go on to the next draft—and the next draft. It is analogous to the hiker who looks up to the top of the mountain, then sets off to arrive there, only to find that she has reached a false summit. The real summit, which had been hidden behind the false one, looms ahead—or perhaps once there it is discovered to be another false summit. But don't be discouraged; you are making progress—and each successive draft, though it may prove to be a false summit, is moving the story closer and closer to completion.

When William Faulkner was asked what advice he would give to young writers, he said:

> At one time I thought the most important thing was talent. I think now that the young man or the young woman must possess or teach himself, training himself, in infinite patience, which is to try and to try until it comes right. He must train himself in ruthless intolerance—that is to throw away anything that is false no matter how much he might love that page or that paragraph.

We have found that students often lose interest in revision because they merely go back over a story from start to finish—making a few changes as they go. They fail to see that an early draft is in a fluid state and can be totally redrafted and/or rearranged: the final scene might be moved to the beginning; the first person might be changed to third; present tense might be changed to past; characters might be dropped or invented; language, scene length, imagery, body language, description, etc., all are evaluated—often separately.

We chose not to include sample pages from a work in progress or examples of successive drafts because how something finds its way on to the page or is changed or deleted is a mysterious, complicated, and always personal process. The most successful "reproductions" of the revision process appear in Janet Burroway's *Writing Fiction* and David Madden's *Revising Fiction,* and in *A Piece of Work,* edited by Jay Woodruff, in which Tobias Wolff and Joyce Carol Oates speak to interviewers about revising their stories. The exercises in this section are designed to take you through various aspects of the revision process, and to help you discover how revision works best for you. Bernard Malamud said, "Revision is one of the true pleasures of writing."

I try to leave out the parts that people skip.
—ELMORE LEONARD

EXERCISE 78

Opening Up Your Story

When stories are in an early draft they sometimes feel thin, in need of more texture—in need of something. This is the precise time when your story is most flexible and capable of being opened up; successive drafts weave the sentences ever more tightly together. At first glance this exercise on opening up your story might seem the most artificial, the most intrusive foray into your work. Keep in mind, however, that even when suggestions come from "outside" the story, your own imagination is still in control of selecting the material, the details, the language, to make many of these suggested additions absolutely organic to your story.

The Exercise

Choose a story to work with that is still in an early draft form. Read it through so you are thoroughly familiar with it and with the characters. Then find a place in the story to complete and insert the following sentences (change the pronoun as necessary).

The last few nights she had a recurring dream (or nightmare) about _____.

Her mother always warned her that _____.

The one thing I couldn't tell him/her/them was _____. (Add this thought to a dramatic scene with two or more characters.)

The telephone rang. It was a wrong number but the caller refused to hang up. Instead, he _____. (Have at least five or six exchanges.)

She made a list: To do, or _____.

Something seemed different _____.

The last time he had worn this was when _____.

If someone said make a wish, she would wish for _____.

As for God, _____.

So this is what it's all about: _____.

People were probably saying . (You can use this as a reality check—that what is being said is true. Or, the character can report what people think and then refute it.)

199

This time last year she was _____.

Secretly, I collected _____. (What is collected, where is it kept, and from whom is it hidden?)

Outside, it was _____. (Make the weather do something—play off the inside atmosphere. Choose a season.)

Suddenly, she remembered she had forgotten to _____.

On TV (or the radio or a CD player) was _____.

She suspected that _____.

The smell of _____ brought back _____.

It became a family story _____.

As a child, he had learned _____.

Now, come up with some of your own inserts.

The Objective

To experience how your semiconscious imagination is capable of conjuring up material that is absolutely organic to your story for each "fill-in" from the above list. Writers who do this exercise are always amazed at how something so seemingly artificial can provide them with effective additions to their stories.

Student Examples

Last night Bobby had *the dream* again that Albert was down in the basement, he had all the bodies in the basement, everyone strapped to a chair in a big circle, and the washer was going, rumbling and ticking like there were rocks in it, and Albert was in the middle of the circle with a beer in his hand and he was singing, spinning around and singing to each body, bending, bowing to each one and Bobby yelled to him Albert what the fuck, what the fuck Albert and Albert sang to him too, sang get your own beer, get your own beer brother Bobby, and that's when he realized what the bumping noise was, it was their shoes, all of their shoes, Albert was washing their shoes in the washer, all their feet were bare, purple, and Albert was still singing to him, singing now I'm cleaning their shoes.

—JIM MEZZANOTTE, "BROTHERS"

That night I'd dreamed that the dolls I'd knitted around the spare rolls of toilet paper were twirling on a dance floor. Their skirts weren't my knitted ones, but the toilet paper itself, unwinding in strands like the trains of wedding gowns.

—JANET TASHJIAN

The one thing I can't say is that I have a feeling we might not make it. A negative attitude in the mountains is a taboo. There were two guys who got lost in a snowstorm on this same mountain just a week before and froze to death. But Donnie knows what he's doing.

—TOM BRADY

The one thing I couldn't tell my brother about was the night Nelson pushed his way into the bathroom of the trailer while I was pulling up my pants. Nelson didn't say a word. He shoved me back into the hard sink and pressed against me, and all I could see was his shaved head, up close the stubble of dark hair just beginning to cover the scabs sliced into his scalp. Momma called out for me to help with dinner, and next thing I'm in the kitchen trying to explain what nearly happened. When things happen that quickly, it's easy to be convinced of anything else.

"Winnie," Momma said, "Nelson only went to wash his hands."

Later on, all the proof you have is a fear that shoots through you every time you smell a certain kind of bathroom cleanser, and that's nothing you can explain to a brother.

—CHRISTINE FLANAGAN

The caller refused to hang up, instead she kept asking me if I knew where Joey was. I told her there was no one here by that name.

"Just tell him it's Maria," she said. "He'll know."

"But there's no Joey here."

"Did he tell you about me?" Her voice rose. "He told me about you, you little slut."

For a second I wondered if this Maria somehow knew me, or she knew Billy, or Samantha, or even my mother. "I'm hanging up," I told her. "Sorry." After I hung up, I realized I had apologized, and that she had only called me the name I had been afraid to say all night.

—BARBARA LEWIS

He was calling for a Mrs. Patterson to tell her that she might win a million dollars in a vacuum-cleaner catalog sweepstakes. I said, "There is no Mrs. Patterson here."

"Can I talk to your mom?" he asked.

"No," I said. "Her name's not Mrs. Patterson."

He said, "Your mother must be Mrs. Luckman. She promised she'd call me back." My mother was Mrs. Luckman but what the man didn't know was that my mother was always promising everyone everything. She had no time for all her promises. I tried not to hurt his feelings. "Mister," I said, "Promises are easy to forget when there's more important things to be remembered." Later I often wondered if he understood me.

—DORY ELZAURDIA

Something seemed different, Solomon stopped showing us magic tricks, and drank a lot more, and Mom and he stayed up later, ever since he discovered it was cucumbers he had planted and watered and worried over and weeded and not the mush melons that were so dear to his heart.

—ERIC MECKLENBURG

As for God, he got invoked so often by both sides that I finally told those dickheads God was sitting this one out. I said the better get the hymns picked and the body buried and hope the devil wasn't the one that wrote the will.

—CARROLL THOMAS

"Let's go," the girl said and the boy took the keys from her, still looking at my brother. *She was probably thinking* we came from some sick family, and this wasn't our fault.

—CHRISTINE POSTOLOS

That summer we saw twelve movies. We went on two-mile walks. We ate out at least one meal a day, sometimes two. *Secretly I collected* paper menus from the restaurants, stacking them neatly underneath the coloring books in my suitcase. I circled the food I ate, adding up the calories. If it was breakfast I usually ordered two poached eggs (160 calories), dry whole-wheat toast (140), and a glass of orange juice (100 to 120). Then I highlighted the foods I wanted to eat, but couldn't.

—Abby Ellin

Secretly I'd taken all the engraved matchbooks from the tables—Lorraine and Gregory, April 29, 1952—and smuggled them out of the reception in the pockets of my coat, in my purse. They were stacked, one up one down, in a box of Totes on the top of my closet.

—Janet Tashjian

Outside, it's what you'd expect when everything else is going wrong—freezing rain and a travel advisory that will keep me and Clive together one night longer than we'd planned.

—David Steiner

The cloying smell of lakewater *reminds me* of my running route at home, along a river.

—Anne L. Severson

The smell of fresh coffee *always brings back memories* of teacher's lounges where we'd try to relax between classes, exchanging stories about students and complaints about the principal. We pretended we were friends, but I truly wonder if we ever were.

—Christopher Horan

As a child he'd learned the trick of being the lightening rod to his parents' arguments and he wondered now if they would thank him or even remember what for him had been dinners in hell.

—Andrew Ornsten

INTERVIEWER: *How much rewriting do you do?*
HEMINGWAY: *It depends. I rewrote the ending to* Farewell to Arms, *the last page of it, thirty-nine times before I was satisfied.*
INTERVIEWER: *Was there some technical problem there? What was it that had stumped you?*
HEMINGWAY: *Getting the words right.*
—Writers at Work

EXERCISE 79

Gifts to Yourself

In addition to bringing your characters and story alive, details are first and foremost gifts to yourself as a writer, something to be used and reused, and quite possibly something that will determine the course of the story. Flannery O'Connor speaks to the mystery and power of the telling detail. "I doubt myself if many writers know what they are going to do when they start out. When I started writing that story ["Good Country People"], I didn't know there was going to be a Ph.D. with a wooden leg in it. I merely found myself one morning writing a description of two women that I knew something about, and before I realized it, I had equipped one of them with a daughter with a wooden leg." And that wooden leg became central to the story.

It is true that a story's powerful details often take on symbolic significance, but we never encourage students to insert symbols into their stories. A symbol is something that stands for something else—it is usually smaller and more mundane than the larger truth it represents. Symbols can arise from a number of things—real details, personal attitudes, habits, acting, and so on. The important thing to remember is that significant detail adds to the texture of the story. It makes the story a more interesting (or surprising) account of what-if reality. A symbol should be a subtle hint about the author's ultimate meaning for the fiction. Do not confuse the two uses. Details, when used and reused well, have a way of becoming symbols without the writer's self-conscious effort to make them so.

The Exercise

Make a list of the important details in an early draft of a story. Then consider if there are any details—gifts to yourself—that have unexplored potential for opening up your story, for taking plot in a different direction. Can you delete superfluous details? How can you reuse an important detail? In fiction, $1 + 1 + 1 = 23$, not 3.

The Objective

To learn what Flannery O'Connor means when she says, "To say that fiction proceeds by the use of details does not mean the simple, mechanical piling-up of detail. Detail has to be controlled by some overall purpose, and every detail has to be put to work for you. Art is selective."

Student Examples

Christopher Horan says, "I don't know what possessed me to have the narrator scrubbing the toilet bowl and wearing rubber gloves when his landlord shows up at the door, but when I had to decide what the narrator had invented, I didn't have to look very far."

> That afternoon the landlord appeared at my door and said he'd waited long enough. I took off my rubber gloves (for the first time in months I'd been scrubbing the toilet bowl) and shook his hand. I thanked him for his patience, told him that of course I sympathized with him and understood that he, too, had bills to pay. Fortunately, I assured him, he wouldn't have to wait much longer. By the end of the week I expected to receive the first payment for my invention, which would make me solvent enough to give him a year's rent if he liked. He let out a deep sigh. Then, as if he knew he would later regret it, he repeated the word "invention." So I told him, trying desperately to sound as if I weren't making it up on the spot, about my patent—my patent for the self-cleaning toilet bowl.

Another student says, "In my story, 'Objects in Mirror Are Closer Than They Appear,' I made my main character a toll collector on the Mass Pike. Because of the repetitive motion of the job, her doctor prescribes special gloves for her carpal tunnel syndrome. As the story progresses, these constricting gloves begin to represent everything that has been repressing her (her mother, religion, etc.). And I use them to end the story."

> The gloves slowed me down a bit but Dr. Larson insisted I wear them all day, every day, to help my throbbing wrists. They reminded me of the way my mother used to tie a long piece of yarn to each of my mittens, thread it through the sleeves of my winter jacket, behind my neck then down the other sleeve.
> —JANET TASHJIAN, PUBLISHED IN *MASSACHUSETTS REVIEW*

The story's last sentence is: "I hung the gloves on the handle of my door and fastened the straps. They immediately filled with the wind and exhaust of the highway, like the automatic reflex of hands, waving goodbye or hello."

The only way, I think, to learn to write short stories is to write them, and then try to discover what you have done. The time to think of technique is when you've actually got the story in front of you.
—FLANNERY O'CONNOR

EXERCISE 80

Show and Tell:
There's a Reason It's Called
Storytelling

from Carol-Lynn Marrazzo

Beginning writers have often been told "show don't tell," and sometimes by writers who tell plenty. Flannery O'Connor observed that "fiction writing is very seldom a matter of saying things; it is a matter of showing things." But there is a difference, however, between "saying" and "telling," and the wise writer is not afraid to tell. As the following story excerpts illustrate, O'Connor and other fine writers blend telling and showing in their stories and novels—and for good reason. When a writer depends solely on showing and neglects the narrative that artfully shapes, characterizes, qualifies, or in some other way informs the character's actions, the reader is forced to extrapolate meaning based upon what is observed—for example, a character's sweating palms or nervous twitch—and the reader, rather than the writer, then creates the story.

Contrary to what you may think or have been led to believe, writers tell their stories and even O'Connor tells plenty. In "Good Country People," the main character, Joy, a cripple and self-cultivated cynic, is transformed by a moment of vulnerability with a Bible salesman. O'Connor shows the action, but tells Joy's transformation. In this and examples that follow, first read the plain text, then read the complete passage including the narrative in italics.

> She sat staring at him. *There was nothing about her face or her round freezing-blue eyes to indicate that this had moved her; but she felt as if her heart had stopped and left her mind to pump her blood. She decided that for the first time in her life she was face to face with real innocence. This boy, with an instinct that came from beyond wisdom, had touched the truth about her.* When after a minute, she said in a hoarse high voice, "All right," *it was like surrendering to him completely. It was like losing her own life and finding it again, miraculously, in his.*
>
> Very gently he began to roll the slack leg up.

The sentence that begins "There was nothing" explains why the "show, don't tell" rule so often fails. We are told that we cannot know through observation alone what is happening within Joy. If you are unconvinced, read just the showing alone again. Ask: Is there any indication Joy has changed? In this passage, telling not only heightens the moment, it reveals it as a moment of rapture.

"Good Country People" and other stories prove that a complementary interplay between telling and showing at the transforming moment in the story is often crucial to the reader's understanding. Following is a key passage from Eudora Welty's "Livvie Is Back." This is the story of a girl married to a sickly old man named Solomon. When Livvie holds and kisses Cash, a young laborer, Welty tells the reader exactly what Livvie realizes about herself and marriage:

> She gathered the folds of his coat behind him and fastened her red lips to his mouth, and *she was dazzled at herself then, the way he had been dazzled at himself to begin with. In that instant she felt something that could not be told—that Solomon's death was at hand, that he was the same to her as if he were dead now.* She cried out, and uttering little cries, turned and ran for the house.

Here the reader is told Livvie's thoughts and feelings about Solomon "that he was the same to her as if he were dead." Welty chose not to leave the moment to showing alone.

Another quick example. In Jane Smiley's story "Lily," Smiley tells in one word what Lily experiences when she betrays her good friend:

> Lily broke into a sweat the moment she stopped speaking, *a sweat of instant regret.*

Lily's response is characterized as "regret." The whole story would be changed if Lily reacted with a sweat of "confusion" or "triumph."

There is nothing economical or reticent about James Joyce's telling in "The Dead" during Gabriel's epiphany, the moment when he internalizes that all with his wife is not as he thought—she was loved once by a boy, a love Gabriel knew nothing about. The physical manifestations of Gabriel's new awareness are, in contrast, quite modest.

> "He is dead," she said at length. "He died when he was only seventeen. Isn't it a terrible thing to die so young as that?"
>
> "What was he?" asked Gabriel, *still ironically.*
>
> "He was in the gasworks," she said.
>
> *Gabriel felt humiliated by the failure of his irony and by the evocation of this figure from the dead, a boy in the gasworks. While he had been full of memories of their secret life together, full of tenderness and joy and desire, she had been comparing him in her mind with another. A shameful consciousness of his own person assailed him. He saw himself as a ludicrous figure, acting as a pennyboy for his aunts, a nervous well-meaning sentimentalist, orating to vulgarians and idealizing his own clownish lusts, the pitiable fatuous fellow he had caught a glimpse of in the mirror. Instinctively* he turned his back more to the light *lest she might see the shame that burned upon his forehead.*
>
> *He tried to keep his tone of cold interrogation but* his voice when he spoke was humble and indifferent.

Telling is also used to good effect in Amy Hempel's story, "In the Cemetery Where Al Jolson Is Buried," in which the first-person narrator is visiting a dying friend in the hospital. Hempel writes:

"I have to go home," I said when she woke up.

She thought I meant home to her house in the Canyon, and I had to say No, *home* home. *I twisted my hands in the time-honored fashion of people in pain. I was supposed to offer something. The Best Friend. I could not even offer to come back.*

I felt weak and small and failed.

Also exhilarated.

Hempel's narrator tells exactly how she feels—conflicted.

A wonderful example of balanced and complementary interplay between showing and telling is the transforming movement in Peter Taylor's "The Gift of the Prodigal." In order to appreciate how remarkable the telling is, first read only those portions of the passage that are *not* italicized.

> *I say to myself, "He really is like something not quite human. For all the jams and scrapes he's been in, he's never suffered any second thoughts or known the meaning of remorse. I ought to have let him hang," I say to myself, "by his own beautiful locks."*
>
> But almost simultaneously what I hear myself saying aloud is "Please don't go, Rick. Don't go yet, son." *Yes, I am pleading with him, and I mean what I say with my whole heart.* He still has his right hand on the doorknob and has given it a full turn. Our eyes meet across the room, *directly, as they never have before in the whole of Ricky's life or mine. I think neither of us could tell anyone what it is he sees in the other's eyes, unless it is a need beyond any description either of us is capable of.*
>
> Presently Rick says, "You don't need to hear my crap."
>
> And I hear my *bewildered* voice saying, "I do . . . I do." And "Don't go, Rick, my boy." My eyes have *even* misted over. But I still meet his eyes across the *now too silent* room. He looks at me *in the most compassionate way imaginable. I don't think any child of mine has ever looked at me so before. Or perhaps it isn't really with compassion as he is viewing me but with the sudden, gratifying knowledge that it is not, after all, such a one-sided business, the business between us.* He keeps his right hand on the doorknob a few seconds longer. Then I hear the latch click and *know he has let go.* Meanwhile, I observe his left hand making that *familiar gesture,* his fingers splayed, his hand tilting back and forth. I am out of my chair now. I go to the desk and bring out two Danlys cigars from another desk drawer, which I keep locked. He is there *ready to receive my offering when I turn around.* He accepts the cigar without smiling, and I give it without smiling, too.

Now ask: If only the "showing" portion of this passage were available, would a reader have any idea what subtle understanding has transpired between father and son? Study the passage carefully and observe Taylor's strategy as he grounds the passage through the father's keen senses (showing) and at the same time gives the reader access to the father's most intimate thoughts and feelings (telling)—all while the action keeps moving forward.

The Exercise

Choose a story in which you think the transforming moment is effectively rendered. Underline the telling portions of that moment and read the passage without the underlined portions. Do this for a number of stories.

Then, turn to a story draft of your own in which you think the transforming moment is not yet effectively rendered. Underline the telling portions of that moment. If you have no "telling," add some, but try to balance the showing and telling to their best combined effect. Do not be afraid to use the world "felt." Note how many times it appeared in the previous examples.

If it seems impossible to tell anything, then you might not know your characters well or you might not know what your story is about.

The Objective

To be able to both show and tell. To experiment with different combinations of showing and telling to enhance your narrative technique and to illuminate the final meaning of your story.

[One must] learn to read as a writer, to search out that hidden machinery, which it is the business of art to conceal and the business of the apprentice to comprehend.

—MARGOT LIVESEY

EXERCISE 81

A Little Gardening,
A Little Surgery

When a story or novel isn't working, it often helps to look at it in a new way—not just on your computer screen or even in hard copy manuscript—but with scissors and tape and a conference table or wall.

In her book *The Writing Life*, Annie Dillard says she has often "written" with the "mechanical aid of a twenty-foot conference table. You lay your pages along the table's edge and pace out your work. You walk along the rows; you weed bits, move bits, and dig out bits, bent over the rows with full hands like a gardener."

Novelist E. L. Doctorow, formerly an editor, when asked about the relationship between editing and the craft of writing, said, "Editing taught me how to break books down and put them back together. . . . You learn how to become very free and easy about moving things around, which a reader would never do. A reader sees a printed book and that's it. But when you see a manuscript as an editor, you say, 'Well this is chapter twenty, but it should be chapter three.' You're at ease in the book the way a surgeon is at ease in a human chest, with all the blood and the guts and everything. You're familiar with the material and you can toss it around and say dirty things to the nurse." Thus, one method for revising, or "reenvisioning," a story is to become very self-conscious about its shape and its components when it is laid out in front of you in pieces.

The Exercise

Choose a story that doesn't seem to be working and cut it apart into the separate components of scenes and narrative passages and flashbacks. Number each piece in the order in which it appears in your story. Then hang the pieces across a wall with tape and absorb what is in front of you. Ask:

- How many scenes are there? Are there too few or too many?

- Are too many of the components the same length?

- Does each scene accomplish something? Can some be combined? Deleted?

- Are there any missing scenes? Unexplored territory?

- Is the material from the "past" in the right places?

■ What would happen if you rearranged the sequence of events?

■ What would happen if you begin with the ending scene and use it to frame the story? Or to foretell the end?

As you ask yourself these questions, pace back and forth and move your story pieces around. Play with them. Experiment. If you have missing scenes, add a piece of paper that says "add scene about." Then, when you are satisfied with the order of your story, number the sections again—ignoring the original numbers. Then compare the old order—and numbers—to the new order. Chances are 9 might now be 3 and 2 and 4 might be combined. Finally, instead of doing "cut and paste" on your computer, retype the story again from scratch—using your new arrangement. Feel the difference, the power of the revised word.

The Objective

To see an early draft of a story as something that isn't etched in stone. Not only are the words and lines capable of being revised, but the story structure itself is often still fluid enough to rearrange and analyze for the questions listed above.

Student Examples

I asked one class to write about this "scissors and tape" process and below are several responses:

> This was a good learning process. I saw the story as a whole, laid out on the floor, while also seeing how individual sections fit into the whole. I then asked myself, truthfully this time because the separated pages were staring me in the face, if the order was the best it could be? I discovered I hadn't been nearly as truthful or careful as I could have been.
>
> —KIM REYNOLDS

> I discovered that Gladys, my incorrigible housekeeper, is not introduced until page 18. In class, Kim Reynolds suggested that I drop Gladys, but I wanted to keep her. Now, I see what Kim means. I could remove all of Gladys' components without affecting—at all—the heart of the story. It's hard to see a scene objectively until you separate it from the rest of the story and dare it to stand on its own. Cutting up a story liberates you; it gives you a kind of "fuck it" attitude when you see how easy it is to shape and move things around.
>
> —LEE HARRINGTON

> I thought cutting things apart and switching them around would somehow damage my overall story. I thought it was pretty close to perfect the way I had it (I was sort of embarrassed by this attitude because I'd never considered myself a "touchy artist" type, but that's a subject for another paper). Then I saw that one scene took up fourteen of seventeen pages. Other sections were much too short and one section repeated

everything I had written in another section. The second draft isn't exactly flying along at the speed of sound, but I'm happy about the way it's coming together now.

—MICHAEL SUMMERS

Mainly I learned that any story is fluid. I will do this for every story now. I've also cut up other stories—in particular, a couple of Alice Munro's, since many of her stories dip into the past. I'm amazed at how long some of her sections of the past really are (like mine!), but in hers every word counts.

—MARYANNE O'HARA

Cutting the story up bought me into the story. I'd felt distanced from it even though I was constantly picking it up and reading it. Now after looking at my story piece by piece the task of filling it out seems more manageable.

—JACKSON HOLZ

If you tell yourself you are going to be at your desk tomorrow, you are by that declaration asking your unconscious to prepare the material.

—NORMAN MAILER

EXERCISE 82

Magnifying Conflict
from David Ray

Great fiction is tense with conflict—between characters, within characters, between characters and forces opposing them. We need only think of Ernest Pontifex's struggles with his father in Samuel Butler's Victorian classic *The Way of All Flesh* or Raskolnikov's struggle between his fixation on murder and his impulse to love and remain loyal to his family and its values in Dostoyevsky's *Crime and Punishment*—or more accurately, his struggle between sanity and insanity. We might recall the heroine of Samuel Richardson's *Pamela,* struggling against the wiles of her employer-seducer. Or we might think of Huck Finn, in his perplexity about the racism he's been taught and his more trustworthy intuition and loyalty to his friend Jim, a runaway slave. In *Moby Dick* there is conflict on many levels, but primarily between hunter and hunted, malefic force and the innocent violence of nature. Any solid work of fiction will provide ready examples. The Japanese poet Kobayashi Issa found a storm of raging conflict even within a dewdrop, the most peaceful thing he could find in nature when he sought a retreat from his grief. The writer who loses touch with his responsibility to energize his fiction with conflict will probably have a very limited or temporary audience.

The Exercise

Go through a completed story and intensify the conflict, magnifying the tension and shrillness at every turn, even to the point of absurdity or hyperbole. Add stress wherever possible, both between characters and within them as individuals. Exaggerate the obstacles they face. Be extreme.

The Objective

To create an awareness of the need for a high level of tension while encouraging a healthy regard for how easily it can become excessive. This exercise is not meant to "improve" the story, although it often provokes new and more dynamic descriptions and dialogue. It raises the writer's consciousness about the need for conflict in fiction.

EXERCISE 83

What's at Stake?

from Ken Rivard

What's at stake in your story? What is in jeopardy in your story? What is at risk? What do your characters stand to win or lose—custody of the kids, a place on a starting lineup, the approval of a tyrannical boss?

Once you can answer that question, then ask if your stakes are high enough to keep readers reading. When they are too low, the story fails to move us. The survival of a tenuous relationship, a minor personal insight, getting through one more day at a tedious job—it's difficult to make such familiar scenarios come alive. You have to overcome the reader's skepticism that the lousy husband, crappy job, or minor realization is worth the fuss and bother in the first place. Why not create a dilemma that immediately snags and holds our attention? Consider the following situations:

- A six-year-old boy disappears for a few hours. Eventually, he's discovered, unharmed, a few blocks from his home, with no memory of what has happened to him. Years later, as a university student on vacation, he drives by the street where he disappeared, notices a young boy, and acts on an irresistible compulsion to lure him into his car. (Ruth Rendell's "The Fallen Curtain")

- An eccentric substitute teacher subverts the 2 + 2 = 4 universe of her fourth-grade students by introducing them to "substitute facts" (such as 6 + 11 = 68), Egyptian cosmology, and the curse of the Hope diamond. One afternoon she explains the use of Tarot cards, and predicts the early death of a particular student. (Charles Baxter's "Gryphon" on page 287)

- For years, a reticent working-class white woman has allowed a devil-may-care friend to talk her into "adventures" without their husbands' knowledge, including slipping away once a week to go tea dancing. At the ballroom, they make the acquaintance of a young black man who becomes their regular dance partner. When the more daring woman dies, her friend screws up her courage for one last afternoon of escape. This time, their dance partner begins communicating gentle, but unmistakable signals of sexual interest. (William Trevor's "Afternoon Dancing")

Inexperienced writers often forget that readers are essentially voyeurs, peering through the window of a story into its characters' lives. Though quite different in structure and style, each of the three stories described above involves us in circumstances full of promise for events to come. How strange will the substitute teacher get before the school administration finds her out? Will the adult kidnapper remember what happened to him as a boy, and is he doomed to replay some dreadful scene? What will the woman do, confronted with possibilities for new adventure, now that her spunky friend isn't there to encourage her?

Beginning writers often agree in principle that high stakes are good, but balk when it comes to actually upping the ante in their own stories. This natural inclination to avoid tension and/or conflict and to avoid putting anything at risk or in jeopardy is a survival skill in the real world, but a death knell to fiction. In order to create a story with high stakes you must make a leap of imaginative faith—that some things, at least for your characters, are unambiguously worth fighting for.

The Exercise

Examine some of your favorite stories and novels and ask: What's at stake? Then examine your own fiction and ask: What's at stake? If you can't answer then you don't know enough about your characters or their lives.

The Objective

To understand that compelling stories are about characters who take risks, put something in jeopardy, or gamble for high stakes in order to get what they want.

Middles have the double and contradictory function of delaying the climax while at the same time preparing the reader for it and fetching him to it.

—JOHN BARTH, *LOST IN THE FUNHOUSE*

It Ain't Over Till It's Over

When men and women began telling tales around evening campfires, surely the most frequent words from their audience were "And then what happened?" Perhaps the only assurance these storytellers had that their story was truly over was someone in the audience saying "Tell us another one." It is this last response—"Tell us another one"—that you want from your readers at the end of your story or novel. If your reader is still saying "And then what happened?" clearly your story isn't over and hasn't achieved the emotional resolution necessary in most stories.

A complete short story should be like a suspended drop of oil, entire unto itself. Or, viewed another way, it should be psychically "resolved." That is, when the reader gets to the last sentence she will understand that the story ends here—she doesn't have to know what happened to the characters beyond this final moment.

The Exercise

Examine each of your stories carefully to make sure it has this psychic resolution. Read them to a friend or fellow student and ask if they think it's finished. One of the hardest things to learn is how to judge your own work; it's eminently reasonable to try it out on a sympathetic—but objective—listener.

The Objective

To master the art of tying up narrative and thematic threads.

A love story has to implicitly include a definition of love.
—BRIAN HINSHAW

215

EXERCISE 85

The Double Ending:
Two Points in Time

Have you ever finished a short story only to feel that perhaps there is more to the story—but at a future time, past your story's current ending? This dilemma—the need for more—calls for the solution of the double ending. It isn't that the first ending is wrong, but rather it is a necessary stepping-stone on the way to the final ending. And once you have written this second ending to the story—at a future time that is past the current ending—you might find that the first ending no longer satisfies the story's arc. The following stories by three superb storytellers illustrate the elegant art and architecture of the double ending.

Sharon Sheehe Stark's story "The Appaloosa House" begins with this first sentence: "My father's girlfriend's name was Delores and my mother went by Dusie because she was one." The daughter narrates the story with biting good humor as she tells how the father is kicked out of the house because of his philandering, but eventually is allowed to return. As a surprise, her "dusie" of a mother paints the house like an Appaloosa horse and is riding the peak when the father arrives home. He joins her on the roof in a joyful reunion, which the daughter has been longing for, but ultimately doesn't trust. There is a space break and the story continues with the daughter jumping ahead to her father's death in the company of a woman not his wife. And then it returns to the moment of joy—a joy that ends the current time of the story, but alas will not last.

Alice Munro's story "Post and Beam" is the story of Lorna, a young mother of two children, married to an older academic who is "very proud" of their post-and-beam house. Lorna has become infatuated with one of her husband's students, Lionel, who hangs around the house and writes her poems. As the story proceeds, Lionel disappears for a while and Polly, Lorna's disgruntled dissatisfied cousin, comes to visit. Near the end of the story, when the family is on a vacation, Lorna imagines that Polly, who was left behind, is going to commit suicide. In order to head this off, Lorna thinks:

> Make a bargain. Believe that it was still possible, up to the last minute it was possible to make a bargain.
>
> It had to be serious, a most final and wrenching promise or offer. Take this. I promise this. . . . Not the children. She snatched that thought away as if she were grabbing them out of the fire. Not Brendan, for an opposite reason. She did not love him enough. . . . Herself? Her looks. . . . It occurred to her that she might be on the wrong track. In a case like this, it might not be up to you to choose. Not up to you to set the terms. You would know them when you met them. You must promise to honor them without knowing what they were going to be. Promise.

When the family arrives home, in fact, Polly is doing quite well for herself and seems to have caught the fancy of Lionel. Lorna hears their companionable voices in the back yard and thinks, "Lionel. She had forgotten all about him." She had forgotten to exempt him when bargaining. The story nears its end with Lorna, isolated and bereft, looking down from an upstairs window on her assembled family and the new duo of Polly and Lionel, who is now lost to her. There is a space break. And then this:

> It was a long time ago that this happened. In North Vancouver, when they lived in the post-and-beam house. When she was twenty-four years old and new to bargaining.

Clearly, Lorna has learned to bargain better—and this no doubt has had something to do with why they no longer live in the post-and-beam house. This is a crucial detail; surely only death or divorce could have moved her husband out of it.

In Jean Thompson's story "Mercy" a divorced and lonely police officer sleeps with a woman after he tells her that her son has been killed in a car accident. He continues to call her, but she avoids him until finally, at the end of the story, he waits outside the place where she works. When he accosts her, she tells him, "Christ. I felt sorry for you. You and your sad-sack face and your stupid badge. It was a mercy fuck. OK." He is devastated. Then a few sentences later the story continues:

> Much later, after he had met and married his second wife, and left the force, and had become accustomed to his new happiness, he was able to see that moment more clearly. She might have been cruel, but she had not been unwise to cast him off. He had only wanted to fill himself up with her grief, because it would take up more space in him than his own imperfect grief . . . But he didn't know that yet, or that things would get better, or that he would not always feel his shame like a sickness. He started the car, and she gave him a little fluttering wave, and the rain dropped like a curtain over the windshield glass and blurred the red of her skirt. She made a pantomime of dodging the rain, turned, and disappeared into the shop. He had been set free from something, although that was another thing he did not yet know.

And there the story ends—although we know that a better future is in store for him.

Note that the double ending allows the writer to use an *extreme* ending for the first ending because it will be mitigated by the one to follow. In "Mercy" the policeman hits bottom in the first ending, when the woman tells him that their earlier encounter was a "mercy fuck." In "Post and Beam" the young wife is also in despair at losing Lionel, at "acquiring Polly," and at returning to her previous situation of a young mother married to a pompous academic. In "The Appaloosa House" the daughter sees her parents at their best: her mother's craziness beguiling the father into coming home once again. Their immense joy on that roof. But it is too extreme to last—and the father's character (character is destiny) asserts itself and he once again cheats on his wife and he and his young fling die in an accident.

The extreme is acceptable in the first ending for some of the following reasons:

- Sometimes, what happens to a character needs time to sink in—to make a character act (as in "Post and Beam").

- A character needs time to heal, but can't immediately (as in "Mercy").

■ A character needs enough to time make a decision (again as in "Post and Beam") or for the inevitable to happen (the break up of the "Post and Beam" marriage).

■ It allows a character to have a satisfying *but temporary* change of character (as in "The Appaloosa House"), but that temporary change cannot last.

The Exercise

Look at your stories that are in draft form and consider whether one of them would benefit from just such a double ending. How might the future of the characters be quite different and produce a truer ending to their story than the current ending? Be sure to set the "second" ending at least two to five years in the future. And on your own, look at the double ending that Richard Russo uses in his story "Joy Ride." After a space break, he writes: "All of this was a long time ago. More than twenty years now, and as I think back on our joy ride that spring, it seems far more remarkable than it did at the time, and what followed more remarkable still." Why did Russo go forward to look back?

The Objective

To give the way you think about your characters' lives—the arc of their stories—more latitude. To understand how the future can be foretold within the confines of the first ending.

When you're in a workshop, your manuscript is given the time of day.
—EDWIN HILL

EXERCISE 86

In-Class Revision

In spite of good intentions, writers often don't put enough time into revising a story, so they never learn to trust the process, and their stories' potential remains unexplored. This exercise suggests ways to revise and shows you how to relax into the revision process. Ideally, the exercise should be done in two consecutive workshops or classes, totaling six to eight hours. Although all questions and suggestions for revision will not apply to all stories, enough will speak to each writer's individual story to make the session rewarding and even fun. Writer Laurence Davies calls this exercise "strategic derangement."

The Exercise

Bring to class a first or second draft of a story—a story you care enough about to spend six to eight hours revising. (Caring about the story is crucial to this exercise's success.) Also bring several highlighters, scissors, and tape. The teacher or workshop leader will ask questions, give instructions, and direct you to various exercises. You will probably find questions and problems that can't be answered or resolved during this session; jot down notes as reminders for the next time you revise this particular story.

- Whose story is it? How does the story reflect this? Is the point of view right for the story? (The point-of-view character owns the story.)

- What does your main character want? Where do you indicate this in the story? How does this drive the story? See Exercise 13, "What Do Your Characters Want?"

- Can you answer the question, "Into what life has this trouble come?" for your point-of-view character? Can you describe the life and identify the trouble?

- What does the reader learn about your main characters in the first third of the story? Is any crucial information withheld from the reader? Do Exercise 11, "What Do You Know About Your Characters?"

- Do your characters have an inner life? See Part 5, "The Interior Landscape of Your Characters." Have you allowed them to use their imaginations?

- How well does your POV character know the other people in his or her life? Allow them to imagine what another character is doing in real time that will affect the story. See Exercise 32.

■ Does your story both show and tell, especially toward the end of the story? See Exercise 79, "Show and Tell: There's a Reason It's Called Storytelling."

■ How many scenes does your story have? See Exercise 80, "A Little Gardening, A Little Surgery." Now for the scissors: Cut your story apart into its components and spread it out somewhere to peruse. Or better yet, hang it up on a long wall.

■ What is the unstable situation of your story? See the introduction to Part 6, "Plot," on page 112.

■ Does your story start in the right place—in the middle? What is the story's "history"?

■ Is your beginning sentence the best way to start your story? See Exercise 3, "Ways to Begin a Story."

■ What is at stake in your story? What is at risk? What can be won or lost? See Exercise 82, "What's at Stake?"

■ Does your story have tension, conflict? See Exercise 81, "Magnifying Conflict."

■ Does something happen in your story? Something that is significant, that carries everything? Is there a change? See Exercise 44, "So, What Happened?" You might not be able to determine this until you cut your story apart.

■ How well have you choreographed your scenes? Highlight the body language in your most important scenes. See Exercise 29, "The Invisible Scene."

■ Does your dialogue serve the story well and move the plot along? Do you use indirect discourse where needed? See Exercise 27, "Telling Talk."

■ Have you developed your story's gifts to yourself? Make a list of the significant details and check to see if you have reused them. See Exercise 78, "Gifts to Yourself."

■ Does your story have enough texture? Open up your story with Exercise 77, "Opening Up Your Story." This exercise should take a while to do. Spend about four minutes each on six to eight "inserts." Have students create other "inserts."

■ Underline the first interesting sentence in your story—interesting for language, characterization, setting, atmosphere—for something. (It should be the first or close to the first sentence.)

■ Is the language of your story interesting? See the introduction to Part 7, "The Elements of Style," page 133.

■ Do your adjectives and adverbs enhance your nouns and verbs? Circle all the adjectives and adverbs in the first two pages. See Exercise 50, "Taboos: Weak Adjectives and Adverbs."

■ Do your sentences vary in length and complexity? See Exercise 49, "A Style of Your Own."

■ Do you know how your story ends? Are there unanswered questions? See Exercise 83, "It Ain't Over Till It's Over."

- What final meaning are you working toward in your story?

- Was your title thrown at the top of the page or chosen with care? Make a list of fifty or one hundred possible titles—take some from within the story. See Exercise 64, "Titles and Keys."

You've accomplished a lot in the past few hours. Now, think about what you have discovered about this story, and sometime in the next day or two return to this story for further revision. Then, bring a new draft in to the next class. Include a page or two in which you discuss the revision process and how it worked for you. How will you proceed in the future?

The Objective

To relax into the revision process and give your story your undivided attention. To see the process as a fluid one—made up of components that are variable, manageable, and yours alone.

- What final meaning are you working toward in your story?

- Was your title thrown at the top of the page or chosen with care? Make a list of fifty or one hundred possible titles—take some from within the story. See Exercise 64, "Titles and Keys."

You've accomplished a lot in the past few hours. Now, think about what you have discovered about this story, and sometime in the next day or two return to this story for further revision. Then, bring a new draft in to the next class. Include a page or two in which you discuss the revision process and how it worked for you. How will you proceed in the future?

The Objective

To relax into the revision process and give your story your undivided attention. To see the process as a fluid one—made up of components that are variable, manageable, and yours alone.

PART ELEVEN

Sudden, Flash, Micro, Nano: Writing the Short Short Story

The short short story is an elusive form—perhaps more mysterious than the short story or novel. In *Sudden Fiction*, Stuart Dybek addresses the editors' question of what is a short short as opposed to a short story. He says, ". . . the short prose piece so frequently inhabits a no-man's land between prose and poetry, narrative and lyric, story and fable, joke and meditation, fragment and whole, that one of its identifying characteristics has been its protean shape. Part of the fun of writing them is the sense of slipping between the seams. Within the constraint of their small boundaries the writer discovers great freedom. In fact, their very limitations of scale often *demand* unconventional strategies. . . . Each writer makes up the form. Each piece is a departure. A departure—but from what?"

The elusiveness of the short short story especially makes itself felt in the workshop. When discussing longer stories or novel excerpts in class we use the language of the art of fiction, asking if the characters are fully fleshed out, does the plot have forward movement, does the metafictional aspect of the story enlarge our understanding of fiction, has the story found its own balance between narrative summary and scene, and so on. When teaching a *short short* story workshop, however, we find ourselves asking only one question of each short short story: *does it work?* Irving Howe in his introduction to *Short Shorts* states, "Writers who do short shorts need to be especially bold. They stake everything on a stroke of inventiveness. Sometimes they have to be prepared to speak out directly, not so much in order to state a theme as to provide a jarring or complicating commentary. . . . And then, almost before it begins, the fiction is brought to a stark conclusion—abrupt, bleeding, exhausting. This conclusion need not complete the action; it has to break it off decisively."

As always, the best teachers are the stories themselves. Noted practitioners include Kafka, Borges, Hemingway, Kawabata, Yukio Mishima, and more recently Grace Paley, Thomas Berger, Luisa Valenzuela, and Diane Williams. Even writers known for longer work have written in this form: Joyce Carol Oates, David Foster Wallace, and Tim O'Brien, among others. There are also many superb anthologies of the short short story. One of the first to appear was Irving and Ilana Wiener Howe's *Short Shorts*, mentioned above, with its informative introduction. Then came the enormously influential *Sudden Fiction*, followed by *Flash Fiction*, *Sudden Fiction International*, and the shortest of all, *Microfiction*, edited by Jerome Stern, which includes many of the winners and finalists of a contest started by Stern, known as the World's Best Short Short Story Contest. One winner of this contest was Brian Hinshaw, then an MFA student at Emerson College. Hinshaw's story, "The Custodian" (page 275), is discussed at length in Ron Wallace's essay "Writers Try Short Shorts" in the *AWP Chronicle* (Vol. 33, No. 6, 2001). (It can be read online by going to Google and keying in "Ronald Wallace" to find his Web site.) Other anthologies of short short stories include *Four Minute Fictions*, edited by Robley Wilson, who first published them in *North American Review*, and *Sudden Stories: The Mammoth Book of Miniscule Stories*, edited by Dinty Moore. Finally, two new magazines by former Emerson students feature the short short story: *Quick Fiction*, edited by Jennifer Cande and Adam Pieroni, publishes stories under 500 words (www.quickfiction.org), and *Night Train*, edited by Rod Siino and Rusty Barnes, runs an intriguing competition twice a year for "Firebox" fiction (www.Nighttrainmagazine.com)—a competition that shares the reading fees with the contest winners. *Esquire* often features a short short story on its last page under the title "Snapfiction." The new and impressive Rose Metal Press, started by Emerson MFA graduates Abigail Beckel and Kathleen Rooney, has made a place for itself in the world of Flash Fiction. Their first book was *Brevity and Echo: An Anthology of Short Short Stories* by Emerson students—stories first published in the "real world." One of the Press's newest books is *The Rose Metal Press Field Guide to Writing Flash Fiction: Tips from Editors, Teachers, and Writers in the Field*, edited by Tara Masih. It includes essays by Ron Carlson, Rusty Barnes, Randall Brown, Stuart Dybek, Tom Hazuka, Julio Ortega, Jayne Anne Phillips, and Robert Shapard, among others. Lots of stories to read. Lessons to learn. Places to publish.

There is no absolute rule for how short or long a short short might be, but we think of it as falling somewhere between 250 words and four or five manuscript pages. It is not a condensed longer story, but rather a story that requires this length and its particular form. The most compelling short short stories often have a narrative thread.

Perhaps because the stories are so short, we encourage you to play around with the exercises—on your own or in a workshop. When assigning Ron Carlson's ABC story (see page 229) we ask students to come up with A words as fast as they can, going around and around the room until someone repeats a word. (They are amazed at how many A words there are—that they know.) Then B words. Then we move to X and Y and Z words. When students bring their ABC stories in, we ask each student to read off their AB and YZ sentences—just to hear the variety. When students are assigned the "Rules of the Game" exercise (page 235), we go around the room compiling a list of games. Sometimes we ask the students to create their own exercises based on a story they've read. One student came up with a superb "Chain" story exercise based on Francine Prose's "Pumpkins" from *Flash Fiction*. At the end of the semester each student is astonished that she has written and revised between ten and fifteen new short short stories. At this time, students put together individual collections in addition to creating a class anthology of short shorts, complete with title page and cover art. Now, it's your turn.

> The business of the poet and novelist is to show the sorriness underlying
> the grandest things, and the grandeur underlying the sorriest things.
> —THOMAS HARDY

EXERCISE 87

Sudden Fiction

from James Thomas

In our introduction to *Sudden Fiction*, Robert Shapard and I recount how we solicited responses to our working first title, "Blasters," and were amazed at the "uproar." Writers not only had opinions about the word for the short short story, but also about their traditions, their present developments, the motives for writing and reading them, how they compare to sonnets, ghazals, folk tales, parables, koans, and other forms. Almost no one agreed entirely on anything, least of all what a short short was. Highly compressed, highly charged, insidious, protean, sudden, alarming, tantalizing, short shorts do confer form on small corners of chaos, and, at their best, can do in a page what a novel does in two hundred.

Question: What is shorter than "sudden fiction?"

Answer: "Flash fiction."

These even shorter stories (all under 750 words) are collected in *Flash Fiction*, edited by Tom Hazuka, Denise Thomas, and myself. Then there is the World's Best Short Short Story Contest, run by Jerome Stern at Florida State University at Tallahassee, whose winners and finalists appear in *Sundog: The Southeast Review*. Will anyone forget the "big wind" or "moiling dogs" from the 1991 winning story, "Baby, Baby, Baby," by François Camoin?

The Exercise

Read, read, read these shortest of stories with joy and amazement at their range and multiplicity of form.

Then write one—fewer than 750 words.

The Objective

To create a world, give it shape—all of a sudden, in a flash.

226

EXERCISE 88

Write a Story Using a Small Unit of Time

Some short stories employ a small, contained unit of time or center on a single event that provides the story with a given natural shape. For example, in Nicholson Baker's short story "Pants on Fire," the narrator puts on a shirt and takes the subway to work—nothing else happens. Raymond Carver's story "Cathedral" takes place in one evening when an old friend comes to visit the narrator's wife (page 306). Luisa Valenzuela's "Vision Out of the Corner of One Eye" captures a fleeting encounter on a bus (page 286). Elizabeth Tallent's story "No One's a Mystery" lasts the length of time it takes for the narrator to receive a gift from her married lover Jack, who also gives her the unwanted truth of their situation, achieving a unity of time and place (page 284). Such unity is a natural for the short short story form.

The Exercise

Make a list yourself of things that are done in small units of time: naming a child or a pet, washing a car, stealing something, waiting or standing in line, packing for a trip, changing the message on an answering machine, teaching a class, getting a haircut, throwing a birthday party, etc. Now write a two-to-four-page story staying within the confines of a particular time unit. For example, a birthday party story would probably last only a few hours, or an afternoon or evening.

The Objective

To recognize the large number of shaped time units in our lives. These units can provide a natural substructure for a story and make the writing of a story seem less daunting.

Student Example

Bouncing

Standing at the kitchen sink, blinking away sleep, he hears his wife's scream "Oh God!" followed by terrible thumping and crashing, which he knows as sure as he's standing there in his boxers is his baby son bouncing down the stairs, just as he's always feared, and he drops the coffee pot and runs to the foot of the staircase in time to catch the startled body as it tumbles off the last carpeted stair, a plastic toddler gate crashing behind and hitting—*Thock!*—the wall, leaving a big hole that could have easily been his son's perfect head, but instead he's holding that head in one hand, cradling the rest of his tense pooh-clad body, staring at the tiny face, contorted in a frozen, soundless scream of fear and wonder, smooth skin turning crimson, breath held for an eternity as he hears his wife's "Please God," echo his own prayers along with his voiced pleading "Breathe, Lorne," when the logjam breaks at last, tears flow and cries like someone is sticking him with a sewing needle erupt out of the suddenly heaving body, threatening to rupture his membranes, and then just as suddenly the cat strolls by, blissfully unconcerned with the drama before her, and the tortured expression of his son clears as sunny as a solstice morning, leaving only a mother and a father, their lives no longer their own.

—KEITH LOREN CARTER, PUBLISHED IN *MID-AMERICAN REVIEW*

Stare. It is the way to educate your eye, and more. Stare. Pry. Listen. Eavesdrop. Die knowing something. You are not here long.
—WALKER EVANS

Solving for X

from Ron Carlson

The following exercise works best if it is done first and discussed afterward.

The Exercise

Write a short story with the following conditions: It is exactly twenty-six sentences in length. Each sentence begins with a word that starts with one of the letters of the alphabet—in order. For example:

> All the excuses had been used. By the time the school doctor saw me, he'd heard everything. Coughing, I began to tell him about the lie which I hoped would save us all. [And so forth.]

Also, you must use one sentence fragment. Oh, and one sentence should be exactly 100 words long and grammatically sound.

The Objective

The objective here is initially obscured by how confused everyone is to have such a strange mission. Tell them to get over it. What the assignment illuminates is form's role in process. Since the imposed form has nothing at all to do with the writer's real agenda, the exercise becomes a fundamental exploration of our sense of story, narrative rise and fall, and process—process most prominently. What a challenge and a comfort knowing how that next sentence begins! The discussions we've had over these ABC stories are some of the strongest and most central, and the issues that arise follow us all semester.

To make a more dramatic point about structure and its relationship to process, divide any group of writers in two and assign only half the above exercise to the first group. Assign the second group the same exercise but make it clear that the twenty-six sentences do not have to be in alphabetical order. Any bets on who has the more difficult task?

Student Example

Tasteful

Anton, my wife's French lover, has been leaving me clues in the kitchen sink. Before I realized what was at work I thought them to be merely lazy with their adulterous business. "Careless, careless," I thought, on finding the clamshells piled on the countertop, some rimmed with lipstick, a red kind I'd never seen before. Determined to leave them to their affair, I said nothing and cleaned up, scrubbing the saucepots and plates (Anton would sometimes have the courtesy to rinse the blackest of the bunch and these gestures were to me like little reliefs).

Eventually, however, a line was crossed, or rather, a line was drawn. For the record, I'd like to put that my initial reaction was not violent in nature; I tore no hair, or cursed or banged my chest in heartfelt agony—in truth, I flinched. Getting home late one evening I found the house in a state of measured disarray: chairs carefully overturned, shelves upset of their volumes (mostly mine), pictures skewed on their hooks, etc., etc. . . . but the dining room was ruined for me alone. Honestly, it appeared as though they had gone to some trouble to give me a show, as the walls were speckled with soup (a pork and potato potage, I determined, after much finger licking), the plates and their contents scattered across the floor (swordfish, in a light virgin oil with mixed greens) while the table itself was strewn with the wreckage of a planned passion; a snow angel of wine stains and silverware to document their deliberate bad fun. In the heart of this scene was a heavy line of salt, running lengthwise down the table, dividing the house into territories of mine and theirs, but like a challenge as well—a dare, if you will. Justifiably, I remained a gentleman and made no effort to erase the line or its litter, but switched off the lights instead, the salt strip illuminating the room like a tail of phosphorus. Knowing hunger myself, I righted a chair and fell to, picking through the leftovers.

Later, weeks later, the taste of this food would remain in my mouth, blooming at the back of my throat into a kind of perpetual gag reflex, an unshakable sweetness, there, just behind my tongue, trimmed out with the unmistakable sting of stomach bile. Momentarily, I believed the nausea to be the announcement of a great nest of ulcers, all growing fat from my ample stress and rotten habits—a consequence of adulthood with which I have learned to live. Nevertheless, the symptoms here refused to match up—they were more violent, unpredictable and stretched to include bouts of strenuous retching, night fever, insomnia and a general bad temper. Of course, no conventional remedy could slake the tides of digestive fluid; chalk tablets, milk of magnesia—even a strong belt of castor oil did nothing but discolor my teeth and extinguish my appetite. Polite as you please, I spent each night splayed across the cool tiles of our shared bathroom, stifling my moans and thumbing eagerly through a French dictionary, my ear pressed to the wall, conjugating his irregular and exclamatory verbs with all the severity of a death sentence.

Quite by accident, I discovered my own antidote.

Regarding the innocence of my intentions, I must say that reckless knife-play has never been customary in my kitchen—however, fortunate slips of the hand are. So, one afternoon, while straying admittedly too far from my task at the chopping block (dicing fresh rhubarb for rhubarb pie), I found myself wandering the house, knife in hand, apparently seeking out some hidden rhubarb, or some such thing. This long and seemingly aimless search ended at last (surprisingly) in my wife's private bed chambers. Under oath (were I ever to find myself in such a civil bind), I would feel obligated to include in my testimony a brief description of my wife's habit of discarding useless and quite obtrusive items onto the floor of her bedroom (including clothes, suitcases, boxes and books—all manner of item and accessory laid out like an obstacle course), as it sheds, I believe, some light on how I managed to plunge, or rather, trip, knife-first into the bed.

Very much by coincidence, the bed was unoccupied and none were duly slain— but oh, those sheets—those stained and soiled and sinned-upon sheets, they did get a running through, by god! Without love, I gathered the tattered remnants of my wife's beloved bed sheets and, seeing no further use for them, and being myself a bit short on rhubarb, I saw no better course than to include them in my pie. XXL Egyptian cotton bed sheets, it turns out, need only a good dousing of sherry before being sealed under a cinnamon crust and put to bake for more than two hours at a medium heat. Yes, and it came out marvelous, tasting in the end something like almond or arsenic, like a poison you build yourself up against, becoming stronger by every bite until the last of the acid is snuffed out and you are at once full—full up forever. Zero states, in the stomach and the heart and all the rest, full up and empty forever, never again to feel hunger or pain, free to eat now for reasons of your own.

—DERRICK ABLEMAN, *NIGHT TRAIN*

Try again. Fail again. Fail better.
—SAMUEL BECKETT

EXERCISE 90

The Journey
of the Long Sentence

The following exercise came from a conversation with the poet Richard Jackson, who values exercises and always does each exercise with his students. He tells his class to write a poem that is one sentence long. He says the sentence should keep pushing and gain momentum. Even in the midst of suspension and qualification, the sentence has to move forward—not just repeating—but adding new information and achieving new emotional levels to finish on a different emotional note at the end. He says that what goes along with this assignment is the assumption that the sentence should radiate out to embrace more of the world, of the complications surrounding details and events and observations and feelings. Then the details become a part of an intricate set of relationships, giving and taking from that set.

Below is the beginning of the poem, printed with permission, without its line breaks from *Alive All Day,* that Jackson wrote with his class for this exercise:

THE OTHER DAY

I just want to say a few words about the other day, an ordinary day I happen to recall because my daughter has just given me a yellow flower, a buttercup, for no reason, though it was important that other day, that ordinary one when the stones stayed stones and were not symbols for anything else, when the stars made no effort to fill the spaces we see between them, though maybe you remember it differently, a morning when I woke to find my hand had flowered on the breast of my wife, a day so ordinary I happened to notice the old woman across the street, hips so large it's useless to try to describe them, struggle off her sofa to pull down the shade that has separated us ever since, her room as lonely as Keats' room on the Piazza di Spagna where there was hardly any space for words, where I snapped a forbidden photo that later showed nothing of his shadow making its way to a window above Bernini's fountain . . .

For other examples of long sentences intrinsic to a writer's style, turn to the work of William Faulkner, Julio Cortazar, Marcel Proust, and David Foster Wallace, all of whom explore and express continuing action with qualification and complication.

The Exercise

Write a short short story that is only one sentence.

The Objective

To develop a sense of how syntax can qualify, develop, and provide an expansive context for our observations in much the same way the brain does, finding a linear order for what are often simultaneous aspects of an observation.

Student Example

One Day Walk Through the Front Door
It got so the only place I could cry was the freeway since traffic jams and the absence of curves made driving and crying less dangerous, unlike surface streets which scattered the pile of flyers on the passenger seat, jumbling the printed images of my sister's face and frightening me beyond tears with the sight of a life slipping out of reach as I pulled into gas stations, cafés, rest stops, a mad woman slapping flyers on walls, in people's faces, blurting *Have you seen her?* . . . until soon I only made calls from phone booths, avoiding the empty apartment I shared with her, talking to police, friends, reporters, even giving phone interviews so sometimes it was my own voice on the news as I drove, *I just hope she's safe, I want her home,* other times my voice shouted back at the radio, *say her name, don't drop the story, oh Jesus, please,* then I'd cry more and believe how alone I felt, surrounded by hundreds of people encased in tinted-glass worlds that could neatly hide any individual horror, until I could only whisper, *please even just her body,* because I had to know or I'd be stranded in this moment forever and I'd never sleep again, but wait, always wait to see her one day just walk through the front door . . . then, finally, my last hope was to hear it from our priest, but it was the car, detached reporting from that radio on the fifth day: they'd found a body, floating in the bay.
—MOLLY LANZAROTTA, HONORABLE MENTION,
WORLD'S BEST SHORT SHORT STORY CONTEST

I'm just trying to look at something without blinking.
—TONI MORRISON

EXERCISE 91

He Said/She Said—But About What!

This exercise was suggested by Jane Berentson, a former student who found, pinned to her office bulletin board, a restaurant review in the form of "he said/she said." The two "voices" were in total disagreement about the restaurant's quality of food, service, etc. I agreed that the structure had promise—but to make it work as fiction there should be a subtext to what is being discussed.

The Exercise

Write a story that is 250 to 500 words long. Use the structure of alternating voices. *He said:* _____. *She said:* _____. *He said:* _____. *She said:* _____. And so on. Use italics and keep it in paragraph form. The two "characters" should disagree about an issue or subject and their dialogue should have a subtext, an emotional truth that is operating on a deeper and perhaps hidden level. As you will see, the student example, "Without a Second Thought" by a student I met at a writers' conference, is not about misplaced keys.

The Objective

To use a simple structure on which to hang a story.

Student Example

Without a Second Thought

He says: Just put the keys in the same place every time. *She says:* It's not that easy. *He says:* Retrace your steps. *She says:* It's better if I try to remember what I was thinking about. *He says:* Let's start at the front door. *She says:* It was dinner I was thinking about, salmon baked in foil. *He says:* Let's walk to the kitchen. *She says:* I was fumbling with the keys, my hands full of groceries, thinking how old it gets being locked out with you already home. *He says:* It's for security. *She says:* They're still in the deadbolt. *He says:* Every time, just put them on the hook behind the front door, on the counter next to the pile of old bills and letters, on the table next to the photograph from the day we spent at the lake, that time you wouldn't jump in the water because you said there were snakes even though I promised you there weren't. *She says:* The last place I'd think to look is on a hook behind the front door. *He says:* The problem is you don't believe me. It's careless. *She says:* It's a habit.

—Kathleen Blackburn, Published in *Field Guide to Flash Fiction*

EXERCISE 92

Rules of the Game

As we mentioned in the introduction, except for length the short short story doesn't have any rules. But the "rules of a game" and the accoutrements that accompany many games—boards, chessmen, checkers, a dictionary—are good material for the short short story form In this exercise, we want you to write a story that somehow uses a familiar game and its rules.

The Exercise

Go around the class and have each person name a game. Continue doing this, round and round, till you have run out of games. You will be surprised how many games there are that most of us know. Shut this book right now and begin. When you return to this exercise, see how many of the following games the class named: Scrabble, Life, Risk, Poker, Candyland, Parcheesi, Monopoly, Trouble, Clue, Trivial Pursuit, bridge, Dictionary, crossword puzzles, Mousetrap, Othello, Chutes and Ladders, checkers, chess, Sorry, backgammon, hearts, canasta, Go, Boggle, Stratego, mah jong, telephone, and so on.

Next, write a story that uses a game in some way. Are the players playing the game? Is the game writing new rules for itself? Is someone calling Parker Brothers to adjudicate a Monopoly move?

The Objective

To show how rules lend themselves to the freedom of the short short story form.

Student Example

Alfalfa

The fight started with a simple cryptogram in the Sunday edition of the *New York Times:* Find a word with the letter combination XYZXYZX, but things escalated, as they inevitably did, and soon it was no longer a friendly contest to see who could solve the puzzle first but a battle fought tooth and nail across a glass coffee table, the outcome of which would be the surest sign yet of who was smarter, thus settling a furtive rivalry that loomed over their new marriage like a cartoon anvil and had recently intensified thanks to comments such as, Oh come on, my twelve-year-old niece knows Bismarck is the capital of North Dakota, Thirty-five across is harebrained, not "hairbrained," and

Well sure, I used to think existentialism was interesting too, but that was back in high school, and even though they were both educated and believed themselves to be above the things about which most newlyweds bickered, they still found themselves arguing over equally trivial matters—the significance of SAT scores, who had actually read Baudelaire in French, or the proper pronunciation of Nabokov—at the same time they both knew these subjects had little to do with the questions they really wanted to ask, the answers they wanted to hear, so now here they were in the middle of a row over a word game, saying nasty things about each other's parents and threatening to give up on the whole damn marriage, emphasizing each point by pounding the table-top when suddenly the glass surface shattered into a thousand tiny pieces and they were left wondering what just happened, until one of them figured it out.

—TERRY THEUMLING, *StoryQuarterly*

Journalism allows its readers to witness history; fiction gives its readers the opportunity to live it.

—JOHN HERSEY

EXERCISE 93

Ten to One

from Hester Kaplan

Part of writing well is the ability to reduce a story to its linguistic essence, while still allowing for rich and complex ideas and images. Imagination and control meet to create effective fiction. Sometimes less really is more. This exercise is always a hit; thanks to Tracy Boothman Duyck for passing it on to me.

The Exercise

Write a complete story in fifty-five words. Your first sentence should have ten words, your second nine, your third eight, and so on until your final sentence consists of a single word.

The Objective

To illustrate that writing's power can often be found in its economy; that precision can lead to surprisingly original results.

Student Example

Ophelia
Tonight I lost my heart to the actress playing Ophelia.
I waited to meet her by the stage door.
She was the last one to come out.
I told her I was in love.
It happens every night, she said.
Let me have your playbill.
To Fred. Love, Ophelia.
She walked away.
Toward Broadway.
Alone.

—FRED MAGEE

237

EXERCISE 94

Make a List

Do you keep a list? A grocery list? A "to-do" list? a list of errands to run, people to call, letters to write, items to pack, books you've read, places you've lived? Almost everyone at some time or other resorts to a list. It might be a list to organize one's day or chores, or a list that is meant to provide you with information about yourself: women you have loved; men you have left; friends who are no longer friends; or excuses you have used, as in Antonia Clark's short short story, "Excuses I Have Already Used" on page 274. One can almost imagine the "protagonist" making up the list in Gregory Burnham's superb story, "Subtotals," from *Flash Fiction*. Interesting correspondences: "Number of dogs: 1. Number of cats: 7." All subtotals, because of course the protagonist is still counting. Then there are the books that are themselves lists: Alexander Theroux's *The Primary Colors* and John Mitchell's *Euphonics: A Poet's Dictionary of Sounds*.

The Exercise

Write a story about a list or write a story that is a list. The list must tell us something about the person making the list, and have an organic structure of its own.

The Objective

To be able to use an ordinary list as a microcosm of your character's life.

Student Examples

List Within a Story

". . . or I'll be some kind of super hero, straight out of the comic books, and my superpower, be it death, breath, magma vomit, hypnosehair, or telekinetic control over mops, pasta, curtains, dishwashers, applesauce, doorknobs, earlobes, comic books, burlap, fog, and monkeys, will allow the elderly and timid to walk through even the toughest neighborhoods with a strut of confidence . . ."

—BRIAN RUUSKA

Story

"Love and Other Catastrophes: A Mix Tape"

"All By Myself" (Eric Carmen). "Looking for Love" (Lou Reed). "I Wanna Dance With Somebody" (Whitney Houston). "Let's Dance" (David Bowie). "Let's Kiss" (Beat

Happening). "Let's Talk About Sex" (Salt N' Pepa). "Like A Virgin" (Madonna). "We've Only Just Begun" (The Carpenters). "I Wanna Be Your Boyfriend" (The Ramones). "I'll Tumble 4 Ya" (Culture Club). "Head Over Heels" (The Go-Go's). "Nothing Compares To You" (Sinéad O'Connor). "My Girl" (The Temptations). "Could This Be Love?" (Bob Marley). "Love and Marriage" (Frank Sinatra). "White Wedding" (Billy Idol). "Stuck in the Middle with You" (Steelers Wheel). "Tempted" (The Squeeze). "There Goes My Baby" (The Drifters). "What's Going On?" (Marvin Gaye). "Where Did You Sleep Last Night?" (Leadbelly). "Whose Bed Have Your Boots Been Under?" (Shania Twain). "Jealous Guy" (John Lennon). "Your Cheatin' Heart" (Tammy Wynette). "Shot Through the Heart" (Bon Jovi). "Don't Go Breaking My Heart" (Elton John and Kiki Dee). "My Achy Breaky Heart" (Billy Ray Cyrus). "Heartbreak Hotel" (Elvis Presley). "Stop, In the Name of Love" (The Supremes). "Try a Little Tenderness" (Otis Redding). "Try (Just a Little Bit Harder)" (Janis Joplin). "All Apologies" (Nirvana). "Hanging on the Telephone" (Blondie). "I Just Called to Say I Love You" (Stevie Wonder). "Love Will Keep Us Together" (Captain and Tennille). "Let's Stay Together" (Al Green). "It Ain't Over 'Till It's Over" (Lenny Kravitz). "What's Love Got To Do With It?" (Tina Turner). "You Don't Bring Me Flowers Anymore" (Barbara Streisand and Neil Diamond). "I Wish You Wouldn't Say That" (Talking Heads). "You're So Vain" (Carly Simon). "Love is a Battlefield" (Pat Benatar). "Heaven Knows I'm Miserable Now" (The Smiths). "Can't Get No Satisfaction" (Rolling Stones). "Must Have Been Love (But It's Over Now)" (Roxette). "Breaking Up is Hard to Do" (Neil Sedaka). "I Will Survive" (Gloria Gaynor). "Hit the Road, Jack" (Mary McCaslin and Jim Ringer). "These Boots Were Made for Walking" (Nancy Sinatra). " All Out of Love" (Air Supply). "All By Myself" (Eric Carmen).

—AMANDA HOLZER, *STORYQUARTERLY, BEST AMERICAN NON-REQUIRED READING 2004*

EXERCISE 95

Questions. Some Answers

Sometimes we ask a question when we already know the answer. Other times we ask a question we do not know the answer to—and never will. Turn to page 283 and read "How Could a Mother?" by Bruce Holland Rogers to experience a story that is all questions. Note how we can deduce the two characters involved, the setting, the situation, and what the answers are to many of the questions as they build on one another, while some of the questions seem meant for the narrator and become personal to the narrator's own life. This exercise was created by writer and teacher Nina Schneider.

Exercise

Come up with a situation in which one person is asking questions of another person. The second person does not answer in the story, though the first person sometimes continues on as if the question has been answered. As the story moves toward its conclusion, several of the last questions should reveal something of the narrator's own emotional landscape.

The Objective

Questions are at the core of fiction. Why? And as the narrator asks, "Why not?" Learn to supply your characters with questions for each other—and especially for themselves. Questions are more important than answers.

Student Example

Where Does the Mind Go?
Can we talk in the hall? It's a little too much in here, don't you think? All these flowers—who even sends them? Do you find it hard to think over the constant beeping? Isn't it like a little hammer beating into your brain after a while? Is he going to be okay alone?

Is he as bad as he looks? Does he look worse than the other people in the ICU? Worse than anyone else you've seen? All the breaks and bruises on his face, are they going to heal? Will he look like he did before? Do you need me to bring in a picture? The most recent we have is from his junior prom, is that all right? God, why can't I stop talking? There's nothing to be nervous about, right? Will you please tell me I don't have anything to be nervous about?

The tests? How long is he going to last? Days? Months? Years? Could he go at any second? What does that mean? Where is that? What about the rest of his brain? Is there anything there? What does that mean for the rest of his body? Can you just tell me straight? Will you use words I can understand?

What do you mean there isn't anything else? At all? Have you looked hard enough? Can you look again? Aren't there other tests? These things change sometimes, right? You've seen miracles around here, right? How many of these patients walk out of here two weeks later? Haven't you seen that before?

Now? Can't we wait and see? Doesn't he still have a little part of his brain? A little is all you need, right? It's not like he used it a whole lot before, right?

Oh, God, why am I making jokes?

I never liked that he rode that bike did you know that? I'd tell him be could get a better part-time job, maybe not killing himself to deliver goddamn packages, and he'd say, "What other job lets you fly like this?" Did he think he was flying when he got hit? Could you see that in the CAT scan? What did you see in there? Is it all broken? Are there parts that are still intact? His sense of smell? His first Christmas? Did you see me? Would he want me to do this?

Can he hear anything? Can he hear my voice out here?

Are you sure that's just it? Isn't there something still there? He's still alive somewhere in there, right? Isn't that what the beeping means? What do you mean, these machines are keeping him alive? What kind of machine can do that? Is there really a plug? Am I the one who does it?

—ANNIE CARDI, PUBLISHED IN *VESTAL REVIEW*

EXERCISE 96

How to . . .

How to do what? you might ask. Well, anything. Think of all the articles written about how to grow herbs indoors, how to lose weight, how to train a dog, how to write a will, how to improve your golf game, tennis serve, swimming stroke, sales techniques, how to—you fill in the blank. But better yet, write a story that uses the language of "how to" as part of the story. The inspiration for this exercise came from the writer Nancy Zafris, and was passed along via Kit Irwin to Toni Clark, who wrote a hilarious story from the point of view of a food photographer titled "How to Shoot a Tomato."

The Exercise

Write a story that is about a character learning how to do something. Or telling someone else how to do it. Make the directions particular to the character and the task at hand—sometimes an inadvertent lesson, such as in Lee Harrington's "How to Become a Country-Western Singer," below.

The Objective

To use the stuff of everyday instruction as the basis for a story. It can be in the story—or the story itself.

Student Example

How to Become a Country-Western Singer
First your girlfriend has to move out, taking everything from the Lovett albums to the leftover beans-and-franks. Then you rush to your secret letter drawer; sure enough, the latest from Dolly-Sue are missing. Minutes later, snow begins to fall. Ice collects on the gutters and eaves. At midnight, black water seeps through the ceiling and onto your white shag rug. Your girlfriend calls while you're on your knees, positioning pots and pans beneath the drips. "You cheat too much," she says. "You're lazy and selfish and you never make me laugh."

   You stand and cough and tell her marriage could change all that.

   "Well, what about those goddamn extension cords?" she says.

   "Extension cords?"

   On the radio, DJ Charles Francis says something about the coldest winter in forty years.

"Can't you string them behind furniture like normal people?" she says. "Not straight across the floor?" She screams something about landmines and subconscious sabotage and slams down the phone.

You step over a few of these cords: bass-amp, floor lamp, mike. Apparently they represent some major character flaw. You try to read them like lifelines on a palm. *Like lifelines on a palm!*

There's a song in this, you tell yourself, and open a bottle of rum. You sit on the rug and listen; if you listen, the music will come.

The popcorn bowl clacks and the mini-wok thwacks. The ice in your glass makes a tinkly-wind-chime sound. But the rhythm needs work. You'll try less ice, more rum. Then you'll add some pathetic lyrics. Later, when the bottle's empty, you can lie among the extension cords and compare the sound of water hitting skin. Maybe it will thud like a broken heart.

—Lee Harrington, Finalist, Best Short Short Story Contest

I think this whole division about realism and magical realism is pointless. Hasn't literature always been magical realism—whether you're talking about the Bible or Kafka? In fact, when you are writing realism—isn't that a kind of "magical realism" in a way? They are words on a page—how real is that. The divisions are arbitrary. I've always been interested in the possibilities underneath the everyday. That's what makes writing fascinating to me—to think about what could be rather than what is. The natural world is the most magical thing of all. Think about death—how hard is that to get your mind around: one minute a person is there and then—where did they go?

—Alice Hoffman

EXERCISE 97

Nanofictions

How short can a story be and still be engaging as a "story?" That was an issue that came up when our student, Michael Hennesey, turned in an exercise on "Nanofiction" for a class assignment. We all know the famous Hemingway story that goes: For sale: Baby shoes. Never worn. Michael's exercise instructed the writer to write five nanofictions—stories that are only three sentences long. When we assigned this exercise to our students, they were also told to put them in an artist's "book." The results were amazing varied and astonishing. One student used a 78 record he'd recorded; another student did a Jacob's ladder; and another used a deck of cards for their nanofictions.

Exercise

Write five very short-short stories—nanofictions. Each should be three sentences long. The five can be connected by character or place or anything, really, though they needn't be.

Objective

To learn how to move immediately to a troubled situation and be able to identify the small details of drama.

Student Examples

Like a Potato or a Turnip

"I can't be late," she said, "or I'll turn into a pumpkin." But I couldn't imagine her in a fairy tale; not with her neatly tied shoelaces, each loop a perfect bunny's ear, and her hands smelling like antibacterial soap. No, she'd probably turn into something much more practical and less, well, *orange*.

—Elisabeth Price

Forgive Me

I'm so tired that even in my dreams I fall asleep before I have a chance to get your clothes off. Somehow, sometime, I promise I'll make it up to you.

—Michael S. Hennessey

From Mrs. Charles Hansone, Two Weeks After Her Seventeenth Birthday, 1947

We're writing to announce that Charlie and I have returned from our trip to Baltimore, which I realize probably struck you all as a bit abrupt. There will be no reception or ceremony. We expect no gifts, as Charlie and I have been planning this for three years, so I think we're all set.

—BRIDGET PELKIE

The Neighbors Who Don't Wave

"Yankees?" I asked cousin Jerry.

"I wasn't going to say it," he said, juicing an orange with his knife for me to suck on, "but I believe it."

—MEGAN BEDFORD

Over Drinks

Jocelyn told us she'd had an affair with her garbage man. He was great with his tongue, she said, but she broke it off because he wouldn't use his hands.

—VANESSA CARLISLE

from Mrs. Charles Hansome, Two Weeks After Her Seventeenth Birthday, 1997

We're writing to announce that Charlie and I have returned from our trip to Baltimore, which I realize probably struck you all as a bit abrupt. There will be no reception or ceremony. We expect no gifts, as Charlie and I have been planning this for three years, so I think we're all set.

—Robert Parke

The Neighbors Who Don't Wave

"Yankees?" I asked cousin Jerry.

"I wasn't going to say it," he said, juicing an orange with his knife for me to suck on, "but I believe it."

—Megan Bedford

Over Drinks

Jocelyn told us she'd had an affair with her garbage man. He was great with his tongue, she said, but she broke it off because he wouldn't use his hands.

—Vanessa Carlisle

PART TWELVE

Learning from the Greats

Everywhere I've been a poet has been there first.

—Freud

The great guides were the books I discovered in the Johns Hopkins library, where my student job was to file books away. One was more or less encouraged to take a cart of books and go back into the stacks and not come out for seven or eight hours. So I read what I was filing. My great teachers (the best thing that can happen to a writer) were Scheherazade, Homer, Virgil, and Boccaccio; also the great Sanskrit taletellers. I was impressed forever with the width as well as the depth of literature. . . .

—John Barth

We hope this book will take you in two directions: first, into your own well of inspiration, your own store of forgotten or overlooked material, and into your own writing and, second, back to the greats who are your true teachers.

One of these teachers, F. Scott Fitzgerald, names his own teachers in the following passage:

> By style, I mean color. . . . I want to be able to do anything with words: handle slashing, flaming descriptions like Wells, and use the paradox with the clarity of Samuel Butler, the breadth of Bernard Shaw and the wit of Oscar Wilde, I want to do the wide sultry heavens of Conrad, the rolled gold sundowns and crazy-quilt skies of Hichens and Kipling as well as the pastelle [*sic*] dawns and twilights of Chesterton. All that is by way of example. As a matter of fact I am a professional literary thief, hot after the best methods of every writer in my generation.

In a letter Fitzgerald again pays homage to a "teacher." He says, "The motif of the 'dying fall' [in *Tender Is the Night*] was absolutely deliberate and did not come from the diminution of vitality but from a definite plan. That particular trick is one that Ernest Hemingway and I worked out—probably from Conrad's preface to *The Nigger* [*of the Narcissus*]." Madison Smartt Bell echoes this sense of learning tricks from a master in his dedication for *The Washington Square Ensemble*. He says, "This book is dedicated to the long patience of my parents with a tip of the trick hat to George Garrett."

The exercises in this next section are meant to show you how to read for inspiration and instruction. Study the letters and journals of writers to discover how they grappled with problems you will encounter in your own fiction. For example, Flaubert worried about the "lack of action" in *Madame Bovary*. In a letter to Louise Colet he says, "The psychological development of my characters is giving me a lot of trouble; and everything, in this novel, depends on it." And he immediately comes up with the solution, "for in my opinion, ideas can be as entertaining as actions, but in order to be so they must flow one from the other like a series of cascades, carrying the reader along midst the throbbing of sentences and the seething of metaphors."

And read what writers say about writing, for example, John Barth's *Lost in the Funhouse*, Elizabeth Bowen's *Collected Impressions*, Raymond Carver's *Fires*, Annie Dillard's *Living by Fiction* and *The Writing Life*, John Gardner's *The Art of Fiction* and *Becoming a Novelist*, E. M. Forster's *Aspects of the Novel*, William Gass's *On Being Blue*, Henry James's prefaces to his novels, Flannery O'Connor's *Mystery and Manners*, Eudora Welty's *The Eye of the Story*, and Virginia Woolf's *A Room of One's Own*, among others. And now on to our exercises for learning from the greats.

The important thing for a writer is to get to your desk before you do.
—HERB GARDNER

EXERCISE 98

Finding Inspiration in Other Sources—Poetry, Nonfiction, Etc.

A writer is someone who reads. We recommend that you read the letters and notebooks of writers, biographies and autobiographies, plays and poetry, history and religion. Reading for writers has always engendered a cross-pollination of ideas and forms. For the writer, everything is a possible source for an epigraph, a title, a story, a novel.

Following are some well-chosen epigraphs.

Joseph Conrad, *Nostromo*
So foul a day clears not without a storm.

—SHAKESPEARE, *KING JOHN*

Joseph Conrad, *Lord Jim*
It is certain my Conviction gains infinitely, the moment another soul will believe in it.

—NOVALIS

Charles Baxter, *First Light*
Life can only be understood backwards; but it must be lived forwards.

—SØREN KIERKEGAARD

Arundhati Roy, *The God of Small Things*
Never again will a single story be told as though it's the only one.

—JOHN BERGER

John Hawkes, *The Blood Oranges*
Is there then any terrestrial paradise where, amidst the whispering of the olive-leaves, people can be with whom they like and have what they like and take their ease in shadows and in coolness?

—FORD MADOX FORD, *THE GOOD SOLDIER*

Margot Livesey, *Homework*
. . . it is children really, perhaps because so much is forbidden to them, who understand from within the nature of crime.

—RENATA ADLER, *PITCH DARK*

249

James Alan McPherson, *Elbow Room*
> I don't know which way I'm travelin'—
>> Far or near,
> All I knows fo' certain is
>> I *cain't* stay *here*.

—STERLING A. BROWN, "LONG GONE"

Nadine Gordimer, *Burger's Daughter*
> I am the place in which something has occurred.

—CLAUDE LÉVI-STRAUSS

Joyce Carol Oates, *Them*
> . . . because we are poor
> Shall we be vicious?

—JOHN WEBSTER, *THE WHITE DEVIL*

Tim O'Brien, *Going After Cacciato*
> Soldiers are dreamers.

—SIEGFRIED SASSOON

Amy Hempel, *Reasons to Live*
> Because grief unites us,
> like the locked antlers of moose
> who die on their knees in pairs.

—WILLIAM MATTHEWS

T. Coraghessan Boyle, *If the River Was Whiskey*
> You know that the best you can expect is to avoid the worst.

—ITALO CALVINO, *IF ON A WINTER'S NIGHT A TRAVELER*

One final example: the "Etymology" and "extracts" preceding the first chapter of Herman Melville's novel *Moby Dick*. In them, Melville quotes from Hakluyt, *Genesis*, Holland's *Plutarch's Morals*, Rabelais, *King Henry*, *Hamlet*, *Paradise Lost*, Thomas Jefferson's *Whale Memorial to the French minister in 1778*, Falconer's *Shipwreck*, Hawthorne's *Twice Told Tales*, and *Whale Song*, among others.

The Exercise

Read widely for inspiration and then use an original text as an epigraph for your own story or novel. For example, think of Stanley Kunitz's wonderful line: "The thing that eats the heart is mostly heart." This would make a superb epigraph to a story collection or novel titled *Mostly Heart*. Begin a story with this line in mind. Or write a story that illustrates this line from John le Carré's *Tinker, Tailor, Soldier, Spy*: "There are moments that are made up of too much stuff for them to be lived at the time they occur."

Choose several of your favorite poems and reread them with an eye toward finding a title or using a line as an epigraph to a story. Or choose a sentence from an essay or popular song.

Read, read, read. Then write, write, write. Sometimes in reverse order.

The Objective

To absorb what we read in a way that allows it to spark our own creativity, to use it as inspiration for our own writing. To build on what has gone before.

We're supposed to be able to get into other skins. We're supposed to be able to render experiences not our own and warrant times and places we haven't seen. That's one justification for art, isn't it—to distribute the suffering? Writing teachers invariably tell students Write about what you know. That's, of course, what you have to do, but on the other hand, how do you know what you know until you've written it? Writing is knowing. What did Kafka know? The insurance business? So that kind of advice is foolish because it presumes that you have to go out to a war to be able to do war. Well, some do and some don't. I've had very little experience in my life. In fact, I try to avoid experience if I can. Most experience is bad.

—E. L. DOCTOROW, *THE WRITER'S CHAPBOOK*

The Sky's the Limit:
Homage to Kafka
and García Márquez
from Christopher Noël

In a *Paris Review* interview, Gabriel García Márquez says,

> At the university in Bogotá, I started making new friends and acquaintances, who introduced me to contemporary writers. One night a friend lent me a book of short stories by Franz Kafka. I went back to the pension where I was staying and began to read *The Metamorphosis*. The first line almost knocked me off the bed. I was so surprised. The first line reads, "As Gregor Samsa awoke that morning from uneasy dreams he found himself transformed in his bed into a gigantic insect. . . ." When I read the line I thought to myself that I didn't know anyone was allowed to write things like that. If I had known, I would have started writing a long time ago. So I immediately started writing.

The Exercise

For inspiration, read Kafka's story, or perhaps García Márquez's "A Very Old Man with Enormous Wings." Then, if you are part of a group, each member should write a fantastical first line and pass it to the left (or right). Each person, after receiving a first line from her neighbor, should then try to make good on its implicit riches, to open up a world from this seed, one that is different from the everyday world but nonetheless full of concrete detail and clear and consistent qualities, rules of being.

Next, write a story of your own.

The Objective

To loosen up your thinking, to countenance a greater range of possibilities, and to see that sometimes even the most apparently frivolous or ludicrous notions, completely implausible even for the slanted implausibility that writers use, can turn out to be just the ticket. What's strange can be made to seem necessary in a story; you can work to solidify the strangeness if, while you're writing, you keep a sort of grim faith at those pivotal moments—whether the first line or the third chapter or the final paragraph—when it seems you are betraying or trivializing your authentic vision of the world.

Student Examples

I scream each time I see that the house is surrounded, and I know this makes Carmen's patience wavery, like the heat mirages. Carmen has always lived in this desert and tells me that it is the normal way for Joshua trees to behave. But how am I to get used to them, all standing there with their arms raised each time I pass the window and forget not to look out. The Joshua trees are moving closer every day, and to me this is ominous, Carmen or no Carmen.

This house, this desert, are supposed to be for my health. Carmen, too, is supposed to be for my health. The doctor in Boston told my son so. Warm climate, a companion, and the old lady will be all set. Well, that doctor didn't know about the ways of the desert. I watch as the Joshua trees group and regroup like some stunted army, never quite making up their minds that they are going to advance. Bradford gets upset on the phone if I talk about the Joshua trees, how they are preparing for some sort of final march. Carmen can see it in the moon, although I don't tell Bradford this lest he think Carmen a bad influence.

—MOLLY LANZAROTTA, "RUNNING WITH THE JOSHUA TREE"

When Rene returned from the army, I felt at first that we should not contradict him, although the letter that had come weeks before clearly stated he was dead.

And sure enough, my cousin Rene did not at all wish to discuss the manner of his dying, which had been described in great detail in the letter from his friend in the army, how he had been dismembered by the rebels in the mountains, how he'd been skinned and scalped, his eyes gouged out and any number of things, to the point that there was nothing left to send home of him, nothing for us to mourn but the letter. I was practiced at this, this sudden grief with no ceremony, and wondered whether soon I would be the last one of this family, too, just one young girl left from so many.

And then Rene wandered in on a night that was gray with the glow of distant explosions, gray himself, covered with the dirt of the mountains and the dust of the desert our town has become. Little Yolanda shrieked when he pulled back the burlap we'd hung over the door of our collapsing home, and, of course, none of us could finish our meal. Rene sat down and ate everything on each of our plates, while his brother Evelio shouted, paced the room and questioned him, and his mother, Luisa, wept and kissed him and pulled on her rosary until it snapped, showering us all with tiny black beads. It seemed that they had cut the voice out of Rene as well, when they killed him, because he did not want to talk at all.

—MOLLY LANZAROTTA, "THE DEATH OF RENE PAZ,"
FROM *CAROLINA QUARTERLY*

If it hadn't been for my long serpentine tail, I wouldn't have lost my job as a cabdriver. It wasn't that management objected so much, God knows good help is hard to find these days, but eventually passengers complained, especially when I became agitated, say, in heavy traffic and whipped my tail into the backseat. I even struck a passenger once, but not on purpose or forcefully, and no permanent damage was done. I apologized afterward. I didn't get many tips.

I tried to make a virtue of my tail by decorating it on holidays, tying bright ribbons around its circumference until it looked like a barber pole, or the lance of a medieval knight. Things seemed to be working, at least until that incident with the motorcycle cop.

"Believe me, Melvin, it's not you," the dispatcher said. "Well, actually, it is you, in a way. But it's not personal," he pleaded, larding his voice with concern to avoid a class action suit. "Insurance is eating me up, man. That pedestrian you hit the other day . . ."

"I can explain that. I was giving a left turn signal . . ."

"Melvin, go to a doctor. Get it taken off. You're a good driver. You got a future."

"But it's part of me. It kind of gives me something to lean against."

He shrugged his shoulders toward the picture of the near-naked woman embracing a tire on the Parts Pups calendar on the wall. "He likes it," he said, as if to her. Then he looked at me. "Okay, Mel, you like it. You live with it. But not here."

And so I was out of a job.

—GENE LANGSTON, "FIRED"

I read Shakespeare directly I have finished writing. When my mind is agape and redhot. Then it is astonishing. I never yet knew how amazing his stretch and speed and word coining power is, until I felt it utterly outpace and outrace my own, seeming to start equal and then I see him draw ahead and to things I could not in my wildest tumult and utmost press of mind imagine.

—VIRGINIA WOOLF, *A WRITER'S DIARY*

EXERCISE 100

Learning from the Greats

Every writer is a reader moved to emulation.

—SAUL BELLOW

Most writers can look back and name the books that seemed to fling open doors for them, books that made them want to go to the typewriter and begin to write one word after another. When asked if one writer had influenced her more than others, Joan Didion replied:

> I always say Hemingway, because he taught me how sentences worked. When I was fifteen or sixteen I would type out his stories to learn how sentences worked. . . . A few years ago when I was teaching a course at Berkeley I reread *A Farewell to Arms* and fell right back into those sentences. I mean they're perfect sentences. Very direct sentences, smooth rivers, clear water over granite, no sinkholes.

While teaching at several writing conferences, we noticed that fiction writers tend to remember what other writers have said about writing—and said eloquently—while poets memorized the poem itself. "Not memorized," the poet Christopher Merrill says, "Commit to heart"—something he requires of all his students. The style and cadences of the Bible verses Abraham Lincoln learned as a boy emerged in his "Gettysburg Address."

The Exercise

Choose a writer you admire, one who has withstood the test of time. Type out that writer's stories or several chapters from a novel. Try to analyze how the sentences work, how their vocabulary differs from your own, how the structure of the story emerges from the language. Feel in your fingers what is different about that prose.

Then, commit your favorite passages to heart.

Next, in a story or novel by the writer you admire, find a place between two sentences that seems like a "crack" that could be "opened up." Next, write your own paragraph or scene and insert it into this place. Now read the entire story including your addition.

The Objective

To understand just how much you need to know to really understand another person's story and how it works—and then add to it. The answer: everything—characterization, plot, tone, style, etc.

Student Examples

Two consecutive sentences from "A Very Old Man with Enormous Wings," by Gabriel García Márquez:

> The Angel was no less stand-offish with him than with other mortals, but he tolerated the most ingenious infamies with the patience of a dog who had no illusions. They both came down with chicken pox at the same time.

A student inserted the following addition between the above two sentences.

The child hung dried crabs and lizards off the fallen Angel's wings, climbed onto his back to grasp the crow feathers in his tiny hands. The child tried to pull the enormous wing wide, imagining they were flying as the chickens ticked his muddy toes. He thought of the Angel as a great, broken doll and spent hours tying colored rags around his dried fig of a head, hanging rosaries around his neck and painting the crevices of his face with soot and red earth, the Angel all the while mumbling in his befuddled sailor's dialect.

When the wise neighbor woman heard words of the Angel's language coming out of the child's mouth, she shook her head and threw more mothballs into the chicken coop. She told Elisenda, "Your child will grow wings or be carried off. He will disappear into the heavens." For a while, Elisenda tried to keep the child in the garden and Pelayo repaired the broken wires of the chicken coop. But the child continued to play on the other side of the wire and the Angel remained so inert that Elisenda ceased to believe it was the Angel's tongue her child spoke at all, but his own made up child's language. Soon the child was once again playing inside the coop, flying on the back of the old man.

—MOLLY LANZAROTTA

Two consecutive sentences from *Lost in the Funhouse,* by John Barth:

> Ambrose's former archenemy.
> Shortly after the mirror room he'd groped along a musty corridor, his heart already misgiving him at the absence of phosphorescent arrows and other signs.

One student inserted this between the above two sentences.

Ambrose wanders aimlessly, loses sight of Peter as Magda chases him beyond the mirrors, into the darkness of the next room. Their laughter echoes and he cannot tell the direction from which it comes. He will not call out to them. He is not lost yet. He will find his way out on his own. The smudges of hand prints on the mirrors reassure Ambrose that he is not the only one to follow this path through the funhouse. In one of the reflections, his arm is around the waist of an exquisite young woman with a figure unusually well developed for her age. He is taller, wearing a sailor's uniform. The image moves away, but Ambrose remains. Glass. *Not a mirror.* Sentence fragments can be used to emphasize discoveries or thoughts that suddenly occur to a character. The point is communicated to the reader without saying "he thought . . ." The fragmented thought may be used in combination with italics to create a feeling of urgency. Ambrose tries creating a path parallel to the one taken by the others but is constantly forced to change direction as the mirrors obscure his goal. At an unordained moment he reaches out to touch what he thinks is another mirror, but turns out in fact to be a passageway.

—ZAREH ARTINIAN

> *Whenever I sit down to write and can't think of anything to say, I write my name—W. Somerset Maugham—over and over again until something happens.*
>
> —W. SOMERSET MAUGHAM

EXERCISE 101

Borrowing Characters

There's no gap that prose cannot bridge.

—HENRY JAMES

Authors have been borrowing characters from other authors' works for years. Some well-known examples are Jean Rhys's wonderful novel *Wide Sargasso Sea,* which provides an account of the early life of Mrs. Rochester, the wife of Mr. Rochester in Charlotte Brontë's *Jane Eyre.* George Macdonald Fraser uses Tom Brown and Flashman from Thomas Hughes's novel, *Tom Brown's School Days.* And there have been any number of continuations of the adventures of Sherlock Holmes; Nicholas Meyer's *The Seven Percent Solution,* Rick Boyer's *The Giant Rat of Sumatra,* and Sena Jeter Nasland's *Sherlock in Love* are three of the best. John Gardner wrote a novel titled *Grendel* about the beast in *Beowulf.* Joseph Heller brought King David once again to life in *God Knows.* Mark Twain also turned to the Bible for *The Diary of Adam and Eve.* Playwright Tom Stoppard borrowed characters from Shakespeare's *Hamlet* for *Rosencrantz and Guildenstern Are Dead. Ahab's Wife,* by Sena Jeter Nasland, begins with this tantalizing sentence: "Captain Ahab was neither my first husband nor my last." David Foster Wallace takes on Lyndon Baines Johnson in "LBJ." In Kafka's short short story "The Truth about Sancho Panza," we learn that Don Quixote was really Panza's demon, whom he called Don Quixote, and then followed "on his crusades, perhaps out of a sense of responsibility, and had of them a great and edifying entertainment to the end of his days."

The Exercise

Take an antagonist or a minor character from a story or novel by someone else—a character who has always intrigued you. Make that person the protagonist in a scene or story of your own. For example, what would Allie Fox's wife say if she were to tell her version of Paul Theroux's *Mosquito Coast,* or write a story about their courtship? And what would Rabbit's illegitimate daughter, from Updike's *Rabbit* novels, say if she could tell her story?

The Objective

To enter into the imaginative world of another writer, to understand that particular world, and to build from it.

EXERCISE 102

What Keeps You Reading?

In *The Eye of the Story,* Eudora Welty writes, "Learning to write may be part of learning to read. For all I know, writing comes out of a superior devotion to reading."

Part of the apprenticeship of being a successful writer is learning to read like a writer, discovering how a particular story catches your attention and keeps you involved right straight through to the end.

The Exercise

Halfway through a story ask yourself several questions: What do I care about? What has been set in motion that I want to see completed? Where is the writer taking me? Then, finish reading the story and see how well the writer met the expectations that she raised for you.

The Objective

To illustrate how the best stories and novels set up situations that are resolved by the time you finish the story or close the book. To learn how to arouse the reader's curiosity or create expectations in the first half of your story or novel, and then to decide to what degree you should feel obliged to meet those expectations.

Mary McCarthy once lost the only manuscript copy of a novel. Interviewer Bob Cromie said to her, "But it's your novel, you can write it again." McCarthy replied, "Oh, I couldn't do that—I know how it ends."

The Literary Scene Circa 1893, 1929, 1948, or . . .?

from George Garrett

The year 1929 saw the publication of major books (in the present view of things) by Faulkner, Fitzgerald, Thomas Wolfe, and others. The Pulitzer Prize, and the lion's share of review space, went to Oliver LaFarge for *Laughing Boy*. Another example: Throughout the 1920s one of the most productive and interesting American novelists, widely reviewed and praised, was Joseph Hergesheimer. One of the very few reviews of a work of fiction by the young William Faulkner was devoted to Hergesheimer and indicates not only that Faulkner took his work very seriously, but also that Hergesheimer influenced Faulkner's own art.

The Exercise

You are given (or draw out of a hat) a year, say, 1929. You are responsible for knowing the literary history of this year as it saw itself. That is, on your honor you do not use books or histories to learn about the literary scene in 1929. You use only the newspapers and magazines of that year. In due time you report on that year to the rest of us. (To make it a bit more interesting, the student who chose 1929 might do a book report on LaFarge's *Laughing Boy*, discovering thereby that it is an excellent novel.)

The Objective

Year after year, to your surprise and to ours, you will report on all kinds of once-famous writers none of us has ever heard of. You will discover that many now-acclaimed masters were ignored or given short shrift in their own time. Thus learn a basic truth—that they did not know or accurately judge their own era and neither can we. It follows that the writer's business is to write. Reputation, or the lack of it, is out of your hands. Persevere. Endure. Maybe prevail.

PART THIRTEEN

Notebooks, Journals, and Memory

Creative wrong memory is a source of art.

—Marcel Proust

As writers, we lead double lives. We live in the world as the people we are. But we also live in the world as writer/observers ready to see a story anywhere, to note a detail that simply couldn't be made up, to record an overheard line of dialogue, to borrow the stories of family and friends, to explore our enemies' points of view, and to sift through memory—did we really have a happy childhood? A writer's notebooks and journals are a testimony to this double life. As Socrates said, "The unexamined life is not worth living." For an illuminating essay on the intersection of autobiography and fiction, rendered with insight and humor, read Stephen Dunn's "Truth: A Memoir," from *Walking Light*.

Journals and notebooks function in several ways. One writer may use them as a repository for the raw material for fiction that he will turn to for inspiration. Another writer may keep a notebook but never look at what he writes again—for him, the act of selecting and writing something down was the valuable exercise, keeping his writer's ear and eye in shape. And yet another writer may use her journal for deepening stories she's already written.

Alexandra Johnson has written eloquently on the practicality and art of keeping a journal in her book *Leaving a Trace: The Art of Transforming a Life into Stories*. Johnson talks of her own experience in keeping a journal, how a museum stub "sparked a sketch about a summer in Italy when I first met someone who lent me an apartment." She identifies patterns hidden in a journal's pages, speaks to the freedom that might come from sharing a journal with a friend or a writing group, and provides exercises for beginning a journal or using the material that has been accumulating unexamined, unused, in your journal for years. In the final pages, Johnson pays tribute to her

261

grandmother who taught her "how to make connections. How to listen. How to observe the world. The real gift she was giving me, though, was the legacy of the imagination, of knowing how to transform stubborn facts into stories, how to recognize that the story not told is often the most interesting one. How every story—and life—is of value." *Leaving a Trace* is a book for every writer's shelf.

A cartoon by William Hamilton speaks to this point. A harassed-looking young woman is seated at a desk, holding several manuscript pages. Her typewriter has been pushed to one side, as she says into the phone, "Frances, can I get back to you? Gordon ran away with the babysitter and I'm trying to see if there's a short story in it." Of course there's a story in it, probably more than one, but now might be a little soon to begin writing about Gordon's flight. Hamilton's young woman needs to take to heart what Wordsworth said about poetry, that it is "emotion recollected in tranquility."

What this young woman should do, since she is determined to find a story, is jot down in a notebook or journal a few details that she doesn't want to lose. Perhaps Gordon left an odd note? Or one of the children asked if Gordon, who had recently lost his Wall Street job, was going to start a babysitting business. Or perhaps the harassed wife discovered she was secretly delighted that Gordon was gone? When she returns to this material and her notes at a later time, she might want to tell the story from Gordon's point of view—a story about a man who leaves his wife because he knows that she will someday leave him. Or from the babysitter's point of view—a story about a babysitter who feels sorry for a husband whose wife begins typing the minute he gets home from work.

Our own exercises are designed to show you some of the possibilities and rewards of keeping a journal or notebook. It is the perfect place to jot down that odd name you found on a program—"Buck Gash"—a name you'll never legally be able to use, but one you want to remember. Or to make a list of all the places you've ever lived. But always be true to your self. In a letter to a Radcliffe student, F. Scott Fitzgerald wrote of the price she must pay for aspiring to be a professional writer:

> You've got to sell your heart, your strongest reactions, not the little minor things that only touch you lightly, the little experiences that you might tell at dinner. This is especially true when you begin to write, when you have not yet developed the tricks of interesting people on paper, when you have none of the technique which it takes time to learn. When, in short, you have only your emotions to sell.

Too many writers avoid their own strongest feelings and stories because they are afraid of them, or because they are afraid of being sentimental. Yet these are the very things that will make beginning work ring true and affect us. Your stories have to matter to you the writer before they can matter to the reader; your story has to affect you, before it can affect us. William Kittredge says, "If you are not *risking* sentimentality, you are not close to your inner self."

Art is art because it is not nature.
—GOETHE

EXERCISE 104

Who Are You? Somebody!

Richard Hugo, in an essay titled "In Defense of Creative Writing Classes," recalls the most important lesson he ever learned, "perhaps the most important lesson one can teach. You are someone and you have a right to your life." He decries the way the world tells us in so many ways that "individual differences do not exist" and that "our lives are unimportant." He says, "A creative writing class may be one of the last places you can go where your life still matters." The same thing is true for the writer who sits alone at her desk.

The Exercise

Buy a notebook to use for just this one exercise. Then, on a regular basis, perhaps at the beginning of your writing time or before you go to bed, write for ten to twenty minutes addressing each of the following subjects:

- List in detail all the places you have lived—one place per page. (This is a good way to begin because it gives the entire notebook a concrete grounding in time and place.) You might even want to get very specific, say, by recounting all the kitchens, or bedrooms.

- Next, recall if you were happy or unhappy in those places.

- Consider your parents' relationship, from their point of view.

- List important family members: brothers and sisters, grandparents, uncles and aunts, cousins. What were the dynamics of your nuclear family, your extended family? (Some of these subjects may take several twenty-minute sessions. Leave space for unfinished business.)

- List smells—indoor and outdoor—and the memories they conjure up.

- How do your clothes define you—or not?

- Do you have any recurring dreams or nightmares? Start a section for dreams.

- Ask yourself, What did I care about when I was five, ten, fifteen, twenty, twenty-five, thirty, etc.? What do I care about now?

- Did anyone ever give you advice that changed your life?

- What are the forks in your road? Imagine the road not taken.

- What is your five-year plan?

These are the kinds of questions that help you define who you are. Now, make up questions of your own to answer in your notebook. In fact, making up questions to bring back the past, to explore the present, and to voice your hopes and expectations for the future is part of the fun of this exercise.

The Objective

To lead an examined life. Your notebook will become a lifetime companion and an invaluable source of material.

Appealing workplaces are to be avoided. One wants a room with no view, so imagination can meet memory in the dark. When I furnished this study seven years ago, I pushed the long desk against a blank wall, so I could not see from either window. Once, fifteen years ago, I wrote in a cinder-block cell over a parking lot. It overlooked a tar-and-gravel roof. This pine shed under trees is not quite so good as the cinder-block study was, but it will do.

"The beginning of wisdom," according to a West African proverb, "is to get you a roof."

—ANNIE DILLARD

EXERCISE 105

People from the Past: Characters of the Future

You don't have anything if you don't have the stories.

—LESLIE MARMON SILKO, CEREMONY

Most of us have an unsettling memory of another child who loomed larger than life as we were growing up. Someone we resented, feared, hated, or envied. It might have been a sibling, a cousin, someone from the neighborhood, or someone from school. Often, that child—perhaps a little older or a little younger—had the power to make us take risks we would never have taken on our own, or had the power to make us miserable. This is the subject of Margaret Atwood's novel *Cat's Eye,* in which artist Elaine Risley is haunted by Cordelia, just such a childhood tormentor and "friend." Well, eventually these children grow up.

The Exercise

First, think about your childhood between the ages of six and twelve and try to recall someone whose memory, even now, has the power to invoke strong, often negative feelings in you. Was that person the class bully, the clown, the daredevil, the town snob, the neighborhood bore, etc? Write down details of what you remember about this person, how she looked and talked. Did you ever have any encounters with this person? Or did you just observe her from a distance?

Next, if you haven't seen this person for ten years or longer, imagine what she is doing now, where she lives, etc. Be specific.

If you had a long acquaintance with this person, or still know her, imagine where she will be ten years from now.

The Objective

To understand how our past is material for our imaginations and how writing well can be the best revenge.

Student Examples

His first name was Frank, or Frankie. We went to a small private day school in California. There were thirteen students in my eighth-grade class and all of us were afraid of Frankie, who was in the ninth grade. He was the school bully, a mean person, bottom line.

Once when I walked into the locker room, Frankie threw a Japanese Ninja throwing star into the wall just next to me. "Damn, I missed," he said. He talked about how his father had hit him with a 2 × 4 and he'd asked him for more. He bragged that his father had shot and killed a black man. Frankie hated everyone.

I can imagine Frankie in ten years. He'll be a white supremacist living in rural Georgia and working in a factory. He'll be married with three kids. He'll keep loaded shotguns and pistols around the house and will threaten to kill the kids. Before he's 35 he'll be doing time for a murder he committed outside a bar.

—HUNTER HELLER

Darlene was two years older than me, heavyset, a great football player. She loved the Dallas Cowboys just like all the guys—although we also liked the cheerleaders. Darlene taught me to ride a bike because she was sick of riding me around on her handlebars. One day, she put me on her Sears ten-speed and pushed me into the street, where I smashed into a parked car. She got mad because I "messed up the paint" on her bike. She says I ruined her first sexual experience one night when all the neighborhood kids were playing "Ring-O-Leveo." According to her, she was under a bush, about to "make her move" on Jeremy Witkins, when I saw her and called out her name and location. We used to smoke Marlboro Reds and drink stolen Budweisers behind the local swimming pool. In the five years I knew her, she never once wore a skirt.

I'll bet Darlene went to Grattenville Trade School—she was tough and good with tools. She probably kept wearing concert-Tees, denim jackets, and eventually got into heavy metal. I wonder if her teeth got straightened and her acne went away and her breasts got even bigger. I can imagine her dropping out of school, fighting with her folks all the time, and scooping ice cream nine to five at Carvel, or selling 36-shot film out the little Fotomat window. She'll buy takeout most nights. I can see her standing in line for a couple of beers and a slice of pepperoni for her live-in boyfriend, a muffler mechanic named Al, who is too high to deal with the counter person.

—DANIEL BIGMAN

EXERCISE 106

An Image Notebook
from Melanie Rae Thon

As playwright and actor Sam Shepard traveled cross-country, he kept a notebook that later became *Motel Chronicles,* a book of poems, images, scenes, and snatches of dialogue that evoke the disorienting experience of being continually on the move. A move or arrival at college often has the same effect. It may be difficult to make sense of all that's happening while you're in the middle of it, just as Shepard couldn't make sense of his experiences. But you can render these moments vividly, as Shepard did, put them together, and see what surfaces. This is a good exercise when you're between stories, unsure of where you want to go next. It keeps you writing without pressure and provides a space where material may surface.

The Exercise

For the length of the semester, keep an "image notebook." Every day, record at least one image. (Date these entries.) Use all your senses. Ask yourself: What's the most striking thing I heard, saw, smelled, touched, tasted today? Images begin with precise sensual detail. One day you may overhear a strange bit of conversation, another you may smell something that triggers a memory of a familiar smell.

Another day you might find a photograph or take one or do a drawing. You might make a collage of words and pictures from magazines. This exercise is very open. Length is variable. Some days you may write a page, another day a line. Don't get behind. Interesting juxtapositions emerge when you're not conscious of how images are colliding. If you do your week's work all at once, you'll lose this mystery.

The Objective

To learn to pay attention to detail. To gather images for later use. To find interesting juxtapositions to use in stories. To find threads of narrative that lead to stories. To become clearer about what's interesting to you.

Student Examples

I think of a white dog in Foot's yard. Big as a husky. White with white eyes, almost white eyes. Leaping to the end of his chain and later running free, dodging cars, but just barely.

I'm remembering the London tube, the man looking at the punked-out girl as if he wanted to kill her, as if she were disgusting, vile—how the tears welled in my eyes, because I knew how it felt to be looked at that way—but she didn't see. She had spiked, red hair, a lime-green miniskirt, torn fishnet stockings, black—a teenager. He was middle-aged, working class? I wonder if he had a daughter of his own. It scared me, the way he looked at her, because I really thought he might leap, might pummel her, might rip her throat.

Down the street the children have made a Snow Snake. This was before the storm. Fifteen feet long, two feet high—sweet-faced serpent. Disappeared now for sure.

There's this point in the perm process where Annette smears gel along the hairline, then wraps cotton under the curlers to keep the solution off my face. It's the gel that gets me. Cool, slick. And I tell her it reminds me of women getting electroshock, how they smeared gel on the head before they applied the electrodes.

Christine tells me this story. Her friend is riding his bicycle but is completely spaced out. He crashes in Harvard Square, runs into a tree. (Where did he find a tree?) Breaks his wrist but doesn't know it. Is just embarrassed. Hops back on the bike. Peddles away. Then the shock hits him and he's down again. When he comes to, he finds himself in a fireman's arms. Christine and I howl. Make our plans for collapse. To wake that way.

The wastepaper basket is the writer's best friend.
—ISAAC BASHEVIS SINGER

Journal Keeping for Writers

from William Melvin Kelley

Everybody has a day to write about, and so writing about the day makes everybody equal. Keeping a diary separates the act of writing from creating character and plot. You can write every day and learn certain fictional techniques without having to invent fiction on command.

The Exercise

Write one page a day. Concentrate on observation and description, not feeling. For example, if you receive a letter, the ordinary reaction is to write in the diary, "I received a letter that made me happy." (Or sad.) Instead, describe the size of the envelope, the quality of the paper, what the stamps looked like.

Keep your diary without using the verb *to be*. Forms of the verb *to be* don't create any vivid images. By avoiding its use, you get into the habit of choosing more interesting verbs. You'll also be more accurate. For example, some people will say "John Smith is a really funny guy," when what they really mean is "John Smith makes me laugh," or "I like John Smith's sense of humor."

Experiment with sentence length. Keep the diary for a week in sentences of ten words or less. Then, try writing each day's account in a single sentence. Avoid use of "and" to connect the parts of the long sentence; try out other conjunctions.

Switch your diary to third person for a while, so that instead of writing *I*, you can write about *he* or *she*. Then, try mixing the point of view. Start the day in third person and switch into first person to comment on the action. By interspersing first- and third-person points of view, you can experiment with stream of consciousness and the interior monologue.

Try keeping your diary in an accent—first the accent of somebody who is learning how to write English, then the accent of somebody learning to speak English.

Keep it in baby talk: Baby want. Baby hurt. Baby want food. Baby want love. Baby walk.

Try making lists for a diary entry—just a record of the nouns of that day: toothbrush, coffee, subway tokens, schoolbooks, gym shoes.

The Objective

To enhance your powers of observation and description without having to juggle the demands of characterization and plot.

EXERCISE 108

Creative Wrong Memory

One of the dangers of writing about something that really happened is the urge to stay too close to the literal truth. Because you don't quite trust your memory of it you come up with a thin narrative with very little texture, or you add details or events the reader may find unconvincing. "It really happened that way" or "It's a true story" is no defense. Also, keep in mind that a recital of just the facts rarely adds up to a satisfying fictional truth, to the emotional truth underlying what really happened.

This is another exercise to show you how to remember what you don't know—how to combine autobiography and imagination to achieve what Proust calls "creative wrong memory."

The Exercise

1. Recall an event or dramatic situation from your childhood and describe the event in one or two sentences at the top of the page.

2. Next, using both words and phrases, make a list of all the things you remember about the event.

3. Now, make a list of all the things you don't remember about that event.

4. Finally, begin a story using several details from the list you remember and several from the list you don't remember—details you have made up. One way to make this work is to link important details before you begin. For example: I remember that Uncle Cal and Aunt Marie had a fight, but not what started it.

The Objective

To enlarge and deepen your autobiographical material by making up what you don't remember and adding it to what you do.

Student Example

Italics indicate the parts that are "made up."

Notes

EVENT: death of a classmate (Albert Parsons)

I REMEMBER: my puzzlement about his sudden disappearance. He was dark-haired and serious. It was fall. Shortly afterwards my favorite uncle died and I went to his funeral at the cathedral and cried. I remember lying in bed, knowing my parents would not be there forever, that they would die. I remember at that moment a terrifying fear and sense of loss.

I DON'T REMEMBER: how Albert Parsons died. An illness? I don't remember how I found out. I don't remember how the others in my class reacted. Nor do I remember how my uncle died or how my aunt and parents reacted.

Beginning of Story

It was a crisp, fall afternoon *with both sides lined up on the field for soccer practice when I saw that Albert Parsons wasn't there. Earlier, in the classroom, I hadn't noticed that Albert was missing.* He was a solemn, dark-haired boy who sat quietly *at the back of the first row; he didn't join in any of the recess games.* But soccer was compulsory *and I was worried that our side, Ayre House, was a man shy for the scrimmage. Things weren't in order.*

"Mister Todd," I yelled to our coach, really our fifth-grade teacher. He wore a topcoat and bowler hat, and was eager to blow his whistle to get us started so he could get away to the sideline for a cigarette.

"Albert Parsons isn't here," I called. "It's not fair."

Mr. Todd swung around, taking the whistle from his mouth. "You a coward, Campbell," he barked. He jerked his head at the other side, Harrington House, whose color was yellow. "You afraid the yellow-bellies over there are going to beat you and you won't end up on the winning side? What's not fair? That you might lose or that Albert Parsons isn't here?"

His outburst of questions startled me. We were all leery of Mr. Todd. More creepy stories were told about him than any of the other teachers; his class loomed ahead of us like a dragon's cave we would have to someday enter.

—DONALD FRASER McNEILL

I can't write without a reader. It's precisely like a kiss—you can't do it alone.

—JOHN CHEEVER

EXERCISE 109

Let Us Write Letters

*Nine-tenths of the letters in which people speak
unreservedly of their inmost feelings are written
after ten at night.*

—Thomas Hardy

Several writers we know save copies of letters written to close friends as a sort of journal, and another writer writes a one-page letter every morning before turning to her fiction. Writing letters can be a form of limbering up. The exercise "Let Us Write Letters" isn't really an exercise but rather the suggestion that we all write more letters—to family and friends (and even to the editorial pages of magazines and newspapers). Robert Watson makes a good case for this in his poem "Please Write: don't phone."

> While there is mail there is hope.
> After we have hung up I can't recall
> Your words, and your voice sounds strange
> Whether from a distance, a bad cold, deceit
> I don't know. When you call I'm asleep
> Or bathing or my mouth is full of toast.
>
> I can't think of what to say.
> "We have rain"? "We have snow"?
>
> Let us write instead: surely our fingers spread out
> With pen and paper touch more of mind's flesh
> Than the sound waves moving from throat to lips
> To phone, through wire, to one ear.
> I can touch the paper you touch.
> I can see you undressed in your calligraphy.
> I can read you over and over.
> I can read you day after day.
> I can wait at the mailbox with my hair combed,
> In my best suit.
> I hang up. What did you say?
> What did I say? Your phone call is gone.
> I hold the envelope you addressed in my hand.
> I hold the skin that covers you.

PART FOURTEEN

A Collection of Short Short Stories

20/20

Linda Brewer

By the time they reached Indiana, Bill realized that Ruthie, his driving companion, was incapable of theoretical debate. She drove okay, she went halves on gas, etc., but she refused to argue. She didn't seem to know how. Bill was used to East Coast women who disputed everything he said, every step of the way. Ruthie stuck to simple observation, like "Look—cows." He chalked it up to the fact that she was from rural Ohio and thrilled to death to be anywhere else.

She didn't mind driving into the setting sun. The third evening out Bill rested his eyes while she cruised along making the occasional announcement.

"Indian paintbrush. A golden eagle."

Miles later he frowned. There was no Indian paintbrush, that he knew of, near Chicago.

The next evening, driving, Ruthie said, "I never thought I'd see a Bigfoot in real life." Bill turned and looked at the side of the road streaming innocently out behind them. Two red spots winked back—reflectors nailed to a tree stump.

"Ruthie, I'll drive," he said. She stopped the car and they changed places in the light of the evening star.

"I'm so glad I got to come with you," Ruthie said. Her eyes were big, blue, and capable of seeing wonderful sights. A white buffalo near Fargo. A UFO above Twin Falls. A handsome genius in the person of Bill himself. This last vision came to her in Spokane and Bill decided to let it ride.

Excuses I Have
Already Used

Antonia Clark

He hit me first. She called me four-eyes. The dog ate it. It's not my turn. Everybody else is doing it. My alarm didn't go off. I didn't know it was due. My grandmother died. It went through the wash. My roommate threw it in the trash. He got me drunk. He said he loved me. He said he'd pull out in time. She pulled right out in front of me. I didn't know how you felt. I was only trying to help. He backed me into a corner. It just slipped out of my hand. I was in a hurry. It was on sale. I needed a little pick-me-up. It calms my nerves. They looked too good to resist. It sounded like such a good deal. Hospitals give me the creeps. He's probably tired of visitors. He didn't even recognize me last time. There were extra expenses this month. My vote wouldn't have counted anyway. The kids were driving me nuts. I didn't have time. My watch must have stopped. I couldn't find the instructions. The dishwasher's broken. Somebody else used it last. I forgot my checkbook. I gave at the office. I've got a headache. I've got my period. It's too hot. I'm too tired. I had to work late. I got stuck in traffic. I couldn't get away. I couldn't let them down. I didn't know how to say no. We were thrown together by circumstance. He made me feel like a woman again. I didn't know what I was doing. It seemed like a good idea at the time. I've been up to my eyeballs. The flight was delayed. The car broke down. My hard drive crashed. I've got a call waiting. I'm flat out. Life is too short. It's too late to go back.

The Custodian

Brian Hinshaw

The job would get boring if you didn't mix it up a little. Like this woman in 14-A, the nurses called her the mockingbird, start any song and this old lady would sing it through. Couldn't speak, couldn't eat a lick of solid food, but she sang like a house on fire. So for a kick, I would get in there with my mop and such, prop the door open with the bucket, and set her going. She was best at the songs you'd sing with a group—"Oh Susanna," campfire stuff. Any kind of Christmas song worked good, too, and it always cracked the nurses if I could get her into "Let it Snow" during a heat spell. We'd try to make her take up a song from the radio or some of the old songs with cursing in them, but she would never go for those. Although I once had her do "How dry I am" while Nurse Winchell fussed with the catheter.

Yesterday, her daughter or maybe granddaughter comes in while 14-A and I were partways into "Auld Lang Syne" and the daughter says "oh oh oh" like she had interrupted scintillating conversation and then she takes a long look at 14-A lying there in the gurney with her eyes shut and her curled-up hands, taking a cup of kindness yet. And the daughter looks at me the way a girl does at the end of an old movie and she says "my god," says "you're an angel," and now I can't do it anymore, can hardly step in her room.

Confirmation Names

Mariette Lippo

We studied the saints, slipped the boys in through a break in the hockey field's fence, and led them to the woods the nuns had deemed "off-limits."

Vicky let a boy read her palm there. He told her her lifeline was short, that she'd better learn reverence for the moment. She cried for weeks before choosing the name Barbara, patron saint of those in danger of sudden death.

Susan said she would only go "so far," but no one knew what that meant. Boys went nuts trying to find out. They loved to untie her waist-long hair, to see it fan underneath her. She loved their love letters, the way they'd straighten up whenever she walked by. She chose Thecla, who'd caused the lions to "forget themselves;" instead of tearing her to shreds, they licked her feet.

Jackie couldn't wait for anything. The nuns told her impatience was her cross. Even the lunches her mother packed would be gone before ten, and she'd be left sorry, wanting more. She'd chosen Anthony, "the Finder," in a last-ditch effort to recover what she'd lost. But the nuns gave her Euphrasia, the virgin, who'd hauled huge rocks from place to place to rid her soul of temptation.

Before mass, we'd check her back for leaves.

None of us, of course, chose Magdalen, the whore. She was the secret patron whose spirit, we believed, watched over us from the trees. She was the woman who'd managed to turn her passion sacred. She was the saint who turned the flesh Divine.

It Would've Been Hot

Melissa McCracken

The first and only night he and I had sex his apartment building burned down and though the "official" cause was 2B's hotplate, I wanted to blame him as I huddled in his winter coat and boxer shorts beside the fire truck—blame him because he'd been reckless and impatient, hadn't used a condom or even the couch, instead mauling me in his hallway, all long before I said, "Do you smell that?" and he threw open the front door, drowning us in choking smoke before he slammed it shut, coughing, and I tried to yell "back stairs" but I couldn't breathe, yet I saw him reach up with the flat of his palm and place it against the now closed door (like in those old school-safety films) just to see, had he bothered, if it would've been hot—the same way he reached out, as the fireman pulled away, and placed his hand against the small of my back in a gesture I guess was meant to be tender but instead was after the fact.

277

My Mother's Gifts

Judith Claire Mitchell

While I sleep, my dead mother revises my poetry. I wake to find my pet adjectives—indigo, lone, cozy—deleted and my childhood traumas—a swan biting my finger, the bearded man who followed me home—inserted. I tend to write about domestic life. Raising tomatoes. Folding towels. My mother adds ice cubes cracking in scotch, wildcats roaming backyards, poets sleeping with poets.

Before she died, my mother bequeathed me her editor, an older man with eyes as blue as Johnny jump-ups and a very deep tan. He takes me to lunch when I'm in the city. He reads my work over sushi. Nice, he says. My mother sits in the chair next to mine, oblivious to my purse on the cushion. She beams when the editor tells me I resemble her. Have you ever twisted your hair in a knot? he asks. Did she leave you any of those wild earrings? My mother leans back, young, beautiful, and lights a cigarette. She never speaks but she expresses herself.

Tell me your happiest memory, the editor says. Then, waving his hand, he erases the question. No, he says. The most bitter.

I pick one at random. An evening before one of her readings. I'm eleven and stretched on her bed while she wriggles into a fuchsia sheath. Let me go with you, I say. When she shakes her head her earrings ring like a New Year's toast. You're too young, she says. Your poems still rhyme. She presses a tissue to her lips, tosses it so it floats toward me. Her goodbye kiss. A hot pink smear.

Write about it, the editor says. What is poetry, after all? Personal stuff. Gossip. My mother pulls out her notebook, starts scribbling.

Before we part, the editor takes my wineglass, rubs away my own lipstick smear with the pad of his thumb. Be safe, he says. He kisses my cheek. He is worried I'll die the same way she did, as if swallowing pills while swimming naked in a neighbor's pool runs in families like poor circulation.

On the drive back to Connecticut my mother writes a new poem for me to claim as my own. It tells how I will actually die—a very old woman with bad knees toppling down steep basement stairs while carrying an overflowing laundry basket. She writes about how embarrassed I'll be when the *Times*' obituary compares our deaths. The poem is wry and clever and hurts my feelings. When we get home I type it up and fax it to the editor. He replies at once. Now we're talking, he says.

Sometimes I question the morality of what we are doing. Other times I wonder if this is how every poet breaks in. Once I gave us both credit—by Catherine and Erica Blessing, I wrote—but next morning there was a slash through her name, a pink lipstick kiss on mine.

My mother never questions anything, never did. Not her borrowed images, not her summers with jaded laureates, not her leaving me home with stepfathers.

Still, why hold a grudge? She's with me now, maybe to stay until I fall down the stairs. And certainly she's generous with her gifts—her talent, her time. Both are boundless.

And yet, there are times I'm ungrateful.

Tonight I lock my bedroom door so I can write a poem about sautéing onions. The words come fast. When I finish I fold the page in half, hide it beneath my pillow. I fall asleep and dream the editor has come to visit. He praises my herb garden and the shape of my calves and my subtle interior rhymes.

It isn't quite dawn when I wake up, first surprised to be alone, then reluctant to admit I'm not. I glance around my bedroom several times to confirm that the windows are locked, the key in the latch. It doesn't matter. I know what woke me: the sound of feet shuffling several inches above the carpet.

I reach under the pillow. I don't have to read the poem to know that it's better. Even the pillowcase smells of raw onion. She has turned paper torn from a notebook into the vegetable's frail husk.

I hold the onion's skin toward the window. Muffled light shines through it. A corner crumbles, scraps of peel fall to my comforter. I rub the opposite corner between my fingers. It disintegrates, too. I rub away the other corners; I rub away the poem's heart. There is still some power in flesh and unburied bones.

Pencil to lined paper, I go at that poem again. I slice away the beginning, chop off the ending, add childhood memories my mother doesn't know I have. I include all she left out, things so simple they would never occur to her. The way a paring knife's handle fits in a palm. A Vidalia's green meat, more tempting and dangerous than any apple. The cook herself— she holds her hair away from the blue burner as she bends over a pan. White slivers turn translucent. She likes how they squirm in the hot, spitting oil.

The raw juice on my fingers, the fumes and smoke in my bedroom, sting my eyes. I keep it anyway. Longer and longer. Better and better. How will I know when to stop?

Cigarette smoke haloes my head. That's easy, my mother says. When the tears come, of course.

The New Year

Pamela Painter

It's late Christmas Eve at Spinelli's when Dominic presents us, the waitstaff, with his dumb idea of a bonus—Italian hams in casings so tight they shimmer like Gilda's gold lamé stockings.

At home, Gilda's waiting up for me with a surprise of her own: my stuff from the last three months is sitting on the stoop. Arms crossed, scarlet nails tapping the satin sleeves of her robe, she says she's heard about Fiona. I balance the ham on my hip and pack my things—CD's, weights, a vintage Polaroid—into garbage bags she's provided free of charge. Then I let it all drop and offer up the ham in both hands, cradling it as if it might have been our child. She doesn't want any explanations—or the ham.

Fiona belongs to Dominic, and we are a short sad story of one night's restaurant despair. But the story's out and for sure I don't want Dominic coming after my ham.

Under Gilda's unforgiving eye, I sling my garbage bags into the trunk of the car and head west. The ham glistens beside me in the passenger's seat. Somewhere in Indiana I strap it into a seat belt.

I stop to call, but Gilda hangs up every time. So I send her pictures of my trip instead: The Ham under the silver arch of St. Louis; The Ham at the Grand Canyon; The Ham in Las Vegas. I'm taking a picture of The Ham in the Pacific when a big wave washes it out to sea. I send the picture anyway: The Ham in the Pacific Undertow. In this picture, you can't tell which of us is missing.

Wants

Grace Paley

I saw my ex-husband in the street. I was sitting on the steps of the new library.

Hello, my life, I said. We had once been married for twenty-seven years, so I felt justified.

He said, What? What life? No life of mine.

I said, O.K. I don't argue when there's real disagreement. I got up and went into the library to see how much I owed them.

The librarian said $32 even and you've owed it for eighteen years. I didn't deny anything. Because I don't understand how time passes. I have had those books. I have often thought of them. The library is only two blocks away.

My ex-husband followed me to the Books Returned desk. He interrupted the librarian, who had more to tell. In many ways, he said, as I look back, I attribute the dissolution of our marriage to the fact that you never invited the Bertrams to dinner.

That's possible, I said. But really, if you remember: first, my father was sick that Friday, then the children were born, then I had those Tuesday-night meetings, then the war began. Then we didn't seem to know them any more. But you're right. I should have had them to dinner.

I gave the librarian a check for $32. Immediately she trusted me, put my past behind her, wiped the record clean, which is just what most other municipal and/or state bureaucracies will *not* do.

I checked out the two Edith Wharton books I had just returned because I'd read them so long ago and they are more apropos now than ever. They were *The House of Mirth* and *The Children,* which is about how life in the United States in New York changed in twenty-seven years fifty years ago. A nice thing I do remember is breakfast, my ex-husband said. I was surprised. All we ever had was coffee. Then I remembered there was a hole in the back of the kitchen closet which opened into the apartment next door. There, they always ate sugar-cured smoked bacon. It gave us a very grand feeling about breakfast, but we never got stuffed and sluggish.

That was when we were poor, I said.

When were we ever rich? he asked.

Oh, as time went on, as our responsibilities increased, we didn't go in need. You took adequate financial care, I reminded him. The children went to camp four weeks a year and in decent ponchos with sleeping bags and boots, just like everyone else. They looked very nice. Our place was warm in winter, and we had nice red pillows and things.

I wanted a sailboat, he said. But you didn't want anything.

Don't be bitter, I said. It's never too late.

No, he said with a great deal of bitterness. I may get a sailboat. As a matter of fact I have money down on an eighteen-foot two-rigger. I'm doing well this year and can look forward to better. But as for you, it's too late. You'll always want nothing.

He had had a habit throughout the twenty-seven years of making a narrow remark which, like a plumber's snake, could work its way through the ear down the throat, halfway to my heart. He would then disappear, leaving me choking with equipment. What I mean is, I sat down on the library steps and he went away.

I looked through *The House of Mirth,* but lost interest. I felt extremely accused. Now, it's true, I'm short of requests and absolute requirements. But I do want *something*.

I want, for instance, to be a different person. I want to be the woman who brings these two books back in two weeks. I want to be the effective citizen who changes the school system and addresses the Board of Estimate on the troubles of this dear urban center.

I *had* promised my children to end the war before they grew up.

I wanted to have been married forever to one person, my ex-husband or my present one. Either has enough character for a whole life, which as it turns out is really not such a long time. You couldn't exhaust either man's qualities or get under the rock of his reasons in one short life.

Just this morning I looked out the window to watch the street for a while and saw that the little sycamores the city had dreamily planted a couple of years before the kids were born had come that day to the prime of their lives.

Well! I decided to bring those two books back to the library. Which proves that when a person or an event comes along to jolt or appraise me I *can* take some appropriate action, although I am better known for my hospitable remarks.

How Could a Mother?

Bruce Holland Rogers

It's better doing this woman to woman, don't you think? Before we get started, is there anything you need? Do you want something to drink? Coffee? A soft drink? Do you need to use the bathroom?

How had the day gone, before all this started? Were you at home the entire day, both you and your boyfriend? Had your boyfriend been drinking? Had you been drinking? How much did he drink during the day? In the evening? And you? How much did you have? Can you estimate? More than a six-pack? More than two six-packs? Was your daughter in the house with you the whole time?

When was it that your daughter—when was it that Josie started to cry? What was your state of mind when you punished her? What were you thinking when she wouldn't stop crying? Did your boyfriend say anything about Josie's crying? What did he say? What did you do to make her stop? Then, what did your boyfriend do? Did you do anything to restrain him? Did you say anything? No, I mean, did you say anything to your boyfriend about what he was doing to your daughter?

Did you try to wake her up right away? Did you check her pulse? Did you listen for her breathing? When was the next time that you checked on her condition?

What time did you wake up? How soon after you woke up did you check on your daughter? You could tell right away? How did you know? Then what did you do? Was the abduction story his idea, or yours? Which car did you take? How did you come to choose Cascadia State Park? Had you been to the area before? When had he been there? Did he say anything to you about why he thought the park would be a good place? Where were you when you called the police to report her missing?

Is there anything you'd like to add?

Does this typescript accurately reflect what you have told me? Do you need more time to read it before you sign?

Can you guess how it feels for me, even with all the practice I have, to ask these questions? Do you wonder what questions I'm not able to ask you? Do you wonder if I have children of my own? Are you a monster? What is a monster? Did you know there were officers like me who handled only cases like this, one after another? Do you have any thoughts about the question no one can answer? Not the one everyone asks, but the one only a mother who has felt her own hands shake with a rage that is bigger than she is can ask? Not that I'd willingly trade the suffering on my side of the table for the suffering on your side, but why haven't I? Why not?

No One's a Mystery

Elizabeth Tallent

For my eighteenth birthday Jack gave me a five-year diary with a latch and a little key, light as a dime. I was sitting beside him scratching at the lock, which didn't seem to want to work, when he thought he saw his wife's Cadillac in the distance, coming toward us. He pushed me down onto the dirty floor of the pickup and kept one hand on my head while I inhaled the musk of his cigarettes in the dashboard ashtray and sang along with Rosanne Cash on the tape deck. We'd been drinking tequila and the bottle was between his legs, resting up against his crotch, where the seam of his Levi's was bleached linen-white, though the Levi's were nearly new. I don't know why his Levi's always bleached like that, along the seams and at the knees. In a curve of cloth his zipper glinted, gold.

"It's her," he said. "She keeps the lights on in the daytime. I can't think of a single habit in a woman that irritates me more than that." When he saw that I was going to stay still he took his hand from my head and ran it through his own dark hair.

"Why does she?" I said.

"She thinks it's safer. Why does she need to be safer? She's driving exactly fifty-five miles an hour. She believes in those signs: 'Speed Monitored by Aircraft.' It doesn't matter that you can look up and see that the sky is empty."

"She'll see your lips move, Jack. She'll know you're talking to someone."

"She'll think I'm singing along with the radio."

He didn't lift his hand, just raised the fingers in salute while the pressure of his palm steadied the wheel, and I heard the Cadillac honk twice, musically; he was driving easily eighty miles an hour. I studied his boots. The elk heads stitched into the leather were bearded with frayed thread, the toes were scuffed, and there was a compact wedge of muddy manure between the heel and the sole—the same boots he'd been wearing for the two years I'd known him. On the tape deck Rosanne Cash sang, "Nobody's into me, no one's a mystery."

"Do you think she's getting famous because of who her daddy is or for herself?" Jack said.

"There are about a hundred pop tops on the floor, did you know that? Some little kid could cut a bare foot on one of these, Jack."

"No little kids get into this truck except for you."

"How come you let it get so dirty?"

"'How come,'" he mocked. "You even sound like a kid. You can get back into the seat now, if you want. She's not going to look over her shoulder and see you."

"How do you know?"

"I just know," he said. "Like I know I'm going to get meat loaf for supper. It's in the air. Like I know what you'll be writing in that diary."

"What will I be writing?" I knelt on my side of the seat and craned around to look at the butterfly of dust printed on my jeans. Outside the window Wyoming was dazzling in the

284

heat. The wheat was fawn and yellow and parted smoothly by the thin dirt road. I could smell the water in the irrigation ditches hidden in the wheat.

"Tonight you'll write, 'I love Jack. This is my birthday present from him. I can't imagine anybody loving anybody more than I love Jack.'"

"I can't."

"In a year you'll write 'I wonder what I ever really saw in Jack. I wonder why I spent so many days just riding around in his pickup. It's true he taught me something about sex. It's true there wasn't ever much else to do in Cheyenne.'"

"I won't write that."

"In two years you'll write, 'I wonder what that old guy's name was, the one with the curly hair and the filthy dirty pickup truck and time on his hands.'"

"I won't write that."

"No?"

"Tonight I'll write, 'I love Jack. This is my birthday present from him. I can't imagine anybody loving anybody more than I love Jack.'"

"No, you can't." he said. "You can't imagine it."

"In a year I'll write, 'Jack should be home any minute now. The table's set—my grandmother's linen and her old silver and the yellow candles left over from the wedding—but I don't know if I can wait until after the trout à la Navarra to make love to him.'"

"It must have been a fast divorce."

"In two years I'll write, 'Jack should be home by now. Little Jack is hungry for his supper. He said his first word today besides "Mama" and "Papa." He said "kaka."'"

Jack laughed. "He was probably trying to finger-paint with kaka on the bathroom wall when you heard him say it."

"In three years I'll write, 'My nipples are a little sore from nursing Eliza Rosamund.'"

"Rosamund. Every little girl should have a middle name she hates."

"'Her breath smells like vanilla and her eyes are just Jack's color of blue.'"

"That's nice," Jack said.

"So, which one do you like?"

"I like yours," he said. "But I believe mine."

"It doesn't matter. I believe mine."

"Not in your heart of hearts, you don't."

"You're wrong."

"I'm not wrong," he said. "And her breath would smell like your milk, and it's kind of a bittersweet smell, if you want to know the truth."

Vision Out of the Corner of One Eye

Luisa Valenzuela

It's true, he put his hand on my ass and I was about to scream bloody murder when the bus passed by a church and he crossed himself. He's a good sort after all, I said to myself. Maybe he didn't do it on purpose or maybe his right hand didn't know what his left hand was up to. I tried to move farther back in the bus—searching for explanations is one thing and letting yourself be pawed is another—but more passengers got on and there was no way I could do it. My wiggling to get out of his reach only let him get a better hold on me and even fondle me. I was nervous and finally moved over. He moved over, too. We passed by another church but he didn't notice it and when he raised his hand to his face it was to wipe the sweat off his forehead. I watched him out of the corner of one eye, pretending that nothing was happening, or at any rate not making him think I liked it. It was impossible to move a step farther and he began jiggling me. I decided to get even and put my hand on his behind. A few blocks later I got separated from him. Then I was swept along by the passengers getting off the bus and now I'm sorry I lost him so suddenly because there were only 7,400 pesos in his wallet and I'd have gotten more out of him if we'd been alone. He seemed affectionate. And very generous.

—Translated by Helen Lane

PART FIFTEEN

A Collection
of Short Stories

Gryphon

Charles Baxter

On Wednesday afternoon, between the geography lesson on ancient Egypt's hand-operated irrigation system and an art project that involved drawing a model city next to a mountain, our fourth-grade teacher, Mr. Hibler, developed a cough. This cough began with a series of muffled throat-clearings and progressed to propulsive noises contained within Mr. Hibler's closed mouth. "Listen to him," Carol Peterson whispered to me. "He's gonna blow up." Mr. Hibler's laughter—dazed and infrequent—sounded a bit like his cough, but as we worked on our model cities we would look up, thinking he was enjoying a joke, and see Mr. Hibler's face turning red, his cheeks puffed out. This was not laughter. Twice he bent over, and his loose tie, like a plumb line, hung down straight from his neck as he exploded himself into a Kleenex. He would excuse himself, then go on coughing. "I'll bet you a dime," Carol Peterson whispered, "we get a substitute tomorrow."

Carol sat at the desk in front of mine and was a bad person—when she thought no one was looking she would blow her nose on notebook paper, then crumple it up and throw it into the wastebasket—but at times of crisis she spoke the truth. I knew I'd lose the dime.

"No deal," I said.

When Mr. Hibler stood us in formation at the door just prior to the final bell, he was almost incapable of speech. "I'm sorry, boys and girls," he said. "I seem to be coming down with something."

"I hope you feel better tomorrow, Mr. Hibler," Bobby Kryzanowicz, the faultless brown-noser, said, and I heard Carol Peterson's evil giggle. Then Mr. Hibler opened the door and

287

we walked out to the buses, a clique of us starting noisily to hawk and laugh as soon as we thought we were a few feet beyond Mr. Hibler's earshot.

Since Five Oaks was a rural community, and in Michigan, the supply of substitute teachers was limited to the town's unemployed community college graduates, a pool of about four mothers. These ladies fluttered, provided easeful class days, and nervously covered material we had mastered weeks earlier. Therefore it was a surprise when a woman we had never seen came into the class the next day, carrying a purple purse, a checkerboard lunchbox, and a few books. She put the books on one side of Mr. Hibler's desk and the lunchbox on the other, next to the Voice of Music phonograph. Three of us in the back of the room were playing with Heever, the chameleon that lived in a terrarium and on one of the plastic drapes, when she walked in.

She clapped her hands at us. "Little boys," she said, "why are you bent over together like that?" She didn't wait for us to answer. "Are you tormenting an animal? Put it back. Please sit down at your desks. I want no cabals this time of the day." We just stared at her. "Boys," she repeated, "I asked you to sit down."

I put the chameleon in his terrarium and felt my way to my desk, never taking my eyes off the woman. With white and green chalk, she had started to draw a tree on the left side of the blackboard. She didn't look usual. Furthermore, her tree was outsized, disproportionate, for some reason.

"This room needs a tree," she said, with one line drawing the suggestion of a leaf. "A large, leafy, shady, deciduous . . . oak."

Her fine, light hair had been done up in what I would learn years later was called a chignon, and she wore gold-rimmed glasses whose lenses seemed to have the faintest blue tint. Harold Knardahl, who sat across from me, whispered, "Mars," and I nodded slowly, savoring the imminent weirdness of the day. The substitute drew another branch with an extravagant arm gesture, then turned around and said, "Good morning. I don't believe I said good morning to all of you yet."

Facing us, she was no special age—an adult is an adult—but her face had two prominent lines, descending vertically from the sides of her mouth to her chin. I knew where I had seen those lines before: *Pinocchio.* They were marionette lines. "You may stare at me," she said to us, as a few more kids from the last bus came into the room; their eyes fixed on her, "for a few more seconds, until the bell rings. Then I will permit no more staring. Looking I will permit. Staring, no. It is impolite to stare, and a sign of bad breeding. You cannot make a social effort while staring."

Harold Knardahl did not glance at me, or nudge, but I heard him whisper "Mars" again, trying to get more mileage out of his single joke with the kids who had just come in.

When everyone was seated, the substitute teacher finished her tree, put down her chalk fastidiously on the phonograph, brushed her hands, and faced us. "Good morning," she said. "I am Miss Ferenczi, your teacher for the day. I am fairly new to your community, and I don't believe any of you know me. I will therefore start by telling you a story about myself."

While we settled back, she launched into her tale. She said her grandfather had been a Hungarian prince; her mother had been born in some place called Flanders, had been a pianist, and had played concerts for people Miss Ferenczi referred to as "crowned heads." She gave us a knowing look. "Grieg," she said, "the Norwegian master, wrote a concerto for piano that was . . ."—she paused—"my mother's triumph at her debut concert in

London." Her eyes searched the ceiling. Our eyes followed. Nothing up there but ceiling tile. "For reasons that I shall not go into, my family's fortunes took us to Detroit, then north to dreadful Saginaw, and now here I am in Five Oaks, as your substitute teacher, for today, Thursday, October the eleventh. I believe it will be a good day: all the forecasts coincide. We shall start with your reading lesson. Take out your reading book. I believe it is called *Broad Horizons,* or something along those lines."

Jeannie Vermeesch raised her hand. Miss Ferenczi nodded at her. "Mr. Hibler always starts the day with the Pledge of Allegiance." Jeannie whined.

"Oh, does he? In that case," Miss Ferenczi said, "you must know it *very* well by now, and we certainly need not spend our time on it. No, no allegiance pledging on the premises today, by my reckoning. Not with so much sunlight coming into the room. A pledge does not suit my mood." She glanced at her watch. "Time *is* flying. Take out *Broad Horizons.*"

She disappointed us by giving us an ordinary lesson, complete with vocabulary and drills, comprehension questions, and recitation. She didn't seem to care for the material, however. She sighed every few minutes and rubbed her glasses with a frilly handkerchief that she withdrew, magician-style, from her left sleeve.

After reading we moved on to arithmetic. It was my favorite time of the morning, when the lazy autumn sunlight dazzled its way through ribbons of clouds past the windows on the east side of the classroom and crept across the linoleum floor. On the playground the first group of children, the kindergartners, were running on the quack grass just beyond the monkey bars. We were doing multiplication tables. Miss Ferenczi had made John Wazny stand up at his desk in the front row. He was supposed to go through the tables of six. From where I was sitting, I could smell the Vitalis soaked into John's plastered hair. He was doing fine until he came to six times eleven and six times twelve. "Six times eleven," he said, "is sixty-eight. Six times twelve is . . ." He put his fingers to his head, quickly and secretly sniffed his fingertips, and said, ". . . seventy-two." Then he sat down.

"Fine," Miss Ferenczi said, "Well now. That was very good."

"Miss Ferenczi!" One of the Eddy twins was waving her hand desperately in the air. "Miss Ferenczi! Miss Ferenczi!"

"Yes?"

"John said that six times eleven is sixty-eight and you said he was right!"

"*Did* I?" She gazed at the class with a jolly look breaking across her marionette's face. "Did I say that? Well, what *is* six times eleven?"

"It's sixty-six!"

She nodded. "Yes. So it is. But, and I know some people will not entirely agree with me, at some times it is sixty-eight."

"When? When is it sixty-eight?"

We were all waiting.

"In higher mathematics, which you children do not yet understand, six times eleven can be considered to be sixty-eight." She laughed through her nose. "In higher mathematics numbers are . . . more fluid. The only thing a number does is contain a certain amount of something. Think of water. A cup is not the only way to measure a certain amount of water, is it?" We were staring, shaking our heads. "You could use saucepans or thimbles. In either case, the water *would be the same.* Perhaps," she started again, "it would be better for you to think that six times eleven is sixty-eight only when I am in the room."

"Why is it sixty-eight," Mark Poole asked, "when you're in the room?"

"Because it's more interesting that way," she said, smiling very rapidly behind her blue-tinted glasses. "Besides, I'm your substitute teacher, am I not?" We all nodded. "Well, then, think of six times eleven equals sixty-eight as a substitute fact."

"A substitute fact?"

"Yes." Then she looked at us carefully. "Do you think," she asked, "that anyone is going to be hurt by a substitute fact?"

We looked back at her.

"Will the plants on the windowsill be hurt?" We glanced at them. There were sensitive plants thriving in a green plastic tray, and several wilted ferns in small clay pots. "Your dogs and cats, or your moms and dads?" She waited. "So," she concluded, "what's the problem?"

"But it's wrong," Janice Weber said, "isn't it?"

"What's your name, young lady?"

"Janice Weber."

"And you think it's wrong, Janice?"

"I was just asking."

"Well, all right. You were just asking. I think we've spent enough time on this matter by now, don't you, class? You are free to think what you like. When your teacher, Mr. Hibler, returns, six times eleven will be sixty-six again, you can rest assured. And it will be that for the rest of your lives in Five Oaks. Too bad, eh?" She raised her eyebrows and glinted herself at us. "But for now, it wasn't. So much for that. Let us go on to your assigned problems for today, as painstakingly outlined, I see, in Mr. Hibler's lesson plan. Take out a sheet of paper and write your names on the upper left-hand corner."

For the next half hour we did the rest of our arithmetic problems. We handed them in and then went on to spelling, my worst subject. Spelling always came before lunch. We were taking spelling dictation and looking at the clock. "Thorough," Miss Ferenczi said. "Boundary." She walked in the aisles between the desks, holding the spelling book open and looking down at our papers. "Balcony." I clutched my pencil. Somehow, the way she said those words, they seemed foreign, mis-voweled and mis-consonanted. I stared down at what I had spelled. *Balconie.* I turned the pencil upside down and erased my mistake. *Balconey.* That looked better, but still incorrect. I cursed the world of spelling and tried erasing it again and saw the paper beginning to wear away. *Balkony.* Suddenly I felt a hand on my shoulder.

"I don't like that word either," Miss Ferenczi whispered, bent over, her mouth near my ear. "It's ugly. My feeling is, if you don't like a word, you don't have to use it." She straightened up, leaving behind a slight odor of Clorets.

At lunchtime we went out to get our trays of sloppy joes, peaches in heavy syrup, coconut cookies, and milk, and brought them back to the classroom, where Miss Ferenczi was sitting at the desk, eating a brown sticky thing she had unwrapped from tightly rubber-banded waxed paper. "Miss Ferenczi," I said, raising my hand. "You don't have to eat with us. You can eat with the other teachers. There's a teacher's lounge," I ended up, "next to the principal's office."

"No, thank you," she said. "I prefer it here."

"We've got a room monitor," I said. "Mrs. Eddy." I pointed to where Mrs. Eddy, Joyce and Judy's mother, sat silently at the back of the room, doing her knitting.

"That's fine," Miss Ferenczi said. "But I shall continue to eat here, with you children. I prefer it," she repeated.

"How come?" Wayne Razmer asked without raising his hand.

"I talked to the other teachers before class this morning," Miss Ferenczi said, biting into her brown food. "There was a great rattling of the words for the fewness of the ideas. I didn't care for their brand of hilarity. I don't like ditto-machine jokes."

"Oh," Wayne said.

"What's that you're eating?" Maxine Sylvester asked, twitching her nose. "Is it food?"

"It most certainly *is* food. It's a stuffed fig. I had to drive almost down to Detroit to get it. I also brought some smoked sturgeon. And this," she said, lifting some green leaves out of her lunchbox, "is raw spinach, cleaned this morning."

"Why're you eating raw spinach?" Maxine asked.

"It's good for you," Miss Ferenczi said. "More stimulating than soda pop or smelling salts." I bit into my sloppy joe and stared blankly out the window. An almost invisible moon was faintly silvered in the daytime autumn sky. "As far as food is concerned," Miss Ferenczi was saying, "you have to shuffle the pack. Mix it up. Too many people eat . . . well, never mind."

"Miss Ferenczi," Carol Peterson said, "what are we going to do this afternoon?"

"Well," she said, looking down at Mr. Hibler's lesson plan, "I see that your teacher, Mr. Hibler, has you scheduled for a unit on the Egyptians." Carol groaned. "Yessss," Miss Ferenczi continued, "that is what we will do: the Egyptians. A remarkable people. Almost as remarkable as the Americans. But not quite." She lowered her head, did her quick smile, and went back to eating her spinach.

After noon recess we came back into the classroom and saw that Miss Ferenczi had drawn a pyramid on the blackboard close to her oak tree. Some of us who had been playing baseball were messing around in the back of the room, dropping the bats and gloves into the playground box, and Ray Schontzeler had just slugged me when I heard Miss Ferenczi's high-pitched voice, quavering with emotions. "Boys," she said, "come to order right this minute and take your seats. I do not wish to waste a minute of class time. Take out your geography books." We trudged to our desks and, still sweating, pulled out *Distant Lands and Their People*. "Turn to page forty-two." She waited for thirty seconds, then looked over at Kelly Munger. "Young man," she said, "why are you still fossicking in your desk?"

Kelly looked as if his foot had been stepped on. "Why am I what?"

"Why are you . . . burrowing in your desk like that?"

"I'm lookin' for the book, Miss Ferenczi."

Bobby Kryzanowicz, the faultless brown-noser who sat in the first row by choice, softly said, "His name is Kelly Munger. He can't ever find his stuff. "He always does that."

"I don't care what his name is, especially after lunch," Miss Ferenczi said. "*Where is your book?*"

"I just found it." Kelly was peering into his desk and with both hands pulled at the book, shoveling along in front of it several pencils and crayons, which fell into his lap and then to the floor.

"I hate a mess," Miss Ferenczi said. "I hate a mess in a desk or a mind. It's . . . unsanitary. You wouldn't want your house at home to look like your desk at school, now, would you?" She didn't wait for an answer. "I should think not. A house at home should be as neat as human hands can make it. What were we talking about? Egypt. Page forty-two. I note from Mr. Hibler's lesson plan that you have been discussing the modes of Egyptian irrigation. Interesting, in my view, but not so interesting as what we are about to cover. The pyramids, and

Egyptian slave labor. A plus on one side, a minus on the other." We had our books open to page forty-two, where there was a picture of a pyramid, but Miss Ferenczi wasn't looking at the book. Instead, she was staring at some object just outside the window.

"Pyramids," Miss Ferenczi said, still looking past the window. "I want you to think about pyramids. And what was inside. The bodies of the pharaohs, of course, and their attendant treasures. Scrolls. Perhaps," Miss Ferenczi said, her face gleeful but unsmiling, "these scrolls were novels for the pharaohs, helping them to pass the time in their long voyage through the centuries. But then, I am joking." I was looking at the lines on Miss Ferenczi's skin. "Pyramids," Miss Ferenczi went on, "were the repositories of special cosmic powers. The nature of a pyramid is to guide cosmic energy forces into a concentrated point. The Egyptians knew that; we have generally forgotten it. Did you know," she asked, walking to the side of the room so that she was standing by the coat closet, "that George Washington had Egyptian blood, from his grandmother? Certain features of the Constitution of the United States are notable for their Egyptian ideas."

Without glancing down at the book, she began to talk about the movement of souls in Egyptian religion. She said that when people die, their souls return to Earth in the form of carpenter ants or walnut trees, depending on how they behaved—"well or ill"—in life. She said that the Egyptians believed that people act the way they do because of magnetism produced by tidal forces in the solar system, forces produced by the sun and by its "planetary ally," Jupiter. Jupiter, she said, was a planet, as we had been told, but had "certain properties of stars." She was speaking very fast. She said that the Egyptians were great explorers and conquerors. She said that the greatest of all the conquerors, Genghis Khan, had had forty horses and forty young women killed on the site of his grave. We listened. No one tried to stop her. "I myself have been in Egypt," she said, "and have witnessed much dust and many brutalities." She said that an old man in Egypt who worked for a circus had personally shown her an animal in a cage, a monster, half bird and half lion. She said that this monster was called a gryphon and that she had heard about them but never seen them until she traveled to the outskirts of Cairo. She wrote the word out on the blackboard in large capital letters: GRYPHON. She said that Egyptian astronomers had discovered the planet Saturn but had not seen its rings. She said that the Egyptians were the first to discover that dogs, when they are ill, will not drink from rivers, but wait for rain, and hold their jaws open to catch it.

"She lies."

We were on the school bus home. I was sitting next to Carl Whiteside, who had bad breath and a huge collection of marbles. We were arguing. Carl thought she was lying. I said she wasn't, probably.

"I didn't believe that stuff about the bird," Carl said, "and what she told us about the pyramids? I didn't believe that, either. She didn't know what she was talking about."

"Oh yeah?" I had liked her. She was strange. I thought I could nail him. "If she was lying," I said, "what'd she say that was a lie?"

"Six times eleven isn't sixty-eight. It isn't ever. It's sixty-six, I know for a fact."

"She said so. She admitted it. What else did she lie about?"

"I don't know," he said. "Stuff."

"What stuff?"

"Well." He swung his legs back and forth. "You ever see an animal that was half lion and half bird?" He crossed his arms. "It sounded real fakey to me."

"It could happen," I said. I had to improvise, to outrage him. "I read in this newspaper my mom bought in the IGA about this scientist, this mad scientist in the Swiss Alps, and he's been putting genes and chromosomes and stuff together in test tubes, and he combined a human being and a hamster." I waited, for effect. "It's called a humster."

"You never." Carl was staring at me, his mouth open, his terrible bad breath making its way toward me. "What newspaper was it?"

"*The National Enquirer,*" I said, "that they sell next to the cash registers." When I saw his look of recognition, I knew I had him. "And this mad scientist," I said, "his name was, um, Dr. Frankenbush." I realized belatedly that this name was a mistake and waited for Carl to notice its resemblance to the name of the other famous mad master of permutations, but he only sat there.

"A man and a hamster?" He was staring at me, squinting, his mouth opening in distaste. "Jeez. What'd it look like?"

When the bus reached my stop, I took off down our dirt road and ran up through the backyard, kicking the tire swing for good luck. I dropped my books on the back steps so I could hug and kiss our dog, Mr. Selby. Then I hurried inside. I could smell brussels sprouts cooking, my unfavorite vegetable. My mother was washing other vegetables in the kitchen sink, and my baby brother was hollering in his yellow playpen on the kitchen floor.

"Hi, Mom," I said, hopping around the playpen to kiss her. "Guess what?"

"I have no idea."

"We had this substitute today, Miss Ferenczi, and I'd never seen her before, and she had all these stories and ideas and stuff."

"Well. That's good." My mother looked out the window in front of the sink, her eyes on the pine woods west of our house. That time of the afternoon her skin always looked so white to me. Strangers always said my mother looked like Betty Crocker, framed by the giant spoon on the side of the Bisquick box. "Listen, Tommy," she said. "Would you please go upstairs and pick your clothes off the floor in the bathroom, and then go outside to the shed and put the shovel and ax away that your father left outside this morning?"

"She said that six times eleven was sometimes sixty-eight!" I said. "And she said she once saw a monster that was half lion and half bird." I waited. "In Egypt."

"Did you hear me?" my mother asked, raising her arm to wipe her forehead with the back of her hand. "You have chores to do."

"I know," I said. "I was just telling you about the substitute."

"It's very interesting," my mother said, quickly glancing down at me, "and we can talk about it later when your father gets home. But right now you have some work to do."

"Okay, Mom." I took a cookie out of the jar on the counter and was about to go outside when I had a thought. I ran into the living room, pulled out a dictionary next to the TV stand, and opened it to the Gs. After five minutes I found it. *Gryphon:* variant of griffin. *Griffin:* "a fabulous beast with the head and wings of an eagle and the body of a lion." Fabulous was right. I shouted with triumph and ran outside to put my father's tools in their proper places.

Miss Ferenczi was back the next day, slightly altered. She had pulled her hair down and twisted it into pigtails, with red rubber bands holding them tight one inch from the ends. She was wearing a green blouse and pink scarf, making her difficult to look at for a full class day. This time there was no pretense of doing a reading lesson or moving on to arithmetic. As soon as the bell rang, she simply began to talk.

She talked for forty minutes straight. There seemed to be less connection between her ideas, but the ideas themselves were, as the dictionary would say, fabulous. She said she had heard of a huge jewel, in what she called the antipodes, that was so brilliant that when light shone into it at a certain angle it would blind whoever was looking at its center. She said the biggest diamond in the world was cursed and had killed everyone who owned it, and that by a trick of fate it was called the Hope Diamond. Diamonds are magic, she said, and this is why women wear them on their fingers, as a sign of the magic of womanhood. Men have strength, Miss Ferenczi said, but no true magic. That is why men fall in love with women but women do not fall in love with men: they just love being loved. George Washington had died because of a mistake he made about a diamond. Washington was not the first *true* President, but she didn't say who was. In some places in the world, she said, men and women still live in the trees and eat monkeys for breakfast. Their doctors are magicians. At the bottom of the sea are creatures thin as pancakes who have never been studied by scientists because when you take them up to air, the fish explode.

There was not a sound in the classroom, except for Miss Ferenczi's voice, and Donna DeShano's coughing. No one even went to the bathroom.

Beethoven, she said, had not been deaf; it was a trick to make himself famous, and it worked. As she talked, Miss Ferenczi's pigtails swung back and forth. There are trees in the world, she said, that eat meat: their leaves are sticky and close up on bugs like hands. She lifted her hands and brought them together, palm to palm. Venus, which most people think is the next closest planet to the sun, is not always closer, and, besides, it is the planet of greatest mystery because of its thick cloud cover. "I know what lies underneath those clouds," Miss Ferenczi said, and waited. After the silence, she said, "Angels. Angels live under those clouds." She said that angels were not invisible to everyone and were in fact smarter than most people. They did not dress in robes as was often claimed but instead wore formal evening clothes, as if they were about to attend a concert. Often angels *do* attend concerts and sit in the aisles, where, she said, most people pay no attention to them. She said the most terrible angel had the shape of the Sphinx. "There is no running away from that one," she said. She said that unquenchable fires burn just under the surface of the earth in Ohio, and that the baby Mozart fainted dead away in his cradle when he first heard the sound of a trumpet. She said that someone named Narzim al Harrardim was the greatest writer who ever lived. She said that planets control behavior, and anyone conceived during a solar eclipse would be born with webbed feet.

"I know you children like to hear these things," she said, "these secrets, and that is why I am telling you all this." We nodded. It was better than doing comprehension questions for the readings in *Broad Horizons*.

"I will tell you one more story," she said, "and then we will have to do arithmetic." She leaned over, and her voice grew soft. "There is no death," she said. "You must never be afraid. Never. That which is, cannot die. It will change into different earthly and unearthly elements, but I know this as sure as I stand here in front of you, and I swear it: you must not be afraid. I have seen this truth with these eyes. I know it because in a dream God kissed me. Here." And she pointed with her right index finger to the side of her head, below the mouth where the vertical lines were carved into her skin.

Absentmindedly we all did our arithmetic problems. At recess the class was out on the playground, but no one was playing. We were all standing in small groups, talking about

Miss Ferenczi. We didn't know if she was crazy, or what. I looked out beyond the playground, at the rusted cars piled in a small heap behind a clump of sumac, and I wanted to see shapes there, approaching me.

On the way home, Carl sat next to me again. He didn't say much, and I didn't either. At last he turned to me. "You know what she said about the leaves that close up on bugs?"

"Huh?"

"The leaves," Carl insisted, "The meat-eating plants. I know it's true. I saw it on television. The leaves have this icky glue that the plants have got smeared all over them and the insects can't get off 'cause they're stuck. I saw it." He seemed demoralized. "She's tellin' the truth."

"Yeah."

"You think she's seen all those angels?"

I shrugged.

"I don't think she has," Carl informed me. "I think she made that part up."

"There's a tree," I suddenly said. I was looking out the window at the farms along County Road H. I knew every barn, every broken windmill, every fence, every anhydrous ammonia tank, by heart. "There's a tree that's . . . that I've seen . . ."

"Don't you try to do it," Carl said. "You'll just sound like a jerk."

I kissed my mother. She was standing in front of the stove. "How was your day?" she asked.

"Fine."

"Did you have Miss Ferenczi again?"

"Yeah."

"Well?"

"She was fine. Mom," I asked, "can I go to my room?"

"No," she said, "not until you've gone out to the vegetable garden and picked me a few tomatoes." She glanced at the sky. "I think it's going to rain. Skedaddle and do it now. Then you come back inside and watch your brother for a few minutes while I go upstairs. I need to clean up before dinner." She looked down at me. "You're looking a little pale, Tommy." She touched the back of her hand to my forehead and I felt her diamond ring against my skin. "Do you feel all right?"

"I'm fine," I said, and went out to pick the tomatoes.

Coughing mutedly, Mr. Hibler was back the next day, slipping lozenges into his mouth when his back was turned at forty-five minute intervals and asking us how much of his prepared lesson plan Miss Ferenczi had followed. Edith Atwater took the responsibility for the class of explaining to Mr. Hibler that the substitute hadn't always done exactly what he, Mr. Hibler, would have done, but we had worked hard even though she talked a lot. About what? he asked. All kinds of things, Edith said. I sort of forgot. To our relief, Mr. Hibler seemed not at all interested in what Miss Ferenczi had said to fill the day. He probably thought it was woman's talk: unserious and not suited for school. It was enough that he had a pile of arithmetic problems from us to correct.

For the next month, the sumac turned a distracting red in the field, and the sun traveled toward the southern sky, so that its rays reached Mr. Hibler's Halloween display on the bulletin board in the back of the room, fading the pumpkin head scarecrow from orange to tan. Every three days I measured how much farther the sun had moved toward the southern horizon by making small marks with my black Crayola on the north wall, ant-sized marks only I knew were there.

And then in early December, four days after the first permanent snowfall, she appeared again in our classroom. The minute she came in the door, I felt my heart begin to pound. Once again, she was different: this time, her hair hung straight down and seemed hardly to have been combed. She hadn't brought her lunchbox with her, but she was carrying what seemed to be a small box. She greeted all of us and talked about the weather. Donna DeShano had to remind her to take her overcoat off.

When the bell to start the day finally rang, Miss Ferenczi looked out at all of us and said, "Children, I have enjoyed your company in the past, and today I am going to reward you." She held up the small box. "Do you know what this is?" She waited. "Of course you don't. It is a Tarot pack."

Edith Atwater raised her hand. "What's a Tarot pack, Miss Ferenczi?"

"It is used to tell fortunes," she said. "And that is what I shall do this morning. I shall tell your fortunes, as I have been taught to do."

"What's fortune?" Bobby Kryzanowicz asked.

"The future, young man. I shall tell you what your future will be. I can't do your whole future, of course. I shall have to limit myself to the five-card system, the wands, cups, swords, pentacles, and the higher arcanes. Now who wants to be first?"

There was a long silence. Then Carol Peterson raised her hand.

"All right," Miss Ferenczi said. She divided the pack into five smaller packs and walked back to Carol's desk, in front of mine. "Pick one card from each one of these packs," she said. I saw that Carol had a four of cups and a six of swords, but I couldn't see the other cards. Miss Ferenczi studied the cards on Carol's desk for a minute. "Not bad," she said. "I do not see much higher education. Probably an early marriage. Many children. There's something bleak and dreary here, but I can't tell what. Perhaps just the tasks of a housewife life. I think you'll do very well, for the most part." She smiled at Carol, a smile with a certain lack of interest. "Who wants to be next?"

Carl Whiteside raised his hand slowly.

"Yes," Miss Ferenczi said, "let's do a boy." She walked over to where Carl sat. After he picked his five cards, she gazed at them for a long time. "Travel," she said. "Much distant travel. You might go into the army. Not too much romantic interest here. A late marriage, if at all. But the Sun in your major arcana, that's a very good card." She giggled. "You'll have a happy life."

Next I raised my hand. She told me my future. She did the same with Bobby Kryzanowicz, Kelly Munger, Edith Atwater, and Kim Foor. Then she came to Wayne Razmer. He picked his five cards, and I could see that the Death card was one of them.

"What's your name?" Miss Ferenczi asked.

"Wayne."

"Well, Wayne," she said, "you will undergo a great metamorphosis, a change, before you become an adult. Your earthly element will no doubt leap higher, because you seem to be a sweet boy. This card, this nine of swords, tells me of suffering and desolation. And this ten of wands, well, that's a heavy load."

"What about this one?" Wayne pointed at the Death card.

"It means, my sweet, that you will die soon." She gathered up the cards. We were all looking at Wayne. "But do not fear," she said. "It is not really death. Just change. Out of your earthly shape." She put the cards on Mr. Hibler's desk. "And now, let's do some arithmetic."

At lunchtime Wayne went to Mr. Faegre, the principal, and informed him of what Miss Ferenczi had done. During the noon recess, we saw Miss Ferenczi drive out of the parking lot in her rusting green Rambler American. I stood under the slide, listening to the other kids coasting down and landing in the little depressive bowls at the bottom. I was kicking stones and tugging at my hair right up to the moment when I saw Wayne come out to the playground. He smiled, the dead fool, and with the fingers of his right hand he was showing everyone how he had told on Miss Ferenczi.

I made my way toward Wayne, pushing myself past two girls from another class. He was watching me with his little pinhead eyes.

"You told," I shouted at him. "She was just kidding."

"She shouldn't have," he shouted back. "We were supposed to be doing arithmetic."

"She just scared you," I said. "You're a chicken. You're a chicken, Wayne. You are. Scared of a little card," I sing-songed.

Wayne fell at me, his two fists hammering down on my nose. I gave him a good one in the stomach and then I tried for his head. Aiming my fist, I saw that he was crying. I slugged him.

"She was right," I yelled. "She was always right! She told the truth!" Other kids were whooping. "You were just scared, that's all!"

And then large hands pulled at us, and it was my turn to speak to Mr. Faegre.

In the afternoon Miss Ferenczi was gone, and my nose was stuffed with cotton clotted with blood, and my lip had swelled, and our class had been combined with Mrs. Mantei's sixth-grade class for a crowded afternoon science unit on insect life in ditches and swamps. I knew where Mrs. Mantei lived: she had a new house trailer just down the road from us, at the Clearwater Park. She was no mystery. Somehow she and Mr. Bodine, the other fourth-grade teacher, had managed to fit forty-five desks into the room. Kelly Munger asked if Miss Ferenczi had been arrested, and Mrs. Mantei said no, of course not. All that afternoon, until the buses came to pick us up, we learned about field crickets and two-striped grasshoppers, water bugs, cicadas, mosquitoes, flies, and moths. We learned about insects' hard outer shell, the exoskeleton, and the usual parts of the mouth, including the labrum, mandible, maxilla, and glossa. We learned about compound eyes, and the four-stage metamorphosis from egg to larva to pupa to adult. We learned something, but not much, about mating. Mrs. Mantei drew, very skillfully, the internal anatomy of the grasshopper on the blackboard. We learned about the dance of the honeybee, directing other bees in the hive to pollen. We found out about which insects were pests to man, and which were not. On lined white pieces of paper we made lists of insects we might actually see, then a list of insects too small to be clearly visible, such as fleas; Mrs. Mantei said that our assignment would be to memorize these lists for the next day, when Mr. Hibler would certainly return and test us on our knowledge.

Some of Our Work
with Monsters

Ron Carlson

Elaine and I had been working in the lab, dismantling the sleep research equipment, when the call came from the Secret Agency. We hadn't planned on a big project so soon. Elaine wanted to go up to Union City to see our son, Grant, and his wife, Karla, and the baby. We missed them, and we needed a break. Grant's the mayor of Union City, and they had just put his name on the water tower over the population, 2,234, and we wanted to go up there and kiss everybody and take a few photographs. Elaine and I joked about wanting some proof that we were grandparents. We'd lived a life looking for proof, and now we had a grandchild. We hadn't realized how much we wanted to be grandparents; we hadn't even thought about that word. Sometimes there's a real gap between a word and the thing, and we have learned that empirical evidence can narrow that gap. Grandfather. Grandmother. Of course, we were still young people, but we needed to see Carlisle, the baby. I had a real interest in holding the baby. A fact, our little fact.

But, when the Secret Agency calls, you listen. These people do all their contracts over the phone, and by the time we hung up the receiver, we were definitely hired. They sent a plane that night, and a driver came to our apartment while we were still packing. We didn't know if we would be gone overnight or for a couple of weeks. He stood in the bedroom doorway in his dark suit and skinny tie.

"How long will we be gone," Elaine asked him, "a day or a couple of weeks?"

"I don't know," the driver said. "I'm just the driver." Elaine is a scrupulous packer; she can pack like nobody. She's experienced at packing. She's gone everywhere and arrived with the right stuff, even Alaska. At least, we think it was Alaska. It was a ten-day job in a snow-packed place. This new job was in the Midwest. The guy on the phone, the Secret Guy, had said the Midwest. It would require warm clothing and some lighter stuff; it could get cold in the spring.

Elaine and I hadn't spoken about it, but we already knew what the job was. It had been in all the papers every day. It was the new monster. The monster was doing a lot of damage and he was responsible for a great deal of harm. Some of the things the monster had done were difficult to listen to. They were terrible. It had been going on for months, but the Secret Agency was closing in. We'd seen it like this before. It takes a while for there to be sightings. Then the evidence piles up, and pretty soon, they're closing in on the monster.

It puts us in a tough spot, but that's why they pay us the big bucks.

The Secret Agency has about ten ways to kill the monster, but only one or two work, and it's never the same ones. These guys spend all their time working up ways to kill the monster. They've done it again and again. Usually they try to kill the monster three or four ways before they find the right way to kill him, and then they do that. It's always a big show, and we've been in it up close where some of the monster got on us.

When we arrived at the airport the driver went through the secret gate and drove us to the unlighted runway and the Secret Airplane. I was pretty worried about the way I'd packed because I'd been warm all day and I think I put in too many light clothes. Cold rain in the forties would render me ineffective. Sleet would render me ineffective. I'd also forgotten my gloves. I knew Elaine would have gloves, an extra pair, but we'd done that before. They don't fit.

As he stopped at the Secret Plane, the driver said, "What are you going to recommend about the monster?"

Elaine said, "You're just the driver; you don't need to know."

The driver said, "I'm also the pilot and the Director of the Mission. Climb aboard. I'm interested to hear your ideas." He changed hats and led us onto the Secret Plane.

The secret airplanes are small but nice. They have a fridge with all the stuff we don't have at home. We don't keep candy in our fridge. Elaine and I have a policy of never going for the fridge right away, but as we begin our descent, we always enjoy a light snack. The Director of the Mission didn't want a snack. He wanted to know what we were going to recommend about the monster.

"You know our recommendation," Elaine told him.

"You make the same recommendation every time," the Director of our Mission told her. "Do you know the facts of this case?"

"We've studied the dossier and we've seen the papers. This is a textbook monster."

"And we need to destroy it before it does more damage or harm." The Director was firm on this. He spoke into the radio, circled the plane, and landed in a dark place.

"We need to study the monster," Elaine said. How many times had we said this? We said this every monster. "You can't kill it. We need to keep it alive."

"Tell that to the next farmer who loses his family and all his livestock and outbuildings," the Director of the Mission said.

"We've met the people who have suffered harm and damage," I told the Director. We had moved into his command tent now, and we were looking at the big maps taped to the table. Elaine and I had met these people at every monster and their stories made us sick and dizzy. They hated us because we wanted to save the monster. These were terrible moments for us, sitting in the rocks and rubble of someone's house, usually smoke rising around us, while the survivor looked at us as if we were the monster. Well, we weren't the monster! We were trying to save the monster so we could study the monster. Sometimes, the monster was one of a kind, and the Secret Agency only wanted to blow it up or hang it or drown it in acid, trying their various methods until they found the one that worked.

"What if it was your family!" The survivors of the monster attacks shouted at us. "What if it was you or you!"

This is when Elaine would say, "Then we hope somebody else would capture and study the monster." But this didn't get through and sometimes the survivors of the monster attacks would come up and act like they were going to strike us or jump on us, but over all these years, none have.

"Where's the monster now?" Elaine said.

"Right here," one of the secret guys said, pointing at the telegrid screen. We looked at the screen and could see the little blip moving through the quadrants.

"It's a big monster," Elaine said. She looked at me. "It's as tall as you are."

"And fast," the Director of the Mission said. "But we've got ways to kill this big, fast monster."

"More than one way, I bet," Elaine said.

"Ten ways," the Director of the Mission said, holding up all ten fingers.

A gust of chilly wind ripped at the command tent and Elaine looked at me. "Did you bring your khaki jacket?" she asked.

"I've only got a sweater vest and my old school scarf."

"Oh Ron," she said, and though it was a scolding, I loved to hear it. "You're going to catch a real cold this time and flu season is approaching."

"Is summer flu season?" A chill shot through me because if I was sick, I wouldn't get to hold the baby. I wanted to hold Carlisle. I had to get to Union City and hold the baby!

Now we could hear the droning of big motors, and the man running the telegrid said, "Here come the big robotdrones." On the screen we could see the six big robotdrones.

"They'll get the monster," the Director said.

"No they won't," Elaine said. "The Secret Agency has tried robotdrones on every monster for the last thirty years and the robotdrones have never ever worked against a single monster."

"They might this time," the Director said.

We all put our faces closer to the green telegrid screen. We watched the robotdrones approach the monster and then turn in different directions and go off the screen. The blip of the monster still roved freely.

"Shoot!" the Director swore. "Where'd they go?"

"Sir," the telegrid man said. "One of the robotdrones is coming this way."

We all filed into the bunker under the mission control tent. It was warm down there out of the wind, and Elaine sat by me on one of the sandbags. "This happened before with a robotdrone," she said. "It chased us and blew up some things."

"Don't you criticize the robotdrone program," the Director of the Mission said. "They'll work it out." Around the dark room we could see everybody's eyeballs. The robotdrone roar grew louder and louder and then the explosion shook the mission control bunker and loose dirt filtered down on us all. We went up into the tent, which was ripped up mostly. The telegrid machine was in flinders. By now night had passed and it was dawn's early light and dust and smoke and some small fires.

"You can't kill this monster," Elaine said to the Director. "We need to study him."

"Somebody get this person away from me," he said. "Call me a command vehicle."

"You know," she said, "as well as I do that this monster is one of a kind."

"They're all one of a kind," he said. "We know that. If they were all alike, we could kill them without any trouble." A truckload of men in army gear arrived and began cleaning up the robotdrone debris. They called orders back and forth. Every few minutes we could hear the other robotdrones exploding in the distance, over here and then way over there.

The command vehicle arrived, a big Winnebago painted army green with ten antennae sticking out of the top. We followed the Director of the Mission aboard and looked at the portable telegrid they had in the module. There was nothing on the screen now except the wiggly lines where the robotdrones had crashed and burned various parts of the country.

"He's not moving now," the Director of the Mission said.

"He's nocturnal," Elaine said.

"We've seen several nocturnal monsters," I said. "In our studies."

The Director of the Mission looked at me.

"If we could capture him and study him," Elaine said, "we'd know a lot more about nocturnal monsters."

I could tell the Director of the Mission did not like to hear the word *nocturnal*. He had a look on his face that indicated he was going to scream if we said it again.

"Let's drive up to the quadrant where the monster was last marked," he said. "And see what we see. We'll lay out the glowing bags of poison; they sometimes work."

"They've never worked," Elaine said. "They're just another way of inflating your budget. We've never had a monster, even those starved monsters in New Zealand, who fell for the glowing poison bags."

"We'll deploy the glowing bags of poison if I say so," the Director of the Mission said. He opened the storage room where we could see the bags glowing.

The driver of the command Winnebago was a young woman in army clothes. She was one of the best drivers we'd ever had and never took any corners too hard. The refrigerators in the command Winnebagos aren't as interesting as the ones in the Secret Airplanes. They have some bottled water and cold cuts, but no candy and no fresh fruit. I made us all a turkey sandwich with cheddar for the long drive to Quadrant 44.

Quadrant 44 was desolate in a windy, springtime way. The prairie here was barren of trees and only marked here and there by humpy bluffs grown with long grass. We stood on one bluff and surveyed the entire area. A herd of cattle grazed nearby in the rippling waves of grass. We could see a long way and there was nothing but a couple spires of smoke on the horizon.

"He's out here somewhere."

"He's lying in the grass or he's found a hole," Elaine said.

"Deploy the glowing bags of poison," the Director of the Mission said.

"We're here to save the monster and study him," I said. "We can't help you deploy the glowing bags of poison."

"They're heavy," the Director of the Mission said. "We need help."

We watched the driver and the Director of the Mission struggle with a glowing bag of poison.

Elaine stood with her arms folded.

"The bags of poison are not effective," I told her. "They won't kill the monster. We've never seen a monster fall for the glowing bags of poison." We could see the driver sweating as she lifted her end of the bag of poison. They could not lift it out of the Command Winnebago, but they were going to keep trying, bumping it along the floor of the vehicle toward the door. The driver was sweating and the Director of the Mission was huffing and puffing.

"O.K.," Elaine said, taking hold of the first bag, "but the Secret Agency is full of big bad baloney." So, this way we helped them deploy the glowing bags of poison. By the time we'd finished, we were all thirsty and we sat drinking bottled water in the Command Winnebago, listening to the wind blow.

"What'd you do before you joined the Secret Agency, Monster Division," Elaine asked him.

"I was in their motor pool. They've got some stuff in there. It isn't a typical motor pool."

"Do they have that One-Man Radar-Deflecting Hovercraft," I asked him. We'd heard the same rumors everyone else had.

"You didn't hear it from me," the Director said. He reached in a small drawer and pulled out a deck of cards. They were shiny black playing cards with the Secret Agency's Insignia in the center. "You want to see some card tricks?" He shuffled the deck and did some good tricks. The Lost Soldier, The Everlasting Three, No Diamonds, and he ended with Big Jack. "Yeah, I was in motor pool, but I had to move up. I didn't make up the Secret Agency's monster policy, but I'm the Director now."

"No family?" Elaine asked him.

"I've got the monster," he said. When he said it, he looked like that one actor, a guy I like.

It was a breezy afternoon on the old prairie. We'd been up all night, the three of us. I didn't know if the driver had been up all night or not. We were all tired in the Command Winnebago out on the empty prairie in the long afternoon. Sleep filled me up like sand in an hourglass and I put my feet up and went out.

The Command Winnebago rocked slightly in the wind. It wasn't unpleasant. I dreamed the same old dreams where I was working in the lab. I had something on the burner and something in the sink and I was missing a vial of something. I was stretched out between the two projects trying to keep them from blowing up. We've had a few unplanned explosions, but fewer than most small research facilities. When things blow up in Elaine's lab, we never spend very much time on recrimination and negative energy. We usually clean up and try something else. In my dream both projects were about to blow, when Elaine came in with her arms full of boxes. I had some trouble in the dream getting her attention, but when I did, she turned off the water and then she turned off the burner, and we ate lunch. In the boxes she had Chinese food and we ate in the dream for a long time.

I woke at midnight. The wind had stopped. Everyone else was still asleep, and the Director of the Mission was a noisy sleeper, the way worried people often can be. Elaine and I had done a ton of sleep research over the years. Our conclusion was that sleep knits up the raveled sleeve of care. Lack of sleep is a factor in most crime, and the worst place to try to sleep is prison. It's a terrible cycle that goes on and on. Our article went on and on. I was glad to see the Director of the Mission sleeping, because he was a man who had important decisions to make every minute, and sleep would help with that.

It was a clear night out, stars, but I could see something else outside the windows. Something was glowing and at first I thought it was the bags of poison we had deployed, but then I saw the shape nearby. I knew what it was, and I quietly woke Elaine. We opened the door on the still prairie and we walked out to the glowing object. It was one of the cows laid out dead and glowing. We could see the other cattle where they lay glowing in the night. They were beautiful and terrible, the kind of thing you don't see twice. Elaine called back to the Director of the Mission who stood in the Command Winnebago doorway, "You've killed all these cattle with your stupid glowing bags of poison."

The Director of the Mission called out to us. "Get back here right now. The monster is coming this way!"

"You've poisoned all the cattle!" Elaine cried out.

"Get back here!" the Director screamed. "He is approaching!"

"He is approaching," the driver called.

We looked around in a complete circle. There was nothing in the quiet world except the square box of the Command Winnebago. The sky was bigger than the earth and it was jostling with stars. The poisoned cows glowed like little scattered campfires.

"We should go back," I said.

Elaine was thinking it over. I loved this feature of hers. She was evaluating what to do. "He's going to think we tried to poison him," I told her.

"Listen," she said.

I'd been listening. There was nothing, except the Director of the Mission calling and calling, get back, come back here now, I order you back here, he's coming, we see him on the screen, come back, etcetera.

"We want to save you!" Elaine called into the night. She was walking further away from the Command Winnebago.

"Did you hear the monster?" I asked her.

"Something," she said.

Behind us I heard the Director of the Mission cry, "I've called in the Space Lasers! Come back here!"

"The Space Lasers don't work!" Elaine said. I knew she was right with this one. The Space Laser was like handing a baby a flashlight; the beams went everywhere. We'd seen the Space Lasers one time in Canada and they wouldn't melt snow.

"Ten seconds!" the Director of the Mission called. Nine, eight, seven, six. . . .

The first big laser beam zipped past us like a flashbulb and then another ran behind us, bright and silent. Pretty soon the whole plain was crisscrossed with great lines of light in a kind of entertainment. The flashes were painful and I had to squint. From time to time in the display, two or three streams of photons would converge and we'd hear the hiss of burning grass. Elaine took my hand and we sat down in the thick prairie grass. She was rapt, and I knew she wanted to know if we might see the rumored Big DeLuxe Lasers. There had been so much talk about these super lasers, the next phase in laser work. The shafts of resonant light hummed back and forth. We'd worked with lasers and we'd had our difficulties. Suddenly, in a flash brighter than a force-four magnesium flare, our shadows were printed on the grassy world in a microsecond, and we saw for a true fact the Big DeLuxe Laser, a rod of light thick as a column in the Supreme Court. It beamed down and then split and fizzled. It hit near the Command Winnebago, and we heard glass break as the windshield exploded and smoke poured out. The Director and the driver stumbled out of the door coughing in the roving lasers. In the flashes the two Secret Agency employees looked like they were doing a jerky puppet dance.

A moment later the Space Lasers abated and the world was dark again and silent, though we couldn't see anything for four of five minutes while our eyes adjusted.

The driver led the Director of the Mission by the elbow over to where we stood in the grass. The Command Winnebago was burning lazily behind us.

"Don't tell me those lasers aren't powerful," the Director of the Mission said.

"We've killed the cattle," Elaine told him. "This happens again and again."

The driver stared in horror at the glowing cow.

The Director was speaking into his phone. "Get me a Gas-Bearing Hovercraft right now," he said. "We're in quadrant 44 near the little fire."

"We saw him on the screen," the woman driver said to us. "He's right here. Did you see him?"

"He's here somewhere," Elaine said. "I could tell, but we had no visual."

The driver went to the Director of the Mission and clenched the front of his khaki shirt in both of her hands. "I'm just a driver," she said, "and I think I'm a good driver, but I'm not a monster person. I'm not a cow killer. What are we doing here? What do I drive now?" She pointed over to the flaming Command Winnebago.

"What's your name, soldier," the Director of the Mission asked her.

The driver let go of the Director of the Mission's shirt and stepped back into a salute, saying, "Corporal Ashton."

The Director of the Mission returned the salute, and he looked into her face like a man reading important news in a letter. "Corporal Ashton, we've been through a lot together on this mission, and now your duty is to get us to Union City." We saw him press a field compass in her palm.

"Hey," I said, "our son is mayor of Union City. They just put his name on the water tower."

"Well, he's going to have his hands full with this guy," the Director said.

"What do you mean?" I asked him.

"Quadrant 44 is right outside Union City. This monster is definitely heading toward Union City. He's on a collision course with Union City. You people," the Director said. "Now how do you feel about save the monster, study the monster?"

Then we heard a humming sound like an old vacuum in the other room of a house, and we spotted the sleek little One-Man Radar-Deflecting Hovercraft sliding over the prairie coming our way. It was as neat as the rumors had it. The craft came up and hovered before us, humming. The pilot was a young guy who peeled off his gas mask and asked the Director, "Did you have lasers? Were the lasers out here?"

"Forget the lasers," the Director said. "Prepare to lay down the Green Gas." We could see the gas tubes on the back of the hovercraft.

"Will do," the young guy said, handing us each a polygold gasmask. He began circling us with the hovercraft in wider and wider circles and then we saw the first plumes of the Green Gas drifting over the ground. It made a pretty layer in the pale night.

"You won't need that gasmask," Elaine told Corporal Ashton, "the gas isn't going to hurt you." The woman had the mask on and looked up from her compass at us. The Director had his mask on.

Elaine dropped her gasmask onto the ground and so did I. She's taken the lead in some of our best work. Now she took my hand and we hurried north toward Union City.

"Be careful of that Green Gas!" the Director said, muffled through his gas mask. "Watch out!"

The Green Gas swirled around our legs as we kicked through it. We'd seen four gases total that the Secret Agency deploys and they haven't had any discernable effect in years. They're all caffeine based, so there's a little stimulation, but it dissipates. We could hear the prairie dogs starting to yip and scramble in the living world. Morning is a blessing everywhere, of course, and I could smell the new day coming for us. The light on the horizon was a pearl crescent prying the edge of the dark firmament.

"I didn't know Quadrant 44 was next to Union City," Elaine said. We stopped and I could just see her worried face in the small light. "It's hard. Everything tests you."

"Life's a real experiment," I said. It was what we always said when we were stymied. We'd been stymied plenty by various stymies.

Behind us I could hear the Director and Corporal Ashton jogging to catch up. The Director had retrieved our gas masks and swung them as he ran. He was in charge of every aspect of this mission.

I turned to Corporal Ashton. "We're going to see our grandson for the first time. We've never even seen him, and finally our work has brought us to this town." Daylight was inventing Union City.

"I loved my grandpa," Corporal Ashton said. The corporal was full of the green gas, and she asked Elaine, "How do you make love last? Is the monster part of it? Do you need a monster?"

This was a discussion Elaine usually took up, but I could see other thoughts on her face. She merely said to the young soldier, "A monster makes falling in love easier, but love can withstand the absence of monsters."

"Don't worry about the monster, Corporal Ashton," the Director of the Mission said. "He's nocturnal."

We came to the railroad trestle and stepped down the gravel bank to the footbridge. We could see the silver water tower on its six tall legs. Then the Director of the Mission said, "After we regroup and get some chow, I'm going to call in the magneto screens."

"Do that," I told him. We both knew too well how stupid the big noisy magneto screens were. They would do nothing but wreck everybody's wristwatch for forty miles.

"His name is Grant?" the Director pointed at the water tower. "Look at those letters." We could see our son's name. We'd all taken a little of the gas and felt stimulated. "They're ten feet tall. You guys sure did something right to raise a mayor like that."

Elaine had let go of my hand now, and I saw her step in front of the Director of the Mission. She had him by the shoulders as if he were a lectern, and she was face to face with him. "Hello," she said. "Listen. What else have you guys got, besides the magnetos? Can you call in the vacuum ray? Come on, look at that tank. This is Union City. There are two thousand people here. You're the Secret Agency; isn't there something you can do?"

A true work of fiction does all of the following things, and does them elegantly, efficiently; it creates a vivid and continuous dream in the reader's mind; it is implicitly philosophical; it fulfills or at least deals with all the expectations it sets up; and it strikes us, in the end, not simply as a thing done but as a shining performance.
—John Gardner

Cathedral

Raymond Carver

This blind man, an old friend of my wife's, he was on his way to spend the night. His wife had died. So he was visiting the dead wife's relatives in Connecticut. He called my wife from his in-laws'. Arrangements were made. He would come by train, a five-hour trip, and my wife would meet him at the station. She hadn't seen him since she worked for him one summer in Seattle ten years ago. But she and the blind man had kept in touch. They made tapes and mailed them back and forth. I wasn't enthusiastic about his visit. He was no one I knew. And his being blind bothered me. My idea of blindness came from the movies. In the movies, the blind moved slowly and never laughed. Sometimes they were led by seeing-eye dogs. A blind man in my house was not something I looked forward to.

That summer in Seattle she had needed a job. She didn't have any money. The man she was going to marry at the end of the summer was in officers' training school. He didn't have any money, either. But she was in love with the guy, and he was in love with her, etc. She'd seen something in the paper: HELP WANTED—*Reading to Blind Man,* and a telephone number. She phoned and went over, was hired on the spot. She'd worked with this blind man all summer. She read stuff to him, case studies, reports, that sort of thing. She helped him organize his little office in the county social-service department. They'd become good friends, my wife and the blind man. How do I know these things? She told me. And she told me something else. On her last day in the office, the blind man asked if he could touch her face. She agreed to this. She told me he touched his fingers to every part of her face, her nose—even her neck! She never forgot it. She even tried to write a poem about it. She was always trying to write a poem. She wrote a poem or two every year, usually after something really important had happened to her.

When we first started going out together, she showed me the poem. In the poem, she recalled his fingers and the way they had moved around over her face. In the poem, she talked about what she had felt at the time, about what went through her mind when the blind man touched her nose and lips. I can remember I didn't think much of the poem. Of course, I didn't tell her that. Maybe I just don't understand poetry. I admit it's not the first thing I reach for when I pick up something to read.

Anyway, this man who'd first enjoyed her favors, the officer-to-be, he'd been her childhood sweetheart. So okay. I'm saying that at the end of the summer she let the blind man run his hands over her face, said goodbye to him, married her childhood etc., who was now a commissioned officer, and she moved away from Seattle. But they'd kept in touch, she and the blind man. She made the first contact after a year or so. She called him up one night from an Air Force base in Alabama. She wanted to talk. They talked. He asked her to send him a tape and tell him about her life. She did this. She sent the tape. On the tape, she told the blind man about her husband and about their life together in the military.

She told the blind man she loved her husband but she didn't like it where they lived and she didn't like it that he was a part of the military-industrial thing. She told the blind man she'd written a poem and he was in it. She told him that she was writing a poem about what it was like to be an Air Force officer's wife. The poem wasn't finished yet. She was still writing it. The blind man made a tape. He sent her the tape. She made a tape. This went on for years. My wife's officer was posted to one base and then another. She sent tapes from Moody AFB, McGuire, McConnell, and finally Travis, near Sacramento, where one night she got to feeling lonely and cut off from people she kept losing in that moving-around life. She got to feeling she couldn't go it another step. She went in and swallowed all the pills and capsules in the medicine chest and washed them down with a bottle of gin. Then she got into a hot bath and passed out.

But instead of dying, she got sick. She threw up. Her officer—why should he have a name? he was the childhood sweetheart, and what more does he want?—came home from somewhere, found her, and called the ambulance. In time, she put it all on a tape and sent the tape to the blind man. Over the years, she put all kinds of stuff on tapes and sent the tapes off lickety-split. Next to writing a poem every year, I think it was her chief means of recreation. On one tape, she told the blind man she'd decided to live away from her officer for a time. On another tape, she told him about her divorce. She and I began going out, and of course she told her blind man about it. She told him everything, or so it seemed to me. Once she asked me if I'd like to hear the latest tape from the blind man. This was a year ago. I was on the tape, she said. So I said okay, I'd listen to it. I got us drinks and we settled down in the living room. We made ready to listen. First she inserted the tape into the player and adjusted a couple of dials. Then she pushed a lever. The tape squeaked and someone began to talk in this loud voice. She lowered the volume. After a few minutes of harmless chitchat, I heard my own name in the mouth of this stranger, this blind man I didn't even know! And then this: "From all you've said about him, I can only conclude—" But we were interrupted, a knock at the door, something, and we didn't ever get back to the tape. Maybe it was just as well. I'd heard all I wanted to.

Now this same blind man was coming to sleep in my house.

"Maybe I could take him bowling," I said to my wife. She was at the draining board doing scalloped potatoes. She put down the knife she was using and turned around.

"If you love me," she said, "you can do this for me. If you don't love me, okay. But if you had a friend, any friend, and the friend came to visit, I'd make him feel comfortable." She wiped her hands with the dish towel.

"I don't have any blind friends," I said.

"You don't have *any* friends," she said. "Period. Besides," she said, "goddamn it, his wife's just died! Don't you understand that? The man's lost his wife!"

I didn't answer. She'd told me a little about the blind man's wife. Her name was Beulah. Beulah! That's a name for a colored woman.

"Was his wife a Negro?" I asked.

"Are you crazy?" my wife said. "Have you just flipped or something?" She picked up a potato. I saw it hit the floor, then roll under the stove. "What's wrong with you?" she said "Are you drunk?"

"I'm just asking," I said.

Right then my wife filled me in with more detail than I cared to know. I made a drink and sat at the kitchen table to listen. Pieces of the story began to fall into place.

Beulah had gone to work for the blind man the summer after my wife had stopped working for him. Pretty soon Beulah and the blind man had themselves a church wedding. It was a little wedding—who'd want to go to such a wedding in the first place?—just the two of them, plus the minister and the minister's wife. But it was a church wedding just the same. It was what Beulah had wanted, he'd said. But even then Beulah must have been carrying the cancer in her glands. After they had been inseparable for eight years—my wife's word, *inseparable*—Beulah's health went into a rapid decline. She died in a Seattle hospital room, the blind man sitting beside the bed and holding on to her hand. They'd married, lived and worked together, slept together—had sex, sure—and then the blind man had to bury her. All this without his having ever seen what the goddamned woman looked like. It was beyond my understanding. Hearing this, I felt sorry for the blind man for a little bit. And then I found myself thinking what a pitiful life this woman must have led. Imagine a woman who could never see herself as she was seen in the eyes of her loved one. A woman who could go on day after day and never receive the smallest compliment from her beloved. A woman whose husband could never read the expression on her face, be it misery or something better. Someone who could wear makeup or not—what difference to him? She could, if she wanted, wear green eyeshadow around one eye, a straight pin in her nostril, yellow slacks and purple shoes, no matter. And then to slip off into death, the blind man's hand on her hand, his blind eyes streaming tears—I'm imagining now—her last thought maybe this: that he never even knew what she looked like, and she on an express to the grave. Robert was left with a small insurance policy and half of a twentypeso Mexican coin. The other half of the coin went into the box with her. Pathetic.

So when the time rolled around, my wife went to the depot to pick him up. With nothing to do but wait—sure, I blamed him for that—I was having a drink and watching the TV when I heard the car pull into the drive. I got up from the sofa with my drink and went to the window to have a look.

I saw my wife laughing as she parked the car. I saw her get out of the car and shut the door. She was still wearing a smile. Just amazing. She went around to the other side of the car to where the blind man was already starting to get out. This blind man, feature this, he was wearing a full beard! A beard on a blind man! Too much, I say. The blind man reached into the back seat and dragged out a suitcase. My wife took his arm, shut the car door, and, talking all the way, moved him down the drive and then up the steps to the front porch. I turned off the TV. I finished my drink, rinsed the glass, dried my hands. Then I went to the door.

My wife said, "I want you to meet Robert. Robert, this is my husband. I've told you all about him." She was beaming. She had this blind man by his coat sleeve.

The blind man let go of his suitcase and up came his hand.

I took it. He squeezed hard, held my hand, and then he let it go.

"I feel like we've already met," he boomed.

"Likewise," I said. I didn't know what else to say. Then I said, "Welcome. I've heard a lot about you." We began to move then, a little group, from the porch into the living room, my wife guiding him by the arm. The blind man was carrying his suitcase in his other hand. My wife said things like, "To your left here, Robert. That's right. Now watch it, there's a chair. That's it. Sit down right here. This is the sofa. We just bought this sofa two weeks ago."

I started to say something about the old sofa. I'd liked that old sofa. But I didn't say anything. Then I wanted to say something else, small-talk, about the scenic ride along the

Hudson. How going *to* New York, you should sit on the right-hand side of the train, and coming *from* New York, the left-hand side.

"Did you have a good train ride?" I said. "Which side of the train did you sit on, by the way?"

"What a question, which side!" my wife said. "What's it matter which side?" she said.

"I just asked," I said.

"Right side," the blind man said. "I hadn't been on a train in nearly forty years. Not since I was a kid. With my folks. That's been a long time. I'd nearly forgotten the sensation. I have winter in my beard now," he said. "So I've been told, anyway. Do I look distinguished, my dear?" the blind man said to my wife.

"You look distinguished, Robert," she said. "Robert," she said. "Robert, it's just so good to see you."

My wife finally took her eyes off the blind man and looked at me. I had the feeling she didn't like what she saw. I shrugged.

I've never met, or personally known, anyone who was blind. This blind man was late forties, a heavy-set, balding man with stooped shoulders, as if he carried a great weight there. He wore brown slacks, brown shoes, a light-brown shirt, a tie, a sports coat. Spiffy. He also had this full beard. But he didn't use a cane and he didn't wear dark glasses. I'd always thought dark glasses were a must for the blind. Fact was, I wished he had a pair. At first glance, his eyes looked like anyone else's eyes. But if you looked close, there was something different about them. Too much white in the iris, for one thing, and the pupils seemed to move around in the sockets without his knowing it or being able to stop it. Creepy. As I stared at his face, I saw the left pupil turn in toward his nose while the other made an effort to keep in one place. But it was only an effort, for that eye was on the roam without his knowing it or wanting it to be.

I said, "Let me get you a drink. What's your pleasure? We have a little of everything. It's one of our pastimes."

"Bub, I'm a Scotch man myself," he said fast enough in this big voice.

"Right," I said. Bub! "Sure you are. I knew it."

He let his fingers touch his suitcase, which was sitting alongside the sofa. He was taking his bearings. I didn't blame him for that.

"I'll move that up to your room," my wife said.

"No, that's fine," the blind man said loudly. "It can go up when I go up."

"A little water with the Scotch?" I said.

"Very little," he said.

"I knew it," I said.

He said, "Just a tad. The Irish actor, Barry Fitzgerald? I'm like that fellow. When I drink water, Fitzgerald said, I drink water. When I drink whiskey, I drink whiskey." My wife laughed. The blind man brought his hand up under his beard. He lifted his beard slowly and let it drop.

I did the drinks, three big glasses of Scotch with a splash of water in each. Then we made ourselves comfortable and talked about Robert's travels. First the long flight from the West Coast to Connecticut, we covered that. Then from Connecticut up here by train. We had another drink concerning that leg of the trip.

I remembered having read somewhere that the blind didn't smoke because, as speculation had it, they couldn't see the smoke they exhaled. I thought I knew that much and that much only about blind people. But this blind man smoked his cigarette down to the nubbin and then lit another one. This blind man filled his ashtray and my wife emptied it.

When we sat down at the table for dinner, we had another drink. My wife heaped Robert's plate with cube steak, scalloped potatoes, green beans. I buttered him up two slices of bread. I said, "Here's bread and butter for you." I swallowed some of my drink. "Now let us pray," I said, and the blind man lowered his head. My wife looked at me, her mouth agape. "Pray the phone won't ring and the food doesn't get cold," I said.

We dug in. We ate everything there was to eat on the table. We ate like there was no tomorrow. We didn't talk. We ate. We scarfed. We grazed that table. We were into serious eating. The blind man had right away located his foods, he knew just where everything was on his plate. I watched with admiration as he used his knife and fork on the meat. He'd cut two pieces of meat, fork the meat into his mouth, and then go all out for the scalloped potatoes, the beans next, and then he'd tear off a hunk of buttered bread and eat that. He'd follow this up with a big drink of milk. It didn't seem to bother him to use his fingers once in a while, either.

We finished everything, including half a strawberry pie. For a few moments, we sat as if stunned. Sweat beaded on our faces. Finally, we got up from the table and left the dirty plates. We didn't look back. We took ourselves into the living room and sank into our places again. Robert and my wife sat on the sofa. I took the big chair. We had us two or three more drinks while they talked about the major things that had come to pass for them in the past ten years. For the most part, I just listened. Now and then I joined in. I didn't want him to think I'd left the room, and I didn't want her to think I was feeling left out. They talked of things that had happened to them—to them!—these past ten years. I waited in vain to hear my name on my wife's sweet lips: "And then my dear husband came into my life"—something like that. But I heard nothing of the sort. More talk of Robert. Robert had done a little of everything, it seemed, a regular blind jack-of-all-trades. But most recently he and his wife had had an Amway distributorship, from which, I gathered, they'd earned their living, such as it was. The blind man was also a ham radio operator. He talked in his loud voice about conversations he'd had with fellow operators in Guam, in the Philippines, in Alaska, and even in Tahiti. He said he'd have a lot of friends there if he ever wanted to go visit those places. From time to time, he'd turn his blind face toward me, put his hand under his beard, ask me something. How long had I been in my present position? (Three years.) Did I like my work? (I didn't.) Was I going to stay with it? (What were the options?) Finally, when I thought he was beginning to run down, I got up and turned on the TV.

My wife looked at me with irritation. She was heading toward a boil. Then she looked at the blind man and said, "Robert, do you have a TV?"

The blind man said, "My dear, I have two TVs. I have a color set and a black-and-white thing, an old relic. It's funny, but if I turn the TV on, and I'm always turning it on, I turn on the color set. It's funny, don't you think?"

I didn't know what to say to that. I had absolutely nothing to say to that. No opinion. So I watched the news program and tried to listen to what the announcer was saying.

"This is a color TV," the blind man said. "Don't ask me how, but I can tell."

"We traded up a while ago," I said.

The blind man had another taste of his drink. He lifted his beard, sniffed it, and let it fall. He leaned forward on the sofa. He positioned his ashtray on the coffee table, then put the lighter to his cigarette. He leaned back on the sofa and crossed his legs at the ankles.

My wife covered her mouth, and then she yawned. She stretched. She said, "I think I'll go upstairs and put on my robe. I think I'll change into something else. Robert, you make yourself comfortable," she said.

"I'm comfortable," the blind man said.

"I want you to feel comfortable in this house," she said.

"I am comfortable," the blind man said.

After she'd left the room, he and I listened to the weather report and then to the sports roundup. By that time, she'd been gone so long I didn't know if she was going to come back. I thought she might have gone to bed. I wished she'd come back downstairs. I didn't want to be left alone with a blind man. I asked him if he wanted another drink, and he said sure. Then I asked if he wanted to smoke some dope with me. I said I'd just rolled a number. I hadn't, but I planned to do so in about two shakes.

"I'll try some with you," he said.

"Damn right," I said. "That's the stuff."

I got our drinks and sat down on the sofa with him. Then I rolled us two fat numbers. I lit one and passed it. I brought it to his fingers. He took it and inhaled.

"Hold it as long as you can," I said. I could tell he didn't know the first thing.

My wife came back downstairs wearing her pink robe and her pink slippers.

"What do I smell?" she said.

"We thought we'd have us some cannabis," I said.

My wife gave me a savage look. Then she looked at the blind man and said, "Robert, I didn't know you smoked."

He said, "I do now, my dear. There's a first time for everything. But I don't feel anything yet."

"This stuff is pretty mellow," I said. "This stuff is mild. It's dope you can reason with," I said. "It doesn't mess you up."

"Not much it doesn't, bub," he said, and laughed.

My wife sat on the sofa between the blind man and me. I passed her the number. She took it and toked and then passed it back to me. "Which way is this going?" she said. Then she said, " I shouldn't be smoking this. I can hardly keep my eyes open as it is. That dinner did me in. I shouldn't have eaten so much."

"It was the strawberry pie," the blind man said. "That's what did it," he said, and he laughed his big laugh. Then he shook his head.

"There's more strawberry pie," I said.

"Do you want some more, Robert?" my wife said.

"Maybe in a little while," he said.

We gave our attention to the TV. My wife yawned again. She said, "Your bed is made up when you feel like going to bed, Robert. I know you must have had a long day. When you're ready to go to bed, say so." She pulled his arm. "Robert?"

He came to and said, "I've had a real nice time. This beats tapes, doesn't it?"

I said, "Coming at you," and I put the number between his fingers. He inhaled, held the smoke, and then let it go. It was like he'd been doing it since he was nine years old.

"Thanks, bub," he said. "But I think this is all for me. I think I'm beginning to feel it," he said. He held the burning roach out for my wife.

"Same here," she said. "Ditto. Me, too." She took the roach and passed it to me. "I may just sit here for a while between you two guys with my eyes closed. But don't let me bother you, okay? Either one of you. If it bothers you, say so. Otherwise, I may just sit here with my eyes closed until you're ready to go to bed," she said. "Your bed's made up, Robert, when you're ready. It's right next to our room at the top of the stairs. We'll show you up when you're ready. You wake me up now, you guys, if I fall asleep." She said that and then she closed her eyes and went to sleep.

The news program ended. I got up and changed the channel. I sat back down on the sofa. I wished my wife hadn't pooped out. Her head lay across the back of the sofa, her mouth open. She'd turned so that her robe had slipped away from her legs, exposing a juicy thigh. I reached to draw her robe back over her, and it was then that I glanced at the blind man. What the hell! I flipped the robe open again.

"You say when you want some strawberry pie," I said.

"I will," he said.

I said, "Are you tired? Do you want me to take you up to your bed? Are you ready to hit the hay?"

"Not yet," he said. "No, I'll stay up with you, bub. If that's all right. I'll stay up until you're ready to turn in. We haven't had a chance to talk. Know what I mean? I feel like me and her monopolized the evening." He lifted his beard and he let it fall. He picked up his cigarettes and his lighter.

"That's all right," I said. Then I said, "I'm glad for the company."

And I guess I was. Every night I smoked dope and stayed up as long as I could before I fell asleep. My wife and I hardly ever went to bed at the same time. When I did go to sleep, I had these dreams. Sometimes I'd wake up from one of them, my heart going crazy.

Something about the church and the Middle Ages was on the TV. Not your run-of-the-mill TV fare. I wanted to watch something else. I turned to the other channels. But there was nothing on them, either. So I turned back to the first channel and apologized.

"Bub, it's all right," the blind man said. "It's fine with me. Whatever you want to watch is okay. I'm always learning something. Learning never ends. It won't hurt me to learn something tonight. I got ears," he said.

We didn't say anything for a time. He was leaning forward with his head turned at me, his right ear aimed in the direction of the set. Very disconcerting. Now and then his eyelids drooped and then they snapped open again. Now and then he put his fingers into his beard and tugged, like he was thinking about something he was hearing on the television.

On the screen, a group of men wearing cowls was being set upon and tormented by men dressed in skeleton costumes and men dressed as devils. The men dressed as devils wore devil masks, horns, and long tails. This pageant was part of a procession. The Englishman who was narrating the thing said it took place in Spain once a year. I tried to explain to the blind man what was happening.

"Skeletons," he said. "I know about skeletons," he said, and he nodded.

The TV showed this one cathedral. Then there was a long, slow look at another one. Finally, the picture switched to the famous one in Paris, with its flying buttresses and its spires reaching up to the clouds. The camera pulled away to show the whole of the cathedral rising above the skyline.

There were times when the Englishman who was telling the thing would shut up, would simply let the camera move around over the cathedrals. Or else the camera would tour the countryside, men in fields walking behind oxen. I waited as long as I could. Then I felt

I had to say something. I said, "They're showing the outside of this cathedral now. Gargoyles. Little statues carved to look like monsters. Now I guess they're in Italy. Yeah, they're in Italy. There's paintings on the walls of this one church."

"Are those fresco paintings, bub?" he asked, and he sipped from his drink.

I reached for my glass. But it was empty. I tried to remember what I could remember. "You're asking me are those frescoes?" I said. "That's a good question. I don't know."

The camera moved to a cathedral outside Lisbon. The differences in the Portuguese cathedral compared with the French and Italian were not that great. But they were there. Mostly the interior stuff. Then something occurred to me, and I said, "Something has occurred to me. Do you have any idea what a cathedral is? What they look like, that is? Do you follow me? If somebody says cathedral to you, do you have any notion what they're talking about? Do you know the difference between that and a Baptist church, say?"

He let the smoke dribble from his mouth. "I know they took hundreds of workers fifty or a hundred years to build," he said. "I just heard the man say that, of course. I know generations of the same families worked on a cathedral. I heard him say that, too. The men who began their life's work on them, they never lived to see the completion of their work. In that wise, bub, they're no different from the rest of us, right?" He laughed. Then his eyelids drooped again. His head nodded. He seemed to be snoozing. Maybe he was imagining himself in Portugal. The TV was showing another cathedral now. This one was in Germany. The Englishman's voice droned on. "Cathedrals," the blind man said. He sat up and rolled his head back and forth. "If you want the truth, bub, that's about all I know. What I just said. What I heard him say. But maybe you could describe one to me? I wish you'd do it. I'd like that. If you want to know, I really don't have a good idea."

I stared hard at the shot of the cathedral on the TV. How could I even begin to describe it? But say my life depended on it. Say my life was being threatened by an insane guy who said I had to do it or else.

I stared some more at the cathedral before the picture flipped off into the countryside. There was no use. I turned to the blind man and said, "To begin with, they're very tall." I was looking around the room for clues. "They reach way up. Up and up. Toward the sky. They're so big, some of them, they have to have these supports. To help hold them up, so to speak. These supports are called buttresses. They remind me of viaducts, for some reason. But maybe you don't know viaducts, either? Sometimes the cathedrals have devils and such carved into the front. Sometimes lords and ladies. Don't ask me why this is," I said.

He was nodding. The whole upper part of his body seemed to be moving back and forth.

"I'm not doing so good, am I?" I said.

He stopped nodding and leaned forward on the edge of the sofa. As he listened to me, he was running his fingers through his beard. I wasn't getting through to him, I could see that. But he waited for me to go on just the same. He nodded, like he was trying to encourage me. I tried to think what else to say. "They're really big," I said. "They're massive. They're built of stone. Marble, too, sometimes. In those olden days, when they built cathedrals, men wanted to be close to God. In those olden days, God was an important part of everyone's life. You could tell this from their cathedral-building. I'm sorry," I said, "but it looks like that's the best I can do for you. I'm just no good at it."

"That's all right, bub," the blind man said. "Hey, listen. I hope you don't mind my asking you. Can I ask you something? Let me ask you a simple question, yes or no. I'm just curious and there's no offense. You're my host. But let me ask if you are in any way religious? You don't mind my asking?"

I shook my head. He couldn't see that, though. A wink is the same as a nod to a blind man. "I guess I don't believe in it. In anything. Sometimes it's hard. You know what I'm saying?"

"Sure, I do," he said.

"Right," I said.

The Englishman was still holding forth. My wife sighed in her sleep. She drew a long breath and went on with her sleeping.

"You'll have to forgive me," I said. "But I can't tell you what a cathedral looks like. It just isn't in me to do it. I can't do any more than I've done."

The blind man sat very still, his head down, as he listened to me.

I said, "The truth is, cathedrals don't mean anything special to me. Nothing. Cathedrals. They're something to look at on late-night TV. That's all they are."

It was then that the blind man cleared his throat. He brought something up. He took a handkerchief from his back pocket. Then he said, "I get it, bub. It's okay. It happens. Don't worry about it," he said. "Hey, listen to me. Will you do me a favor? I got an idea. Why don't you find us some heavy paper? And a pen. We'll do something. We'll draw one together. Get us a pen and some heavy paper. Go on, bub, get the stuff," he said.

So I went upstairs. My legs felt like they didn't have any strength in them. They felt like they did after I'd done some running. In my wife's room, I looked around. I found some ballpoints in a little basket on her table. And then I tried to think where to look for the kind of paper he was talking about.

Downstairs, in the kitchen, I found a shopping bag with onion skins in the bottom of the bag. I emptied the bag and shook it. I brought it into the living room and sat down with it near his legs. I moved some things, smoothed the wrinkles from the bag, spread it out on the coffee table.

The blind man got down from the sofa and sat next to me on the carpet.

He ran his fingers over the paper. He went up and down the sides of the paper. The edges, even the edges. He fingered the corners.

"All right," he said. "All right, let's do her."

He found my hand, the hand with the pen. He closed his hand over my hand. "Go ahead, bub, draw," he said. "Draw. You'll see. I'll follow along with you. It'll be okay. Just begin now like I'm telling you. You'll see. Draw," the blind man said.

So I began. First I drew a box that looked like a house. It could have been the house I lived in. Then I put a roof on it. At either end of the roof, I drew spires. Crazy.

"Swell," he said. "Terrific. You're doing fine," he said. "Never thought anything like this could happen in your lifetime, did you, bub? Well, it's a strange life, we all know that. Go on now. Keep it up."

I put in windows with arches. I drew flying buttresses. I hung great doors. I couldn't stop. The TV station went off the air. I put down the pen and closed and opened my fingers. The blind man felt around over the paper. He moved the tips of his fingers over the paper, all over what I had drawn, and he nodded.

"Doing fine," the blind man said.

I took up the pen again, and he found my hand. I kept at it. I'm no artist. But I kept drawing just the same.

My wife opened up her eyes and gazed at us. She sat up on the sofa, her robe hanging open. She said, "What are you doing? Tell me, I want to know."

I didn't answer her.

The blind man said, "We're drawing a cathedral. Me and him are working on it. Press hard," he said to me. "That's right. That's good," he said. "Sure. You got it, bub. I can tell. You didn't think you could. But you can, can't you? You're cooking with gas now. You know what I'm saying? We're going to really have us something here in a minute. How's the old arm?" he said. "Put some people in there now. What's a cathedral without people?"

My wife said, "What's going on? Robert, what are you doing? What's going on?"

"It's all right," he said to her. "Close your eyes now," the blind man said to me.

I did it. I closed them just like he said.

"Are they closed?" he said. "Don't fudge."

"They're closed," I said.

"Keep them that way," he said. He said, "Don't stop now. Draw."

So we kept on with it. His fingers rode my fingers as my hand went over the paper. It was like nothing else in my life up to now.

Then he said, "I think that's it. I think you got it," he said. "Take a look. What do you think?"

But I had my eyes closed. I thought I'd keep them that way for a little longer. I thought it was something I ought to do.

"Well?" he said. "Are you looking?"

My eyes were still closed. I was in my house. I knew that. But I didn't feel like I was inside anything.

"It's really something," I said.

Eleven

Sandra Cisneros

What they don't understand about birthdays and what they never tell you is that when you're eleven, you're also ten, and nine, and eight, and seven, and six, and five, and four, and three, and two, and one. And when you wake up on your eleventh birthday you expect to feel eleven, but you don't. You open your eyes and everything's just like yesterday, only it's today. And you don't feel eleven at all. You feel like you're still ten. And you are—underneath the year that makes you eleven.

Like some days you might say something stupid, and that's the part of you that's still ten. Or maybe some days you might need to sit on your mama's lap because you're scared, and that's the part of you that's five. And maybe one day when you're all grown up maybe you will need to cry like if you're three, and that's okay. That's what I tell Mama when she's sad and needs to cry. Maybe she's feeling three.

Because the way you grow old is kind of like an onion or like the rings inside a tree trunk or like my little wooden dolls that fit one inside the other, each year inside the next one. That's how being eleven years old is.

You don't feel eleven. Not right away. It takes a few days, weeks even, sometimes even months before you say Eleven when they ask you. And you don't feel smart eleven, not until you're almost twelve. That's the way it is.

Only today I wish I didn't have only eleven years rattling inside me like pennies in a tin Band-Aid box. Today I wish I was one hundred and two instead of eleven because if I was one hundred and two I'd have known what to say when Mrs. Price put the red sweater on my desk. I would've known how to tell her it wasn't mine instead of just sitting there with that look on my face and nothing coming out of my mouth.

"Whose is this?" Mrs. Price says, and she holds the red sweater up in the air for all the class to see. "Whose? It's been sitting in the coatroom for a month."

"Not mine," says everybody. "Not me."

"It has to belong to somebody." Mrs. Price keeps saying, but nobody can remember. It's an ugly sweater with red plastic buttons and a collar and sleeves all stretched out like you could use it for a jump rope. It's maybe a thousand years old and even if it belonged to me I wouldn't say so.

Maybe because I'm skinny, maybe because she doesn't like me, that stupid Sylvia Saldivar says. "I think it belongs to Rachel." An ugly sweater like that, all raggedy and old, but Mrs. Price believes her. Mrs. Price takes the sweater and puts it right on my desk, but when I open my mouth nothing comes out.

"That's not, I don't, you're not . . . Not mine," I finally say in a little voice that was maybe me when I was four.

"Of course it's yours," Mrs. Price says. "I remember you wearing it once." Because she's older and the teacher, she's right and I'm not.

Not mine, not mine, not mine, but Mrs. Price is already turning to page thirty-two, and math problem number four. I don't know why but all of a sudden I'm feeling sick inside, like the part of me that's three wants to come out of my eyes, only I squeeze them shut tight and bite down on my teeth real hard and try to remember today I am eleven, eleven. Mama is making a cake for me for tonight, and when Papa comes home everybody will sing Happy birthday, happy birthday to you.

But when the sick feeling goes away and I open my eyes, the red sweater's still sitting there like a big red mountain. I move the red sweater to the corner of my desk with my ruler. I move my pencil and books and eraser as far from it as possible. I even move my chair a little to the right. Not mine, not mine, not mine.

In my head I'm thinking how long till lunchtime, how long till I can take the red sweater and throw it over the schoolyard fence, or leave it hanging on a parking meter, or bunch it up into a little ball and toss it in the alley. Except when math period ends Mrs. Price says loud and in front of everybody. "Now, Rachel, that's enough," because she sees I've shoved the red sweater to the tippy-tip corner of my desk and it's hanging all over the edge like a waterfall, but I don't care.

"Rachel," Mrs. Price says. She says it like she's getting mad. "You put that sweater on right now and no more nonsense."

"But it's not—"

"Now!" Mrs. Price says.

This is when I wish I wasn't eleven, because all the years inside of me—ten, nine, eight, seven, six, five, four, three, two, and one—are pushing at the back of my eyes when I put one arm through one sleeve of the sweater that smells like cottage cheese, and then the other arm through the other and stand there with my arms apart like if the sweater hurts me and it does, all itchy and full of germs that aren't even mine.

That's when everything I've been holding in since this morning, since when Mrs. Price put the sweater on my desk, finally lets go, and all of a sudden I'm crying in front of everybody. I wish I was invisible but I'm not. I'm eleven and it's my birthday today and I'm crying like I'm three in front of everybody. I put my head down on the desk and bury my face in my stupid clown-sweater arms. My face all hot and spit coming out of my mouth because I can't stop the little animal noises from coming out of me, until there aren't any more tears left in my eyes, and it's just my body shaking like when you have the hiccups, and my whole head hurts like when you drink milk too fast.

But the worst part is right before the bell rings for lunch. That stupid Phyllis Lopez, who is even dumber than Sylvia Saldívar, says she remembers the red sweater is hers! I take it off right away and give it to her, only Mrs. Price pretends like everything's okay.

Today I'm eleven. There's a cake Mama's making for tonight, and when Papa comes home from work we'll eat it. There'll be candles and presents and everybody will sing Happy birthday, happy birthday to you, Rachel, only it's too late.

I'm eleven today. I'm eleven, ten, nine, eight, seven, six, five, four, three, two, and one, but I wish I was one hundred and two. I wish I was anything but eleven, because I want today to be far away already, far away like a runaway balloon, like a tiny o in the sky, so tiny-tiny you have to close your eyes to see it.

White Angel

Michael Cunningham

We lived then in Cleveland, in the middle of everything. It was the sixties—our radios sang out love all day long. This of course is history. It was before the city of Cleveland went broke, before its river caught fire. We were four. My mother and father, Carlton, and me. Carlton turned sixteen the year I turned nine. Between us were several brothers and sisters, weak flames quenched in our mother's womb. We are not a fruitful or many-branched line. Our family name is Morrow.

Our father was a high school music teacher. Our mother taught children called "exceptional," which meant that some could name the day Christmas would fall in the year 2000 but couldn't remember to take down their pants when they peed. We lived in a tract called Woodlawn—neat one- and two-story houses painted optimistic colors. The tract bordered a cemetery. Behind our back yard was a gully choked with brush and, beyond that, the field of smooth, polished stones. I grew up with the cemetery and didn't mind it. It could be beautiful. A single stone angel, small-breasted and determined, rose amid the more conservative markers close to our house. Farther away, in a richer section, miniature mosques and Parthenons spoke silently to Cleveland of man's enduring accomplishments. Carlton and I played in the cemetery as children and, with a little more age, smoked joints and drank Southern Comfort there. I was, thanks to Carlton, the most criminally advanced nine-year-old in my fourth-grade class. I was going places. I made no move without his counsel.

Here is Carlton several months before his death, in an hour so alive with snow that earth and sky are identically white. He labors among the markers, and I run after, stung by snow, following the light of his red knitted cap. Carlton's hair is pulled back into a ponytail, neat and economical, a perfect pine cone of hair. He is thrifty, in his way.

We have taken hits of acid with our breakfast juice. Or, rather, Carlton has taken a hit, and I, in consideration of my youth, have been allowed half. This acid is called windowpane. It is for clarity of vision, as Vicks is for decongestion of the nose. Our parents are at work, earning the daily bread. We have come out into the cold so that the house, when we reenter it, will shock us with its warmth and righteousness. Carlton believes in shocks.

"I think I'm coming on to it," I call out. Carlton has on his buckskin jacket, which is worn down to the shine. On the back, across his shoulder blades, his girlfriend has stitched an electric blue eye. As we walk I speak into the eye. "I think I feel something," I say.

"Too soon," Carlton calls back. "Stay loose, Frisco. You'll know when the time comes."

I am excited and terrified. We are into serious stuff. Carlton has done acid half a dozen times before, but I am new at it. We slipped the tabs into our mouths at breakfast, while our mother paused over the bacon. Carlton likes taking risks.

Snow collects in the engraved letters on the headstones. I lean into the wind, trying to decide whether everything around me seems strange because of the drug or just because

318

everything truly is strange. Three weeks earlier, a family across town had been sitting at home, watching television, when a single-engine plane fell on them. Snow swirls around us, seeming to fall up as well as down.

Carlton leads the way to our spot, the pillared entrance to a society tomb. This tomb is a palace. Stone cherubs cluster on the peaked roof, with their stunted, frozen wings and matrons' faces. Under the roof is a veranda, backed by cast-iron doors that lead to the house of the dead proper. In summer this veranda is cool. In winter it blocks the wind. We keep a bottle of Southern Comfort here.

Carlton finds the bottle, unscrews the cap, and takes a good, long draw. He is studded with snowflakes. He hands me the bottle, and I take a more conservative drink. Even in winter, the tomb smells mossy. Dead leaves and a yellow M&M's wrapper, worried by the wind, scrape on the marble floor.

"Are you scared?" Carlton asks me.

I nod. I never think of lying to him.

"Don't be, man," he says. "Fear will screw you right up. Drugs can't hurt you if you feel no fear."

I nod.

We stand sheltered, passing the bottle. I lean into Carlton's certainty as if it gave off heat.

"We can do acid all the time at Woodstock," I say.

"Right on. Woodstock Nation. Yow!"

"Do people really *live* there?" I ask.

"Man, you've got to stop asking that. The concert's over, but people are still there. It's a new nation. Have faith."

I nod again, satisfied. There is a different country for us to live in. I am already a new person, renamed Frisco. My old name was Robert.

"We'll do acid all the time," I say.

"You better believe we will." Carlton's face, surrounded by snow and marble, is lit. His eyes are vivid as neon. Something in them tells me he can see the future, a ghost that hovers over everybody's head. In Carlton's future we all get released from our jobs and schooling. Awaiting us all, and soon, is a bright, perfect simplicity. A life among the trees by the river.

"How are you feeling, man?" he asks me.

"Great," I tell him, and it is purely the truth. Doves clatter up out of a bare tree and turn at the same instant, transforming themselves from steel to silver in snow-blown light. I know then that the drug is working. Everything before me has become suddenly, radiantly itself. How could Carlton have known this was about to happen? "Oh," I whisper. His hand settles on my shoulder.

"Stay loose, Frisco," he says. "There's not a thing in this pretty world to be afraid of. I'm here."

I am not afraid. I am astonished. I had not realized until this moment how real everything is. A twig lies on the marble at my feet, bearing a cluster of hard brown berries. The broken-off end is raw, white, fleshy. Trees are alive.

"I'm here," Carlton says again, and he is.

Hours later, we are sprawled on the sofa in front of the television, ordinary as Wally and the Beav. Our mother makes dinner in the kitchen. A pot lid clangs. We are undercover agents. I am trying to conceal my amazement.

Our father is building a grandfather clock from a kit. He wants to have something to leave us, something for us to pass along. We can hear him in the basement, sawing and pounding. I know what is laid out on his sawhorses—a long, raw wooden box, onto which he glues fancy moldings. A pearl of sweat meanders down his forehead as he works. Tonight I discovered my ability to see every room of the house at once, to know every single thing that goes on. A mouse nibbles inside the wall. Electrical wires curl behind the plaster, hidden and patient as snakes.

"Sh-h-h," I say to Carlton, who has not said anything. He is watching television through his splayed fingers. Gunshots ping. Bullets raise chalk dust on a concrete wall. I have no idea what we are watching.

"Boys?" our mother calls from the kitchen. I can, with my new ears, hear her slap hamburger into patties. "Set the table like good citizens," she calls.

"O.K., Ma," Carlton replies, in a gorgeous imitation of normality. Our father hammers in the basement. I can feel Carlton's heart ticking. He pats my hand, to assure me that everything's perfect.

We set the table, fork knife spoon, paper napkins triangled to one side. We know the moves cold. After we are done I pause to notice the dining room wallpaper: a golden farm, backed by mountains. Cows graze, autumn trees cast golden shade. This scene repeats itelf three times, on three walls. "Zap," Carlton whispers. "Zzzzzoom."

"Did we do it right?" I ask him.

"We did everything perfect, little son. How are you doing in there, anyway?" He raps lightly on my head.

"Perfect, I guess." I am staring at the wallpaper as if I were thinking of stepping into it.

"You guess. You guess? You and I are going to other planets, man. Come over here."

"Where?"

"Here. Come here." He leads me to the window. Outside, snow skitters under the street lamps. Ranch-style houses hoard their warmth but bleed light into the gathering snow.

"You and I are going to fly, man," Carlton whispers, close to my ear. He opens the window. Snow blows in, sparking on the carpet. "Fly," he says, and we do. For a moment we strain up and out, the black night wind blowing in our faces—we raise ourselves up off the cocoa-colored deep-pile wool-and-polyester carpet by a sliver of an inch. I swear it to this day. Sweet glory. The secret of flight is this: You have to do it immediately, before your body realizes it is defying the laws.

We both know we have taken momentary leave of the earth. It does not strike either of us as remarkable, any more than does the fact that airplanes sometimes fall from the sky, or that we have always lived in Ohio and will soon leave for a new nation. We settle back down. Carlton touches my shoulder.

"You wait, Frisco," he says. "Miracles are happening. Goddam miracles."

I nod. He pulls down the window, which reseals itself with a sucking sound. Our own faces look back at us from the cold, dark glass. Behind us, our mother drops the hamburgers into the skillet. Our father bends to his work under a hooded light bulb, preparing the long box into which he will lay clockwork, pendulum, a face. A plane drones by overhead, invisible in the clouds. I glance nervously at Carlton. He smiles his assurance and squeezes the back of my neck.

March. After the thaw. I am walking through the cemetery, thinking about my endless life. One of the beauties of living in Cleveland is that any direction feels like progress. I've memorized the map. We are by my calculations 350 miles shy of Woodstock, New York. On this raw new day I am walking east, to the place where Carlton and I keep our bottle. I am going to have an early nip, to celebrate my bright future.

When I get to our spot I hear low moans coming from behind the tomb. I freeze, considering my options. The sound is a long, drawn-out agony with a whip at the end, a final high C, something like "ooooooOw." A wolf's cry run backward. What decides me on investigation rather than flight is the need to create a story. In the stories Carlton likes best, people always do the foolish, risky thing. I find I can reach decisions this way—by thinking of myself as a character in a story told by Carlton.

I creep around the side of the monument, cautious as a badger, pressed up close to the marble. I peer over a cherub's girlish shoulder. What I find is Carlton on the ground with his girlfriend, in a jumble of clothes and bare flesh. Carlton's jacket, the one with the embroidered eye, is draped over the stone, keeping watch.

I hunch behind the statue. I can see the girl's naked arms, and the familiar bones of Carlton's spine. The two of them moan together in the brown winter grass. Though I can't make out the girl's expression, Carlton's face is twisted and grimacing, the cords of his neck pulled tight. I had never thought the experience might be painful. I watch, trying to learn. I hold on to the cherub's cold wings.

It isn't long before Carlton catches sight of me. His eyes rove briefly, ecstatically skyward, and what do they light on but his brother's small head, sticking up next to a cherub's. We lock eyes and spend a moment in mutual decision. The girl keeps on clutching at Carlton's skinny back. He decides to smile at me. He decides to wink.

I am out of there so fast I tear up divots. I dodge among the stones, jump the gully, clear the fence into the swing-set-and-picnic-table sanctity of the back yard. Something about that wink. My heart beats fast as a sparrow's.

I go into the kitchen and find our mother washing fruit. She asks what's going on. I tell her nothing is. Nothing at all.

She sighs over an apple's imperfection. The curtains sport blue teapots. Our mother works the apple with a scrub brush. She believes they come coated with poison.

"Where's Carlton?" she asks.

"Don't know," I tell her.

"Bobby?"

"Huh?"

"What exactly is going on?"

"Nothing," I say. My heart works itself up to a hummingbird's rate, more buzz than beat.

"I think something is. Will you answer a question?"

"O.K."

"Is your brother taking drugs?"

I relax a bit. It's only drugs. I know why she is asking. Lately police cars have been cruising past our house like sharks. They pause, take note, glide on. Some neighborhood crackdown. Carlton is famous in these parts.

"No," I tell her.

She faces me with the brush in one hand, an apple in the other. "You wouldn't lie to me, would you?" She knows something is up. Her nerves run through this house. She can feel dust settling on the tabletops, milk starting to turn in the refrigerator.

"No," I say.

"Something's going on," she sighs. She is a small, efficient woman who looks at things as if they gave off a painful light. She grew up on a farm in Wisconsin and spent her girlhood tying up bean rows, worrying over the sun and rain. She is still trying to overcome her habit of modest expectations.

I leave the kitchen, pretending sudden interest in the cat. Our mother follows, holding her brush. She means to scrub the truth out of me. I follow the cat, his erect black tail and pink anus.

"Don't walk away when I'm talking to you," our mother says.

I keep walking, to see how far I'll get, calling "Kittykittykitty." In the front hall, our father's homemade clock chimes the half hour. I make for the clock. I get as far as the rubber plant before she collars me.

"I told you not to walk away," she says, and cuffs me a good one with the brush. She catches me on the ear and sets it ringing. The cat is out of there quick as a quarter note.

I stand for a minute, to let her know I've received the message. Then I resume walking. She hits me again, this time on the back of the head, hard enough to make me see colors. "Will you *stop?*" she screams. Still, I keep walking. Our house runs west to east. With every step I get closer to Yasgur's farm.

Carlton comes home whistling. Our mother treats him like a guest who's overstayed. He doesn't care. He is lost in optimism. He pats her cheek and calls her "Professor." He treats her as if she were harmless, and so she is.

She never hits Carlton. She suffers him the way farm girls suffer a thieving crow, with a grudge so old it borders on reverence. She gives him a scrubbed apple and tells him what she'll do if he tracks mud on the carpet.

I am waiting in our room. He brings the smell of the cemetery with him—its old snow and wet pine needles. He rolls his eyes at me, takes a crunch of his apple. "What's happening, Frisco?" he says.

I have arranged myself loosely on my bed, trying to pull a Dylan riff out of my harmonica. I have always figured I can bluff my way into wisdom. I offer Carlton a dignified nod.

He drops onto his own bed. I can see a crushed crocus stuck to the black rubber sole of his boot.

"Well, Frisco," he says. "Today you are a man."

I nod again. Is that all there is to it?

"*Yow,*" Carlton says. He laughs, pleased with himself and the world. "That was so perfect."

I pick out what I can of "Blowin' in the Wind."

Carlton says, "Man, when I saw you out there spying on us I thought to myself, *Yes.* Now *I'm* really here. You know what I'm saying?" He waves his apple core.

"Uh-huh," I say.

"Frisco, that was the first time her and I ever did it. I mean, we'd talked. But when we finally got down to it, there you were. My brother. Like you *knew.*"

I nod, and this time for real. What happened was an adventure we had together. All right. The story is beginning to make sense.

"Aw, Frisco," Carlton says. "I'm gonna find you a girl, too. You're nine. You been a virgin too long."

"Really?" I say.

"*Man.* We'll find you a woman from the sixth grade, somebody with a little experience. We'll get stoned and all make out under the trees in the boneyard. I want to be present at your deflowering, man. You're gonna need a brother there."

I am about to ask, as casually as I can manage, about the relationship between love and bodily pain, when our mother's voice cuts into the room. "You did it," she screams. "You tracked mud all over the rug."

A family entanglement follows. Our mother brings our father, who comes and stands in the doorway with her, taking in evidence. He is a formerly handsome man. His face has been worn down by too much patience. He has lately taken up some sporty touches—a goatee, a pair of calfskin boots.

Our mother points out the trail of muddy half-moons that lead from the door to Carlton's bed. Dangling over the end of the bed are the culprits themselves, voluptuously muddy, with Carlton's criminal feet still in them.

"You see?" she says. "You see what he thinks of me?"

Our father, a reasonable man, suggests that Carlton clean it up. Our mother finds that too small a gesture. She wants Carlton not to have done it in the first place. "I don't ask for much," she says. "I don't ask where he goes. I don't ask why the police are suddenly so interested in our house. I ask that he not track mud all over the floor. That's all." She squints in the glare of her own outrage.

"Better clean it right up," our father says to Carlton.

"And that's it?" our mother says. "He cleans up the mess and all is forgiven?"

"Well, what do you want him to do? Lick it up?"

"I want some consideration," she says, turning helplessly to me. "That's what I want."

I shrug, at a loss. I sympathize with our mother but am not on her team.

"All right," she says. "I just won't bother cleaning the house anymore. I'll let you men handle it. I'll sit and watch television and throw my candy wrappers on the floor."

She starts out, cutting the air like a blade. On the way she picks up a jar of pencils, looks at it, and tosses the pencils on the floor. They fall like fortune-telling sticks, in pairs and criss-crosses.

Our father goes after her, calling her name. Her name is Isabel. We can hear them making their way across the house, our father calling "Isabel, Isabel, Isabel," while our mother, pleased with the way the pencils looked, dumps more things onto the floor.

"I hope she doesn't break the TV," I say.

"She'll do what she needs to do," Carlton says.

"I hate her," I say. I am not certain about that. I want to test the sound of it, to see if it's true.

"She's got more balls than any of us, Frisco," he says. "Better watch what you say about her."

I keep quiet. Soon I get up and start gathering pencils, because I prefer that to lying around and trying to follow the shifting lines of allegiance. Carlton goes for a sponge and starts in on the mud.

"You get shit on the carpet, you clean it up," he says. "Simple."

The time for all my questions about love has passed, and I am not so unhip as to force a subject. I know it will come up again. I make a neat bouquet of pencils. Our mother rages through the house.

Later, after she has thrown enough and we three have picked it all up, I lie on my bed thinking things over. Carlton is on the phone to his girlfriend, talking low. Our mother, becalmed but still dangerous, cooks dinner. She sings as she cooks, some slow forties number that must have been all over the jukes when her first husband's plane went down in the Pacific. Our father plays his clarinet in the basement. That is where he goes to practice, down among his woodworking tools, the neatly hung hammers and awls that throw oversized shadows in the light of the single bulb. If I put my ear to the floor, I can hear him, pulling a long, low tomcat moan out of that horn. There is some strange comfort in pressing my ear to the carpet and hearing our father's music leaking up through the floorboards. Lying down, with my ear to the floor, I join in on my harmonica.

That spring our parents have a party to celebrate the sun's return. It has been a long, bitter winter, and now the first wild daisies are poking up on the lawns and among the graves.

Our parents' parties are mannerly affairs. Their friends, schoolteachers all, bring wine jugs and guitars. They are Ohio hip. Though they hold jobs and meet mortgages, they think of themselves as independent spirits on a spying mission. They have agreed to impersonate teachers until they write their novels, finish their dissertations, or just save up enough money to set themselves free.

Carlton and I are the lackeys. We take coats, fetch drinks. We have done this at every party since we were small, trading on our precocity, doing a brother act. We know the moves. A big, lipsticked woman who has devoted her maidenhood to ninth-grade math calls me Mr. Right. An assistant vice principal in a Russian fur hat asks us both whether we expect to vote Democratic or Socialist. By sneaking sips I manage to get myself semicrocked.

The reliability of the evening is derailed halfway through, however, by a half dozen of Carlton's friends. They rap on the door and I go for it, anxious as a carnival sharp to see who will step up next and swallow the illusion that I'm a kindly, sober nine-year-old child. I'm expecting callow adults, and what do I find but a pack of young outlaws, big-booted and wild-haired. Carlton's girlfriend stands in front, in an outfit made up almost entirely of fringe.

"Hi, Bobby," she says confidently. She comes from New York, and is more than just locally smart.

"Hi," I say. I let them all in despite a retrograde urge to lock the door and phone the police. Three are girls, four boys. They pass me in a cloud of dope smoke and sly-eyed greeting.

What they do is invade the party. Carlton is standing on the far side of the rumpus room, picking the next album, and his girl cuts straight through the crowd to his side. She has the bones and the loose, liquid moves some people consider beautiful. She walks through that room as if she'd been sent to teach the whole party a lesson.

Carlton's face tips me off that this was planned. Our mother demands to know what's going on here. She is wearing a long, dark red dress that doesn't interfere with her shoulders. When she dresses up, you can see what it is about her, or what it was. She is the source of Carlton's beauty. I have our father's face.

Carlton does some quick talking. Though it is against our mother's better judgment, the invaders are suffered to stay. One of them, an Eddie Haskell for all his leather and hair, tells her she is looking good. She is willing to hear it.

So the outlaws, house-sanctioned, start to mingle. I work my way over to Carlton's side, the side unoccupied by his girlfriend. I would like to say something ironic and wised-up, something that will band Carlton and me against every other person in the room. I can feel the shape of the comment I have in mind, but, being a tipsy nine-year-old, can't get my mouth around it. What I say is "Shit, man."

Carlton's girl laughs. I would like to tell her what I have figured out about her, but I am nine, and three-quarters gone on Tom Collinses. Even sober, I can only imagine a sharp-tongued wit.

"Hang on, Frisco," Carlton tells me. "This could turn into a real party."

I can tell by the light in his eyes what is going down. He has arranged a blind date between our parents' friends and his own. It's a Woodstock move—he is plotting a future in which young and old have business together. I agree to hang on, and go to the kitchen, hoping to sneak a few knocks of gin.

There I find our father leaning up against the refrigerator. A line of butterfly-shaped magnets hovers around his head. "Are you enjoying this party?" he asks, touching his goatee. He is still getting used to being a man with a beard.

"Uh-huh."

"I am, too," he says sadly. He never meant to be a high school music teacher. The money question caught up with him.

"What do you think of this music?" he asks. Carlton has put the Stones on the turntable. Mick Jagger sings "19th Nervous Breakdown." Our father gestures in an openhanded way that takes in the room, the party, the whole house—everything the music touches.

"I like it," I say.

"So do I." He stirs his drink with his finger, and sucks on the finger.

"I *love* it," I say, too loud. Something about our father leads me to raise my voice. I want to grab handfuls of music out of the air and stuff them into my mouth.

"I'm not sure I could say I love it," he says. "I'm not sure if I could say that, no. I would say I'm friendly to its intentions. I would say that if this is the direction music is going in, I won't stand in its way."

"Uh-huh," I say. I am already anxious to get back to the party but don't want to hurt his feelings. If he senses he's being avoided, he can fall into fits of apology more terrifying than our mother's rages.

"I think I may have been too rigid with my students," our father says. "Maybe over the summer you boys could teach me a few things about the music young people are listening to these days."

"Sure," I say loudly. We spend a minute waiting for the next thing to say.

"You boys are happy, aren't you?" he asks. "Are you enjoying this party?"

"We're having a great time," I say.

"I thought you were. I am, too."

I have by this time gotten myself to within jumping distance of the door. I call out, "Well, goodbye," and dive back into the party.

Something has happened in my absence. The party has started to roll. Call it an accident of history and the weather. Carlton's friends are on decent behavior, and our parents' friends have decided to give up some of their wine-and-folksong propriety to see what they can learn. Carlton is dancing with a vice principal's wife. Carlton's friend Frank, with his ancient-child face and I.Q. in the low sixties, dances with our mother. I see that our father has followed me out of the kitchen. He positions himself at the party's edge; I leap into its center. I invite the fuchsia-lipped math teacher to dance. She is only too happy. She is big and graceful as a parade float, and I steer her effortlessly out into the middle of everything. My mother, who is known around school for Sicilian discipline, dances freely, which is news to everybody. There is no getting around her beauty.

The night rises higher and higher. A wildness sets in. Carlton throws new music on the turntable—Janis Joplin, the Doors, the Dead. The future shines for everyone, rich with the possibility of more nights exactly like this. Even our father is pressed into dancing, which he does like a flightless bird, all flapping arms and potbelly. Still, he dances. Our mother has a kiss for him.

Finally I nod out on the sofa, blissful under the drinks. I am dreaming of flight when our mother comes and touches my shoulder. I smile up into her flushed, smiling face.

"It's hours past your bedtime," she says, all velvet motherliness. I nod. I can't dispute the fact.

She keeps on nudging my shoulder. I am a moment or two apprehending the fact that she actually wants me to leave the party and go to bed. "No," I tell her.

"Yes," she smiles.

"No," I say cordially, experimentally. This new mother can dance, and flirt. Who knows what else she might allow?

"Yes." The velvet motherliness leaves her voice. She means business of the usual kind. I get myself off the sofa and I run to Carlton for protection. He is laughing with his girl, a sweaty question mark of hair plastered to his forehead. I plow into him so hard he nearly goes over.

"Whoa, Frisco," he says. He takes me up under the arms and swings me a half turn. Our mother plucks me out of his hands and sets me down, with a good, farm-style hold on the back of my neck.

"Say good night, Bobby," she says. She adds, for the benefit of Carlton's girl, "He should have been in bed before this party started."

"No," I holler. I try to twist loose, but our mother has a grip that could crack walnuts.

Carlton's girl tosses her hair and says, "Good night, baby." She smiles a victor's smile. She smoothes the stray hair off Carlton's forehead.

"No," I scream again. Something about the way she touches his hair. Our mother calls our father, who comes and scoops me up and starts out of the room with me, holding me like a live bomb. Before I go, I lock eyes with Carlton. He shrugs and says, "Night, man." Our father hustles me out. I do not take it bravely. I leave flailing, too furious to cry, dribbling a thread of spittle.

Later I lie alone on my narrow bed, feeling the music hum in the coiled springs. Life is cracking open right there in our house. People are changing. By tomorrow, no one will be quite the same. How can they let me miss it? I dream up revenge against our parents, and worse for Carlton. He is the one who could have saved me. He could have banded with me against them. What I can't forgive is his shrug, his mild-eyed "Night, man." He has joined the adults. He has made himself bigger and taken size from me. As the Doors thump "Strange Days," I hope something awful happens to him. I say so to myself.

Around midnight, dim-witted Frank announces he has seen a flying saucer hovering over the back yard. I can hear his deep, excited voice all the way in my room. He says it is like a blinking, luminous cloud. I hear half the party struggling out through the sliding glass door in a disorganized whooping knot. By that time everyone is so delirious a flying saucer would be just what was expected. That much celebration would logically attract an answering happiness from across the stars.

I get out of bed and sneak down the hall. I will not miss alien visitors for anyone, not even at the cost of our mother's wrath or our father's disappointment. I stop at the end of the hallway, though, embarrassed to be in pajamas. If there really are aliens, they will think I am the lowest member of the house. While I hesitate over whether to go back to my room to change, people start coming back inside, talking about a trick of the mist and an airplane. People resume their dancing.

Carlton must have jumped the back fence. He must have wanted to be there alone, singular, in case they decided to take somebody with them. A few nights later I will go out and stand where he could have been standing. On the far side of the gully, now a river swollen with melted snow, the cemetery will gleam like a lost city. The moon will be full. I will hang around just as Carlton must have, hypnotized by the silver light on the stones, the white angel raising her arms across the river.

According to our parents the mystery is why he ran back to the house full tilt. Something in the graveyard may have scared him, he may have needed to break its spell, but I think it's more likely that when he came back to himself he just couldn't wait to return to the music and the people, the noisy disorder of continuing life.

Somebody has shut the sliding glass door. Carlton's girlfriend looks lazily out, touching base with her own reflection. I look, too. Carlton is running toward the house. I hesitate. Then I figure he can bump his nose. It will be a good joke on him. I let him keep coming. His girlfriend sees him through her own reflection, starts to scream a warning just as Carlton hits the glass.

It is an explosion. Triangles of glass fly brightly through the room. I think that for him, it must be more surprising than painful, like hitting water from a great height. He stands blinking for a moment. The whole party stops, stares, getting its bearings. Bob Dylan sings "Just Like a Woman." Carlton reaches up curiously to take out the shard of glass that is stuck in his neck, and that is when the blood starts. It shoots out of him. Our mother screams. Carlton steps forward into his girlfriend's arms and the two of them fall together. Our mother throws herself down on top of him and the girl. People shout their accident wisdom. Don't lift him. Call an ambulance. I watch from the hallway. Carlton's blood spurts, soaking into the carpet, spattering people's clothes. Our mother and father both try to plug the wound with their hands, but the blood just shoots between their fingers. Carlton looks more puzzled than anything, as if he can't quite follow this turn of events. "It's all right," our father tells him, trying to stop the blood. "It's all right, just don't move, it's all right." Carlton nods, and holds our father's hand. His eyes take on an astonished light. Our mother screams, "Is anybody *doing* anything?" What comes out of Carlton grows darker, almost black. I watch. Our father tries to get a hold on Carlton's neck while Carlton keeps trying to take his hand. Our mother's hair is matted with blood. It runs down her face. Carlton's girl holds him to her breasts, touches his hair, whispers in his ear.

He is gone by the time the ambulance gets there. You can see the life drain out of him. When his face goes slack our mother wails. A part of her flies wailing through the house, where it will wail and rage forever. I feel our mother pass through me on her way out. She covers Carlton's body with her own.

He is buried in the cemetery out back. Years have passed—we are living in the future, and it has turned out differently from what we'd planned. Our mother has established her life of separateness behind the guest room door. Our father mutters his greetings to the door as he passes.

One April night, almost a year to the day after Carlton's accident, I hear cautious footsteps shuffling across the living room floor after midnight. I run out eagerly, thinking of ghosts, but find only our father in moth-colored pajamas. He looks unsteadily at the dark air in front of him.

"Hi, Dad," I say from the doorway.

He looks in my direction. "Yes?"

"It's me. Bobby."

"Oh, Bobby," he says. "What are you doing up, young man?"

"Nothing," I tell him. "Dad?"

"Yes, son."

"Maybe you better come back to bed. O.K.?"

"Maybe I had," he says. "I just came out here for a drink of water, but I seem to have gotten turned around in the darkness. Yes, maybe I better had."

I take his hand and lead him down the hall to his room. The grandfather clock chimes the quarter hour.

"Sorry," our father says.

I get him into bed. "There," I say. "O.K.?"

"Perfect. Could not be better."

"O.K. Good night."

"Good night. Bobby?"

"Uh-huh?"

"Why don't you stay a minute?" he says. "We could have ourselves a talk, you and me. How would that be?"

"O.K.," I say. I sit on the edge of his mattress. His bedside clock ticks off the minutes. I can hear the low rasp of his breathing. Around our house, the Ohio night chirps and buzzes. The small gray finger of Carlton's stone pokes up among the others, within sight of the angel's white eyes. Above us, airplanes and satellites sparkle. People are flying even now toward New York or California, to take up lives of risk and invention.

I stay until our father has worked his way into a muttering sleep.

Carlton's girlfriend moved to Denver with her family a month before. I never learned what it was she'd whispered to him. Though she'd kept her head admirably during the accident, she lost it afterward. She cried so hard at the funeral that she had to be taken away by her mother—an older, redder-haired version of her. She started seeing a psychiatrist three times a week. Everyone, including my parents, talked about how hard it was for her, to have held a dying boy in her arms at that age. I'm grateful to her for holding my brother while he died, but I never once heard her mention the fact that though she had been through something terrible, at least she was still alive and going places. At least she had protected herself by trying to warn him. I can appreciate the intricacies of her pain. But as long as she was in Cleveland, I could never look her straight in the face. I couldn't talk about the wounds she suffered. I can't even write her name.

Don't think of biography as a history of accomplishment but as a history of desire.

—BIOGRAPHER ON NPR

The Pillows

Dagoberto Gilb

While I was at the Albuquerque airport bar—Pueblo turquoise and sandstone—waiting to meet my girlfriend, a woman offered to buy me a drink. She was better than good-looking. We each ordered a frozen margarita, did a *salud*, and I walked her politely to her gate, and she kissed my lips as she went to the plane at the very last minute—she had a first-class seat. I came back to the bar and ordered both a shot and another margarita. In less than fifteen minutes my girlfriend's plane was supposed to arrive. It was one of those days when I was a man. My head was shaking when a starched white shirt and tie, coat slung over the shoulder, came up to me.

"George," he said. His speech was timid and a little too formal. It was always hard for me to figure out these guys who wore business suits. "You don't remember me? From El Paso. Austin High?"

It took me a few seconds to connect. "Ibáñez?"

I was right. I stood up and shook his hand harder than he did mine. "How's it going, Daniel?" I said his first name with a Spanish pronunciation, un-Americanized. I was conscious of this immediately, and I was sure he remembered me as the guy who didn't like it back in the old days when an Anglo coach or teacher would say it their way, like they were right and the other was wrong. I was still that same guy, even though my own legal name was Jorge, like my father and his father. It's just that I didn't happen to like my name in Spanish. I thought George was better. And that was always my point anyway: Our choice, not theirs.

Danny and I went to Austin High School a hundred years ago, though we didn't hang out together. He was a better student than me, and that was probably why we never had any of the same classes. But we started elementary at the same time, at Crockett, and that was enough for us to know each other forever. It must've been around sixth or seventh that we separated off. We played on the same Little League team one season. He was left field, sometimes third base. I played short and pitched. He was fast, I was strong. We made the city play-offs that year.

"So you get back much?" I asked.

"I'm living there," he said.

"Really?" Everybody who grew up in El Paso hated it and left when they could, as soon as possible. There was nothing to do, and no jobs, let alone good-paying ones. If you were raised there, it seemed like any other city was better. You sensed this if you hadn't ever gotten away, and knew when you had. The best thing about El Paso was that people thought you were cool and tough for growing up there.

"It's what I'm doing here. Flying back."

"Really?" Leaving El Paso was for good. Moving back was almost unheard of. There were two possible explanations. You had no choice—desperate, tragic economics—or your parents, who of course were still there, were old, and somebody had to take care of them. That was cultural, and the best part of El Paso. "You actually have a job El Chuco? *Pues, ¿qué haces hay?*"

"I'm a newspaper editor."

"Like a reporter?"

"No. Though I used to be a reporter. I did that in Dallas, then in L.A. I took the job in El Paso as the paper's editor." He looked at me carefully, like he was wondering if I was aware how much his suit was worth. "I was the first Hispanic to have it."

"First Hispanic, huh?"

He caught my sound like he did when I pronounced his name. It's an ancient discussion made new again—who we are, where we're from. Like saying you were "Spanish," how they called us years ago, this one implied the light-skinned Iberian Peninsula too. No one I ever knew in El Paso, Tejas, dark or *güero,* had a single relative from *pinche* Spain. These words were a way to avoid saying you had Mexican descent, that Mexico was too low-class. Even if it was out of public fashion, I felt like I was the last one to still say I was a Chicano. Maybe it was a dead issue left over from the old days, but not to me.

"Congratulations," I told him, letting it loose. "That *is* great. I bet El Paso's up to like ninety percent of us Mexicans by now. *Que duro,* that town. Yeah, it's about fucking time they noticed us living there. That's great. You gotta be proud. You should be."

I'd made him happy.

"I can't imagine the newspaper having stories about people from the neighborhood," I went on. "Did they ever?"

"It was bad. Gangs and graffiti stories. Sometimes about how to make tamales."

Even as he told me this he was somber, too dry. "So you're kicking ass. That's great, Daniel."

"I did all right." He paused and looked off.

"Really," I said. The pause was loud. I told him about my art.

"What're you doing here?" he asked.

"*Mi locura,*" I said. "I'm broke, but I got a girlfriend . . ."

"I saw her," he said.

"You saw her?"

"Yeah, you lucky bastard."

"You mean that woman at this bar?"

"Couldn't miss her."

"She ain't her, man. My baby hasn't gotten off the plane yet."

He laughed. "And I can't find one."

"She's coming in from Denver, and I'm waiting here for her plane."

"And this other, you just met her?"

"She lives in New York City and says she was out here for a shoot. Do you believe it? Says she's a model. Sat right up next to me and started talking and shit."

"What a lucky bastard. If I were you I'd go out and buy a stack of lottery tickets immediately. You may never be so hot again as long as you live."

"*Sabes qué,* Daniel, *tienes razón,* that's smart business advice."

Smiling, we're both shaking our heads now. My girlfriend's 747 was gleaming in the windows as it approached the gate. The bar was directly across from it.

"So what'd you mean?" I asked. "You get fired from your job or something?"

He sighed, surprised, I thought, by what I'd heard from his voice.

"Well, I quit. I decided I had to move on."

I was watching for my girlfriend.

"I need that job right now," I said. "So, *¿qué te pasó?* You burned out on El Paso?"

"El Paso's all right. It's not Albuquerque, but it is getting better. You should come down. You could stay at my place." He started watching for my girlfriend too. "No, it was a woman. Romance, love." He wasn't sure I was listening, and I wasn't. "So I decided to quit."

"*Hay viene,*" I said.

"That's her?"

"Yeah."

"You *are* a lucky bastard. You find two, and I can't even keep one."

"*¿Bien fea, verdad?*"

"You lucky bastard."

"I am, I know. *Pues, también she's married.*"

Now he was shaking his head like I was before he came up to me. "Let me give you my number before you take off," he said. "Visit anytime. Especially now."

"You don't know what you're offering, dude. I may be sleeping on your couch next week. *No traes una* business card or something?"

"It's old . . . ." He touched the wallet in his back pocket, and he felt around for a pen in his jacket, and he stared at my girlfriend standing over there. "Don't you think you better get her?"

I followed her eyes as her body pivoted, searching for me in the long, well-lit aisle beyond the darkened airport bar. "Let her find me. She will any minute, watch."

"You're too much." He pulled out his wallet and scribbled on the back of a card.

I was pocketing it as she saw me. The eyes closed, the face looked at the ceiling, her head began saying no. When it stopped, she moved with a huge grin toward me.

Not a month later I was at his apartment. He'd offered it to me for the utilities while he was in Mexico and Central America for the next six weeks. The timing was a magic potion—I couldn't pay the rent on my studio, hadn't in two months, and my landlord wasn't a patron of the arts.

"This here is some view," I said. "You forget the big picture, you know, of where you're from." I held on to a wooden post on the wide old wooden deck of this old plastered apartment, below me the compact El Paso downtown, and the darkened slot that was the concreted Rio Grande, and Ciudad Juárez beyond that, and then the blackened plain of the desert. The lights of the city all around shook like moonlight broken up in a calm lake.

"If this were L.A.," Danny said, handing me another cold bottle of Negra Modelo beer, "this would be Mulholland Drive, and it would cost beaucoup." No cans of American for him, only the imports.

"A *chingo* of bucks, for sure," I translated. Maybe his Spanish wasn't so perfect anymore and that was why he avoided using it—all of us spoke English best, began leaving the other in the house once we were old enough to ride a bike a few blocks—but, though I didn't know why, he was still thinking about being Mexican somehow: Besides the beer, he played Tejano music on the stereo, and a black felt sombrero was on the wall.

"So what's going on with your women?" he asked.

I took a swallow. "Women?"

"The ones I saw."

I'd forgotten about the one at the bar. "She called me once. Told me to come to New York."

He interrupted. "Is she a Latina?"

I wasn't sure what that was about. "De Califas. I think she's *una de los que,* one of those *que* don't even know how we say California. Don't know *ni una palabra* of Spanish."

"She was sexy."

She was a good-looking woman, I remembered, but I hadn't thought about her.

He laughed too loud and finished his bottle, chugging like a frat boy. "You want another?"

I was only half done. "Sure," I said. I gulped mine down as we moved inside, to be agreeable. "My problem is Lisita. You know, *la otra.*"

"She's a beauty, George." He shook his head as he plucked off a bottle cap like this took strength. It bounced on the ceramic tile counter and onto the floor. I picked it up. "She's not a Latina, is she?" He handed the bottle to me, and attacked another with his opener.

Here we were standing, staring at *the* Mexican-Chicano border, and he still dug around for distant labels. "No, *pura* white girl, and not Latina." I couldn't help mocking that word ever so subtly, even though I realized this wasn't a time for a disagreement over something so stupid. "I only call her Lisita. Her name's Lisa."

"She was a beautiful woman, she really was a beauty." He looked at me like he was about to say something important, but drank instead.

Danny was getting buzzed. He was drinking so fast, already almost finishing the beer he'd just opened.

"Does it matter to you?" he asked. "Does it matter if she's Anglo or Latina?"

"My wife was from here. *Pura chuqueña.* She went to La Jeff."

"So this Lisa, who's married, right?"

I nodded.

"You two are serious?" He spoke like he was doing an interview.

"Depends on what room her husband's in."

He didn't even smile.

"It always gets serious, no matter what it starts like."

Danny went for another Negra Modelo without offering me one—I'd barely sipped this one yet—and we went to the living room. It had two wooden-sashed windows on the south wall, and they were open, and wind blew enough for the shades that were half down to lift and slap. There was a big couch against another wall, and across from it the TV set and a stereo system and a few racks of CDs and cassettes and a tall, stuffed bookcase. His desk was a scratched-up dining room table with a computer on it pushed against the wall and under the windows. That was where he sat. I took the couch.

"Pretty comfortable," I said. "You might have to worry that I won't let you in when you get back."

"Use the computer if you want," he said.

"I never write a postcard."

"You're welcome to it."

"I'll probably set up outside on the porch. If that's okay." There really wasn't enough room inside. I'd been expecting a much bigger place, probably because I assumed Danny made big bucks.

"Of course."

"I've never been one to paint outdoors before."

"You'll have to watch out for the wind," he said. The shade puffed out with it. He was draining this next bottle too fast too, though he did seem to be slowing down in another way, sinking into the swivel chair at the dining room table. "It'll blow hard."

"I swear, you're like divine intervention," I told him. "I'm supposed to be getting money by the end of the month. I didn't want to have to borrow money."

"It helps me out too," he said. "It's better if somebody's here. The thieves, they get to the porch, crawl through a window." He got up for another beer. "So what are you planning after this?" he said from the kitchen. "You going back to Albuquerque?"

"*Sabes que,* I really don't know. *La cosa es que,* I really don't."

He sat down again and set the beer on the table—maybe to let his arm rest. He rubbed his eyes.

"So what about you?" I finally asked. "You don't exactly seem pumped about going."

"I guess it's obvious," he said.

"*Pues,* you did drink all the beers."

"I'm sorry."

"I'm joking, dude."

"I am sorry. I am. Oh. Yeah. Well. I'm sorry." Shaking his head, but not in wonder. "It's because of Mary."

I felt like that might be where he left it. "Mary," I said. It was all I could think of to say.

"She lives in Albuquerque."

"That's what you were up there for?"

"Well. Yeah. Mostly."

"You broke up."

"It's been going on. We tried for almost five years."

I didn't say anything.

"She was an Anglo girl."

That took me by surprise. Not that she was, but how he said she was.

"All I ever wanted was to get married. I wanted a house. I wanted a couple of kids. I wanted to read the Sunday paper in an overstuffed chair."

"Really." I wasn't sure what else to say.

"I couldn't understand. I can't."

"What does she do?"

"Teaches art."

"She could've moved here for that."

"She likes her job. I couldn't get my job up there in Albuquerque."

I could only raise my eyebrows and nod.

"I'm happy as an editor. I'm good too. But I decided I had to move on. I had to take some risks. I have to do more."

"And so that's why you're taking this trip to Méjico?"

"Mostly." He was drinking more reasonably now. Sips. "Be a man."

"Be a man?"

"Yeah. Have adventure. Stop thinking like a soft editor. What I was didn't work, you know. It didn't work out."

"You'll meet another woman. I'm sure of it. You can't miss."

"Yeah, probably. Maybe when I'm down there. A woman from my own culture."

I sipped some beer. He sipped some beer.

"What do you think?" Danny asked. "You think it's better we stay with our own?"

This all had taken me so much by surprise. I saw how Indian his dark face was—the eyes, the nostrils. The deep, quiet frown.

He didn't wait for me. "I love that woman, I still love that woman. I just don't know why she doesn't love me."

What could I say?

"See? I get mad one minute, sad the next," he told me. "You done?"

"I guess so."

I was almost finished with mine, he was only halfway on his. He carried them into the kitchen.

"I got a futon in here," he said at a closet. He took it and two sheets and a blanket out for me. He went into his bedroom and came out with a pillow. "I'll be getting up early in the morning. Finish packing, make a couple of phone calls."

I unrolled the futon and threw one sheet over it. The wind was blowing with a gritty howl and whistle. I loved the sound, its invisible power and beauty. It reminded me of what I missed about El Paso. The simple things. Sun, and moon, and stars, and dirt, and wind. Day and night. Before I turned off the lamp, I grabbed the pillow he'd put on the couch: I couldn't believe how filthy it was, so much so that its dirty gloss bled through the white pillowcase. I didn't even want to put the back of my head on it, so I used the blanket for that instead, and pulled the other sheet over me.

It was early in the morning when we got up. Too early for me, but I didn't say so. I rerolled the futon and folded the sheets and the blanket and put them in a pile on the couch, pillow on top. Danny packed and I read magazines. He had every magazine in print, months of them, three big piles. It was what he was going to do, write for these magazines, and he'd studied the market. He'd bought cushioned nylon bags for his camera and lenses. He worried about his laptop, using it, losing it. He needed to make some calls at his desk, the table. No, he said to me, it's okay, you can stay. First it was his mom and dad. In case he didn't come back, he told me, if anything happened. He called his sister and his brother. He talked to each of them for a long time about his career. He sounded confident, self-assured. I wanted to leave, take a walk, but I didn't want him to worry about me, because I was driving him to the airport. He was worried about so much. This trip, which so many people I knew had taken, worried him. His flight was to Mexico City, where he was meeting up with a friend, and then they'd travel in a jeep together. The city worried him, driving through the country worried him. I sat on the couch for a long time, reading, studying photos, while he was in the bedroom. He was a long time in there. When he finally came out he asked me if I was ready. Everything but the ticket, I said. He had most of his belongings in a backpack. I carried a small tote down the apartment stairs—we were loud, and it echoed on the hardwood floors—and we stopped for Mr. Palacios. I'd sort of met him the day before, when I got here. The old man had opened the door and asked if I was looking for someone. He knew everything, Danny had told me. He saw everything, every coming and every going. He liked to talk. As we got to the bottom of the stairs, near his door, it opened and Danny introduced me. He explained how I'd be staying there until he got back. Mr. Palacios nodded. *Andale, bien bien, ni modo, mucho gusto.* Though I knew we weren't, I asked him if we were related—the same last name and all. He didn't think so, he told me. He was born in Parral. No relatives here except his wife. I knew we weren't, I said, I was just joking around because we had the same last name. He went on, not reacting. She'd had two children previous. They'd had one, a man with a family of his own now, and lost one. We have to go, Danny interrupted. Down the front building stairs, and we tossed his bags in the back of my pickup. We got on I-10 and headed for Airway Boulevard. It was warm out, but the wind was still blowing, so the windows were only cracked.

"I wanted to call her. I had this overwhelming urge to call her."

"It'd be all right if you did."

"I wanted to tell her. I hate that I can't talk to her. This doesn't even matter, I still feel the same for her. I wouldn't even go on this trip. It isn't what I want. I wouldn't need to go if, you know, if we were together, or going to be."

"You should call her, dude. Call her from the airport. You'll have plenty of time. I'll bet she'd like it."

"I just can't."

"That's not so bad either. Maybe you shouldn't. But, *sabes que,* it'd be okay if you did. You guys were together what, five years?"

"I wanted us to live together. An apartment for a while. I wanted her to live with me. I thought she'd agree to that."

"But she didn't. Well, you're both working. Distances. *Es bien duro.*"

"Tell me what you think about this. That in all the time, in all that time, she never once told me she loved me."

I wanted my window down anyway. "That's, well, I'm not sure what you're saying."

"That she never did. Not once."

"But you guys were together a lot? Went places?" My real thought was about sex.

"We had *great* times. Especially the first years. Lots of fun. We loved being together. And I know she did. I know. It's why I don't understand."

"Well," I said, "I think you should make the best of this trip. Get away for a while. I think shaking it up is good. And, *de todos modos,* you told me how you can get jobs everywhere. This either works out for you, or you get another good job after you get back. Either way, dude."

I double-parked near a skycap booth for his airline. We said good-bye to each other hurriedly, shaking hands.

I slumped onto the couch when I got back. I was sleepy and didn't want to start working yet. I lifted up the pillowcase and I looked at the pillow again. Dead was the only way I could describe it. It once had silky, blue stripes, and then I remembered, with sudden clearness, having a pillow exactly like this when I was maybe ten years old, even younger. It was my favorite pillow. It was probably my mom's first. She'd given it to me when she got a new one, or when one was ruined and she bought a pair. This could be the same pillow, decades later. I went into the bedroom. His other pillow was a match. He had two of them. Two dead, decomposing pillows, discolored not by stains or misuse but by age, the passage of time. He'd been given them, by his mom, and they weren't torn, and he kept them. He didn't notice how black the white stripes between the blue had become, how gray the blue ones. He'd had them so long, for so many years, and he'd kept them, and couldn't see that they needed to be thrown away.

The couch, if comfortable, was old, unattractive, indistinctive. Not damaged in any way, not a tear, not a spill, but it hadn't been cleaned ever either, and it was turning brown, a black film on the armrests from the oil of human hands. Everything in the apartment, it occurred to me, was like the couch. Furniture that functioned but was never more than functional new. Never beautiful, never worth taking care of, not worth paying attention to but for the function. Like particleboard with paper veneer, it would never be "antique" or "kitsch." And all of it brown like the walls, the ceilings, like the shades. Nothing with brilliant color. Not a red, not a white, not even a faded bright color. Except for that sombrero, the walls were empty. Not a picture, not a tacked-up poster, nothing.

I imagined his Mary on the bed. She is passionate, wanting, in the throes. I imagine her body all alert, hear her breathing fast, feel her perspire, and she reaches, climbs, and peaks. When she is spent, as she drops back into time, naked, her blood still rushing, when her head—eyes and nose and mouth—rests on one of these disgusting pillows.

The two pillows I bought at the department store weren't the cheapest, but close. I liked them. The covers had a satiny sheen, in a pattern of long-stemmed, leafy flowers. I went ahead and bought a set of sheets with pillowcases too. The clerk put them in the biggest bag I'd ever been given. The pillows were plump, overripe, bursting. The front door of the apartment building was locked and the key to the apartment didn't fit. I had to ring the bell. Mr. Palacios came.

"You don't have a key?" he asked.

It felt like the bag barely fit through the door. "I guess he forgot."

"It's only locked at night."

"You think I could get one from you?"

Mr. Palacios wasn't sure.

"You don't have an extra?"

"I'll have to ask Mr. Nevárez, the owner."

"I'll pay you if you want." I reached for my wallet. I took out five dollars. "When you get a chance."

He took the cash. "New pillows," he said.

I swore he wanted to open the bag and touch them. I swore he wanted to talk about these new pillows.

"Look at it this way," I told Lisita. "She's either an artist or she teaches it. So she loves beauty. She lives for the idea of beauty. She *desires* it. Can you see what I'm saying? What other reason to be in art?"

"Why do you suppose he hasn't tried to make it better?"

"He told me. He thought of this place as temporary, and five years later he's still here."

"Is he a good-looking man?"

"He is. And he's in good shape. He's athletic."

"Those *are* the worst pillows I've ever seen."

"I can't imagine a woman getting in a bed with those pillows. I can't imagine a woman wanting to, even to take a nap."

"It is an awful bed." She rocked up and down on it. "How are we going to sleep on it?"

"But you see what I'm saying about beauty, right? Don't you see the conflict? Say she has this lust, this sexual passion, which is the raw form of what drives us into art in the first place, and she's here, with these pillows, in a place, a situation if you think about it, that is absent of what she deeply wants and loves most."

Lisita had stopped listening. "How do you know they were here all the time?"

I hadn't even considered that.

"It's a bachelor's pad. You're being hard on him. He's a guy."

"*Pues,* I'm a guy you know."

"Palacios." She was still on the bed. She was waiting.

"What I mean . . ." I stopped for a few seconds: Lisita was so uniquely sexy that it caught me once in a while. She was pure want of woman, something powerful and undeniable and not visible. "*Lo que digo,* I mean I don't go around saying this all the time. I've never worried about pillows before."

"I care about pillows. You're right about that. Women care more about pillows than men. I like these ones you bought."

"*Quelá,* mommy! I'm talking about *beauty.* That I never realized how much I take it for granted in my life. Put it this way. I want a woman to like getting in my bed."

"Shut up about your women."

"It's not what I'm saying."

"Oh, Palacios."

"What I'm trying to say is that lots of men don't know about women. That a woman won't fall in love with a man that doesn't care about beauty."

"Oh, Palacios," she said, crawling up on the bed. "Are you going to get on this bed with me, Palacios?"

I don't know what I loved most about making love to Lisita. What I think of is her face. That punishing shock of desire all over it. So pleasurable it scared her. I loved making love to her, loved making her love it.

"I'm leaving these pillows," I told her afterward. "I don't think I should leave the sheets though. I don't want him to . . . well, you know, and I don't want it to seem like a personal thing."

"He could've put his best ones away."

"I'm thinking he'll see these new pillows . . ."

Her fingers traced the small of my back and the top of my butt and she sighed as her breasts pressed against my chest and she kissed my neck, under my ears, to my lips. "I love being with you," she said. "I love it too much."

It was early evening when we got out for a drive. I took her over to the neighborhood, by Austin, the high school Danny and I went to, and I stopped my truck across the street from where I grew up, a stone house that was painted white when I lived there and had been repainted pink. Lace curtains in the windows. There was a cherry, stock '64 Impala on the front yard, a Corolla in the rutted driveway. The house was so much like all the others, and as still as a photograph twenty-five years old. I was full of this selfish pride, full of a private joy about our neighborhood, about our culture. I lied. I didn't tell her it was my house but that it was an old friend's.

The next three days we drove under that desert sun and sky, moon and stars, in the wind and air. We drove up the river through the cotton fields and ate *rellenos* at Chopes and swung back and drove down to the San Eli mission, smelling the burning skin of green chile all around. We ate at Kiki's and Delicious and Lucy's and we walked El Paso Street across the bridge and onto Juárez Avenue and we drank at the Kentucky Club. We hiked, until we were out of breath, up a loose rock path in McKelligon Canyon to a high point where my dad buried our dog when she died, in a grave heaped with boulders, protected by agave and ocotillo. We drove slow past the brick house over by Washington Park where my wife grew up and where we'd lived together with her parents those first years. I'd wanted to go, get away, so bad.

And, like those first days, and the others when she flew down, it was the bed, my sheets, with the pillows. Her breasts and waist and hips, nipples, lips, *lengua, nalgas, panocha*. Never enough.

"It's so wonderful here," she said. "El Paso is such a sweet town. I could live here. We could live here."

I didn't say.

"I love you," Lisita said. "I want to be with you," she said.

No, I decided not to. Not for the obvious, that he'd be offended, that he'd take it as a personal criticism. Which would be bad after he'd been so generous to me. No, that wasn't it. It just seemed like too much for him to suddenly learn. Not the embarrassment of realizing that he'd been sleeping on disgusting pillows, even offering them to guests. Much as that might be too much too. But no, it wasn't that. It was if he did see it as I did. The revelation of the repulsive truth. And yes, I did believe it was absolutely true, an easy call. I did. He would look at these new pillows, and he would look at those dead ones, and he would think of the years that had passed, how he'd wasted so many, how simple it might've been and how he'd messed up. No, I didn't want that responsibility. I didn't want to be the one. I couldn't be sure how he, how anyone, would take it, would respond.

I had to get them out of the apartment and into my truck. At first I thought of dropping them from the porch, then picking them up from the side of the house. Which would have kept Mr. Palacios from seeing me go down the stairs with them, unless he saw what I did do, and that would be much worse, much more memorable. I already worried that he would tell Danny about the pillows anyway. The day you left, I could hear him say, he bought these two pillows that he carried upstairs in the biggest sack I ever saw. After six weeks, I'd learned there was no telling when he might be awake, and when he was awake, and he heard, he opened the door. Though he didn't need to open the door every time. In the afternoon to early evening it was usually already open. He had the TV on, a Mexican station blaring. I worried about walking them down in the middle of the night too, because I didn't want him to rush out and open the door then either. In my stocking feet, down the hall and the stairs and out the door? Unless he saw me, and with the pillows. He'd cracked it open on me between two and three A.M. a couple of times. Once he'd met Lisita, he asked me about her every time I came down without her, which had been most of the days I'd been staying in the apartment.

I was making it too big a deal? Exaggerating the possibility of Mr. Palacios seeing me? If I did, I did, and anyway I finally figured it out: I took the clothes out of my suitcase and put the pillows in and zipped it up. I walked down the stairs.

I heard the door opening.

"Moving out?" Mr. Palacios asked.

I kept my hand on the suitcase handle, but rested it on the floor. "Daniel's here tomorrow night. He's taking his apartment from me."

"Tomorrow night?"

"Yeah," I said, "so I'm getting my things out now."

I carried the suitcase to my truck. Left it, and I went back. Mr. Palacios's door was wide open now, and the TV was on. I brought down a couple of easels, my paint boxes. After a couple of those trips, I unzipped the suitcase and took the pillows out and went back to the building with it empty again.

I passed his door and up the stairs and when I looked behind me I saw him standing under the threshold watching me go up. I made two other trips. Then I repacked my clothes in the suitcase.

He was standing at his door, suspicious.

"You forgot something?"

I acted guilty. "Yeah," I laughed.

Now he watched me more carefully. A few hours later, when I was moved out, I cleaned up what mess I'd made, and I locked the door behind me.

"You mind giving him this key when he gets here? He told me it's a spare, so he can get in with his. And here's the other too."

He looked them both over. "Tomorrow night?"

"He's supposed to be here tomorrow night."

We both waited.

"Well, it was good to meet you, Mr. Palacios."

. . . what is useful is eavesdropping, listening, talking to people in an informal way, sitting around tables swapping stories, listening to kids. I might take notes, too. And I keep huge notebook sketches. I have one that's just physical descriptions: faces postures, walks, the way somebody's elbows point outward, their complexion, the cast of their eyes, any scars, pockmarks, peculiar gaits, accents, odd ways of holding the mouth. So all these things I'll write down at odd moments as I travel . . . And when I approach a new novel, I know the characters I want and will look through to see if I can find a physical description that fits.

—E. ANNIE PROULX

How to Talk to a Hunter

Pam Houston

When he says "Skins or blankets?" it will take you a moment to realize that he's asking which you want to sleep under. And in your hesitation he'll decide that he wants to see your skin wrapped in the big black moose hide. He carried it, he'll say, soaking wet and heavier than a dead man, across the tundra for two—was it hours or days or weeks? But the payoff, now, will be to see it fall across one of your white breasts. It's December, and your skin is never really warm, so you will pull the bulk of it around you and pose for him, pose for his camera, without having to narrate this moose's death.

You will spend every night in this man's bed without asking yourself why he listens to top-forty country. Why he donated money to the Republican Party. Why he won't play back his messages while you are in the room. You are there so often the messages pile up. Once you noticed the bright green counter reading as high as fifteen.

He will have lured you here out of a careful independence that you spent months cultivating; though it will finally be winter, the dwindling daylight and the threat of Christmas, that makes you give in. Spending nights with this man means suffering the long face of your sheepdog, who likes to sleep on your bed, who worries when you don't come home. But the hunter's house is so much warmer than yours, and he'll give you a key, and just like a woman, you'll think that means something. It will snow hard for thirteen straight days. Then it will really get cold. When it is sixty below there will be no wind and no clouds, just still air and cold sunshine. The sun on the windows will lure you out of bed, but he'll pull you back under. The next two hours he'll devote to your body. With his hands, with his tongue, he'll express what will seem to you like the most eternal of loves. Like the house key, this is just another kind of lie. Even in bed; especially in bed, you and he cannot speak the same language. The machine will answer the incoming calls. From under an ocean of passion and hide and hair you'll hear a woman's muffled voice between the beeps.

Your best female friend will say, "So what did you think? That a man who sleeps under a dead moose is capable of commitment?"

This is what you learned in college: A man desires the satisfaction of his desire; a woman desires the condition of desiring.

The hunter will talk about spring in Hawaii, summer in Alaska. The man who says he was always better at math will form the sentences so carefully it will be impossible to tell if you are included in these plans. When he asks you if you would like to open a small guest ranch way out in the country, understand that this is a rhetorical question. Label these conversations future perfect, but don't expect the present to catch up with them. Spring is an inconceivable distance from the December days that just keep getting shorter and gray.

He'll ask you if you've ever shot anything, if you'd like to, if you ever thought about teaching your dog to retrieve. Your dog will like him too much, will drop the stick at his feet every time, will roll over and let the hunter scratch his belly.

One day he'll leave you sleeping to go split wood or get the mail and his phone will ring again. You'll sit very still while a woman who calls herself something like Janie Coyote leaves a message on his machine: She's leaving work, she'll say, and the last thing she wanted to hear was the sound of his beautiful voice. Maybe she'll talk only in rhyme. Maybe the counter will change to sixteen. You'll look a question at the mule deer on the wall, and the dark spots on either side of his mouth will tell you he shares more with this hunter than you ever will. One night, drunk, the hunter told you he was sorry for taking that deer, that every now and then there's an animal that isn't meant to be taken, and he should have known that deer was one.

Your best male friend will say, "No one who needs to call herself Janie Coyote can hold a candle to you, but why not let him sleep alone a few nights, just to make sure?"

The hunter will fill your freezer with elk burger, venison sausage, organic potatoes, fresh pecans. He'll tell you to wear your seat belt, to dress warmly, to drive safely. He'll say you are always on his mind, that you're the best thing that's ever happened to him, that you make him glad that he's a man.

Tell him it don't come easy, tell him freedom's just another word for nothing left to lose.

These are the things you'll know without asking: The coyote woman wears her hair in braids. She uses words like "howdy." She's man enough to shoot a deer.

A week before Christmas you'll rent *It's a Wonderful Life* and watch it together, curled on your couch, faces touching. Then you'll bring up the word "monogamy." He'll tell you how badly he was hurt by your predecessor. He'll tell you he couldn't be happier spending every night with you. He'll say there's just a few questions he doesn't have the answers for. He'll say he's just scared and confused. Of course this isn't exactly what he means. Tell him you understand. Tell him you are scared too. Tell him to take all the time he needs. Know that you could never shoot an animal; and be glad of it.

Your best female friend will say, "You didn't tell him you loved him, did you?" Don't even tell her the truth. If you do you'll have to tell her that he said this: "I feel exactly the same way."

Your best male friend will say, "Didn't you know what would happen when you said the word 'commitment'?"

But that isn't the word that you said.

He'll say, "Commitment, monogamy, it all means just one thing."

The coyote woman will come from Montana with the heavier snows. The hunter will call you on the day of the solstice to say he has a friend in town and can't see you. He'll leave you hanging your Christmas lights; he'll give new meaning to the phrase "longest night of the year." The man who has said he's not so good with words will manage to say eight things about his friend without using a gender-determining pronoun. Get out of the house quickly. Call the most understanding person you know who will let you sleep in his bed.

Your best female friend will say, "So what did you think? That he was capable of living outside his gender?"

When you get home in the morning there's a candy tin on your pillow. Santa, obese and grotesque, fondles two small children on the lid. The card will say something like "From your not-so-secret admirer." Open it. Examine each carefully made truffle. Feed them, one at a time, to the dog. Call the hunter's machine. Tell him you don't speak chocolate.

Your best female friend will say, "At this point, what is it about him that you could possibly find appealing?"

Your best male friend will say, "Can't you understand that this is a good sign? Can't you understand that this proves how deep he's in with you?" Hug your best male friend. Give him the truffles the dog wouldn't eat.

Of course the weather will cooperate with the coyote woman. The highways will close, she will stay another night. He'll tell her he's going to work so he can come and see you. He'll even leave her your number and write "Me at Work" on the yellow pad of paper by his phone. Although you shouldn't, you'll have to be there. It will be you and your nauseous dog and your half-trimmed tree all waiting for him like a series of questions.

This is what you learned in graduate school: In every assumption is contained the possibility of its opposite.

In your kitchen he'll hug you like you might both die there. Sniff him for coyote. Don't hug him back.

He will say whatever he needs to to win. He'll say it's just an old friend. He'll say the visit was all the friend's idea. He'll say the night away from you has given him time to think about how much you mean to him. Realize that nothing short of sleeping alone will ever make him realize how much you mean to him. He'll say that if you can just be a little patient, some good will come out of this for the two of you after all. He still won't use a gender-specific pronoun.

Put your head in your hands. Think about what it means to be patient. Think about the beautiful, smart, strong, clever woman you thought he saw when he looked at you. Pull on your hair. Rock your body back and forth. Don't cry.

He'll say that after holding you it doesn't feel right holding anyone else. For "holding," substitute "fucking." Then take it as a compliment.

He will get frustrated and rise to leave. He may or may not be bluffing. Stall for time. Ask a question he can't immediately answer. Tell him you want to make love on the floor. When he tells you your body is beautiful say, "I feel exactly the same way." Don't, under any circumstances, stand in front of the door.

Your best female friend will say, "They lie to us, they cheat on us, and we love them more for it." She'll say, "It's our fault; we raise them to be like that."

Tell her it can't be your fault. You've never raised anything but dogs.

The hunter will say it's late and he has to go home to sleep. He'll emphasize the last word in the sentence. Give him one kiss that he'll remember while he's fucking the coyote woman. Give him one kiss that ought to make him cry if he's capable of it, but don't notice when he does. Tell him to have a good night.

Your best male friend will say, "We all do it. We can't help it. We're self-destructive. It's the old bad-boy routine. You have a male dog, don't you?"

The next day the sun will be out and the coyote woman will leave. Think about how easy it must be for a coyote woman and a man who listens to top-forty country. The coyote woman would never use a word like "monogamy"; the coyote woman will stay gentle on his mind.

If you can, let him sleep alone for at least one night. If you can't, invite him over to finish trimming your Christmas tree. When he asks how you are, tell him you think it's a good idea to keep your sense of humor during the holidays.

Plan to be breezy and aloof and full of interesting anecdotes about all the other men you've ever known. Plan to be hotter than ever before in bed, and a little cold out of it. Remember that necessity is the mother of invention. Be flexible.

First, he will find the faulty bulb that's been keeping all the others from lighting. He will explain, in great detail, the most elementary electrical principles. You will take turns placing the ornaments you and other men, he and other women, have spent years carefully choosing. Under the circumstances, try to let this be a comforting thought.

He will thin the clusters of tinsel you put on the tree. He'll say something ambiguous like "Next year you should string popcorn and cranberries." Finally, his arm will stretch just high enough to place the angel on the top of the tree.

Your best female friend will say, "Why can't you ever fall in love with a man who will be your friend?"

Your best male friend will say, "You ought to know this by now: Men always cheat on the best women."

This is what you learned in the pop psychology book: Love means letting go of fear.

Play Willie Nelson's "Pretty Paper." He'll ask you to dance, and before you can answer he'll be spinning you around your wood stove, he'll be humming in your ear. Before the song ends he'll be taking off your clothes, setting you lightly under the tree, hovering above you with tinsel in his hair. Through the spread of the branches the all-white lights you insisted on will shudder and blur, outlining the ornaments he brought: a pheasant, a snow goose, a deer.

The record will end. Above the crackle of the wood stove and the rasp of the hunter's breathing you'll hear one long low howl break the quiet of the frozen night: your dog, chained and lonely and cold. You'll wonder if he knows enough to stay in his doghouse. You'll wonder if he knows that the nights are getting shorter now.

Would You Know
It Wasn't Love?

Hester Kaplan

When Walt thinks about his daughter Rosie and her disintegrating marriage, he can't help thinking about himself too. He's not moved to pity, either for his own sick self or for Rosie and Tim; what he feels instead is the misery and waste of this breaking-up of lives. He's edgy now when he's always been patient, but he's a man with a disease, out of control sometimes, sometimes hateful, he knows, but forgiven. His wife Helen, well ahead of him into Rosie's mess already, has bags under her eyes and a penchant for salty things which she eats until her mouth swells up. After dinner, Walt caught her gulping glass after glass of water at the kitchen sink. He felt as though he'd walked in on something he shouldn't have seen, but he couldn't look away. Recently Helen has stopped acknowledging his private moments—the time his swollen fingers refused to hold a glass, so that it fell and shattered on the floor, when his morning stiffness had him groping at the wall for something to lean against. He knows she's witnessed them. He's seen her worried shadow pass by, heard her gasp.

On the downstairs extension in his study off the kitchen, and Helen upstairs on the bedroom phone, he talks to Rosie. Walt wants to understand what's going on, but she sniffles more than she speaks a full sentence so that, again, he isn't sure what the problem is. After Rosie says good bye to her parents, Walt and Helen stay on the line. Tim *is* brooding and inscrutable, Walt says to Helen—has she ever met a man who wasn't?—but does that mean Rosie should walk away from her marriage? It's an old theme he's brought up: the fear that they've babied their youngest daughter to the point of hobbling her.

Walt thinks it's strange—but also a little easier—to talk to Helen tonight over the phone so they don't have to look at each other. He can imagine that she's not quite as familiar to him, nor he so familiar to her, that they might come up with something they haven't said before.

The operator interrupts before Helen can answer, so Walt walks upstairs to finish the conversation. Helen turns to him as he enters the bedroom, and in the light of her reading lamp he sees the chapping around her thin mouth, like cheap lipstick. He wonders, too tired for passion, how long it has been since they've really kissed, tongues and all, with his hands on her solid body; certainly not since the start of Rosie's crisis.

"Why are you telling me this about Tim?" Helen asks him angrily, and her face blushes red. Her eyes are a cold blue. "Inscrutable? Brooding? Those are ridiculous words. What am I supposed to do with them? Are they going to help the situation somehow?"

Walt has no answer for his wife. He hadn't intended to sound so coldhearted, only firm.

Helen returns to the student papers she's correcting for tomorrow, and Walt goes downstairs to his study again. When he kneels slowly in front of the closet, he almost expects to find that the rheumatoid arthritis has reached his knees, as his doctor has warned it might

344

one of these days. But he is relieved to be spared so far and digs around in the back where he keeps all his cassette tapes: of his lectures, the babies' chatter, of his girls' clumsy and beautiful recitals and plays, of school speeches and dinner parties, Helen's singing tipsy at his forty-seventh birthday party. He's sentimental about these sounds the way others are about photographs.

The sharp plastic boxes are a comfort to him. Walt is aware that he's a technological oddity these days, preferring his inoffensive, nonobtrusive tape recorder and cassettes when he could get sound *and* picture with a camcorder the size of his palm, the minor heft of a small melon. One day he intends to do something with all of the tapes he's collected, turn them into a kind of family history he might listen to when he's finally crippled. Through old corduroy pants, Walt's bones begin to grind against the floor, and it takes him a while to locate the cassette he's after. He finds it near the back finally, and stands up.

Walt pushes the play button on his recorder, sits in his armchair the cat has scratched bare, and listens. His study needs repainting, he sees. The bad light plays up how much they've let slide in the past two years since he's been sick, as though the only thing to focus on is the mysterious course his body is taking. He remembers four years earlier deciding to leave the tape running even as his favorite dog vomited under the kitchen table, as Helen dropped an empty pan on the floor and the dishwasher started with its splash of water. It was the noise behind the negotiations he'd wanted to record as much as the discussion itself of the wedding's guest list and the meaning of an open bar. Helen and Rosie had hardly protested against the taping and what their own words might hold them to later on, and then only because they understood it was expected of them, just as the taping was expected of him.

But Walt hears now, very clearly with nothing to distract him in his quiet house, that Tim was not so sure about being recorded, collected. The boy clears his throat too often and says almost nothing, as though it wasn't his wedding they were planning, but someone else's entirely. Again and again, over side A and B of the cassette, Walt hears Tim clear his thick throat. He swears it sounds like thunder rumbling behind Rosie's voice full of premarriage optimism. If ambivalence makes a noise, this is it, Walt thinks, and he turns off the tape recorder with a jab of his thumb.

"You motherfucker," he mumbles, though he is not quite sure who he is naming.

Walt knows the tape isn't going to tell him what to do about his daughter's problems. After all, it didn't tell him that his adored dog was going to die two weeks after the tape was made, choked to death on a splintered pork chop bone dug out of the kitchen garbage. It didn't tell Walt that the reason he sometimes winced from pain as he held a pencil, or answered his wife irritably when he didn't mean to, was the onset of arthritis that wasn't going to go away.

As he puts the cassette back in its box, he knows that there's nothing really *to do* but let Rosie come back home for a while, as she wants. Helen has said yes, of course, immediately, come to us, we're here, but Walt already feels the burden of having her home again. He sees in the wrinkles of his face, his thinning hair, his thickening joints, a man who has no room for this sort of thing at the moment, a man who has no idea how much room is left at all. But Rosie is still his daughter, and he adores her, even if he doesn't feel like being anyone's father right now.

The following Tuesday, it is close to eight as Walt nears the Greyhound bus station, but the expressway is crowded even for a weekday in early December, and the traffic has stopped moving. Helen, on her way out to her reading group earlier, told him to take

Cambridge Street downtown, but he's ignored her advice. Walt knows he'll be late meeting Rosie's bus from New York, and he worries about her in a familiar way. Rosie is twenty-five years old, has a job as a paralegal, an apartment on 73rd Street, a husband—is he still that? Someday she'll have kids. She's an independent person, he'd like to believe, but will she know enough to come and look outside for her father instead of expecting that he'll find her?

Walt remembers asking Rosie the same about Tim once: Does he know to meet us in your office? Meaning, is this man you're in love with, the one your mother is sure you'll marry just by the tone of your voice when you talk about him, capable of thinking of others? Walt had been in Manhattan for a conference at NYU. After lunch, he took a bus uptown to meet Rosie at work; Tim was supposed to meet them there too. As he watched the city through the sooty window, Walt found it hard to believe that his daughter lived in a place where there were so many things to do, to go wrong, and so many people to choose from. He carried in his briefcase a glass paperweight he'd bought for her in a store off Washington Square that morning.

Rosie's office was a small room off a hallway of other small rooms inhabited by women bent over papers or keyboards, fingering their earrings. She had a picture of her parents on her desk, which made Walt feel a little weak, and she put the paperweight next to it. When Tim didn't show up, and Walt and Rosie ran out of things to say after a while—easy without the clutter of the family—Rosie began to look miserable, her dark eyes watered, and she pulled hair loose from her ponytail. It was a habit she and her sister shared, as they shared their mother's thin face and his high forehead.

"I don't know, honey," Walt said gently, and looked at his watch, "maybe he thought we were going to meet him downstairs. Do you remember what you told him?" He hated it when his daughter acted stupid and here she was stupid about love, the worst of all things. It made him feel sorry for both of them.

Tim was on a bench in the building's courtyard, reclining long-legged and reading a book, when Walt and Rosie came out. He'd picked a spot shaded by a cherry tree in bloom, too beautiful for the city. Tim seemed content, so why should he think others wouldn't be, that they might be waiting for him.

"He doesn't have a watch," Rosie whispered to her father. She was clearly charmed by this, Walt saw, by her prince in a garden. Tim unfolded slowly to meet them. Rosie bounced on her tiptoes, her heels lifted out of her blue pumps, and Walt noticed she smelled a bit sweaty. She should be wearing red, rubber-tipped sneakers, he thought to himself, and approached Tim.

"Thought we were going to miss you," Walt said, and raised his eyebrows. It was a voice he often used with his students, a gentle challenge. The boy would not look at him. Tim's surprisingly handsome face was darkened by a two-day-old beard.

"No way," Tim said, and picked at the blossoms of the cherry tree. "Where do you want to go now?"

As if, Walt thought, this alone isn't enough for one father for one day, not to mention your dirty fingernails, your lack of a sense of time and expectations, your hold on my baby daughter. You'll take her away from me; I suppose I'll always dislike you for that. But he put his arm across Tim's shoulders, the way he had with his other daughter's boyfriend because he knew it would make Rosie happy.

"Whatever you two would like," Walt said, "is fine by me."

Later, when Walt told Helen about Tim, she laughed. "Pure jealousy," she'd said. "Fathers and their daughters. Rosie's a grown-up, let her go. You're the one who always says we baby her too much."

Mothers, Walt thinks now, looking for his daughter in the crowd bulging at the bus station entrance, accept when they have to, let go when they must, but watch out; they'll also turn their back on whoever hurts their child so quickly you'll feel the wind cut your face. Fathers, though, are rigid in the end; they suffer for their hearts that have been won so easily. Or is it my episodes of pain, Walt wonders, that's made my chest feel so tight lately?

He circles the station again but doesn't see Rosie in front. Now he'll be damned if he's going to look around for a parking place when it's cold and dark and he's in prime mugging territory. If Rosie really wants to come home so badly, she'll look outside for him. Walt pops one of his books-on-tape into the player and drives around the block—the traffic pattern is oval, with a light at each end. He's so engrossed by the true-life story of a baseball player (his other daughter gave it to him his last birthday) that it takes him a second to realize the person in the green parka trotting alongside the car and tapping at the window when he stops at a red light is Rosie, and not someone trying to take his car. She looks so much like his little girl, like both of his little girls at the point when their faces took their final beautiful shapes, her eyes bright with lack of under-standing and the red Greyhound sign, that he wonders what year it is, and what year he'd like it to be.

When he unlocks the door, Rosie throws her duffel bag in the back seat. He can't help but be dismayed by the size of it, the amount of stuff she's packed for what he thinks is going to be a short visit home. She slips into the front seat and is slightly out of breath when Walt leans over and pulls her face to his lips. Her skin smells of diesel fumes and Jergens, Helen's lotion, so familiar he doesn't want to let her go. Walt notices that Rosie hasn't worn a hat and the tips of her ears are flaming cold, and he wants to touch them. Rosie seems light-hearted for the moment as they drive back to Cambridge, chatting about the bus ride, looking around at the familiar sights, avoiding any mention of Tim, or why she has come home. Walt again feels a touch of dismay at this, at how easily she can leave one thing and fall into another, like an experienced traveler crossing time zones.

He remembers driving four hours one July when she was thirteen to pick her up at camp mid-session. She was miserable, she'd said in her letters, she felt like she was in jail. The black flies by the lake were torture. Walt had glared at the camp director, his daughter's warden in khaki shorts, while Rosie had skipped—skipped!—off to her cabin to get her things, which naturally were not ready, as though this was a game. On the way home they'd stopped for lunch at a diner, and over grilled cheese and thick chocolate milk Rosie told him about the wonderful things she'd done for the past few weeks. He couldn't understand her chang-ing from misery to delight so quickly. He felt his solitude shattered—the prospect of both girls away at the same time, just him and Helen alone—but also his loneliness abating.

"Got a couple of days off from work?" Walt asks. They are almost home, and he wants to know how long she'll be staying.

"Until Monday," she sighs, "but I may quit anyway. I'm not crazy about the job." Walt knows by the way she's caught her breath that she's looking at his twisted hands on the steer-ing wheel. When he looks down too, he sees rocks under his skin.

"Well, being crazy about something isn't always the standard to measure things by, Rosie. In fact, the older you get, the less good a standard it becomes." When he realizes how sad and defeated this sounds, he pats her on the knee and tells her that he's looking forward to spend-ing time with her. "I'm really glad you're visiting."

During his standard end-of-the-semester lecture, Walt is aware of the wheels of the tape recorder that he's placed on the lectern going round and round, a tiny hiss only he can hear. He thinks of the letting out and taking up of the tape, and looks at Diana Lux's long legs in their black pants. She is in his sociology course on community structures, a small, bright head in the first row. Walt is not really listening to what he's saying—he can always rewind later to make sure he hasn't lost his rhythm, just his breath—but wondering if Diana still calls her parents Mommy and Daddy.

Rosie, who has been installed in her old room for a week now—the Monday to return to work come and gone—has taken to calling her parents Walt and Helen, has taken to phoning her older sister long distance every night. She emerges from her room after a conversation with Tim looking sleepy and red-eyed. Walt would like to call his daughter selfish and spoiled for the way she's descended upon them, but he calls her Rosita and Rosebud instead, and when she needs some money, or she asks him to get her a soda while he's up, he gives it to her. He sits with her at the kitchen table and they talk, they play Scrabble at night. She visited him at his office and they went to the Museum of Fine Arts, and afterward, at the gift shop, he bought her a silk scarf with a Matisse print on it.

The day after, when he woke in the morning, he felt as though his upper body was encased in cement. He called for his daughter down the hall. Helen had already left for work. Rosie drove him into Boston to the doctor's, dropped him off and parked the car so he wouldn't be late for the appointment. She was there when he finished, went with him to the pharmacy, and asked how he felt.

Her voice was wobbly with concern, so he showed her his new prescription for Auranofin. "These pills are made from gold extract," he told her. The doctor said they would slow the progression, a word Walt found particularly menacing. "If I take enough of them," he added, not to worry his daughter, "maybe you can melt me down into a pair of earrings."

Meanwhile, Helen has gone from salt to sugar, Walt notices, and hovers over Rosie's problems. Her mouth has stopped swelling; now she has pimples tiny as grains of sand and grease on the sides of her nose, and she talks a lot.

Diana Lux's face is so bright Walt can hardly stand it, and he looks down at his hands on the oak lectern. He would like Diana to tell him that he doesn't look old enough to have two grown women children, or that he's too old to have one tear at his heart, but he knows she's unlikely to be thinking anything so complex.

Rosie found a therapist in Cambridge, and tells her parents when she joins them for dinner in the kitchen. "I need a safe place right now," she says. Walt thinks she's looking thin and exotic dressed in black with her hair loose. Her earrings, though, are like something his secretary would wear, big gold globs, panic buttons. "She thinks I didn't feel safe with Tim."

"He didn't beat you up?" Helen says, half stating, half asking. They both hold their breath for her answer.

"No, of course not," Rosie says. All she's eaten is a breadstick, Walt sees, and he wonders why this detail takes up so much space in his head.

"Of course not? Is that so obvious?" he asks. His mouth is full of chicken and he swallows. "The way you ran out of there, I thought maybe he did hit you or something, maybe you're afraid to go back. *That* at least I can make sense of." He is very angry, and both women look a little scared of what's happening to him.

"It doesn't have to be physical abuse, Dad," she says. Helen nods. "There are other kinds." He wonders at her authority now as she talks with someone else's words.

He is Dad again suddenly. He remembers a time when his daughters came to him with stomachaches, and he could soothe them with a story. Later it was cramps that bothered them, they soothed each other, and stayed far away from him. It was like being fenced off from a place you used to live. He wanted to break back in.

"Please. In my day," he starts, and spews a fleck of food onto the table, "you didn't just leave because you didn't feel 'safe.' What is this shit anyway about safety? This has always been your problem, Rosie, you never feel you have to stick with anything, you can run home any time you like. Your mother and I are to blame for that too, I'll admit. You come, we take you in."

The women tilt their heads at similar angles.

"She's your daughter, for God's sake," Helen says. "Of course we take her in."

Walt sees that Rosie is close to tears. He puts his napkin on his plate—something he knows Helen hates—and leaves the table. In his study, he hears Helen and Rosie talking in the kitchen, and thinks how easily Helen has become a complete mother again, how little she fights this return. Walt feels bad for what he's said but justified in saying it. In a while, he puts in the cassette from his afternoon's lecture.

He can't believe that the voice he hears is his own, and he adjusts the tone on the machine. He sounds flat, dated is how he really thinks of it, the voice of a half-asleep man. From time to time, a staccato cough punctuates his drone, and he imagines that it's Diana Lux trying to rouse him and get his attention, even at this moment in the privacy of his own home, calling him to imagine her in her dorm room in her flannel pajamas. He pictures her tumbling like a gymnast over futons and beanbag chairs, like a doll with string joints.

The light from the kitchen blinds him momentarily. "What are you doing?" Helen asks. It's not accusatory, just curious.

"Listening to today's lecture," he says. "Do you think my voice sounds funny?"

She puts her fingers to her lips. Being married to him for so many years has made her a good listener. "Not really, a little nasal maybe. Why, do you?"

"I thought it sounded flat. Old."

Helen sits on the arm of his chair. She smells like dish soap and chocolate. "Maybe you need new batteries."

He pats her leg in wool pants. "Maybe *you* need new batteries," he jokes.

Helen smiles and gets up to straighten a picture on the wall. It happens, by chance, to be one of Rosie at twelve, knocked slightly askew by the swiveling arm of his desk lamp.

"In my day . . ." Helen starts, doing her imitation of Walt, putting her head down on her chest so that a double chin appears and her eyebrows meet, ". . . in my day . . ." She stops, looks at him, and talks in her own voice. "In your day, Walt? My day and your day are the same, remember? You didn't have that day—and what day was it, anyway?—without me." Walt shrugs.

"Rosie's talking to Tim," Helen adds, matter-of-factly. How easily we pass these things by, Walt thinks, and feels affection for his wife and his long marriage. They've never talked about what will happen if one day he can't move anymore.

"Yes? And what's this about her finding a shrink here? That has the ring of long-term," Walt says. "Doesn't she have to go home at some point? What about her job? And what the hell is she doing about her marriage? Isn't that the problem at hand, as they say?"

Now Helen shrugs, and Walt knows that she too would really like to be done with this— after all, for several years they've been living a different kind of life—but can't bring herself to say so, won't allow herself. Rosie has always been trouble in one way or another, a baby is always—lovely, painful trouble.

"And since we're talking about marriage, how's ours?" he asks and holds his arms open to her. It's as close as he can come to apologizing at the moment.

"I'm not really thinking about it," Helen says, which doesn't surprise or hurt him. She holds his hands, and can't help but massage them a little. "I'm thinking about Rosie now, what she's going to do." Before she leaves the room, Helen kisses his forehead and reminds him to take his gold pills.

Walt has been told by Helen that Tim is coming up from New York Tuesday evening, but on the day he pretends he's forgotten and stays at work and eats dinner at the Faculty Club. He hopes Diana Lux will appear at his late office hours. When she doesn't, he thinks spitefully about giving her a C for the semester—she is mediocre at best. When he gets home just after nine, Helen's car is gone, and he remembers it's her reading group night. This means that now he'll actually have to talk to Tim instead of letting Helen buffer for him, excuse her husband's behavior. The house is warm and dark and smells like tomato soup, and in fact, when he goes into the kitchen, that's just what the smell is. Two empty bowls, skimmed with red, bisected by spoons, are on the table uncleared. Walt smells Tim too, salty and male, and thinks how much fathers are like dogs.

By the time Walt reaches the top of the stairs, he can hear that his daughter and her husband are at it—he can't bring himself to think making love or even screwing at that moment—and the sounds are so easy for him to make out, he's at first delighted by his acuity and then horrified by it. Has he ever listened to other people—Jesus, his daughter!—making love except in the movies? She giggles, he groans, long breaths are let out and grabbed back in. The duet has the most incredible, indescribable fluid life, and he can't bear it.

He reaches into his blazer pocket for the recorder he always carries in case he wants to tape random thoughts or reminders, or just the noise of what happens. If you didn't know who or what was making the sounds behind the door, would you know what it was? he wonders. He thinks of a radio contest he used to listen to as a boy where you tried to identify certain sounds—a sewing machine whirring, crackers being broken, a cat licking herself. Can I pretend this is not my daughter, he thinks now, but just noise too? Would you know it wasn't love?

Walt turns the recorder on and lays it on the rug outside the door. He sits in his bedroom in the dark, sliding toward the floor on the slippery bedspread, and waits until it is quiet. Then he retrieves the machine, its red ON light like a rat's eye in the dark hall.

"Dad?" Rosie says from inside as he picks it up. He is frozen in a painful crouch and wonders if he'll be able to rise again. Her voice sounds full, as though her throat has been opened.

"Oh, hi," Walt says, straining, not to be defeated. He can just imagine Tim, arms behind his head, bare-chested, hairy armpits, staring at the ceiling. "It's late, sweetheart. I'll see you in the morning." He makes a point of shutting his bedroom door loudly, just as he's made a point not to acknowledge Tim.

When Helen comes home and upstairs, Walt says he has a surprise for her. A small smile crosses her face—at fifty-three, she does want to believe in good surprises still, miracle cures. When he plays the tape for her, her eyes widen as though she's spotted something across the room and leans toward it. She is holding the book from her group against her chest.

"Guess," Walt says. "Guess what it is."

"What is this? Jesus Christ," she says, and rushes for the recorder, but she can't immediately find the button to turn it off, and for a second, turns up the volume. "This is sick, really crazy," she says, but hands the machine back to Walt and sits down on the bed next to him. "What are you doing?" she pleads.

"I don't want them screwing in my house," he says, firmly. "If she doesn't love him, she shouldn't be screwing him either. Should I have to listen to this?"

"Oh, Walt," Helen moans. "You sound like an old man." Her eyes narrow. "Rosie doesn't know what she wants. They're married, they're adults, they're allowed not to know. No one made you listen."

"They should go home."

Helen shakes her head at him. "Why are you doing this?" She is disappointed and crying when she says, "Don't make us hate you."

The next morning Helen leaves early to teach a class, and when Walt goes downstairs for coffee, Rosie and Tim are at the kitchen table, posed over empty bowls again, their dark heads together. He sees that Tim's bare feet are resting on top of Rosie's under the table. Walt cannot bring himself to talk directly to them, but says a general hello to the room, and touches his daughter on the shoulder as he makes his way to the stove. Tim says hi. Rosie, still in her bathrobe, doesn't say anything. She is not capable of hurting her father. Walt wonders if Helen has told them something, warned them about him, and the shame of what he's done, what he's listened to, makes him back away quickly.

"I'm going to be working here today," he announces, and moves into his study. "So . . . I guess I'll see you." An hour later, his other daughter calls, but she wants to talk to Rosie and not to him, and he wonders how far his poison has spread. By mid-afternoon Walt can't stand the whispering between Tim and Rosie, both the urging and the caressing that's gone on for hours, and he goes to his office.

Several days later, Diana Lux comes to Walt's office to discuss why her term paper is going to be late. He admires her for not lying to him, but simply telling him that it's late because she didn't start it early enough. He commends her parents for teaching her honesty and self-reliance, although at the moment he finds it extremely unappealing. He makes his hands into a pyramid on top of his desk. She doesn't appear to notice the almost purple hue to his skin.

"Fine," Walt says. Diana's sweatshirt has *University of Wisconsin* on it. They are nowhere near Wisconsin, and Walt suspects it's where her boyfriend goes to school, a big-chested blond sort of guy. "Drop it off in my box when you're finished."

"That's okay?" She's done something strange to her hair, so that her bangs point to the ceiling. She sits like a ballerina, with only her pointed toes touching the floor. He doesn't answer her. "Really?"

I'm not your father, Walt thinks, furious, and damned if I'm going to have to say it twice to reassure you and make you feel good about yourself, good about screwing up but being honest about it.

"It's up to you," he says, coldly. "It's your decision, your grade."

Walt knows that she thinks she's been pardoned, when he's done nothing of the sort for her.

Later, when he straightens the papers on his desk before going home, he sees that Diana has left her pen. It's a fake fat tortoiseshell thing, with bite marks on the cap. He can't help thinking that her father must have given it to her as he sent her away, and that now she feels she's really lost something important to her, all her good luck and love in that cheap pen. He doesn't understand how the pen got on his desk unless she put it there, and he can't remember her moving toward him.

When Walt gets home, he knows that Tim has gone. He also knows that Rosie is still in the house; she has not gone with him. He can't understand why people act like this, so inconclusive with their own lives, so dependent on other people to hold them up, but if anyone's to blame for Rosie being like that, he supposes that he is—he is her father. He sees Helen is home too, early, that life in his house is taking place without him.

When he calls for Helen and Rosie, ready to be forgiven—he's sick, he's scared, he'll tell them, he's hateful and he hates his body—they don't answer. He feels a terrible need to be included.

Upstairs, he hears voices again behind a closed door, this time in the bathroom. The water is running into the clawfoot tub, and he listens to Helen and Rosie talking quietly to each other. When he puts his hand out to touch the door, he swears he can feel the steam that clouds the bathroom, then Rosie's little sobs and sniffs, and Helen's comfort that finally shakes the house.

He pushes the door open the smallest bit. He wants to witness as well as hear for once, and sees Helen sitting on a stool next to the tub. Rosie's head is resting against her mother's thigh, while one hand trails along the edge, her fingers dripping water onto the floor. They don't notice him there, and he doesn't want to be seen.

Walt suddenly remembers a photograph he saw in *Life* years before, black-and-white, of a Japanese mother bathing her deformed and half-grown child in a wooden tub. There was no pleasure on either of their faces, but it wasn't displeasure or pain either, which had surprised him. The girl's hands were stiff claws, unable to hold the cloth, and her mother had to keep the hair back from her child's eyes. He had stared at the picture without understanding why. Back then he had simply shut the magazine and put it away. Now he admits to himself what he had been thinking about: that if the child had died, or if her mother had chosen not to care for her, to keep her, then there would be no bath, there would be no moment.

Walt is crying as he shuts the door and goes downstairs into his study. In a while, he hears that the water has been turned off in the bathroom and the drain opened to let it out. In a gush, it rushes down from the second floor, down through the pipes that run through the wall of his study, splashing toward the sewer below him. It's a warm sound, warm as Helen wrapping a towel around Rosie, warm as he wrapped his last baby in a blanket and held her to his chest, warm as though the water's running over him. It sounds too much like life being washed out of his house, and he can't imagine there ever being a time when he'd want to hear it again.

Shiloh

Bobbie Ann Mason

Leroy Moffitt's wife, Norma Jean, is working on her pectorals. She lifts three-pound dumb-bells to warm up, then progresses to a twenty-pound barbell. Standing with her legs apart, she reminds Leroy of Wonder Woman.

"I'd give anything if I could just get these muscles to where they're real hard," says Norma Jean. "Feel this arm. It's not as hard as the other one."

"That's 'cause you're right-handed," says Leroy, dodging as she swings the barbell in an arc.

"Do you think so?"

"Sure."

Leroy is a truckdriver. He injured his leg in a highway accident four months ago, and his physical therapy, which involves weights and a pulley, prompted Norma Jean to try building herself up. Now she is attending a body-building class. Leroy has been collecting temporary disability since his tractor-trailer jackknifed in Missouri, badly twisting his left leg in its socket. He has a steel pin in his hip. He will probably not be able to drive his rig again. It sits in the backyard, like a gigantic bird that has flown home to roost. Leroy has been home in Kentucky for three months, and his leg is almost healed, but the accident frightened him and he does not want to drive any more long hauls. He is not sure what to do next. In the meantime, he makes things from craft kits. He started by building a miniature log cabin from notched Popsicle sticks. He varnished it and placed it on the TV set, where it remains. It reminds him of a rustic Nativity scene. Then he tried string art (sailing ships on black velvet), a macramé owl kit, a snap-together B-17 Flying Fortress, and a lamp made out of a model truck, with a light fixture screwed in the top of the cab. At first the kits were diversions, something to kill time, but now he is thinking about building a full-scale log house from a kit. It would be considerably cheaper than building a regular house, and besides, Leroy has grown to appreciate how things are put together. He has begun to realize that in all the years he was on the road he never took time to examine anything. He was always flying past scenery.

"They won't let you build a log cabin in any of the new subdivisions," Norma Jean tells him.

"They will if I tell them it's for you," he says, teasing her. Ever since they were married, he has promised Norma Jean he would build her a new home one day. They have always rented, and the house they live in is small and nondescript. It does not even feel like a home, Leroy realizes now.

Norma Jean works at the Rexall drugstore, and she has acquired an amazing amount of information about cosmetics. When she explains to Leroy the three stages of complexion care, involving creams, toners, and moisturizers, he thinks happily of other petroleum

353

products—axle grease, diesel fuel. This is a connection between him and Norma Jean. Since he has been home, he has felt unusually tender about his wife and guilty over his long absences. But he can't tell what she feels about him. Norma Jean has never complained about his traveling; she has never made hurt remarks, like calling his truck a "widow-maker." He is reasonably certain she has been faithful to him, but he wishes she would celebrate his permanent homecoming more happily. Norma Jean is often startled to find Leroy at home, and he thinks she seems a little disappointed about it. Perhaps he reminds her too much of the early days of their marriage, before he went on the road. They had a child who died as an infant, years ago. They never speak about their memories of Randy, which have almost faded, but now that Leroy is home all the time, they sometimes feel awkward around each other, and Leroy wonders if one of them should mention the child. He has the feeling that they are waking up out of a dream together—that they must create a new marriage, start afresh. They are lucky they are still married. Leroy has read that for most people losing a child destroys the marriage—or else he heard this on *Donahue*. He can't always remember where he learns things anymore.

At Christmas, Leroy bought an electric organ for Norma Jean. She used to play the piano when she was in high school. "It don't leave you," she told him once. "It's like riding a bicycle."

The new instrument had so many keys and buttons that she was bewildered by it at first. She touched the keys tentatively, pushed some buttons, then pecked out "Chopsticks." It came out in an amplified fox-trot rhythm, with marimba sounds.

"It's an orchestra!" she cried.

The organ had a pecan-look finish and eighteen preset chords, with optional flute, violin, trumpet, clarinet, and banjo accompaniments. Norma Jean mastered the organ almost immediately. At first she played Christmas songs. Then she bought *The Sixties Songbook* and learned every tune in it, adding variations to each with the rows of brightly colored buttons.

"I didn't like these old songs back then," she said. "But I have this crazy feeling I missed something."

"You didn't miss a thing," said Leroy.

Leroy likes to lie on the couch and smoke a joint and listen to Norma Jean play "Can't Take My Eyes Off You" and "I'll Be Back." He is back again. After fifteen years on the road, he is finally settling down with the woman he loves. She is still pretty. Her skin is flawless. Her frosted curls resemble pencil trimmings.

Now that Leroy has come home to stay, he notices how much the town has changed. Subdivisions are spreading across western Kentucky like an oil slick. The sign at the edge of town says "Pop: 11,500"—only seven hundred more than it said twenty years before. Leroy can't figure out who is living in all the new houses. The farmers who used to gather around the courthouse square on Saturday afternoons to play checkers and spit tobacco juice have gone. It has been years since Leroy has thought about the farmers, and they have disappeared without his noticing.

Leroy meets a kid named Stevie Hamilton in the parking lot at the new shopping center. While they pretend to be strangers meeting over a stalled car, Stevie tosses an ounce of marijuana under the front seat of Leroy's car. Stevie is wearing orange jogging shoes and a T-shirt that says CHATTAHOOCHEE SUPER-RAT. His father is a prominent doctor who lives in one of the expensive subdivisions in a new white-columned brick house that looks like a funeral parlor. In the phone book under his name there is a separate number, with the listing "Teenagers."

"Where do you get this stuff?" asks Leroy. "From your pappy?"

"That's for me to know and you to find out," Stevie says. He is slit-eyed and skinny.

"What else you got?"

"What you interested in?"

"Nothing special. Just wondered."

Leroy used to take speed on the road. Now he has to go slowly. He needs to be mellow. He leans back against the car and says, "I'm aiming to build me a log house, soon as I get time. My wife, though, I don't think she likes the idea."

"Well, let me know when you want me again," Stevie says. He has a cigarette in his cupped palm, as though sheltering it from the wind. He takes a long drag, then stomps it on the asphalt and slouches away.

Stevie's father was two years ahead of Leroy in high school. Leroy is thirty-four. He married Norma Jean when they were both eighteen, and their child Randy was born a few months later, but he died at the age of four months and three days. He would be about Stevie's age now. Norma Jean and Leroy were at the drive-in, watching a double feature (*Dr. Strangelove* and *Lover Come Back*), and the baby was sleeping in the back seat. When the first movie ended, the baby was dead. It was the sudden infant death syndrome. Leroy remembers handing Randy to a nurse at the emergency room, as though he were offering her a large doll as a present. A dead baby feels like a sack of flour. "It just happens sometimes," said the doctor, in what Leroy always recalls as a nonchalant tone. Leroy can hardly remember the child anymore, but he still sees vividly a scene from *Dr. Strangelove* in which the President of the United States was talking in a folksy voice on the hot line to the Soviet premier about the bomber accidentally headed toward Russia. He was in the War Room, and the world map was lit up. Leroy remembers Norma Jean standing catatonically beside him in the hospital and himself thinking: Who is this strange girl? He had forgotten who she was. Now scientists are saying that crib death is caused by a virus. Nobody knows anything, Leroy thinks. The answers are always changing.

When Leroy gets home from the shopping center, Norma Jean's mother, Mabel Beasley, is there. Until this year, Leroy has not realized how much time she spends with Norma Jean. When she visits, she inspects the closets and then the plants, informing Norma Jean when a plant is droopy or yellow. Mabel calls the plants "flowers," although there are never any blooms. She always notices if Norma Jean's laundry is piling up. Mabel is a short, overweight woman whose tight, brown-dyed curls look more like a wig than the actual wig she sometimes wears. Today she has brought Norma Jean an off-white dust ruffle she made for the bed; Mabel works in a custom-upholstery shop.

"This is the tenth one I made this year," Mabel says. "I got started and couldn't stop."

"It's real pretty," says Norma Jean.

"Now we can hide things under the bed," says Leroy, who gets along with his mother-in-law primarily by joking with her. Mabel has never really forgiven him for disgracing her by getting Norma Jean pregnant. When the baby died, she said that fate was mocking her.

"What's that thing?" Mabel says to Leroy in a loud voice, pointing to a tangle of yarn on a piece of canvas.

Leroy holds it up for Mabel to see. "It's my needlepoint," he explains. "This is a *Star Trek* pillow cover."

"That's what a woman would do," says Mabel. "Great day in the morning!"

"All the big football players on TV do it," he says.

"Why, Leroy, you're always trying to fool me. I don't believe you for one minute. You don't know what to do with yourself—that's the whole trouble. Sewing!"

"I'm aiming to build us a log house," says Leroy, "Soon as my plans come."

"Like *heck* you are," says Norma Jean. She takes Leroy's needlepoint and shoves it into a drawer. "You have to find a job first. Nobody can afford to build now anyway."

Mabel straightens her girdle and says, "I still think before you get tied down y'all ought to take a little run to Shiloh."

"One of these days, Mama," Norma Jean says impatiently.

Mabel is talking about Shiloh, Tennessee. For the past few years, she has been urging Leroy and Norma Jean to visit the Civil War battleground there. Mabel went there on her honeymoon—the only real trip she ever took. Her husband died of a perforated ulcer when Norma Jean was ten, but Mabel, who was accepted into the United Daughters of the Confederacy in 1975, is still preoccupied with going back to Shiloh.

"I've been to kingdom come and back in that truck out yonder," Leroy says to Mabel, "but we never yet set foot in that battleground. Ain't that something? How did I miss it?"

"It's not even that far," Mabel says.

After Mabel leaves, Norma Jean reads to Leroy from a list she has made. "Things you could do," she announces. "You could get a job as a guard at Union Carbide, where they'd let you set on a stool. You could get on at the lumberyard. You could do a little carpenter work, if you want to build so bad. You could—"

"I can't do something where I'd have to stand up all day."

"You ought to try standing up all day behind a cosmetics counter. It's amazing that I have strong feet, coming from two parents that never had strong feet at all." At the moment Norma Jean is holding on to the kitchen counter, raising her knees one at a time as she talks. She is wearing two-pound ankle weights.

"Don't worry," says Leroy. "I'll do something."

"You could truck calves to slaughter for somebody. You wouldn't have to drive any big old truck for that."

"I'm going to build you this house," says Leroy. "I want to make you a real home."

"I don't want to live in any log cabin."

"It's not a cabin. It's a house."

"I don't care. It looks like a cabin."

"You and me together could lift those logs. It's just like lifting weights."

Norma Jean doesn't answer. Under her breath, she is counting. Now she is marching through the kitchen. She is doing goose steps.

Before his accident, when Leroy came home he used to stay in the house with Norma Jean, watching TV in bed and playing cards. She would cook fried chicken, picnic ham, chocolate pie—all his favorites. Now he is home alone much of the time. In the mornings, Norma Jean disappears, leaving a cooling place in the bed. She eats a cereal called Body Buddies, and she leaves the bowl on the table, with the soggy tan balls floating in a milk puddle. He sees things about Norma Jean that he never realized before. When she chops onions, she stares off into a corner, as if she can't bear to look. She puts on her house slippers almost precisely at nine o'clock every evening and nudges her jogging shoes under the couch. She saves bread heels for the birds. Leroy watches the birds at the feeder. He notices the peculiar way goldfinches fly past the window. They close their wings, then fall, then spread their wings to catch and lift themselves. He wonders if they close their eyes when they fall. Norma Jean closes her eyes when they are in bed. She wants the lights turned out. Even then, he is sure she closes her eyes.

He goes for long drives around town. He tends to drive a car rather carelessly. Power steering and an automatic shift make a car feel so small and inconsequential that his body is hardly involved in the driving process. His injured leg stretches out comfortably. Once or twice he has almost hit something, but even the prospect of an accident seems minor in a car. He cruises the new subdivisions, feeling like a criminal rehearsing for a robbery. Norma Jean is probably right about a log house being inappropriate here in the new subdivisions. All the houses look grand and complicated. They depress him.

One day when Leroy comes home from a drive he finds Norma Jean in tears. She is in the kitchen making a potato and mushroom-soup casserole, with grated-cheese topping. She is crying because her mother caught her smoking.

"I didn't hear her coming. I was standing here puffing away pretty as you please," Norma Jean says, wiping her eyes.

"I knew it would happen sooner or later," says Leroy, putting his arm around her.

"She don't know the meaning of the word 'knock,'" says Norma Jean. "It's a wonder she hadn't caught me years ago."

"Think of it this way," Leroy says. "What if she caught me with a joint?"

"You better not let her!" Norma Jean shrieks. "I'm warning you, Leroy Moffitt!"

"I'm just kidding. Here, play me a tune. That'll help you relax."

Norma Jean puts the casserole in the oven and sets the timer. Then she plays a ragtime tune, with horns and banjo, as Leroy lights up a joint and lies on the couch, laughing to himself about Mabel's catching him at it. He thinks of Stevie Hamilton—a doctor's son pushing grass. Everything is funny. The whole town seems crazy and small. He is reminded of Virgil Mathis, a boastful policeman Leroy used to shoot pool with. Virgil recently led a drug bust in a back room at a bowling alley, where he seized ten thousand dollars' worth of marijuana. The newspaper had a picture of him holding up the bags of grass and grinning widely. Right now, Leroy can imagine Virgil breaking down the door and arresting him with a lungful of smoke. Virgil would probably have been alerted to the scene because of all the racket Norma Jean is making. Now she sounds like a hard-rock band. Norma Jean is terrific. When she switches to a Latin-rhythm version of "Sunshine Superman," Leroy hums along. Norma Jean's foot goes up and down, up and down.

"Well, what do you think?" Leroy says, when Norma Jean pauses to search through her music.

"What do I think about what?"

His mind has gone blank. Then he says, "I'll sell my rig and build us a house." That wasn't what he wanted to say. He wanted to know what she thought—what she *really* thought—about them.

"Don't start in on that again," says Norma Jean. She begins playing "Who'll Be the Next in Line?"

Leroy used to tell hitchhikers his whole life story—about his travels, his hometown, the baby. He would end with a question: "Well, what do you think?" It was just a rhetorical question. In time, he had the feeling that he'd been telling the same story over and over to the same hitchhikers. He quit talking to hitchhikers when he realized how his voice sounded—whining and self-pitying, like some teenage-tragedy song. Now Leroy has the sudden impulse to tell Norma Jean about himself, as if he had just met her. They have known each other so long they have forgotten a lot about each other. They could become reacquainted. But when the oven timer goes off and she runs to the kitchen, he forgets why he wants to do this.

The next day, Mabel drops by. It is Saturday and Norma Jean is cleaning. Leroy is studying the plans of his log house, which have finally come in the mail. He has them spread out on the table—big sheets of stiff blue paper, with diagrams and numbers printed in white. While Norma Jean runs the vacuum, Mabel drinks coffee. She sets her coffee cup on a blueprint.

"I'm just waiting for time to pass," she says to Leroy, drumming her fingers on the table.

As soon as Norma Jean switches off the vacuum, Mabel says in a loud voice, "Did you hear about the datsun dog that killed the baby?"

Norma Jean says, "The word is 'dachshund.'"

"They put the dog on trial. It chewed the baby's legs off. The mother was in the next room all the time." She raises her voice. "They thought it was neglect."

Norma Jean is holding her ears. Leroy manages to open the refrigerator and get some Diet Pepsi to offer Mabel. Mabel still has some coffee and she waves away the Pepsi.

"Datsuns are like that," Mabel says. "They're jealous dogs. They'll tear a place to pieces if you don't keep an eye on them."

"You better watch out what you're saying, Mabel," says Leroy.

"Well, facts is facts."

Leroy looks out the window at his rig. It is like a huge piece of furniture gathering dust in the backyard. Pretty soon it will be an antique. He hears the vacuum cleaner. Norma Jean seems to be cleaning the living room rug again.

Later, she says to Leroy, "She just said that about the baby because she caught me smoking. She's trying to pay me back."

"What are you talking about?" Leroy says, nervously shuffling blueprints.

"You know good and well," Norma Jean says. She is sitting in a kitchen chair with her feet up and her arms wrapped around her knees. She looks small and helpless. She says, "The very idea, her bringing up a subject like that! Saying it was neglect."

"She didn't mean that," Leroy says.

"She might not have *thought* she meant it. She always says things like that. You don't know how she goes on."

"But she didn't really mean it. She was just talking."

Leroy opens a king-sized bottle of beer and pours it into two glasses, dividing it carefully. He hands a glass to Norma Jean and she takes it from him mechanically. For a long time, they sit by the kitchen window watching the birds at the feeder.

Something is happening. Norma Jean is going to night school. She has graduated from her six-week body-building course and now she is taking an adult-education course in composition at Paducah Community College. She spends her evenings outlining paragraphs.

"First you have a topic sentence," she explains to Leroy. "Then you divide it up. Your secondary topic has to be connected to your primary topic."

To Leroy, this sounds intimidating. "I never was any good in English," he says.

"It makes a lot of sense."

"What are you doing this for, anyhow?"

She shrugs. "It's something to do." She stands up and lifts her dumbbells a few times. "Driving a rig, nobody cared about my English."

"I'm not criticizing your English."

Norma Jean used to say, "If I lose ten minutes' sleep, I just drag all day." Now she stays up late, writing compositions. She got a B on her first paper—a how-to theme on soup-based casseroles. Recently Norma Jean has been cooking unusual foods—tacos, lasagna, Bombay chicken. She doesn't play the organ anymore, though her second paper was called "Why Music Is Important to Me." She sits at the kitchen table, concentrating on her outlines, while Leroy plays with his log house plans, practicing with a set of Lincoln Logs. The thought of getting a truckload of notched, numbered logs scares him, and he wants to be prepared. As he and Norma Jean work together at the kitchen table, Leroy has the hopeful thought that they are sharing something, but he knows he is a fool to think this. Norma Jean is miles away. He knows he is going to lose her. Like Mabel, he is just waiting for time to pass.

One day, Mabel is there before Norma Jean gets home from work, and Leroy finds himself confiding in her. Mabel, he realizes, must know Norma Jean better than he does.

"I don't know what's got into that girl," Mabel says. "She used to go to bed with the chickens. Now you say she's up all hours. Plus her a-smoking. I like to died."

"I want to make her this beautiful home," Leroy says, indicating the Lincoln Logs. "I don't think she even wants it. Maybe she was happier with me gone."

"She don't know what to make of you, coming home like this."

"Is that it?"

Mabel takes the roof off his Lincoln Log cabin. "You couldn't get *me* in a log cabin," she says: "I was raised in one. It's no picnic, let me tell you."

"They're different now," says Leroy.

"I tell you what," Mabel says, smiling oddly at Leroy.

"What?"

"Take her on down to Shiloh. Y'all need to get out together, stir a little. Her brain's all balled up over them books."

Leroy can see traces of Norma Jean's features in her mother's face. Mabel's worn face has the texture of crinkled cotton, but suddenly she looks pretty. It occurs to Leroy that Mabel has been hinting all along that she wants them to take her with them to Shiloh.

"Let's all go to Shiloh," he says. "You and me and her. Come Sunday."

Mabel throws up her hands in protest. "Oh, no, not me. Young folks want to be by theirselves."

When Norma Jean comes in with groceries, Leroy says excitedly, "Your mama here's been dying to go to Shiloh for thirty-five years. It's about time we went, don't you think?"

"I'm not going to butt in on anybody's second honeymoon," Mabel says.

"Who's going on a honeymoon, for Christ's sake?" Norma Jean says loudly.

"I never raised no daughter of mine to talk that-a-way," Mabel says.

"You ain't seen nothing yet," says Norma Jean. She starts putting away boxes and cans, slamming cabinet doors.

"There's a log cabin at Shiloh," Mabel says. "It was there during the battle. There's bullet holes in it."

"When are you going to *shut up* about Shiloh, Mama?" asks Norma Jean.

"I always thought Shiloh was the prettiest place, so full of history," Mabel goes on. "I just hoped y'all could see it once before I die, so you could tell me about it." Later, she whispers to Leroy, "You do what I said. A little change is what she needs."

"Your name means 'the king,'" Norma Jean says to Leroy that evening. He is trying to get her to go to Shiloh, and she is reading a book about another century.

"Well, I reckon I ought to be right proud."

"I guess so."

"Am I still king around here?"

Norma Jean flexes her biceps and feels them for hardness. "I'm not fooling around with anybody, if that's what you mean," she says.

"Would you tell me if you were?"

"I don't know."

"What does *your* name mean?"

"It was Marilyn Monroe's real name."

"No kidding!"

"Norma comes from the Normans. They were invaders," she says. She closes her book and looks hard at Leroy. "I'll go to Shiloh with you if you'll stop staring at me."

On Sunday, Norma Jean packs a picnic and they go to Shiloh. To Leroy's relief, Mabel says she does not want to come with them. Norma Jean drives, and Leroy, sitting beside her, feels like some boring hitchhiker she has picked up. He tries some conversation, but she answers him in monosyllables. At Shiloh, she drives aimlessly through the park, past bluffs and trails and steep ravines. Shiloh is an immense place, and Leroy cannot see it as a battleground. It is not what he expected. He thought it would look like a golf course. Monuments are everywhere, showing through the thick clusters of trees. Norma Jean passes the log cabin Mabel mentioned. It is surrounded by tourists looking for bullet holes.

"That's not the kind of log house I've got in mind," says Leroy apologetically.

"I know *that*."

"This is a pretty place. Your mama was right."

"It's O.K.," says Norma Jean. "Well, we've seen it. I hope she's satisfied."

They burst out laughing together.

At the park museum, a movie on Shiloh is shown every half hour, but they decide that they don't want to see it. They buy a souvenir Confederate flag for Mabel, and then they find a picnic spot near the cemetery. Norma Jean has brought a picnic cooler, with pimiento sandwiches, soft drinks, and Yodels. Leroy eats a sandwich and then smokes a joint, hiding it behind the picnic cooler. Norma Jean has quit smoking altogether. She is picking cake crumbs from the cellophane wrapper, like a fussy bird.

Leroy says, "So the boys in gray ended up in Corinth. The Union soldiers zapped 'em finally. April 7, 1862."

They both know that he doesn't know any history. He is just talking about some of the historical plaques they have read. He feels awkward, like a boy on a date with an older girl. They are still just making conversation.

"Corinth is where Mama eloped to," says Norma Jean.

They sit in silence and stare at the cemetery for the Union dead and, beyond, at a tall cluster of trees. Campers are parked nearby, bumper to bumper, and small children in bright clothing are cavorting and squealing. Norma Jean wads up the cake wrapper and squeezes it tightly in her hand. Without looking at Leroy, she says, "I want to leave you."

Leroy takes a bottle of Coke out of the cooler and flips off the cap. He holds the bottle poised near his mouth but cannot remember to take a drink. Finally he says, "No, you don't."

"Yes, I do."

"I won't let you."

"You can't stop me."

"Don't do me that way."

Leroy knows Norma Jean will have her own way. "Didn't I promise to be home from now on?" he says.

"In some ways, a woman prefers a man who wanders," says Norma Jean. "That sounds crazy, I know."

"You're not crazy."

Leroy remembers to drink from his Coke. Then he says, "Yes, you *are* crazy. You and me could start all over again. Right back at the beginning."

"We *have* started all over again," says Norma Jean. "And this is how it turned out."

"What did I do wrong?"

"Nothing."

"Is this one of those women's lib things?" Leroy asks.

"Don't be funny."

The cemetery, a green slope dotted with white markers, looks like a subdivision site. Leroy is trying to comprehend that his marriage is breaking up, but for some reason he is wondering about white slabs in a graveyard.

"Everything was fine till Mama caught me smoking," says Norma Jean, standing up. "That set something off."

"What are you talking about?"

"She won't leave me alone—*you* won't leave me alone." Norma Jean seems to be crying, but she is looking away from him. "I feel eighteen again. I can't face that all over again." She starts walking away. "No, it *wasn't* fine. I don't know what I'm saying. Forget it."

Leroy takes a lungful of smoke and closes his eyes as Norma Jean's words sink in. He tries to focus on the fact that thirty-five hundred soldiers died on the grounds around him. He can only think of that war as a board game with plastic soldiers. Leroy almost smiles, as he compares the Confederates' daring attack on the Union camps and Virgil Mathis's raid on the bowling alley. General Grant, drunk and furious, shoved the Southerners back to Corinth, where Mabel and Jet Beasley were married years later, when Mabel was still thin and good-looking. The next day, Mabel and Jet visited the battleground, and then Norma Jean was born, and then she married Leroy and they had a baby, which they lost, and now Leroy and Norma Jean are here at the same battleground. Leroy knows he is leaving out a lot. He is leaving out the insides of history. History was always just names and dates to him. It occurs to him that building a house out of logs is similarly empty—too simple. And the real inner workings of a marriage, like most of history, have escaped him. Now he sees that building a log house is the dumbest idea he could have had. It was clumsy of him to think Norma Jean would want a log house. It was a crazy idea. He'll have to think of something else, quickly. He will wad the blueprints into tight balls and fling them into the lake. Then he'll get moving again. He opens his eyes. Norma Jean has moved away and is walking through the cemetery, following a serpentine brick path.

Leroy gets up to follow his wife, but his good leg is asleep and his bad leg still hurts him. Norma Jean is far away, walking rapidly toward the bluff by the river, and he tries to hobble toward her. Some children run past him, screaming noisily. Norma Jean has reached the bluff, and she is looking out over the Tennessee River. Now she turns toward Leroy and waves her arms. Is she beckoning to him? She seems to be doing an exercise for her chest muscles. The sky is unusually pale—the color of the dust ruffle Mabel made for their bed.

What I strive for in my writing (and what I tell my students to work for) is not feeling. As a writer, you do not want to write feelings. You want to fabricate understanding so the reader can come into the work and then feel what he feels.

—SUE MILLER, NEWSLETTER INTERVIEW, EMERSON COLLEGE

Sheep

Thomas McNeely

Before the sheriff came to get him, Lloyd found the sheep out by the pond. He'd counted head that morning and come up one short. He did the count over because he was still hazy from the night before. And he'd woken with a foul smell in his nose. So he had gone into Mr. Mac's house—it was early morning; the old man would be dead to the world— and filled his canteen with white lightning. He felt shaky and bad and the spring morning was cold. He shouldn't have gone to town the night before.

The sheep lay on its side in some rushes. A flow of yellowish mucus was coming from its nose, and its eyes were sickly thin slits that looked afraid. Lloyd thought the sheep honorable—it had gone off to die so that it wouldn't infect the rest of the flock. Lloyd knew that the sheep's sickness was his fault and that he couldn't do anything about it, but he squatted down next to the animal and rubbed its underside. In this hour before sunrise, when the night dew was still wet, the warmth and animal smell felt good. Lloyd moved his hands in circles over the sheep's lightly furred pink skin and lines of blue veins, its hard cage of ribs, its slack, soft belly. Across the pond, the sun peeked red through the Panhandle dust over a low line of slate-gray clouds. With his free hand, Lloyd took his canteen from a pocket in his jacket, clamped it between his knees, opened it, and drank. For a moment the liquor stung the sides of his tongue, then dissolved in him like warm water. The sheep's lungs lifted up and down; its heart churned blood like a slowly pounding fist. Soon the sun broke free and the pond, rippled by a slight breeze, ignited in countless tiny candle flames. When Lloyd was a child, Mr. Mac used to tell him that at the Last Judgment the pond would become the Lake of Fire, into which all sinners would be cast. Lloyd could still picture them falling in a dark stream, God pouring them out like a bag of nails. The sheep closed its eyes against the light.

When Sheriff Lynch walked up behind him, Lloyd started. He still caressed the sheep, but it was dead and beginning to stiffen. His canteen felt almost empty; it fell from his fingers. By the sun, Lloyd saw it was almost noon. Big, black vultures wheeled so high above that they looked the size of mockingbirds. Uneasiness creeping on him, Lloyd waited for the sheriff to speak.

Finally the sheriff said, "Son, looks like that sheep's dead."

"Yessir," Lloyd said, and tried to stand, but his legs were stiff and the liquor had taken his balance.

"You look about half-dead yourself." The sheriff picked up Lloyd's canteen from the dry grass, sniffed it, and shook his head. "You want to turn out like Mr. Mac? A pervert?"

Lloyd waggled his head no. He thought how he must look: his long blond hair clumped in uncombed cowlicks, the dark reddish-gray circles around his eyes, his father's dirty herding jacket hanging off his broad, slumped shoulders. Sheriff Lynch stood there, his figure tall and straight. He wore a star-shaped golden badge hitched on a belt finely tooled with wildflowers. His face was burnt the rust color of Dumas County soil, the lines on it deep, like the sudden ravines there into which cattle sometimes fell. His eyes were an odd steely blue, which seemed not to be that color itself but to reflect it. He studied Lloyd.

"That probably doesn't make much of a difference now," he said, lowering his eyes as if embarrassed.

"What?" Lloyd said, though he'd heard him.

"Nothing. We just need to ask you some questions."

Lloyd wondered if Mr. Mac had found out about the sheep somehow. "But I ain't stole nothin'," he said.

"I'm fairly sure of that," the sheriff said. A grin flickered in a corner of his mouth, but it was sad and not meant to mock Lloyd. "Come on. You know the drill. Hand over your knife and shears and anything else you got."

After Lloyd put his tools in a paper bag, the sheriff squatted next to the sheep and ran his hand over its belly. His hand was large and strong and clean, though etched with red-brown creases.

When they got up to the house, Lloyd saw three or four law cars parked at odd angles, as if they'd stopped in a hurry. Their lights whirled around and dispatch radios crackled voices that no one answered. Some policemen busied themselves throwing clothes, bottles and other junk out of Lloyd's shack, which was separated from the house by a tool shed. Others were carrying out cardboard boxes. Lloyd recognized one of the men, name of Gonzales, who'd picked Lloyd up for stealing a ten-speed when he was a kid. Lloyd waved at him and called out, but Gonzales just set his dark eyes on him for a moment and then went back to his business. Mr. Mac stood on the dirt patch in front of the house, his big sloppy body looking like it was about to fall over, talking to a man in a suit.

"If you're gonna drag that pond," he said, his eyes slits in the harsh, clear sunlight, "you're gonna have to pay me for the lost fish. I'm a poor old man. I ain't got nothin' to do with thisayre mess."

The man started to say something to him, but Mr. Mac caught sight of Lloyd. His face spread wide with a fear Lloyd had never seen in him; then his eyes narrowed in disgust. He looked like he did when he saw ewes lamb, or when he punished Lloyd as a child.

"Mr. Mac," Lloyd said, and took a step toward him, but the old man held up his hands as if to shield his face.

"Mr. Mac." Lloyd came closer. "I 'pologize 'bout that 'er sheep. I'll work off the cost to you someway."

Mr. Mac stumbled backwards and pointed at Lloyd; his face was wild and frightened again. He shouted to the man in the suit, "Look at 'im! Look at 'im! A seed of pure evil!"

Lloyd could feel his chest move ahead of his body toward Mr. Mac. He wanted to explain about the sheep, but the old man kept carrying on. The sheriff's hand, firm but kind, gripped his arm and guided him toward a police car.

The sheriff sat bolt upright on the passenger side and looked straight ahead as the rust-colored hills passed by outside. A fingerprint-smudged Plexiglas barrier ran across the top of the front seat and separated him from Lloyd. As always, the hair on the nape of the sheriff's neck looked freshly cut. Lloyd had expected him to take his shears and bowie knife, but why were they tearing up his shack? And what was Mr. Mac going on about? Still drunk, probably. He would ask the sheriff when they got to the jail. His thoughts turned to the sheep. He should've put it out of its misery, slit its throat and then cut its belly for the vultures. Not like at slaughter, when he would've had to root around with his knife and bare hands and clean out its innards. What a Godawful stink sheep's insides had! But this would've been easy. It wouldn't have taken a minute.

In the jail two guards Lloyd didn't know sat him down inside a small white room he'd never seen before. The man in a suit who had been talking to Mr. Mac came in, with Sheriff Lynch following. Lloyd hadn't gotten to ask the sheriff what was going on. The man put what looked like a little transistor radio on the table and pressed a button and began to talk.

"Is it okay if we tape-record this interview?" he asked Lloyd.

Lloyd shrugged and smiled a who's-this-guy? smile at the sheriff. The sheriff gave him a stern, behave-yourself look.

"Sure," Lloyd said. "I ain't never been recorded before."

"Okay," the man said. He said all their names, where they were, what date and time it was. Then he opened a file folder. Lloyd didn't like his looks: he had a smile that hid itself, that laughed at you in secret. Mr. Mac could get one of those. And the man talked in one of those citified accents, maybe from Dallas.

"Okay," the man said. "My name is Thomas Blanchard. I am a special agent with the Federal Bureau of Investigation. I work in the serial-homicide division." He shot his eyes up at Lloyd, as if to catch him at something. "Do you understand what that means?"

"Which part?" Lloyd said.

"Serial homicide—serial murder."

"Nope."

"It means to kill more than once—sometimes many people in a row."

"Okay," Lloyd said.

The man gave him another once-over, and said, "You are being held as a material witness in seventeen murders that have occurred in and around this area. You have not been charged in any of them. Should you be charged, you will have the right to counsel, but at this time you have no such right per se. However, as a witness, should you wish to retain counsel, that is also your right. Do you wish to do so?"

Lloyd tried to put the man's words together. Blanchard bunched up his shoulders, like a squirrel ready to pounce. The sheriff leaned back his chair and studied the ceiling.

After he had drawn out the silence, Lloyd said, "I don't know. I'm still pretty drunk to think about suchlike. Would I have to pay for him?"

Blanchard's hand snaked out to the tape recorder, but the sheriff looked at Lloyd and said, "Lloyd, you think you're too drunk to know what you're sayin'? I mean, to the point of makin' things up or disrememberin'?"

"Oh, no," Lloyd said. The sheriff asked him if he was sure, and he said yes. Then the sheriff told him that to retain a lawyer meant he would have to pay for one. In that case, Lloyd said, he didn't want one.

"Sheriff," he said. "What's this all about?"

The sheriff told him he would find out.

But he didn't, not really. Blanchard asked Lloyd about the night before. He'd gone to Genie's Too, where the old Genie's used to be. He'd brought a canteen of Mr. Mac's stuff with him for set-ups, because they'd lost their liquor license. He saw all the usual people there: Candy, Huff, Wishbone, Firefly. Dwight, Genie's old man, did the colored-baby dance, flopping around this brown rag doll and flashing up its skirt. Everybody seemed to be having a real good time. Big plastic bottles were on nearly every table; people talking—men arguing, women listening. People leaned on each other like scarecrows, dancing slow and close, others just close, doing a little bump-and-grind.

Blanchard asked him if he had met anyone, danced with anyone. Lloyd grinned and blushed and sought out the Sheriff, who smiled this time. Lloyd said, "I always been shy. I guess it's my rearing, out on that old ranch. And they got their own group there at Genie's, everybody always foolin' with everyone else's."

By the end of his answer the sheriff's smile had gone.

Blanchard asked Lloyd the same thing about ten different ways—had he seen anyone new there? The questions got on his nerves. He said, "Sheriff, now what's this about?"

The sheriff told him to have some patience.

Blanchard asked about places in Amarillo, Lubbock, Muleshoe, Longview, Lamesa, Reno, Abilene—bars Lloyd had sneaked away to when he wanted to be alone. The ones he could remember were all about the same as Genie's, each with its own little crowd. Blanchard mentioned places from so long ago that Lloyd began to feel as if he were asking about a different person. He drifted off into thinking about Mr. Mac.

Mr. Mac, when Lloyd would ask him where they were, used to say that all he needed to know was that they were in the United States of America. He used to tell Lloyd that where they were was just like Scotland, and then he'd start laughing to himself until his laughs trailed off into coughs. The sheriff had never, ever laughed at him like that. He didn't have those kind of jokes inside him.

Blanchard began asking personal questions: Did he have a girlfriend? Had he ever? No. How long had he been out at the ranch? All his life—about thirty years, according to Mr. Mac. Was he a virgin?

"Now, sheriff, have I got to answer that?" In truth, he didn't know what he was because, as he often reflected, he didn't know whether what Mr. Mac had done made him not a virgin.

Perhaps sensing this, the sheriff told him, no, he didn't have to answer any more questions. In fact, it might be better to quit for the day. "I'm afraid though, son, we're gonna have to hold you as a suspect."

"Suspect of what?" said Lloyd, a sweat creeping on him like the cold rain when he herded in winter.

Lloyd woke to the stink of his own sweat, and he seemed wholly that sweat and that stench—the stench was him, his soul. The overhead light had been switched on. It was a bare bulb caged by heavy wire. He glanced at the steel place he was in: steel walls, floor, ceiling, toilet, stool, table. Everything was bolted down. The steel door had a small square high window made of meshed security glass, and a slot near its bottom, with a sliding cover, for passing food. Lloyd hid his face in the crook of his arm and shook and wished he could go to Mr. Mac's for some white lightning.

The door clanked open. Lloyd could tell it was the sheriff even though he kept his face hidden and his eyes shut tight. The sheriff put a plastic plate on the table and said, "I was afraid of this." Then he left.

Maybe the food would help. Lloyd stood up, but his legs felt wobbly and his eyes couldn't focus right. He lurched to the stool, planted himself on it, and held the edge of the table. When he picked up the plastic fork, it vibrated in his fingers. His touch sent a jangling electrical charge through his arm and down his back. The harder he gripped, the more it felt as though he were trying to etch stone with a pencil, yet only this concentration made any steadiness possible. Keeping his face close to the plate, he scooped the watery scrambled eggs into his mouth. He fell to his knees and threw up in the toilet. Curled face-down on the floor, Lloyd felt a prickly, nauseous chill seep into his muscles and begin to paralyze him.

Someone not Sheriff Lynch, who seemed by his step to be burly and ill-tempered, grabbed Lloyd's shoulder and twisted his body so that he faced the ceiling. The floor felt cold and hard against the back of his head. The man spread Lloyd's eyelids, opened his shirt, and put a cold metal disc on his chest. Lloyd had not noticed until now, but his heart was racing—much faster than the sheep's. That seemed so long ago. Mr. Mac was angry with him. The man started to yank down Lloyd's pants. Lloyd moved his lips to say no! No! But his limbs and muscles had turned to cement. His mouth gaped open, but he couldn't catch any air. The chill sweat sprang returned. He was a boy again. Mr. Mac's heaviness pressed the air from his lungs, pinned him from behind, faceless, pushing the dull tearing pain into him; he choked Lloyd's thin gasps with old-man smells of sweat and smoke and liquor and his ragged, grunting breath. The man rubbed something on Lloyd's right buttock and then pricked it with a needle. He left without pulling up Lloyd's pants.

His body softened, and the cement dissolved; a cushiony feeling spread through him, as though his limbs were swaddled in plush, warm blankets. He could breathe. He could not smell himself anymore. "Son," he heard the sheriff say. "Put your pants on."

The two of them sat in the little white room, this time without Blanchard.

"Sheriff." Lloyd's words seemed to float out of his mouth. "Sheriff, what's all thisayre 'bout?"

Sheriff Lynch sat across the table. His face changed faintly as animals and unknown faces, then the spirits of Mr. Mac and Blanchard, passed through it. He popped a peppermint Life Saver, sucked on it hard, and pulled back into focus.

"Let me ask you a question first, son, and then I'll answer yours." He reached down next to his chair and put two Ziplock bags with Lloyd's shears and bowie knife in them on the table. Both the shears and knife were tagged, as if they were in hock. The Sheriff pressed them a few times with the tips of his long rust-colored fingers, lightly, as though to make sure they were there, or to remind them to stay still. "Now," he said. "I think I already know the answer to this question, but I need to know from you." He pressed them again. "Are these your knife and shears?"

How should he answer? The sheriff leaned back, waiting, a look on his face that said he didn't want to hear the answer.

"Maybe," Lloyd said.

"Maybe." The sheriff joined his hands behind his head, pointed his eyes up and away, as though he were considering this as a possible truth.

"Maybe," Lloyd said.

"Lloyd Wayne Dogget," the sheriff said, turning his not-blue eyes on him. "How long have I known you? I knew your daddy and your grandpappy when they were alive. I know more about you than you know about you. And you ain't never been able to lie to me and get clear with it. So I'll ask you again—are these your knife and shears?"

Mr. Mac had given Lloyd the shears when he was sixteen. They were long and silvery. At the end of each day of shearing, after cutting the sheep's coarse, billowy hair, Lloyd would sharpen them on a strop and oil them with a can of S'OK to keep off the rust. The merry old man on the green can, a pipe in his mouth, always reminded him of Mr. Mac.

"What if I say yes?" Lloyd said.

Sheriff Lynch sucked on the Life Saver and blew out a breath. He leaned close to Lloyd and put his elbows on the table. "To tell you the truth," he said, "it doesn't make a whit's difference." He pressed the plastic bags again. "There's blood on these tools matches the type of a young lady people saw you leave Genie's with, a young lady who turned up murdered. And I confiscated these two things from you. So it doesn't make a whit's difference what you say, whether you lie or not. I'm just trying to give you a chance to get right with yourself, to be a man." He sank back and ran his hands through his stubbly, iron-gray hair as he bowed his head and looked at the bags. He massaged his clean-cut neck. "Maybe to get right with the Lord, too. I don't know. I don't believe in that kind of thing, but sometimes it helps people."

To Lloyd, the sheriff seemed embarrassed about something. Lloyd wanted to help him. But he was also afraid; he could not remember any young lady, only smiling dark-red lips, the curve of a bare upper arm, honky-tonk music, Dwight flinging the colored-baby doll around.

"Okay, sheriff," he said. "Since it don't make any difference, you know they're mine."

The sheriff escorted him to the showers, where he took Lloyd's street clothes and gave him an orange inmate's jumpsuit and a pair of regulation flip-flops. After Lloyd had showered and changed, the sheriff told him he was under arrest for capital murder, read him his rights, and handcuffed him. They got in his car, Lloyd riding in the front seat, and drove the two blocks to the courthouse. The judge asked him if he had any money or expected any help, and he said no, which was the truth.

Every morning, Sheriff Lynch came to Lloyd's cell and walked with him down to the little white room, where Lloyd talked with his lawyer. When the sheriff opened the door to the room, Lloyd watched his lawyer and the sheriff volley looks under their pleasantries. He remembered a cartoon he'd seen: Brutus and Popeye have each grabbed one of Olive Oyl's rubbery arms. They were stretching her like taffy. He couldn't remember how it ended.

Raoul Schwartz, the lawyer Lloyd had been assigned, said the judge had granted Lloyd a competency hearing, but not very much money to do it with. He, Schwartz, would have to conduct the tests himself and then send them to a psychiatrist for evaluation. In two months the psychiatrist would testify and the judge would decide whether Lloyd was competent to stand trial. Schwartz said they had a lot of work to do. Schwartz said he was there to help.

Schwartz was everything the sheriff was not. He had short, pale, womanish fingers that fluttered through papers, fiddled with pencils, took off his wire-rimmed granny glasses and rubbed the bridge of his nose. When he got impatient, which was often, his fingers scratched at a bald spot on the top of his forehead. Lloyd thought he might have rubbed his hair off this way.

Schwartz wouldn't let him wriggle out of questions, sometimes asking the same ones many times, like Blanchard. He asked about Lloyd's whole life. Sometimes the glare of the white room and Schwartz's drone were like being in school again, and Lloyd would lay his head down on the slick-topped table between them and put his cheek to its cool surface. "Come on, Lloyd," Schwartz would say. "We've got work to do."

Also unlike the sheriff, Schwartz cussed, which was something Lloyd could never abide, and the little man's Yankee accent raked the words across Lloyd's nerves even worse than usual. When Lloyd told him that Sheriff Lynch had been out to talk to Mr. Mac after a teacher had spotted cigarette burns on his arms, Schwartz murmured, "Excellent, excellent. Fucking bastard."

"Who's the effing bastard?"

"Mr. Mac." Schwartz's head popped up just as Blanchard's had when he'd wanted to catch Lloyd at something, only this time it was Lloyd who had caught Schwartz in a lie.

Schwartz began giving Lloyd tests. Lloyd was worried that he might fail them, but he didn't say anything; he had already gotten the impression this man thought he was stupid. But it was the tests that were stupid. First Schwartz asked him about a million yes-or-no questions. Everything from "Do you think your life isn't worth living?" (no) to "Do you ever see things that aren't there?" (sometimes, in the woods). Then came the pictures. One showed a man and a boy standing in opposite corners of a room. At first Lloyd just said what he saw. But this wasn't good enough; Schwartz said he had to interpret it. "Tell me what you think is going to happen next," he said. When Lloyd looked at it closely, he figured the boy had done something wrong and was about to get a good belt-whipping. Schwartz seemed pleased by this. Finally, and strangest of all, Schwartz showed him some blobs of ink and asked him to make something out of them. If Schwartz hadn't been so serious, Lloyd would have thought it was a joke. But when he studied them (Schwartz had used that word—"interpret"—again), Lloyd could see all different kinds of faces and animals, as he had when he'd talked to Sheriff Lynch about his knife and shears.

It only took one little thing to know what the sheriff thought about this testing.

One morning the sheriff walked Lloyd down the hallway without a word, and when he unlocked the door to the white room, he stepped back, held it open, and swooped out his hand in front of Lloyd like a colored doorman.

"Mr. Dogget," he said, for the first time making fun of Lloyd in some secret way.

The sheriff turned and let the door close without so much as a glance at Schwartz. Lloyd wanted to apologize to the sheriff. He was beginning to understand that it came down to this: the worse the sheriff looked, the better he, Lloyd, looked. He felt he was betraying the sheriff, with the help of this strange, foul-mouthed little man. Schwartz seemed to see everything upside-down. When Lloyd had told him about Mr. Mac, even though Schwartz said it must have been awful, Lloyd could tell that in some way he was pleased. When he had told Schwartz about times when a lot of hours passed without him knowing it, like when he'd sat with that sheep, or about drinking at least a canteen of Mr. Mac's white lightning every day for the past few years, Schwartz began scribbling and shooting questions at him. Same thing with the pills and reefer and acid and speed he'd done in his twenties. Even the gas huffing when he was just a kid. Lloyd felt dirty remembering all of it. Schwartz wanted details. Lloyd could almost see Schwartz making designs out of what he told him, rearranging things to make him look pitiful.

"I don't want to do no testin' today," Lloyd said as soon as the door had shut. He sat and leaned back in his chair, arms dangling, chest out.

"Okay," Schwartz said. "What do you want to do?"

"I been thinkin'," Lloyd said. "It don't make no difference if I was drunk or not. That don't excuse what I did."

"But you don't know what you did."

"That don't make no difference. They got the proof."

"They have evidence, Lloyd, not proof."

Another bunch of upside-down words. "But if I can't remember it, then ain't what they got better than what I can say?"

"Lloyd," Schwartz said, his head in his hands, massaging his bald spot. "We've been over this about every time we've talked. I know that it doesn't make common sense at first. But our criminal-justice system—that misnomer—is predicated upon the idea of volition. It means you have to commit a crime with at least an inkling of intention. You can't be punished in the same way when you don't have any idea what you're doing."

This kind of talk made Lloyd's head ache. "All I know," he said, "is I don't want to go foolin' around with truth. It's like the sheriff says—I got to get right with myself and be a man."

"The sheriff says this?" Schwartz's head popped up.

Lloyd nodded.

"Do you talk to the sheriff often?"

"I been knowing Sheriff Lynch since forever. He's like my daddy."

"But do you talk to him? How often do you talk to him?"

"Every chance I get." Lloyd felt queasy. He knew he'd said something he shouldn't have. But his pride in his friendship with the sheriff, perhaps because it was imperiled, drove him to exaggerate. "When we come from my cell, mostly. But any time I want, really. I can call on him any time."

"I don't think it's a good idea for you to be talking to him about your case," Schwartz said.

"And why not?"

"Because anything—anything—you say to him becomes evidence. As a matter of fact, I don't think it's a good idea for you to talk to him at all."

"So who'm I gonna talk to? Myself? You?"

For the next couple of days the sheriff didn't speak to Lloyd unless Lloyd spoke to him first. Schwartz must have done something. But the sheriff never looked at him hard or seemed angry. He mainly kept his words short and his eyes to the floor, as if he was sad and used to his sadness. Lloyd wanted to tell him how he was trying to get right but it was hard. Eventually Lloyd realized that even if he had said this, the sheriff probably wouldn't believe him. If he were trying to get right, then he wouldn't be letting this Schwartz character make him look pitiful. Each morning Lloyd rose early, dressed, and rubbed his palms to dry them as he sat on the edge of his bunk, waiting. When he walked in front of the sheriff down the hallway to the white room, Lloyd could feel the sheriff's eyes taking him in. He tried to stand up straight and walk with manly strides, but the harder he tried, the smaller and more bent over he felt. He was careful not to wrinkle his prison outfit, pressing it at night between his mattress and a piece of plywood the sheriff had given him for his back. He combed his hair as best he could without a mirror.

At night Lloyd lay on his cot and thought about Schwartz. Of course, Schwartz had tricked him into more tests. Next they were going to take pictures of his brain. Lloyd studied Schwartz's words: "volition," "interpret," "diminished responsibility." They all meant you couldn't be punished for your mistakes. This didn't square with Lloyd; he had been punished for plenty of mistakes. That was what Mr. Mac had punished him for; that was what the sheep died of. When you missed one on a head count and it got lost and fell into a ravine; when you forgot to give one a vaccination and it got sick, like the one that had died before Lloyd was taken away, you were punished. But how could he expect Schwartz, a womanish city boy, to understand this?

On one side were Schwartz and the law, and on the other were the sheep and God and the earth and Sheriff Lynch and Mr. Mac and everything else Lloyd had ever known. Who was he to go against all that—to hide from that terrible, swift sword the Almighty would wield on the Final Day? His fear was weak and mortal; it drove him out of his cell to plot with this fellow sinner to deceive God. Some nights Lloyd moaned in agony at the deceit of his life. For in his pride he had latched onto the notion that since he could not remember his gravest sins (and he believed they were all true, they must be true), that he should not have to pay for them in this life. Oh, he would pay for them in eternity, but he flinched at paying here. What upside-down thinking! What cowardice in the face of sins that were probably darker, cloaked as they were in his drunken forgetting, than any he could have committed when he had "volition," as Schwartz called it. Because Lloyd did not know his sins, he could not accept his punishment; but for the same reason, they seemed to him unspeakably heinous.

Lloyd lay on his bunk in the darkness and thought about the pictures he had seen of his brain. Two officers he didn't know had driven him to a hospital in Lubbock to get them taken. The hearing was in a week. Schwartz had pointed out patches in the pictures' rainbow colors, scratching his bald spot and pacing. He'd said that although parts of Lloyd's brain were damaged so that alcohol could cause longer and more severe blackouts in him than in normal people, such damage might not be enough for the court to recognize him as incompetent. And the rest of the tests had proved that he had a dissociative condition but not multiple-personality disorder. Lloyd had wanted to ask if Schwartz thought he was incompetent, but he figured he wouldn't get a straight answer.

In the darkness of the steel room Lloyd touched his head to try and feel the colored patches of heat and coolness that the pictures showed in his brain. He imagined he could sense some here and there. He had come a long way—not many people knew what their brains looked like. But the thought that he might be incompetent frightened him. What if some day one of those big machines they put over his head was put over his chest and a picture was taken of his soul? What would it look like? He saw a dark-winged creature with tearing claws, cloaked in a gray mist.

The knock came to Lloyd in a half-dream, and at first he thought he had imagined the sheriff's voice. The whole jail was quiet; all the inmates were covered in the same darkness.

"Lloyd? Lloyd? You awake, son?" The voice didn't sound exactly like the sheriff's, but Lloyd knew that's who it was. He rose and went to the door, too sleepy to be nervous. He peered out the square window. The glare of the hallway made him squint. The sheriff stood in silhouette, but his steely eyes glinted. Looking at him through the crosshatches of wire in the security glass, Lloyd thought that he, too, looked caged.

"I'm awake, sheriff."

The door opened, and the sheriff said, "Come on." Lloyd could smell whiskey. He followed the sheriff out past the booking area. Everything was still and deserted in the bare fluorescent light. Gonzales dozed in a chair at the front desk with a porno magazine in his lap. The sheriff opened the door to his office, making the same mocking gesture as before, though this time he seemed to be trying to share his joke with Lloyd. He snapped the door's lock and sat down behind his desk. A single shaded lamp glowed in a corner, casting shadows from the piles of paper on the desk and reflecting golden patches from the plaques on the walls.

The sheriff pointed at a low-backed leather chair and told Lloyd to have a seat. "Excuse me gettin' you out of bed, son. I figured this was the only time we could talk."

"It's no trouble."

"You can prob'ly tell I been drinkin'," the sheriff said. "I don't do it as a habit, but I apologize for that, too. I been doin' it more lately. I do it when I'm sick at heart. At least that's my excuse to myself, which is a Goddamned poor one unbefitting a man, if you ask me. But I am. Sick at heart."

He took a long pull from a coffee mug. Lloyd followed it with his eyes, and the sheriff caught him.

"And no," he said, "you can't have any. One of us got to stay sober, and I want you to remember what I'm gonna tell you." He leaned across the desk. "You know what a vacuum is, son? I mean in a pure sense, not the one you clean with."

Lloyd shook his head.

"Well. A vacuum is a place where there ain't anything, not even air. Every light bulb"—the Sheriff nodded at the lamp behind him—"is a vacuum. Space is mostly vacuum. Vacuum tubes used to be in radios. And so on. A place where there ain't nothin'. Is that signifyin' for you?"

Lloyd nodded.

"Good. So we, because we're on this earth with air to breathe, we are in a place that's not a vacuum that's in the middle of a vacuum, which is space. Think of a bubble floating out in the air." The Sheriff made a big circle above the desk with his fingertips. "That's what the earth is like, floating in space. Are you followin' me?"

"I think so."

"Well, are you or aren't you?" the sheriff said with sudden violence. Not waiting for an answer, he yanked open his desk drawer and took out a large folding map of the world. He tumbled it down the front of his desk, weighted its top corners with a tape dispenser and a stapler, and came around the desk to stand next to Lloyd. He told Lloyd what it was and said, "I study this all the time. Do you know where we are right now?"

To Lloyd, the shapes on the map looked like those inkblots. By reading, he found the United States and then Texas, and then he gave up. He shrugged his shoulders. "I don't know, Sheriff."

"That's okay," the sheriff said gently. He pointed to a dot in the Panhandle which someone had drawn with a ballpoint pen. Cursive letters next to it said "Dumas." "This is where we are. Two specks within that dot, on the dark side of the earth, floating in space. Over here"—he pointed to Hong Kong—"it's lunchtime. Japs eatin' their noodles or whatever. Here"—he pointed to London—"people just risin', eatin' their sausages and egg sandwiches."

He stepped back, behind Lloyd, and put his hands on the chair. The heat of his body and the smell of his breath washed over Lloyd.

"But look, son," the sheriff said, "how many places there are. It's some time everywhere, and everybody is doin' something."

The sheriff stood there for a few moments. Lloyd felt as he had when he was a child and watched TV—he couldn't imagine how all those people got inside that little box. Now he couldn't fathom people inside the little dots. The world was vast and stranger than he had ever imagined.

"We are all here doin' things," the sheriff said, "inside this bubble that is not a vacuum. We all breathe the same air, and everything we do nudges everything else." He stepped over and propped himself on the edge of his desk, next to the map, and crossed his legs. The lamp's soft light cast him in half shadow.

"And this is why I'm sick at heart. Because I thought I knew you. Separation is the most terrible thing there is, especially for a man like me." The sheriff gestured to take in the whole room. "This is what I got. It ain't much. You and I aren't that far apart, son. Both of us solitary. But what you done, son, and I do believe you did all that, that separates a man from the whole world. And that's why I said you need to get right with yourself."

Lloyd bowed his head.

"You don't need to tell me you ain't done that." The sheriff's voice rose and quickened, began to quiver. "You and I both know you ain't. But that itself—a negativity, a vacuum—ain't nothing to breathe in. Things die without air. So what I'm askin' you is, I want to do my own competency exam, for my own self. This is between Lloyd Wayne Dogget and Archibald Alexander Lynch. I need to know what's inside you to know what's inside myself. So you tell that lawyer of yours I'll stipulate to whatever he wants. Remember that word—'stipulate.' Now get out a' here." He turned from Lloyd and began folding the map with shaking hands. The corner weighted by the tape dispenser tore. Lloyd could not move.

"Shit," the sheriff muttered. He wheeled unsteadily on Lloyd, his eyes wide with panic and surprise at what he'd said. Lloyd could tell he was afraid, but not of him, as Mr. Mac had been. The sheriff was afraid he might break out of the bubble in which he lived. "Git!" he yelled. "Go tell Gonzales to take you back! Get outta here before I say somethin' foolish!"

"He wants you to do *what*?" Schwartz paced in the little white room, looking at the floor.

Lloyd was sitting at the table, turning his head to follow Schwartz. Was Schwartz right with himself? He repeated what the sheriff had told him.

"What does that son of a bitch want?" Schwartz said to himself.

"I wish you'd stop cussing around me."

Schwartz made a distracted noise.

"I mean it," Lloyd said. "It's offensive."

Schwartz made another noise. He had gathered his lips into a pucker with his fingers, and he looked at the floor as he paced.

"Especially cussing on the sheriff." When Schwartz didn't answer, Lloyd said, "Are you hearing me? Don't cuss on the sheriff."

"I don't know what kind of game he's trying to play." Schwartz did not stop or raise his eyes from the floor. "But I would guess he's trying to trick some kind of confession out of you."

"Sheriff don't play no games with me," Lloyd said. "He don't have no tricks. You're the one with all the tricks."

"I'll take that as a compliment."

"Sheriff's the one tryin' to help me get right."

"Sheriff's the one tryin' to help you get dead," Schwartz said, mimicking Lloyd.

"Okay, man." Lloyd stood up and pushed the chair away. It squealed on the floor, and Schwartz stopped. Lloyd saw that his own fists were clenched. He hesitated.

"What are you gonna do, Lloyd? Beat me up? Go ahead. I've been expecting this."

"You think I'm stupid," Lloyd said. "And all them tests is to make me look pitiful and incompetent. What do you think that's done to my trying to get right?"

"What do you think that means, Lloyd—'getting right'?" Schwartz moved close to him. He stared straight at Lloyd as he spoke. "It means giving up."

That night, and for the nights and days to come, Lloyd turned over in his mind all he had seen and heard. What he had known was like some foreign language that now he couldn't understand. The worlds of Schwartz and the sheriff, of man and God, of what was in the law and what was in the fields, began to blur, and yet between them grew a chasm in which he hung suspended. He tried to remember what had happened in the places Blanchard had said he'd been, but he couldn't. He could not make them connect the way the sheriff had said all the people in all those dots on the map did. An indifference grew around him, a thin glass glazing that separated him from the rest of humankind.

The sheriff led him down the hallway to the white room without a word or a look, and left him with Schwartz. The hearing was the next day. Lloyd felt as though he were about to take another test. He had fought with Schwartz tooth and nail over the sheriff's proposal, and in the end had gotten his way by threatening to fire him. After Lloyd sat down across the table from him, Schwartz explained that he and the sheriff had struck a deal: the sheriff had stipulated not to testify about his "competency exam," as he called it, on the condition that he not have to reveal to Schwartz beforehand what it was going to be about.

"I don't like this," Schwartz said, pacing, clicking the top of a ballpoint pen so that it made a *tick-tick* sound like a clock. He sat down again, his elbows on the table and hands joined as though in prayer, and brought his face close to Lloyd's.

"I want to tell you the truest thing I've ever seen, Lloyd. I've seen a man executed. When you are executed in Texas, you are taken to a powder-blue room. This is the death chamber, where the warden, a physician, and a minister will stand around the gurney. Since executions can only take place in Texas between midnight and dawn, it will have that eerie feeling of a room brightly lit in the middle of the night. Before this, in an anteroom, a guard will tell you to drop your pants. Then he will insert one rubber stopper in your penis and another in your anus, to prevent you from urinating and defecating when your muscles relax after you have died. When you are lying on the gurney, the guard will secure your arms, legs, and chest to it with leather straps. The guard will insert a needle, which is attached to an IV bag, into your left arm. Above you will be fluorescent lighting, and a microphone will hang suspended from the ceiling. The warden—I think it's still Warden Pearson—will ask whether you have any last words. When you're finished, three chemicals will be released into your blood: sodium thiopental, a sedative that is supposed to render you unconscious; pancuronium bromide, a muscle relaxant, to collapse your diaphragm and lungs; potassium chloride, a poison that will stop your heart.

"I could tell that my client could feel the poison entering his veins. I had known him for the last three of his fifteen years on death row; he was old enough to be my father. At his execution, I was separated from him by a piece of meshed security glass. There was nothing I could do when he began writhing and gasping for breath. The poison—later I found out it was the potassium chloride, to stop his heart—had been injected before the thiopental. Imagine a dream in which your body has turned to lead, in which you can't move and are sinking in water. You have the sensations given you by your nerves and understood in your brain, but you can't do anything about them. You struggle against your own body. But really, it is unimaginable—what it is like to try to rouse your own heart.

"What if everything goes as planned? A nice, sleepy feeling—the sedative tricking your nerves—will dissolve your fear. The question is, will you want it taken away, fear being the only thing that binds you to life? Will you want to hold on to that, like the survivor of a shipwreck clinging to a barnacled plank? Will you struggle, in the end, to be afraid?"

Schwartz slumped back in his chair and began again to *tick-tick* the top of his pen, so that it made a sound like a clock. The whiteness and silence of the room seemed to annihilate time, as though the two men could sit there waiting forever. They fell on Lloyd like a thin silting of powdered glass.

"You spend a lot of time thinkin' about that, don't you?" Lloyd said.

"Yes."

"You told me that to scare me, didn't you?"

"Yes."

Lloyd thought that Schwartz may have gotten right with himself, in his own way, by seeing what he had seen and thinking on it. But something still didn't add up.

"How do you know I'd be afraid?" Lloyd said. "How do you know that would be the last thing I'd feel?"

"I don't know that." Schwartz *tick-ticked* the pen. "You can never know. That's what's terrible about death."

"Lots of things you don't know when you're alive. So what's the difference?"

Schwartz's fingers stopped, and he stared at Lloyd as though he had seen him purely and for the first time. A knock at the door broke the brief, still moment, and Sheriff Lynch entered. He carried under his arm a stack of manila folders, which he put down on the table. Schwartz rose, studying Lloyd. He shook the sheriff's hand when it was offered. His eyes, though, were fixed on Lloyd. The sheriff caught this, but smiled pleasantly and told Schwartz it was good to see him again.

"Lloyd," he said, and nodded at him. He lifted a chair from the corner, put it at the head of the table, and sat.

"I think I need a little more time to consult with my client," Schwartz said.

The sheriff pressed his fingers a few times on top of the folders. "Okay. How much time do you think you'll need?"

"We don't need no more time," Lloyd said, rocking back and forth in his chair. "I'm ready."

"I'd like to look at what you've got there first."

"But that wasn't the agreement, Mr. Schwartz."

"Come on," Lloyd said. "I'm ready."

"Why don't you listen to your client?"

Looking from Lloyd to the sheriff, Schwartz paled. He seemed pinned in place for a moment; then took off his glasses and rubbed them on his shirt. He put them on again. Sheriff Lynch stared at the stack of folders, his fingertips resting on them like a pianist's, his expression one of patient indulgence toward a child who was finishing a noisy tantrum. Lloyd clenched his hands between his thighs, wondering what would be revealed to him.

"Do you mind if I stand?" Schwartz said.

"Go right ahead." Sheriff Lynch pressed his fingers again to the top folder, as if for luck or in valediction, took it from the stack and opened it in front of Lloyd. Lloyd did not see what was there at first, because Schwartz had made a sudden movement toward the table, but Sheriff Lynch, with the slightest warning lift of his hand, checked him. He faced Schwartz a moment and then turned to Lloyd.

"Go ahead, son," he said. "Tell me what you see."

When Lloyd looked down, he was disappointed. It was another one of those crazy tests. There were shapes of red and pink and green and black. It was the inkblot test, only in color. He studied it more closely to try and make sense of it. He realized it was a picture of something. He realized what it was.

"I think I got it," he said to the sheriff. The sheriff nodded to help him along. "It's a sheep," Lloyd said.

"Look at it a little more closely, son." Lloyd saw Schwartz again move and the sheriff again check him while keeping his neutral blue eyes on Lloyd. Lloyd went back to the picture. He had missed some details.

"It's a sheep gutted after slaughter," he said.

"Turn the picture over, son," the sheriff said. This time, Schwartz did not move and the sheriff did not hold up his hand. Paper-clipped to the backside of the picture Lloyd found a smaller photo of a young woman. She had straight brown hair, wore blue jeans and a red-and-white checkered blouse, and sat in a lawn chair, smiling to please the person who held the camera.

"Now turn the picture over again," the sheriff said, in his steady, calm voice. "What do you see?"

Lloyd tried to puzzle it out, but he couldn't. There must be something he wasn't seeing. He studied the picture. As he followed the shapes and colors of the sheep's emptied body, a trickle of pity formed in him for all three of them—the woman, the sheep and himself—and dropped somewhere inside him. The glaze over him tightened. He could only tell the sheriff that he saw a sheep.

After the sheriff left, gathering the folders under his arm, the room went back to its silence.

"If I'd known," Schwartz said, "I would've had him testify."

"What?" Lloyd said. "If you'd known what?"

"Never mind." Shielding his face with his pale fingers, Schwartz lay his other hand on Lloyd's shoulder. "Never mind, Lloyd. You're perfect the way you are."

They had sat there a long time, the sheriff opening a folder in front of him, asking him the same questions, and then putting it aside. And in each folder Lloyd had seen the same things: a gutted sheep and a pretty young woman. He knew that the sheriff was trying to do something to help him get right, but as the glaze thickened, that chance seemed ever more remote. Before he left, the sheriff had nodded to Lloyd, to acknowledge that he had found his answer, but his gesture was as distant as that of a receding figure waving a ship out to sea. With each drop of pity Lloyd felt himself borne away yet drowning, so that he knew the heart of the man in the execution chamber, suffocating and unable to move, and he wondered how he would survive in this new and airless world.

Brownies

ZZ Packer

By our second day at Camp Crescendo, the girls in my Brownie troop had decided to kick the asses of each and every girl in Brownie Troop 909. Troop 909 was doomed from the first day of camp; they were white girls, their complexions a blend of ice cream: strawberry, vanilla. They turtled out from their bus in pairs, their rolled-up sleeping bags chromatized with Disney characters: Sleeping Beauty, Snow White, Mickey Mouse; or the generic ones cheap parents bought: washed-out rainbows, unicorns, curly-eyelashed frogs. Some clutched Igloo coolers and still others held on to stuffed toys like pacifiers, looking all around them like tourists determined to be dazzled.

Our troop was wending its way past their bus, past the ranger station, past the colorful trail guide drawn like a treasure map, locked behind glass.

"Man, did you smell them?" Arnetta said, giving the girls a slow once-over, "They smell like Chihuahuas. *Wet* Chihuahuas." Their troop was still at the entrance, and though we had passed them by yards, Arnetta raised her nose in the air and grimaced.

Arnetta said this from the very rear of the line, far away from Mrs. Margolin, who always strung our troop behind her like a brood of obedient ducklings. Mrs. Margolin even looked like a mother duck—she had hair cropped close to a small ball of a head, almost no neck, and huge, miraculous breasts. She wore enormous belts that looked like the kind that weightlifters wear, except hers would be cheap metallic gold or rabbit fur or covered with gigantic fake sunflowers, and often these belts would become nature lessons in and of themselves. "See," Mrs. Margolin once said to us, pointing to her belt, "this one's made entirely from the feathers of baby pigeons."

The belt layered with feathers was uncanny enough, but I was more disturbed by the realization that I had never actually *seen* a baby pigeon. I searched weeks for one, in vain—scampering after pigeons whenever I was downtown with my father.

But nature lessons were not Mrs. Margolin's top priority. She saw the position of troop leader as an evangelical post. Back at the A.M.E. church where our Brownie meetings were held, Mrs. Margolin was especially fond of imparting religious aphorisms by means of acrostics—"Satan" was the "Serpent Always Tempting and Noisome"; she'd refer to the "Bible" as "Basic Instructions Before Leaving Earth." Whenever she quizzed us on these, expecting to hear the acrostics parroted back to her, only Arnetta's correct replies soared over our vague mumblings. "Jesus?" Mrs. Margolin might ask expectantly, and Arnetta alone would dutifully answer, "Jehovah's Example, Saving Us Sinners."

Arnetta always made a point of listening to Mrs. Margolin's religious talk and giving her what she wanted to hear. Because of this, Arnetta could have blared through a megaphone that the white girls of Troop 909 were "wet Chihuahuas" without so much as a blink from Mrs. Margolin. Once, Arnetta killed the troop goldfish by feeding it a french fry covered in ketchup, and when Mrs. Margolin demanded that she explain what had happened, claimed the goldfish had been eyeing her meal for *hours,* then the fish—giving in to temptation—had leapt up and snatched a whole golden fry from her fingertips.

"*Serious* Chihuahua," Octavia added, and though neither Arnetta nor Octavia could *spell* "Chihuahua," had ever *seen* a Chihuahua, trisyllabic words had gained a sort of exoticism within our fourth-grade set at Woodrow Wilson Elementary. Arnetta and Octavia would flip through the dictionary, determined to work the vulgar-sounding ones like "Djibouti" and "asinine" into conversation.

"*Caucasian* Chihuahuas," Arnetta said.

That did it. The girls in my troop turned elastic: Drema and Elise doubled up on one another like inextricably entwined kites; Octavia slapped her belly; Janice jumped straight up in the air, then did it again, as if to slam-dunk her own head. They could not stop laughing. No one had laughed so hard since a boy named Martez had stuck a pencil in the electric socket and spent the whole day with a strange grin on his face.

"Girls, girls," said our parent helper, Mrs. Hedy. Mrs. Hedy was Octavia's mother, and she wagged her index finger perfunctorily, like a windshield wiper. "Stop it, now. Be good." She said this loud enough to be heard, but lazily, bereft of any feeling or indication that she meant to be obeyed, as though she could say these words again at the exact same pitch if a button somewhere on her were pressed.

But the rest of the girls didn't stop; they only laughed louder. It was the word "Caucasian" that got them all going. One day at school, about a month before the Brownie camping trip, Arnetta turned to a boy wearing impossibly high-ankled floodwater jeans and said, "What are you? *Caucasian?*" The word took off from there, and soon everything was Caucasian. If you ate too fast you ate like a Caucasian, if you ate too slow you ate like a Caucasian. The biggest feat anyone at Woodrow Wilson could do was to jump off the swing in midair, at the highest point in its arc, and if you fell (as I had, more than once) instead of landing on your feet, knees bent Olympic gymnast–style, Arnetta and Octavia were prepared to comment. They'd look at each other with the silence of passengers who'd narrowly escaped an accident, then nod their heads, whispering with solemn horror, "*Caucasian.*"

Even the only white kid in our school, Dennis, got in on the Caucasian act. That time when Martez stuck a pencil in the socket, Dennis had pointed and yelled, "That was *so* Caucasian!"

When you lived in the south suburbs of Atlanta, it was easy to forget about whites. Whites were like those baby pigeons: real and existing, but rarely seen or thought about. Everyone had been to Rich's to go clothes shopping, everyone had seen white girls and their mothers coo-cooing over dresses; everyone had gone to the downtown library and seen white businessmen swish by importantly, wrists flexed in front of them to check the time as though they would change from Clark Kent into Superman at any second. But those images were as fleeting as cards shuffled in a deck, whereas the ten white girls behind us— *invaders,* Arnetta would later call them—were instantly real and memorable, with their long, shampoo-commercial hair, straight as spaghetti from the box. This alone was reason for envy and hatred. The only black girl most of us had ever seen with hair that long was Octavia, whose hair hung past her butt like a Hawaiian hula dancer's. The sight of Octavia's mane prompted other girls to listen to her reverentially, as though whatever she had to say would somehow activate their own follicles. For example, when, on the first day of camp, Octavia made as if to speak, and everyone fell silent. "Nobody," Octavia said, "calls us niggers."

At the end of that first day, when half of our troop made their way back to the cabin after tag-team restroom visits, Arnetta said she'd heard one of the Troop 909 girls call Daphne a nigger. The other half of the girls and I were helping Mrs. Margolin clean up the pots and pans from the campfire ravioli dinner. When we made our way to the restrooms to wash up and brush our teeth, we met up with Arnetta midway.

"Man, I completely heard the girl," Arnetta reported. "Right, Daphne?"

Daphne hardly ever spoke, but when she did, her voice was petite and tinkly, the voice one might expect from a shiny new earring. She'd written a poem once, for Langston Hughes Day, a poem brimming with all the teacher-winning ingredients—trees and oceans, sunsets and moons—but what cinched the poem for the grown-ups, snatching the win from Octavia's musical ode to Grandmaster Flash and the Furious Five, were Daphne's last lines:

You are my father, the veteran
When you cry in the dark
It rains and rains and rains in my heart

She'd always worn clean, though faded, jumpers and dresses when Chic jeans were the fashion, but when she went up to the dais to receive her prize journal, pages trimmed in gold, she wore a new dress with a velveteen bodice and a taffeta skirt as wide as an umbrella. All the kids clapped, though none of them understood the poem. I'd read encyclopedias the way others read comics, and I didn't get it. But those last lines pricked me, they were so eerie, and as my father and I ate cereal, I'd whisper over my Froot Loops, like a mantra, *You are my father, the veteran. You are my father, the veteran, the veteran, the veteran,*" until my father, who acted in plays as Caliban and Othello and was not a veteran, marched me up to my teacher one morning and said, "Can you tell me what's wrong with this kid?"

I thought Daphne and I might become friends, but I think she grew spooked by me whispering those lines to her, begging her to tell me what they meant, and I soon understood that two quiet people like us were better off quiet alone.

"Daphne? Didn't you hear them call you a nigger?" Arnetta asked, giving Daphne a nudge.

The sun was setting behind the trees, and their leafy tops formed a canopy of black lace for the flame of the sun to pass through. Daphne shrugged her shoulders at first, then slowly nodded her head when Arnetta gave her a hard look.

Twenty minutes later, when my restroom group returned to the cabin, Arnetta was still talking about Troop 909. My restroom group had passed by some of the 909 girls. For the most part, they deferred to us, waving us into the restrooms, letting us go even though they'd gotten there first.

We'd seen them, but from afar, never within their orbit enough to see whether their faces were the way all white girls appeared on TV—ponytailed and full of energy, bubbling over with love and money. All I could see was that some of them rapidly fanned their faces with their hands, though the heat of the day had long passed. A few seemed to be lolling their heads in slow circles, half purposefully, as if exercising the muscles of their necks, half ecstatically, like Stevie Wonder.

"We can't let them get away with that," Arnetta said, dropping her voice to a laryngitic whisper. "We can't let them get away with calling us niggers. I say we teach them a lesson." She sat down cross-legged on a sleeping bag, an embittered Buddha, eyes glimmering acrylic-black. "We can't go telling Mrs. Margolin, either. Mrs. Margolin'll say something about doing unto others and the path of righteousness and all. Forget that shit." She let her eyes flutter irreverently till they half closed, as though ignoring an insult not worth returning. We could all hear Mrs. Margolin outside, gathering the last of the metal campware.

Nobody said anything for a while. Usually people were quiet after Arnetta spoke. Her tone had an upholstered confidence that was somehow both regal and vulgar at once. It demanded a few moments of silence in its wake, like the ringing of a church bell or the playing of taps. Sometimes Octavia would ditto or dissent to whatever Arnetta had said, and this was the signal that others could speak. But this time Octavia just swirled a long cord of hair into pretzel shapes.

"*Well?*" Arnetta said. She looked as if she had discerned the hidden severity of the situation and was waiting for the rest of us to catch up. Everyone looked from Arnetta to Daphne. It was, after all, Daphne who had supposedly been called the name, but Daphne sat on the bare cabin floor, flipping through the pages of the Girl Scout handbook, eyebrows arched in mock wonder, as if the handbook were a catalogue full of bright and startling foreign costumes. Janice broke the silence. She clapped her hands to broach her idea of a plan.

"They gone be sleeping," she whispered conspiratorially, "then we gone sneak into they cabin, then we'll put daddy longlegs in they sleeping bags. Then they'll wake up. Then we gone beat 'em up till they're as flat as frying pans!" She jammed her fist into the palm of her hand, then made a sizzling sound.

Janice's country accent was laughable, her looks homely, her jumpy acrobatics embarrassing to behold. Arnetta and Octavia volleyed amused, arrogant smiles whenever Janice opened her mouth, but Janice never caught the hint, spoke whenever she wanted, fluttered around Arnetta and Octavia futilely offering her opinions to their departing backs. Whenever Arnetta and Octavia shooed her away, Janice loitered until the two would finally sigh and ask, "What *is* it, Miss Caucausoid? What do you *want?*"

"Shut up, Janice," Octavia said, letting a fingered loop of hair fall to her waist as though just the sound of Janice's voice had ruined the fun of her hair twisting.

Janice obeyed, her mouth hung open in a loose grin, unflappable, unhurt.

"All right," Arnetta said, standing up. "We're going to have a secret meeting and talk about what we're going to do."

Everyone gravely nodded her head. The word "secret" had a built-in importance, the modifier form of the word carried more clout than the noun. A secret meant nothing; it was like gossip: just a bit of unpleasant knowledge about someone who happened to be someone other than yourself. A secret *meeting*, or a secret *club* was entirely different.

That was when Arnetta turned to me as though she knew that doing so was both a compliment and a charity.

"Snot, you're not going to be a bitch and tell Mrs. Margolin, are you?"

I had been called "Snot" ever since first grade, when I'd sneezed in class and two long ropes of mucus had splattered a nearby girl.

"Hey," I said. "Maybe you didn't hear them right—I mean—"

"Are you gonna tell on us or not?" was all Arnetta wanted to know, and by the time the question was asked, the rest of our Brownie troop looked at me as though they'd already decided their course of action, me being the only impediment.

Camp Crescendo used to double as a high-school-band and field hockey camp until an arcing field hockey ball landed on the clasp of a girl's metal barrette, knifing a skull nerve and paralyzing the right side of her body. The camp closed down for a few years and the girl's teammates built a memorial, filling the spot on which the girl fell with hockey balls, on which they had painted—all in nail polish—get-well tidings, flowers, and hearts. The balls were still stacked there, like a shrine of ostrich eggs embedded in the ground.

On the second day of camp, Troop 909 was dancing around the mound of hockey balls, their limbs jangling awkwardly, their cries like the constant summer squeal of an amusement park. There was a stream that bordered the field hockey lawn, and the girls from my troop settled next to it, scarfing down the last of lunch: sandwiches made from salami and slices of tomato that had gotten waterlogged from the melting ice in the cooler, From the stream bank, Arnetta eyed the Troop 909 girls, scrutinizing their movements to glean inspiration for battle.

"Man," Arnetta said, "we could bumrush them right now if that damn lady would *leave*."

The 909 troop leader was a white woman with the severe pageboy hairdo of an ancient Egyptian. She lay on a picnic blanket, sphinx-like, eating a banana, sometimes holding it out in front of her like a microphone. Beside her sat a girl slowly flapping one hand like a bird with a broken wing. Occasionally, the leader would call out the names of girls who'd attempted leapfrogs and flips, or of girls who yelled too loudly or strayed far from the circle.

"I'm just glad Big Fat Mama's not following us here," Octavia said. "At least we don't have to worry about her." Mrs. Margolin, Octavia assured us, was having her Afternoon Devotional, shrouded in mosquito netting, in a clearing she'd found. Mrs. Hedy was cleaning mud from her espadrilles in the cabin.

"I handled them." Arnetta sucked on her teeth and proudly grinned. "I told her we was going to gather leaves."

"Gather leaves," Octavia said, nodding respectfully. "That's a good one. Especially since they're so mad-crazy about this camping thing." She looked from ground to sky, sky to ground. Her hair hung down her back in two braids like a squaw's. "I mean, I really don't know why it's even called *camping*—all we ever do with Nature is find some twigs and say something like, 'Wow, this fell from a tree.'" She then studied her sandwich. With two disdainful fingers, she picked out a slice of dripping tomato, the sections congealed with red slime. She pitched it into the stream embrowned with dead leaves and the murky effigies of other dead things, but in the opaque water, a group of small silver-brown fish appeared. They surrounded the tomato and nibbled.

"Look!" Janice cried. "Fishes! Fishes!" As she scrambled to the edge of the stream to watch, a covey of insects threw up tantrums from the wheatgrass and nettle, a throng of tiny electric machines, all going at once. Octavia sneaked up behind Janice as if to push her in. Daphne and I exchanged terrified looks. It seemed as though only we knew that Octavia was close enough—and bold enough—to actually push Janice into the stream. Janice turned around quickly, but Octavia was already staring serenely into the still water as though she was gathering some sort of courage from it. "What's so funny?" Janice said, eyeing them all suspiciously.

Elise began humming the tune to "Karma Chameleon," all the girls joining in, their hums light and facile. Janice also began to hum, against everyone else, the high-octane opening chords of "Beat It."

"I love me some Michael Jackson," Janice said when she'd finished humming, smacking her lips as though Michael Jackson were a favorite meal. "I *will* marry Michael Jackson."

Before anyone had a chance to impress upon Janice the impossibility of this, Arnetta suddenly rose, made a sun visor of her hand, and watched Troop 909 leave the field hockey lawn.

"Dammit!" she said. "We've got to get them *alone*."

"They won't ever be alone," I said. All the rest of the girls looked at me, for I usually kept quiet. If I spoke even a word, I could count on someone calling me Snot. Everyone seemed to think that we could beat up these girls; no one entertained the thought that they might fight *back*. "The only time they'll be unsupervised is in the bathroom."

"Oh shut up, Snot," Octavia said.

But Arnetta slowly nodded her head. "The bathroom," she said. "The bathroom," she said, again and again. "The bathroom! The bathroom!"

According to Octavia's watch, it took us five minutes to hike to the restrooms, which were midway between our cabin and Troop 909's. Inside, the mirrors above the sinks returned only the vaguest of reflections, as though someone had taken a scouring pad to their surfaces to obscure the shine. Pine needles, leaves, and dirty, flattened wads of chewing gum covered the floor like a mosaic. Webs of hair matted the drain in the middle of the floor. Above the sinks and below the mirrors, stacks of folded white paper towels lay on a long metal counter. Shaggy white balls of paper towels sat on the sinktops in a line like corsages on display. A thread of floss snaked from a wad of tissues dotted with the faint red-pink of blood. One of those white girls, I thought, had just lost a tooth.

Though the restroom looked almost the same as it had the night before, it somehow seemed stranger now. We hadn't noticed the wooden rafters coming together in great V's. We were, it seemed, inside a whale, viewing the ribs of the roof of its mouth.

"Wow. It's a mess," Elise said.

"You can say that again."

Arnetta leaned against the doorjamb of a restroom stall. "This is where they'll be again," she said. Just seeing the place, just having a plan seemed to satisfy her. "We'll go in and talk to them. You know, 'How you doing? How long'll you be here?' That sort of thing. Then Octavia and I are gonna tell them what happens when they call any one of us a nigger."

"I'm going to say something, too," Janice said.

Arnetta considered this. "Sure," she said. "Of course. Whatever you want."

Janice pointed her finger like a gun at Octavia and rehearsed the line she'd thought up, "'We're gonna teach you a *lesson*!' That's what I'm going to say." She narrowed her eyes like a TV mobster. "'We're gonna teach you little girls a lesson!'"

With the back of her hand, Octavia brushed Janice's finger away. "You couldn't teach me to shit in a toilet."

"But," I said, "what if they say, 'We didn't say that? We didn't call anyone an N-I-G-G-E-R.'"

"Snot," Arnetta said, and then sighed. "Don't think. Just fight. If you even know how."

Everyone laughed except Daphne. Arnetta gently laid her hand on Daphne's shoulder. "Daphne. You don't have to fight. We're doing this for you."

Daphne walked to the counter, took a clean paper towel, and carefully unfolded it like a map. With it, she began to pick up the trash all around. Everyone watched.

"C'mon," Arnetta said to everyone. "Let's beat it." We all ambled toward the doorway, where the sunshine made one large white rectangle of light. We were immediately blinded, and we shielded our eyes with our hands and our forearms.

"Daphne?" Arnetta asked. "Are you coming?"

We all looked back at the bending girl, the thin of her back hunched like the back of a custodian sweeping a stage, caught in limelight. Stray strands of her hair were lit near-transparent, thin fiber-optic threads. She did not nod yes to the question, nor did she shake her head no. She abided, bent. Then she began again, picking up leaves, wads of paper, the cotton fluff innards from a torn stuffed toy. She did it so methodically, so exquisitely, so humbly, she must have been trained. I thought of those dresses she wore, faded and old, yet so pressed and clean. I then saw the poverty in them; I then could imagine her mother, cleaning the houses of others, returning home, weary.

"I guess she's not coming."

We left her and headed back to our cabin, over pine needles and leaves, taking the path full of shade.

"What about our secret meeting?" Elise asked.

Arnetta enunciated her words in a way that defied contradiction: "We just had it."

It was nearing our bedtime, but the sun had not yet set.

"Hey, your mama's coming," Arnetta said to Octavia when she saw Mrs. Hedy walk toward the cabin, sniffling. When Octavia's mother wasn't giving bored, parochial orders, she sniffled continuously, mourning an imminent divorce from her husband. She might begin a sentence, "I don't know what Robert will do when Octavia and I are gone. Who'll buy him cigarettes?" and Octavia would hotly whisper, "*Mama*," in a way that meant: Please don't talk about our problems in front of everyone. Please shut up.

But when Mrs. Hedy began talking about her husband, thinking about her husband, seeing clouds shaped like the head of her husband, she couldn't be quiet, and no one could dislodge her from the comfort of her own woe. Only one thing could perk her up—Brownie songs. If the girls were quiet, and Mrs. Hedy was in her dopey, sorrowful mood, she would say, "Y'all know I like those songs, girls. Why don't you sing one?" Everyone would groan, except me and Daphne. I, for one, liked some of the songs.

"C'mon, everybody," Octavia said drearily. "She likes the Brownie song best."

We sang, loud enough to reach Mrs. Hedy:

"I've got something in my pocket;
It belongs across my face.
And I keep it very close at hand
in a most convenient place.
I'm sure you couldn't guess it
If you guessed a long, long while.
So I'll take it out and put it on—
It's a great big Brownie smile!"

The Brownie song was supposed to be sung cheerfully, as though we were elves in a workshop, singing as we merrily cobbled shoes, but everyone except me hated the song so much that they sang it like a maudlin record, played on the most sluggish of rpms.

"That was good," Mrs. Hedy said, closing the cabin door behind her. "Wasn't that nice, Linda?"

"Praise God," Mrs. Margolin answered without raising her head from the chore of counting out Popsicle sticks for the next day's craft session.

"Sing another one," Mrs. Hedy said. She said it with a sort of joyful aggression, like a drunk I'd once seen who'd refused to leave a Korean grocery.

"God, Mama, get over it," Octavia whispered in a voice meant only for Arnetta, but Mrs. Hedy heard it and started to leave the cabin.

"Don't go," Arnetta said. She ran after Mrs. Hedy and held her by the arm. "We haven't finished singing." She nudged us with a single look. "Let's sing the 'Friends Song.' For Mrs. Hedy."

Although I liked some of the songs, I hated this one:

Make new friends
But keep the o-old,
One is silver
And the other gold.

If most of the girls in the troop could be any type of metal, they'd be bunched-up wads of tinfoil, maybe, or rusty iron nails you had to get tetanus shots for.

"No, no, no," Mrs. Margolin said before anyone could start in on the "Friends Song." "An uplifting song. Something to lift her up and take her mind off all these earthly burdens."

Arnetta and Octavia rolled their eyes. Everyone knew what song Mrs. Margolin was talking about, and no one, no one, wanted to sing it.

"Please, no," a voice called out. "Not 'The Doughnut Song.'"

"Please not 'The Doughnut Song,'" Octavia pleaded.

"I'll brush my teeth two times if I don't have to sing 'The Doughnut—'"

"Sing!" Mrs. Margolin demanded.

We sang:

"Life without Jesus is like a do-ough-nut!
Like a do-ooough-nut!
Like a do-ooough-nut!
Life without Jesus is like a do-ough-nut!
There's a hole in the middle of my soul!"

There were other verses, involving other pastries, but we stopped after the first one and cast glances toward Mrs. Margolin to see if we could gain a reprieve. Mrs. Margolin's eyes fluttered blissfully. She was half asleep.

"Awww," Mrs. Hedy said, as though giant Mrs. Margolin were a cute baby, "Mrs. Margolin's had a long day."

"Yes indeed," Mrs. Margolin answered. "If you don't mind, I might just go to the lodge where the beds are. I haven't been the same since the operation."

I had not heard of this operation, or when it had occurred, since Mrs. Margolin had never missed the once-a-week Brownie meetings, but I could see from Daphne's face that she was concerned, and I could see that the other girls had decided that Mrs. Margolin's operation must have happened long ago in some remote time unconnected to our own. Nevertheless, they put on sad faces. We had all been taught that adulthood was full of sorrow and pain, taxes and bills, dreaded work and dealings with whites, sickness and death. I tried to do what the others did. I tried to look silent.

"Go right ahead, Linda," Mrs. Hedy said. "I'll watch the girls." Mrs. Hedy seemed to forget about divorce for a moment; she looked at us with dewy eyes, as if we were mysterious, furry creatures. Meanwhile, Mrs. Margolin walked through the maze of sleeping bags until she found her own. She gathered a neat stack of clothes and pajamas slowly, as though doing so was almost painful. She took her toothbrush, her toothpaste, her pillow. "All right!" Mrs. Margolin said, addressing us all from the threshold of the cabin. "Be in bed by nine." She said it with a twinkle in her voice, letting us know she was allowing us to be naughty and stay up till nine-fifteen.

"C'mon everybody," Arnetta said after Mrs. Margolin left. "Time for us to wash up."

Everyone watched Mrs. Hedy closely, wondering whether she would insist on coming with us since it was night, making a fight with Troop 909 nearly impossible. Troop 909 would soon be in the bathroom, washing their faces, brushing their teeth—completely unsuspecting of our ambush.

"We won't be long," Arnetta said. "We're old enough to go to the restrooms by ourselves."

Ms. Hedy pursed her lips at this dilemma. "Well, I guess you Brownies are almost Girl Scouts, right?"

"Right!"

"Just one more badge," Drema said.

"And about," Octavia droned, "a million more cookies to sell." Octavia looked at all of us, *Now's our chance,* her face seemed to say, but our chance to do *what,* I didn't exactly know.

Finally, Mrs. Hedy walked to the doorway where Octavia stood dutifully waiting to say goodbye but looking bored doing it. Mrs. Hedy held Octavia's chin. "You'll be good?"

"Yes, Mama."

"And remember to pray for me and your father? If I'm asleep when you get back?"

"Yes, Mama."

When the other girls had finished getting their toothbrushes and washcloths and flashlights for the group restroom trip, I was drawing pictures of tiny birds with too many feathers. Daphne was sitting on her sleeping bag, reading.

"You're not going to come?" Octavia asked.

Daphne shook her head.

"I'm gonna stay, too," I said. "I'll go to the restroom when Daphne and Mrs. Hedy go."

Arnetta leaned down toward me and whispered so that Mrs. Hedy, who'd taken over Mrs. Margolin's task of counting Popsicle sticks, couldn't hear. "No, Snot. If we get in trouble, you're going to get in trouble with the rest of us."

We made our way through the darkness by flashlight. The tree branches that had shaded us just hours earlier, along the same path, now looked like arms sprouting menacing hands. The stars sprinkled the sky like spilled salt. They seemed fastened to the darkness, high up and holy, their places fixed and definite as we stirred beneath them.

Some, like me, were quiet because we were afraid of the dark; others were talking like crazy for the same reason.

"Wow!" Drema said, looking up. "Why are all the stars out here? I never see stars back on Oneida Street."

"It's a camping trip, that's why," Octavia said. "You're supposed to see stars on camping trips."

Janice said, "This place smells like my mother's air freshener."

"These woods are *pine*," Elise said. "Your mother probably uses *pine* air freshener."

Janice mouthed an exaggerated "Oh," nodding her head as though she just then understood one of the world's great secrets.

No one talked about fighting. Everyone was afraid enough just walking through the infinite deep of the woods. Even though I didn't fight to fight, was afraid of fighting, I felt I was part of the rest of the troop; like I was defending something. We trudged against the slight incline of the path, Arnetta leading the way.

"You know," I said "their leader will be there. Or they won't even be there. It's dark already. Last night the sun was still in the sky. I'm sure they're already finished."

Arnetta acted as if she hadn't heard me. I followed her gaze with my flashlight, and that's when I saw the squares of light in the darkness. The bathroom was just ahead.

But the girls were there. We could hear them before we could see them.

"Octavia and I will go in first so they'll think there's just two of us, then wait till I say, 'We're gonna teach you a lesson,'" Arnetta said. "Then, bust in. That'll surprise them."

"That's what I was supposed to say," Janice said.

Arnetta went inside, Octavia next to her. Janice followed, and the rest of us waited outside.

They were in there for what seemed like whole minutes, but something was wrong. Arnetta hadn't given the signal yet. I was with the girls outside when I heard one of the Troop 909 girls say, "NO. That did NOT happen!"

That was to be expected, that they'd deny the whole thing. What I hadn't expected was *the voice* in which the denial was said. The girl sounded as though her tongue were caught in her mouth. "That's a BAD word!" the girl continued. "We don't say BAD words!"

"Let's go in," Elise said.

"No," Drema said, "I don't want to. What if we get beat up?"

"Snot?" Elise turned to me, her flashlight blinding. It was the first time anyone had asked my opinion, though I knew they were just asking because they were afraid.

"I say we go inside, just to see what's going on."

"But Arnetta didn't give us the signal," Drema said. "She's supposed to say, 'We're gonna teach you a lesson,' and I didn't hear her say it."

"C'mon," I said. "Let's just go in."

We went inside. There we found the white girls—about five girls huddled up next to one big girl. I instantly knew she was the owner of the voice we'd heard. Arnetta and Octavia inched toward us as soon as we entered.

"Where's Janice?" Elise asked, then we heard a flush. "Oh."

"I think," Octavia said, whispering to Elise, "they're retarded."

"We ARE NOT retarded!" the big girl said, though it was obvious that she was. That they all were. The girls around her began to whimper.

"They're just pretending," Arnetta said, trying to convince herself. "I know they are."

Octavia turned to Arnetta. "Arnetta. Let's just leave."

Janice came out of a stall, happy and relieved, then she suddenly remembered her line, pointed to the big girl, and said, "We're gonna teach you a lesson."

"Shut up, Janice," Octavia said, but her heart was not in it. Arnetta's face was set in a lost, deep scowl. Octavia turned to the big girl and said loudly, slowly, as if they were all deaf,

"We're going to leave. It was nice meeting you, O.K.? You don't have to tell anyone that we were here. O.K.?"

"Why not?" said the big girl, like a taunt. When she spoke, her lips did not meet, her mouth did not close. Her tongue grazed the roof of her mouth, like a little pink fish. "You'll get in trouble. I know. *I* know."

Arnetta got back her old cunning. "If you said anything, then you'd be a tattletale."

The girl looked sad for a moment, then perked up quickly. A flash of genius crossed her face. "I *like* tattletale."

"It's all right, girls. It's gonna be all right!" the 909 troop leader said. All of Troop 909 burst into tears. It was as though someone had instructed them all to cry at once. The troop leader had girls under her arm, and all the rest of the girls crowded about her. It reminded me of a hog I'd seen on a field trip, where all the little hogs gathered about the mother at feeding time, latching onto her teats. The 909 troop leader had come into the bathroom, shortly after the big girl had threatened to tell. Then the ranger came, then, once the ranger had radioed the station, Mrs. Margolin arrived with Daphne in tow.

The ranger had left the restroom area, but everyone else was huddled just outside, swatting mosquitoes.

"Oh. They *will* apologize," Mrs. Margolin said to the 909 troop leader, but she said this so angrily, I knew she was speaking more to us than to the other troop leader. "When their parents find out, every one a them will be on punishment."

"It's all right, it's all right," the 909 troop leader reassured Mrs. Margolin. Her voice lilted in the same way it had when addressing the girls. She smiled the whole time she talked. She was like one of those TV-cooking-show women who talk and dice onions and smile all at the same time.

"See. It could have happened. I'm not calling your girls fibbers or anything." She shook her head ferociously from side to side, her Egyptian-style pageboy flapping against her cheeks like heavy drapes. "It *could* have happened. See. Our girls are *not* retarded. They are *delayed* learners." She said this in a syrupy instructional voice, as though our troop might be delayed learners as well. "We're from the Decatur Children's Academy. Many of them just have special needs."

"Now we won't be able to walk to the bathroom by ourselves!" the big girl said.

"Yes you will," the troop leader said, "but maybe we'll wait till we get back to Decatur—"

"I don't want to wait!" the girl said. "I want my Independence badge!"

The girls in my troop were entirely speechless. Arnetta looked stoic, as though she were soon to be tortured but was determined not to appear weak. Mrs. Margolin pursed her lips solemnly and said, "Bless them, Lord. Bless them."

In contrast, the Troop 909 leader was full of words and energy. "Some of our girls are echolalic—" She smiled and happily presented one of the girls hanging onto her, but the girl widened her eyes in horror, and violently withdrew herself from the center of attention, sensing she was being sacrificed for the village sins. "Echolalic," the troop leader continued. "That means they will say whatever they hear, like an echo—that's where the word comes from. It comes from 'echo.'" She ducked her head apologetically, "I mean, not all of them have the most *progressive* of parents, so if they heard a bad word, they might have repeated it. But I guarantee it would not have been *intentional*."

Arnetta spoke. "I saw her say the word. I heard her." She pointed to a small girl, smaller than any of us, wearing an oversized T-shirt that read: "Eat Bertha's Mussels."

The troop leader shook her head and smiled, "That's impossible. She doesn't speak. She can, but she doesn't."

Arnetta furrowed her brow. "No. It wasn't her. That's right. It was *her*."

The girl Arnetta pointed to grinned as though she'd been paid a compliment. She was the only one from either troop actually wearing a full uniform: the mocha-colored A-line shift, the orange ascot, the sash covered with badges, though all the same one—the Try-It patch. She took a few steps toward Arnetta and made a grand sweeping gesture toward the sash. "See," she said, full of self-importance, "I'm a Brownie." I had a hard time imagining this girl calling anyone a "nigger"; the girl looked perpetually delighted, as though she would have cuddled up with a grizzly if someone had let her.

On the fourth morning, we boarded the bus to go home.

The previous day had been spent building miniature churches from Popsicle sticks. We hardly left the cabin. Mrs. Margolin and Mrs. Hedy guarded us so closely, almost no one talked for the entire day.

Even on the day of departure from Camp Crescendo, all was serious and silent. The bus ride began quietly enough. Arnetta had to sit beside Mrs. Margolin; Octavia had to sit beside her mother. I sat beside Daphne, who gave me her prize journal without a word of explanation.

"You don't want it?"

She shook her head no. It was empty.

Then Mrs. Hedy began to weep. "Octavia," Mrs. Hedy said to her daughter without looking at her, "I'm going to sit with Mrs. Margolin. All right?"

Arnetta exchanged seats with Mrs. Hedy. With the two women up front, Elise felt it safe to speak. "Hey," she said, then she set her face into a placid, vacant stare, trying to imitate that of a Troop 909 girl. Emboldened, Arnetta made a gesture of mock pride toward an imaginary sash, the way the girl in full uniform had done. Then they all made a game of it, trying to do the most exaggerated imitations of the Troop 909 girls, all without speaking, all without laughing loud enough to catch the women's attention.

Daphne looked down at her shoes, white with sneaker polish. I opened the journal she'd given me. I looked out the window, trying to decide what to write, searching for lines, but nothing could compare with what Daphne had written, *"My father, the veteran,"* my favorite line of all time. It replayed itself in my head, and I gave up trying to write.

By then, it seemed that the rest of the troop had given up making fun of the girls in Troop 909. They were now quietly gossiping about who had passed notes to whom in school. For a moment the gossiping fell off, and all I heard was the hum of the bus as we sped down the road and the muffled sounds of Mrs. Hedy and Mrs. Margolin talking about serious things.

"You know," Octavia whispered, "why did *we* have to be stuck at a camp with retarded girls? You know?"

"*You* know why," Arnetta answered. She narrowed her eyes like a cat. "My mama and I were in the mall in Buckhead, and this white lady just kept looking at us. I mean, like we were foreign or something. Like we were from China."

"What did the woman say?" Elise asked.

"Nothing," Arnetta said. "She didn't say nothing."

A few girls quietly nodded their heads.

"There was this time," I said, "when my father and I were in the mall and—"

"Oh shut up, Snot," Octavia said.

I stared at Octavia, then rolled my eyes from her to the window. As I watched the trees blur, I wanted nothing more than to be through with it all: the bus ride, the troop, school—all of it. But we were going home. I'd see the same girls in school the next day. We were on a bus, and there was nowhere else to go.

"Go on, Laurel," Daphne said to me. It seemed like the first time she'd spoken the whole trip, and she'd said my name. I turned to her and smiled weakly so as not to cry, hoping she'd remember when I'd tried to be her friend, thinking maybe that her gift of the journal was an invitation of friendship. But she didn't smile back. All she said was, "What happened?"

I studied the girls, waiting for Octavia to tell me to shut up again before I even had a chance to utter another word, but everyone was amazed that Daphne had spoken. The bus was silent. I gathered my voice. "Well," I said. "My father and I were in this mall, but *I* was the one doing the staring." I stopped and glanced from face to face. I continued. "There were these white people dressed like Puritans or something, but they weren't Puritans. They were Mennonites. They're these people who, if you ask them to do a favor, like paint your porch or something, they have to do it. It's in their rules."

"That sucks," someone said.

"C'mon," Arnetta said. "You're lying."

"I am not."

"How do you know that's not just some story someone made up?" Elise asked, her head cocked full of daring. "I mean, who's gonna do whatever you ask?"

"It's not made up. I know because when I was looking at them, my father said, 'See those people? If you ask them to do something, they'll do it. Anything you want.'"

No one would call anyone's father a liar—then they'd have to fight the person. But Drema parsed her words carefully. "How does your *father* know that's not just some story? Huh?"

"Because," I said, "he went up to the man and asked him would he paint our porch, and the man said yes. It's their religion."

"Man, I'm glad I'm a Baptist," Elise said, shaking her head in sympathy for the Mennonites.

"So did the guy do it?" Drema asked, scooting closer to hear if the story got juicy.

"Yeah," I said. "His whole family was with him. My dad drove them to our house. They all painted our porch. The woman and girl were in bonnets and long, long skirts with buttons up to their necks. The guy wore this weird hat and these huge suspenders."

"Why," Arnetta asked archly, as though she didn't believe a word, "would someone pick a *porch*? If they'll do anything, why not make them paint the whole *house*? Why not ask for a hundred bucks?"

I thought about it, and then remembered the words my father had said about them painting our porch, though I had never seemed to think about his words after he'd said them.

"He said," I began, only then understanding the words as they uncoiled from my mouth, "it was the only time he'd have a white man on his knees doing something for a black man for free."

I now understood what he meant, and why he did it, though I didn't like it. When you've been made to feel bad for so long, you jump at the chance to do it to others. I remembered the Mennonites bending the way Daphne had bent when she was cleaning the restroom. I remembered the dark blue of their bonnets, the black of their shoes. They painted the porch as though scrubbing a floor. I was already trembling before Daphne asked quietly, "Did he thank them?"

I looked out the window. I could not tell which were the thoughts and which were the trees. "No," I said, and suddenly knew there was something mean in the world that I could not stop.

Arnetta laughed. "If I asked them to take off their long skirts and bonnets and put on some jeans, would they do it?"

And Daphne's voice, quiet, steady: "Maybe they would. Just to be nice."

The Whore's Child

Richard Russo

Sister Ursula belonged to an all but extinct order of Belgian nuns who conducted what little spiritual business remained to them in a decrepit old house purchased by the diocese seemingly because it was unlikely to outlast them. Since it was on Forest Avenue, a block from our house, I'd seen Sister Ursula many times before the night she turned up in class, but we never had spoken. She drove a rusted-out station wagon that was always crowded with elderly nuns who needed assistance getting in and out. Though St. Francis Church was only a few blocks away, that was too far to walk for any of them except Sister Ursula, her gait awkward but relentless. "You should go over there and introduce yourself someday," Gail, my wife, suggested more than once. "Those old women have been left all alone." Her suspicion was later confirmed by Sister Ursula herself. "They are waiting for us to die," she confessed. "Impatient of how we clutch to our miserable existences."

"I'm sure you don't mean that," I said, an observation that was to become my mantra with her, and she, in turn, seemed to enjoy hearing me say it.

She appeared in class that first night and settled herself at the very center of the seminar despite the fact that her name did not appear on my computer printout. Fiction writing classes are popular and invariably over-subscribed at most universities, and never more so than when the writer teaching it has recently published a book, as I had done the past spring. Publishing the kind of book that's displayed in strip-mall bookstores bestows a celebrity on academic writers and separates them from their scholar colleagues, whose books resemble the sort of dubious specialty items found only in boutiques and health food stores. I'd gotten quite a lot of press on my recent book, my first in over a decade, and my fleeting celebrity might have explained Sister Ursula's presence in my classroom the first chilly evening of the fall semester, though she gave no indication of this, or that she recognized me as her neighbor.

No, Sister Ursula seemed innocent not only of me but also of all department and university protocol. When informed that students petition to take the advanced fiction writing class by means of a manuscript submission the previous term, and that its prerequisites were beginning and intermediate courses, Sister Ursula disputed neither the existence nor the wisdom of these procedures. Nor did she gather her things and leave, which left me in an odd position. Normally it's my policy not to allow unregistered students to remain in class, because doing so encourages their mistaken belief that they can wheedle, cajole or flatter their way in. In the past I'd shown even football players the door without the slightest courtesy or ceremony, but this was a different challenge entirely. Sister Ursula herself was nearly as big as a linebacker, yet more persuasive than this was her body language, which suggested that once settled, she was not used to moving. And since she was clearly settled, I let her stay.

After class, however, I did explain why it would be highly unprofessional of me to allow her to remain in the advanced fiction workshop. After all, she freely admitted she'd never attempted to write a story before, which, I explained, put her at an extreme disadvantage. My mistake was in not leaving the matter there. Instead I went on. "This is a storytelling class, Sister. We're all liars here. The whole purpose of our enterprise is to become skilled in making things up, of substituting our own truth for *the* truth. In this class we actually prefer a well-told lie," I concluded, certain that this would dissuade her.

She patted my hand, as you might the hand of a child. "Never you mind," she then assured me, adjusting her wimple for the journey home. "My whole life has been a lie."

"I'm sure you don't mean that," I told her.

In the convent, Sister Ursula's first submission began, *I was known as the whore's child. Nice opening,* I wrote in the margin, as if to imply that her choice had been a purely artistic one. It wasn't, of course. She was simply starting with what was for her the beginning of her torment. She was writing—and would continue to write—a memoir. By mid-semester I would give up asking her to invent things.

The first installment weighed in at a robust twenty-five pages, which detailed the suffering of a young girl taken to live in a Belgian convent school where the treatment of the children was determined by the social and financial status of the parents who had abandoned them there. As a charity case and the daughter of a prostitute, young Sister Ursula (for there could be no doubt that she *was* the first-person narrator) found herself at the very bottom of the ecclesiastical food chain. What little wealth she possessed—some pens and paper her father had purchased for her the day before they left the city, along with a pretty new dress—was taken from her, and she was informed that henceforth she would have no use for such pitiful possessions. Her needs—food, a uniform and a single pair of shoes—would be provided for her, though she would doubtless prove unworthy to receive them. The shoes she was given were two sizes too small, an accident, Sister Ursula imagined, until she asked if she might exchange them for the shoes of a younger girl that were two sizes too large, only to be scorned for her impertinence. So before long she developed the tortured gait of a cripple, which was much imitated by the other children, who immediately perceived in her a suitable object for their cruelest derision.

The mockery of her classmates was something Sister Ursula quickly accommodated, by shunning their companionship. In time she grew accustomed to being referred to as "the whore's child," and she hoped that the children would eventually tire of calling her this if she could manage to conceal how deeply it wounded her. During periods of recreation in the convent courtyard she perfected the art of becoming invisible, avoiding all games and contests when, she knew, even those on her own team would turn on her. What she was not prepared for was the cruelty she suffered at the hands of the nuns, who seemed to derive nearly as much satisfaction from tormenting her as their charges—beginning with her request to exchange shoes. She had not merely been told that this was not permitted, but was given a horrible explanation as to why this was so. The chafing of the too small shoes had caused her heels to bleed into her coarse white socks and then into the shoes themselves. Only a wicked child, Sister Veronique explained, would foul the shoes she'd been given with her blood, then beg to exchange them for the shoes of an innocent child. Did she think it fair, the old nun wondered out loud, that another child, one who had not only a virtuous mother but also a father, be asked to wear the polluted shoes of a whore's child?

Worse than the sting of the old nun's suggestion that anything Sister Ursula touched immediately became contaminated was the inference that trailed in the wake of her other remark. The innocent girl had not only a virtuous mother—Sister Ursula knew what this meant—*but also a father,* which seemed to imply that she herself didn't have one. Of course she knew that she did have a father, a tall, handsome father who had promised to rescue her from this place as soon as he could find work. Indeed, it was her father who had brought her to the convent, who had assured Mother Superior that she was a good girl and not at all wicked. How then had Sister Veronique concluded that she had no father? The young girl tried to reason it through but became confused. She knew from experience that evil, by its very nature, counted for more in the world than good. And she understood that her mother's being a prostitute made her "the whore's child," that her mother's wickedness diminished her father's value, but did it negate his very existence? How could such a thing be? She dared not ask, and so the old nun's remark burrowed even deeper, intensifying a misery that already bordered on despair.

Sister Ursula's first installment ended here, and her fellow students approached the discussion of it as one would an alien spacecraft. Several had attended Catholic schools where they'd been tutored by nuns, and they weren't sure, despite my encouragement, that they were allowed to be critical of this one. The material itself was foreign to them; they'd never encountered anything like it in the workshop. On the plus side, Sister Ursula's story had a character in it, and the character was placed in a dire situation, and those were good things for stories to do. On the other hand, the old nun's idiom was imperfect, her style stiff and old-fashioned, and the story seemed to be moving forward without exactly getting anywhere. It reminded them of stories they'd heard other elderly people tell, tales that even the tellers eventually managed to forget the point of, narratives that would gradually peter out with the weak insistence that all these events really did happen. "It's a victim story," one student recognized. "The character is being acted on by outside forces, but she has no choices, which means there can be no consequences to anything she does. If she doesn't participate in her own destiny, where's the story?"

Not having taken the beginning and intermediate courses, Sister Ursula was much enlightened by these unanticipated critiques, and she took feverish notes on everything that was said. "I liked it, though," added the student who'd identified it as a victim story. "It's different." By which he seemed to mean that Sister Ursula herself was different.

The old nun stopped by my office the day after, and it was clear she was still mulling the workshop over. "To be so much . . . a victim," she said, searching for the right words, "it is not good?"

"No," I smiled. Not in stories, not in life, I was about to add, until I remembered that Sister Ursula still wasn't making this distinction, and my doing so would probably confuse her further. "But maybe in the next installment?" I suggested.

She looked at me hopefully.

"Maybe your character will have some choices of her own as your story continues?" I prodded.

Sister Ursula considered this possibility for a long time, and I could tell by looking at her that the past wasn't nearly as flexible as she might have wished.

She was about to leave when she noticed the photograph of my daughter that I keep on my desk. "Your little girl," she said, "is a great beauty?"

"Yes," I said, indicating that it was okay to pick up the photo if she wanted to.

"Sometimes I see her when I am driving by," she explained. When I didn't say anything, she added, "Sometimes I don't see her anymore?"

"She and her mother are gone now," I explained, the sentence feeling syntactically strange, as if English were my second language, too. "They're living in another state."

Sister Ursula nodded uncertainly, as if deliberating whether "state" meant a condition or a place, then said, "She will return to this state?"

It was my turn to nod. "I hope so, Sister."

And so I became a Catholic, began the second installment of Sister Ursula's story, and again I scribbled *nice opening* in the left margin before hunkering down. I'd had students like Sister Ursula before, and they'd inspired the strictly enforced twenty-five page limit in all my workshops. I noted that for this second submission she had narrowed her margins, fiddled with the font, wedging the letters closer together. The spacing didn't look quite double, maybe 1.7. Venial sins.

Having had no religious training prior to entering the convent, Sister Ursula was for some time unable to recite prayers with the other children, further evidence, if any were needed, of the moral depravity inherent to being the offspring of a whore. She discovered it was not an easy task, learning prayers to the cadence of public ridicule, but learn them she did, and though the rote recitation was, in the beginning, a torment, it eventually became a comfort. Most of the prayers she fought to memorize were adamant about the existence of a God who, at least in the person of the crucified Christ, was infinitely more loving and understanding and forgiving than the women He'd led to the altar as His brides.

To be loved and understood and forgiven seemed to Sister Ursula the ultimate indulgence, and thus she became a denizen of the convent chapel, retreating there at every opportunity from the taunts and jeers of the other children and the constant crowlike reprimands of the nuns. She liked the smell of the place—damp and cool and clean—especially when she had it to herself, when it wasn't filled with the bodies of stale old nuns and sweaty children. Often she could hide in the chapel for an hour or more before one of the side doors would finally creak open, momentarily flooding the floor with bright light. Then the long dark shadow of a nun would fall across Sister Ursula where she knelt in prayer at the foot of the cross, and she would have no choice but to rise and be led back to her torment, often by a twisted ear.

In addition to the authorized prayers she'd memorized, Sister Ursula composed others of her own. She prayed that Sister Veronique, who had suggested that she had no father and who worked in the convent stable, might be kicked in the head by a horse and paralyzed for life. She prayed that Sister Joseph, who used her command of the kitchen to ensure that charity children were given the poorest food in the smallest quantities, might one day slip and fall into one of her boiling vats. Required herself to spend most holidays at the convent, Sister Ursula prayed that the children who were allowed to go home might perish in railway accidents. Sometimes, in an economical mood, she prayed that the convent might burn to the ground, and the air fill with black ash. She saw nothing wrong with offering such prayers, particularly since none of them, no matter how urgent, were ever answered. She felt a gentle trust in the Jesus of the Cross who hung above the main altar of the convent chapel. He seemed to know everything that was in her heart and to understand that nothing dwelt there that wasn't absolutely necessary to her survival. He would not begrudge her these prayers.

In truth, Jesus on the cross reminded Sister Ursula of her father who she knew had never wanted to see her packed off to the convent, and who missed her every day, just as she missed him. Like Jesus, her father was slender and handsome and sad; and unable to find work and married to a woman who was his shame. He was, like Jesus, stuck where he was. Yet if the prayers she had struggled to memorize were true, there was hope. Had not Jesus shed His crown of thorns, stepped down from the cross to become the light and salvation of the world, raising up with Him the lowly and the true of heart? Sister Ursula, when she wasn't praying that a horse kick Sister Veronique in the head, fervently prayed that her father might one day be free. The first thing he would do, she felt certain, was come for her, and so every time the chapel's side door opened, she turned toward the harsh light with a mixture of hope and fear, and though it was always a nun whose dark silhouette filled the doorway, she held tenaciously to the belief that soon it would be her father standing there.

One Christmas season—was it her third year at the convent school?—Sister Ursula was summoned to the chamber of Mother Superior, who told her to ready herself for a journey. This was a full week before any of the other students would be permitted to leave for the Christmas holiday, and Sister Ursula was instructed to tell no one of her impending departure. Indeed, Mother Superior seemed flustered, and this gave Sister Ursula heart. During her years of secret, vengeful prayer she'd indulged many fantasies of dramatic liberation, and often imagined her father's arrival on horseback, his angry pounding at the main gate, his purposeful stride through the courtyard and into the chapel. Perhaps Mother Superior's anxiety stemmed from the fact that her father was already on his way to effect just such a rescue.

At the appointed hour, Sister Ursula waited, as instructed, by the main gate, beyond which no men save priests were permitted entry, and awaited her father's arrival. She hoped he would come by a coach or carriage that then would convey them to the village train station, but if necessary she was more than happy to make the journey on foot, so long as she and her father were together. She had better shoes now, though she still hobbled like a cripple. And so when a carriage came into view in the dusty road beyond the iron gate, her heart leapt up— until she recognized it as the one belonging to the convent. Inside sat not her father but Sister Veronique, who had not been kicked in the head by a horse despite three years' worth of Sister Ursula's dogged prayers. When the carriage drew to a halt, Sister Ursula understood that her hopes had been led astray by her need and that she was to be banished from the convent, not rescued from it. She did not fear a worse existence than her present one, because a worse existence was not within her powers of imagination. Rather, what frightened her was the possibility that if she was taken from the convent school, her father no longer would know where to find her when the time came. This terrible fear she kept to herself. She and Sister Veronique did not speak a word on the long journey to the city.

Late that evening they arrived at a hospital and were taken to the charity ward, only to learn that Sister Ursula's mother had expired just after they had left the convent that morning. A nun dressed all in white informed Sister Veronique that it would be far better for the child not to see the deceased, and a look passed between them. All that was left by way of a keepsake was a brittle, curling, scallop-edged photograph, which the white nun gave to Sister Ursula, who had offered no reaction to the news that her mother was dead. Since arriving at the hospital, Sister Ursula had lapsed into a state of paralytic fear that it was her father who had fallen ill there. Instead, it seemed at least one of her prayers had been answered: her father was free.

But where was he? When she summoned the courage to ask, the two nuns exchanged another glance, in which it was plain that the white nun shared Sister Veronique's belief that she had no father, and Sister Ursula saw, too, that it would be useless for her, a child, to try to convince the white nun otherwise. Her fury supported her during their train ride, but then, when the convent came into view from the carriage, Sister Ursula broke down and began to sob. To her surprise, if not comfort, Sister Veronique placed a rough, callused hand on her shoulder and said softly, "Never mind, child. You will become one of us now." In response Sister Ursula slid as far away from the old nun as she could and sobbed even harder, knowing it must be true.

"Are we ever going to meet the father?" one student wanted to know. "I mean, she yearns for him, and he gets compared to Christ, but we never see him directly. We're, like, *told* how to feel about him. If he doesn't ever show up, I'm going to feel cheated."

Sister Ursula dutifully noted this criticism, but you had only to look at the old woman to know that the father was not going to show up. Anybody who felt cheated by this could just join the club.

The day after Sister Ursula's second workshop, my doorbell rang at seven-thirty in the morning. I struggled out of bed, put on a robe and went to the door. Sister Ursula stood on the porch, clearly agitated. The forlorn station wagon idled at the curb with its full cargo of curious, myopic nuns, returning, I guessed, from morning Mass. The yard was strewn with dry, unraked November leaves, several of which had attached themselves to the bottom of Sister Ursula's flowing habit.

"Must he be in the story? Must he return?" Sister Ursula wanted to know. As badly as she had wanted her father to appear in life, she needed, for some reason, to exclude him from the narrative version.

"He's already *in* the story," I pointed out cinching my robe tightly at the waist.

"But I never saw him after she died. This is what my story is about."

"How about a flashback?" I suggested. "You mentioned there was one Christmas holiday . . ."

But she was no longer listening. Her eyes, slate gray, had gone hard. "She died of syphilis."

I nodded, feeling something harden in me too. Behind me I heard the bathroom door open and close, and I thought I saw Sister Ursula's gaze flicker for an instant. She might have caught a glimpse of Jane, the woman I was involved with, and I found myself hoping she had.

"My father's heart was broken."

"How do you know that, if you never saw him again?"

"He loved her." she explained. "She was his ruin."

It was my hatred that drew me deeper into the Church, began Sister Ursula's third installment the words cramped even more tightly on exactly twenty-five pages, and this elicited my now standard comment in the margin. As a writer of opening sentences, Sister Ursula was without peer among my students.

In the months following her mother's death, an explanation had occurred to Sister Ursula. Her father, most likely, had booked passage to America to search for work. Such journeys, she knew, were fraught with unimaginable peril, and perhaps he now lay at the bottom of the ocean. So it was that she gradually came to accept the inevitability of Sister

Veronique's cruel prophecy. She would become one of those whom she detested. Ironically, this fate was hastened by the prophet's untimely death when she was kicked by a horse, not in the head as Sister Ursula had prayed, but in the chest, causing severe internal hemorrhaging and creating an opening in the stable. During her long sojourn at the convent, Sister Ursula had learned to prefer the company of animals to that of humans, and so at the age of sixteen, already a large, full woman like her mother, she became herself a bride of Christ.

Sister Ursula's chronicle of the years following her vows, largely a description of her duties in the stable, featured several brief recollections of the single week she'd spent at home in the city during the Christmas holiday of that first year she entered the convent school. During that holiday she'd seen very little of her mother—a relief, since Sister Ursula dreaded the heat of her mother's embrace and the cloying stench of her whore's perfume. Rather, her beloved father took her with him on his rounds, placing her on a convenient bench outside the dark buildings he entered, telling her how long he would be, how high a number she would have to count to before he would return. Only a few times did she have to count higher. "Did you find work, Father?" she asked each time he reappeared. It seemed to Sister Ursula that in buildings as large and dark as the ones he entered, with so many other men entering and exiting, there should have been work in one of them, but there was none. Still, that they were together was joy enough. Her father took her to the wharf to see the boats, to a small carnival where a man her father knew let her ride a pony for free and finally to a bitter cold picnic in the country where they ate warm bread and cheese. At the end of each of these excursions her father promised again that she would not have to remain much longer in the convent school, that another Christmas would find them together.

The installment ended with Sister Ursula taking her final vows in the same chapel that for years had been her refuge from the taunts of children for whom she would always be the whore's child. There, at the very altar of God, Sister Ursula, like a reluctant bride at an arranged marriage, indulged her fantasy of rescue right up to the last moment. When asked to proclaim her irrevocable devotion to God and the one true Church, she paused and turned toward the side door of the chapel, the one she'd always imagined her father would throw open, and willed her father's shadow to emerge from the blinding light and scatter these useless women and hateful children before him.

But the door remained shut, the chapel dark except for the flickering of a hundred candles, and so Sister Ursula became a bride.

"Isn't there a lot of misogyny in this story?" observed a male student who I happened to know was taking a course with the English department's sole radical feminist, and was therefore alert to all of misogyny's insidious manifestations. By stating this opinion in the form of a question, perhaps he was indicating that the distrust and even hatred of women evident in Sister Ursula's memoir might be okay in this instance because the author was, sort of, a woman.

At any rate, he was right to be cautious. What would you expect, a chorus of his female classmates sang out. The whole thing takes place in a girls' school. There were only two men in the story and one was Jesus, so the statistical sample was bound to be skewed. No, read correctly, Sister Ursula was clearly a feminist.

"I *would* like to see more of the mother, though," one young woman conceded. "It was a major cop-out for her to die before they could get to the hospital."

"You wanted a deathbed scene?" said another. "Wouldn't that be sort of melodramatic?"

Here the discussion faltered. Melodrama was a bad thing, almost as bad as misogyny.

"Why was the daughter sent for?" wondered someone else. "If the mother didn't love her, why send for her?"

"Maybe the father sent for her?"

"Then why wasn't he there himself?"

"I know I was the one," interrupted another, "who wanted to see more of the father after the last submission, but now I think I was wrong. All that stuff with her father over the Christmas holiday? It was like we kept hearing what we already knew. And *then* he's not there at the hospital when the mother dies. I'm confused." He turned to me. "Aren't you?"

"Maybe somebody in the hospital contacted the convent," another student suggested, letting me off the hook.

"For a dying prostitute in a charity ward? How would they even know where the daughter was unless the mother told them?"

Everyone now turned to Sister Ursula, who under this barrage of questions seemed to have slipped into a trance.

"I don't care," said another student, one of the loners in the back of the room. "I *like* this story. It feels real." The fourth and final installment of Sister Ursula's story was only six and a half pages long with regular margins, normal fonts and standard double-spacing.

My life as a nun has been one of terrible hatred and bitterness, it began. I considered writing, *You don't mean that,* in the margin, but refrained. Sister Ursula always meant what she said. It was now late November, and she hadn't veered a centimeter from literal truth since Labor Day. These last, perfunctory pages summarized her remaining years in the convent until the school was partially destroyed by fire. It was then that Sister Ursula came to America. Still a relatively young woman, she nonetheless entertained no thoughts of leaving the order she had always despised. She had become, as Sister Veronique predicted, one of them.

Once, in her late forties, she had returned to Belgium to search for her father, but she had little money and found no trace of him. It was as if, as Sister Veronique had always maintained, the man had never existed. When her funds were exhausted, Sister Ursula gave up and returned to America to live out what remained of her life among the other orphans of her order. This was her first college course, she explained, and she wanted the other students to know that she had enjoyed meeting them and reading their stories, and thanked them for helping her with hers. All of this was contained in the final paragraph of the story, an unconsciously postmodern gesture.

"This last part sort of fizzled out," one student admitted, clearly pained to say this after its author had thanked her readers for their help. "But it's one of the best stories we've read all semester."

"I liked it too," said another, whose voice didn't fall quite right.

Everyone seemed to understand that there was more to say, but no one knew what it might be. Sister Ursula stopped taking notes and silence descended on the room. For some time I'd been watching a young woman who'd said next to nothing all term, but who wrote long, detailed reports on all the stories. She'd caught my attention now because her eyes were brimming with tears. I sent her an urgent telepathic plea. No. Please don't.

"But the girl in the story never *got* it," she protested.

The other students, including Sister Ursula, all turned toward her. "Got what?"

I confess, my own heart was in my throat.

"About the father," she said. "He was the mother's pimp, right? Is there another explanation?"

"So," Sister Ursula said sadly, "I was writing what you call a fictional story after all."

It was now mid-December, my grades were due, and I was puzzling over what to do about Sister Ursula's. She had not turned in a final portfolio of revised work to be evaluated, nor had she returned to class after her final workshop, and no matter how hard I tried, I couldn't erase from my memory the image of the old nun that had haunted me for weeks, of her face coming apart in terrible recognition of the willful lie she'd told herself over a lifetime.

So I'd decided to pay her a visit at the old house where she and five other elderly nuns had been quartered now for nearly a decade in anticipation of their order's dissolution. I had brought the gift of a Christmas tree ornament, only to discover that they had no tree, unless you counted the nine-inch plastic one on the mantel in the living room. Talk about failures of imagination. In a house inhabited by infirm, elderly women, who did I suppose would have put up and decorated a tree?

Sister Ursula seemed surprised to see me standing there on her sloping porch, but she led me into a small parlor off the main hall. "We must be very still," she said softly. "Sister Patrice has fallen ill. I am her nurse, you see. I am nurse to all of them."

In the little room we took seats opposite each other across a small gateleg table. I must have looked uncomfortable, because Sister Ursula said, "You have always been very nervous of me, and you should not. What harm was in me has wasted away with my flesh."

"It's just that I was bitten by a nun as a child," I explained.

Sister Ursula, who'd said so many horrible things about nuns, looked momentarily shocked. Then she smiled. "Oh, I understand that you made a joke," she said. "I thought that you might be . . . what was that word the boy in our class used to describe those like me?"

I had to think a minute. "Oh, a misogynist?"

"Yes, that. Would you tell me the truth if I asked you do you like women?"

"Yes, I do. Very much."

"And I men, so we are the same. We each like the opposite from us."

Which made me smile. And perhaps because she had confided so much about herself, I felt a sudden, irrational urge to confide something in return. Something terrible, perhaps. Something I believed to be true. That my wife had left because she had discovered my involvement with a woman I did not love, who I had taken up with, I now realized, because I felt cheated when the book I'd published in the spring had not done well, cheated because my publisher had been irresponsibly optimistic, claiming the book would make me rich and famous, and because I'd been irresponsibly willing to believe it, so that when it provided neither fame nor fortune, I began to look around for a consolation prize and found her. I am not a good man, I might have told Sister Ursula. I have not only failed but also betrayed those I love. If I said such things to Sister Ursula, maybe she would find some inconsistency in my tale, some flaw. Maybe she'd conclude that I was judging myself too harshly and find it in her heart to say, "You don't mean that."

But I kept my truths to myself, because she was right. I *was* "nervous of her."

After an awkward moment of silence, she said, "I would like to show you something, if you would like to see it?"

Sister Ursula struggled heavily to her feet and left the room, returning almost immediately. The old photograph was pretty much as described—brown and curled at its scalloped edges, the womanly image at its center faded nearly into white. But still beautiful. It might have been the photo of a young Sister Ursula, but of course it wasn't. Since there was nothing to say, I said nothing, merely put it down on the small table between us.

"You? You had loving parents?"

I nodded. "Yes."

"You are kind. This visit is to make sure that I am right, I understand. But I am wondering for a long time. You also knew the meaning of my story?"

I nodded.

"From the beginning?"

"No, not from the beginning."

"But the young woman was correct? Based on the things that I wrote, there could be no other . . . interpretation?"

"Not that I could see."

"And yet *I* could not see."

There was a sound then, a small, dull thud from directly overhead. "Sister Patrice," Sister Ursula informed me, and we got to our feet. "I am needed. Even a hateful nun is sometimes needed."

At the front door, I decided to ask. "One thing," I said. "The fire . . . that destroyed the school?"

Sister Ursula smiled and took my hand. "No," she assured me. "All I did was pray."

She looked off across the years, though, remembering. "Ah, but the flames," she said, her old eyes bright with a young woman's fire. "They reached almost to heaven."

Leave of Absence

Jennifer Shaff

When I first discovered Spock in my basement, I made him promise to take me off this crazy planet. I really didn't need to be here anymore, and he agreed to my deal. If I helped him hide his alienness from the general population, he promised to bring me into space, circle the sun with a slingshot effect, and land in the future, with his spaceship. He was scrounging for material to build a communication device and needed rides to the dump, tools from our shed, and my brother's old transistor radio for the wires and circuits. I cleaned off the laundry table in the basement so he could work, gave him my last set of AA batteries, and let him take apart my Mac Classic for the hard drive. The last thing he needed, he told me, was a big, flat piece of metal, and I was happy to oblige him.

But by the time I was driving Spock to the School Bus Demolition Derby at the county fair, so he could cut a large chunk of metal out of a busted bus, I was starting to feel nervous about where I was going and confused about what everything meant. I even slammed on the brakes in front of one of those "Do Not Pass" signs along Highway H. "I can't pass this point, Spock!" I yelled at him. "What if there's a hole up ahead and we fall into it?" The sky was turning the pale, smoggy blue of late afternoon, but the warm, summer breezes blowing through the car windows were not relaxing me.

"Lisa, there is a high probability that the DO NOT PASS sign means no one can pass you as you drive your vehicle. Your behavior is illogical," he replied.

"I just don't know." I pulled my hands away from the steering wheel, but they were shaking so much, I put them back and gripped the faux leather covering even tighter. "I don't know anything." An emotional man would have recognized my hysteria and tried to calm me with soothing words, but Spock, of course, had no emotions and could barely recognize the dangerous situation he was in—sitting in the passenger seat as I put my idling Ford Fiesta into park in the middle of a road that cut a cornfield in half. Lately, I had been forgetting things I used to know—what highway signs meant, how far to stop behind a flashing school bus, what to do with the dirty kitty litter—things that were somewhat insignificant, but necessary for everyday life. For a moment, I wondered if Spock's mind meld had messed up my memory, confused my knowledge of signs, made me forget important things, but then I remembered my parents' crumpled car in the ditch and I realized the mind meld wasn't that powerful. I wish it had been.

When Spock first landed in Wisconsin, he snuck in a basement window of the duplex I had lived in with my parents and now lived in alone. He must have been digging through old boxes, looking for wires, because the scratchy noises coming from the basement made me think squirrels were getting in again, so I tiptoed down the stairs with the junior size baseball bat and almost had time to scream when I felt someone grab my shoulder from behind. Next thing I knew, I was lying on the floor and this old Jewish-looking man was kneeling over me, chanting, and touching my face. "My mind to your mind . . . my thoughts to your thoughts . . . my mind . . ." I didn't automatically recognize him and, for some reason, thought I was eleven years old again and getting in trouble for skipping Hebrew school. Then, all of a sudden, I understood that this strange man was Spock. He had done the Vulcan Nerve Pinch on me to keep me quiet, was doing the mind meld so that we would know everything about each other, and wasn't Jewish, even if he sort of looked that way. "Appearances can be deceiving," my father always said, though he was talking about cars. Maybe it's a good thing Spock did the mind meld which allowed us to share memories. I probably wouldn't have believed him if he'd just told me he was from the future, but I still wondered if his Vulcan desert memories were blocking some of mine. I wanted to think that Spock had the memories I couldn't access, so I could trust him with confusing highway signs, but I couldn't be sure. He didn't know what to do with the kitty litter either and sent Oscar outside to "drop his excrement in the shrubbery." Oscar didn't come back for a week.

Now Spock peered through my windshield at the sharp curve ahead of us. "In the past when you have slowed your vehicle on this highway to show me grazing, domesticated animals, other cars have driven around you. They 'pass' you. Since passing would be dangerous behavior at this juncture, given the speed capabilities of your automobiles and the curve in the road, it is highly probable that sign refers to automobiles passing other, slower automobiles."

"Yeah, but what if it means I can't pass this point? Don't pass right here—this sign!" I almost started crying. "What if there's a hole up ahead in the road from some old construction?"

For some reason, Spock always considered what I said and gave me one of his thoughtful pauses before continuing. "Lisa, a hole in the road should not cause you to panic."

"What?!" I shrieked as a truck beeped behind us, grew rapidly in my rearview mirror, then beeped again as Spock and I watched it drive around my stopped car and disappear beyond the curve.

"That automobile would not have to engage in an illegal and dangerous maneuver, if you would accelerate."

"You're not worried about a hole?" I asked.

"A hole will not impede the progress of your vehicle."

"Yes it would, Spock! We'd be stuck in a hole."

"Does your vehicle have vertical thrusters?" he asked.

"Up and down?! Jeez! No, Spock! This is a Ford Fiesta. It doesn't go up and down. If we're in a hole, we're stuck. This vehicle has forward and backward. Forward and backward—that's it!" I didn't know why I was so upset. Maybe I was worried that Spock wouldn't find the metal he needed from the side of a dented-up old school bus. Maybe I was worried that he wouldn't like the School Bus Demolition Derby, wouldn't find it as entertaining as my dad and I used to when we went every year and cheered at the first scent of a burning engine.

"Please continue driving forward cautiously for our safety. I can assist you in any difficulties ahead." For some reason, when he spoke like that, I believed him, so I tightened my ponytail by grabbing at two long chunks of hair and separating them until the rubber band was tight on the back of my head, took the car out of park, shifted into first gear and then second. As we gained speed on the empty road, I wiped my eyes on my sleeve, took a few deep, diaphragm breaths, and gradually began to lose my fear of leftover holes. "This is a very quiet road," Spock observed from the passenger seat—using my own words to describe highways with only a few cars. Recently, he'd begun picking up some of my phrases.

"I'm taking you on the back roads to the fair grounds, Spock—more scenic and less crowded. Hey," I said. One of his ears was poking out of the knit, green acrylic of the Packers hat I made him wear. "Pull your hat down." I suddenly sounded like my own father, shouting out the door for me to wear a hat, scarf, or a jacket over the Wiota Middle School sweatsuit I wear to teach physical education to sixth, seventh, and eighth grade students. I had figured I could live with my parents for the first year of teaching to save for a condo in Evanston, but then the rental unit opened up and I got along fine with my parents, except for my father's fear of breezes and my mother's almost mythic quest to find me an attractive, available, intelligent Jewish male in southern Wisconsin. "Maybe it's not dairy and meat that don't mix, but the dairy state and Jews," I would always tease her. "Oh hush," she'd say and offer potential sons of acquaintances as if simply saying their names got them into jewelry stores picking out diamonds. "Millie Hempel over in Jackson has three gorgeous sons. One is named Ron, I think."

"The Minnie we visited in the geriatric home? How old are her sons? I'm only twenty-four, Mom." When she said not Minnie, but Millie, I leaned back on the kitchen counter and said, "You mean the Millie with the cross-dressing son." My mother, truly confused, set down the ladle she had been using to pour liquid, strawberry jelly from the pot into the tight row of sanitized Mason jars and said, "Millie doesn't have . . . what are you . . .?"

"Stop teasing your mother." My father stood in the doorway, smelling of fresh cut grass and diesel fuel. When I tried to look innocent, he pointed a finger at me and said, "Stop."

"Dad," I said. "I can find my own husband, when I'm ready. I'm living on my side of the duplex and paying you rent, so I shouldn't have to take this. She should hound Martin."

"Your brother's another story. Let your mother love you how she knows," he said with finality as he walked past me into the family room and settled into his recliner. "Preseason Packers tonight," he shouted back into the kitchen to change the subject, so I walked into the family room and sat on the couch. "You know they're letting me coach the football team for sixth graders and it's going to be boys *and* girls. Isn't that great?"

"That's great, Lisa. Very modern. See Elena," he spoke loudly so his voice would carry into the kitchen. "Our daughter is very modern—that's all."

"Millie's sons are modern!" Mom shouted back in her high voice which carried into the family room, over to Mrs. Sorensen's house next door, and easily across half the county. "Not modern enough to be cross dressers, but they're modern!"

Sitting in my car, I wondered if in the future, where Spock lived, men and women played on the same professional sports teams. Would Spock understand human athletic games? He adjusted his hat and asked, "What type of metal is used in school bus construction?"

"You know, I'm not really sure." We had driven into the more populated section of Highway H, so we passed ranch homes set at the end of half-mile driveways and acres of mowed, green lawn. "But like I said, this stuff is heavy because they build the buses strong to protect the kids."

"Do the children have any other protective devices at their disposal during the demolition derby?" he asked in his quiet, not-trying-to-judge-humans way.

I stared at Spock in confusion, forgetting safety and good driving habits. "Oh no, Spock. The kids aren't still in the buses. These are old buses they don't use for school anymore."

His eyebrow arched in relief. "These are the crappy, almost broken ones. But the metal—the body is good metal, like I told you. We can get some after the derby. You have your laser thing right?"

"I have the equipment to obtain the piece I need," he said.

"Good." I laughed at his question. "No kids in there, Spock, jeez . . . we're not that bad on this planet."

Although I tried to be accommodating, Spock was so exact about everything that he annoyed me, but then I realized a person with his concern for specifics would be good at flying spaceships. Once I asked him what it felt like to die and then come back to life on the Genesis planet, but he reminded me that he didn't have feelings. Before I could rephrase the question to "What was it like to be reborn on the Genesis planet?" he switched topics and asked if I had thought of a way to disguise him. That's when I gave him Dad's Packers hat to cover his ears and some of Dad's old clothes to wear instead of his Starfleet uniform. But he still sounded odd when he spoke, because he called me "daughter" in public sometimes, which wasn't the plan. I wanted him to pretend I was his daughter, not call me "daughter." By the time I started taking him to restaurants, I was used to hearing, "Daughter, please order the appropriate dishes for me." He liked hummus from Cafe Lebanon, and the tofu from the Chinese take-out place, but not McDonald's salads.

Showing Spock the Earth, or what I knew of it, was sometimes bizarre because the easy places became problematic and the difficult places, the ones I avoided, became even more problematic. For instance, when Spock expressed interest in my religious background, I didn't want to take him to temple, because he wouldn't know what to do. "You could instruct me in the proper behaviors," he suggested as he sat at my kitchen table eating Chinese leftovers. I told him it was too complex. I didn't tell him that I hadn't gone to temple in years. "But my disguise is predicated on my being interpreted as an 'old Jewish man,' as you so often say. Perhaps I should learn more about your heritage." I told him not to worry, but he insisted.

"Fine," I said and rented *Fiddler on the Roof* from the video store, set him up with the remote, a bowl of air popped popcorn, and my brother's old copy of *E.T.* I wanted him to see that we suspected there might be alien life. He could learn about my ancestors and then how humans in the present would deal with aliens.

"Fascinating," he said after the movie marathon. "Should I learn a musical instrument?" He kicked the recliner footrest down.

"No, Spock," I said as I leaned back on the couch. "That's not the point."

"Perhaps if E.T. had learned to vocalize better, he would be pressured to relocate on Earth instead of having to leave the planet."

"Spock! Those are two separate movies!"

"The similarities are remarkable."

Sometimes for a logical Vulcan he was completely dense. "Spock, one is about Jewish people in Russia—like my ancestors—and the other is an alien—like you, from another planet."

"When the winter comes," he asked, "will we be forced to leave the duplex?"

As we drove through another cornfield, I rolled up my window and turned on the air conditioning. To get to the fairgrounds, I needed to turn onto Route 117 which was right past the pull-off people used when they climbed Thompson's Hill, so I told Spock we could stop there on the way and get a great view of a whole cabbage farm. "I have been curious about Earth's agricultural production methods at this time," he said. I turned onto the dusty patch along the road that everyone parked on, matting down the grass till it gave up and turned to dirt and stones for car tires to crunch over. When we opened the car doors, the sun and dust and weedy smell from knee-high brush hit our senses like a brick wall, like a car hitting a brick wall, like a car hitting another car at eighty-five miles per hour. And I remembered how different walking in a field of weeds smelled depending on if it were day or night, or even noon or 8:00 AM. The smell was always different in warm weather and I wondered—picturing my parents' car flipped over into the weeds alongside the highway, in the dark, with the tires spinning and the headlights still on—what their last smell was. My parents always drove with the windows open, if it was warm enough. What did the weeds smell like that night?

After our short hike up Thompson's Hill to check out the cabbage farm, and then back to the car, I pulled onto Highway H and then turned onto Route 117. Spock said "That view was intriguing," and I nodded. "Cabbage has a distinct aroma," he said.

"We'll get that last piece of metal you need, radio your ship, and get the hell out of here. We're almost near the state line." I rolled my window down to get fresh air.

"When we took this route to dine at the Lebanese restaurant, you informed me of the state boundary," he reminded me.

"Oh, yes." I smiled at the memory. "I brought you to Chicago for Lebanese food—good for vegans." He agreed.

The first time I made dinner for Spock, he didn't even know what kind of vegetarian he was. When I asked him if he was lacto-ovo or vegan, he replied that he was Vulcan and I said everybody knew that. What type of vegetarian? He looked puzzled. When I asked about milk, he announced that he consumed dairy products as an infant through breast-feeding, as if we didn't have breasts on this planet and he was some cosmic La Leche representative. Okay, I told him, then you eat cheese. No, he did not. Milk? He refused. Eggs? He asked if eggs were considered "dairy," which frustrated me because I never thought eggs should be on that level of the food pyramid either, I was just asking. My sixth graders always assumed eggs were there because they were white, like milk, and Spock was not turning out to be any easier as a student. I put the box of mac and cheese back on the shelf and found an old can of kidney beans and some rice.

Spock was difficult to live with, and not only because he was vegetarian. I had to hide him from Mrs. Sorensen next door, and it didn't help that she was trying to feed me through my grief with plates of caramel brownies and huge tins of cowboy casserole. Every time I saw her, she would hand me another dish of food and say, "Your parents are with God now, dear." She'd offer to help me clean the house too, but I didn't let her in. I didn't want her to see Spock. "You're always driving off somewhere," she said. "Where do you go?" I told her I was attending to my parents' affairs and had to go to a bank in Milwaukee. "Oh dear," she said. "Couldn't your brother do that?"

"My brother's busy gardening in Oconomowoc," I told her.

"Oh, is that his business now?" Mrs. Sorensen was trying to be friendly, but looked so nervous around me that I made Spock sleep in the basement for a few days, till she went off to Florida to visit her grandchildren. Then I let him stay in the guest room.

It also didn't help that my friend Joanie always called to check in on me when I was boiling dinner. I told her I was fine as I peeled the paper off a can of beans and wiped the top off before opening it. "I've been worried about you since you started the leave of absence," she said. "The kids really missed you at the end of the year. And we don't see you jogging down at the track."

"I'm taking a break from exercising," I told her.

"And Frank was wondering if you wanted to help with his Little League team. It'd be good for you to get out."

"No, I'm taking a break from coaching too." I dumped the beans in the colander and rinsed off the slimy fluid.

"Frank went over and mowed your lawn, you know. He knocked, but you weren't there." When I didn't respond, I heard her take a deep breath through the phone. "I'm not the only one worried about you. We just want to help."

"You can't." I started to get angry. "My parents died and I want to be alone for a while. Is that so bad?"

"No, hon." She was backpedaling. "No. You just never wanted to be alone before and your brother didn't stay long and I know that made you sad. I'm here for you, okay? Are you still seeing that psychiatrist?"

"No. He was crazy. Listen, I'm cooking and I gotta go. I'll call if I need anything."

"Promise?" I heard her ask as I hung up.

Spock asked who had communicated with me and I actually told him to shut up, which was rude, but I was confused. My parents had just died and I wasn't angry that they left me in the middle of a huge state with my brother five hours away and a community of people who thought that if I would just coach something, I would feel better. I wasn't angry that I was left alone on the flattest, most boring part of the planet to instruct young children how to throw a ball and eat vegetables. I wasn't angry, just really sad because that's how a person is supposed to be when loved ones die, not jealous, not angry, but sad. Only when I talked to Spock, I didn't feel sad anymore, but sometimes I got angry with him.

When we pulled into the gravel parking lot of the fair grounds, along with everyone else in the county it seemed, I rolled up my window to keep the dust out and told Spock to do the same. The gravel section of the parking lot gave way to bumpy portions of grass and then dried mud which spit out sheets of dust. A sad-looking teenaged boy used a white flag to point us to our parking spot, itched his face with his other hand and continued walking backwards and pointing at the cars that pulled in behind us. Most people came for the School Bus Demolition Derby at night, but some had been there all day getting their animals judged, their homemade sauerkraut tasted, or their nerves thrilled on the carnival rides. Spock stared out at the rows of cars we needed to walk through to get to the ticket booth and into the fair and I thought he might not want to walk that far, so I said, "It's not that far," as I pulled up my emergency brake and turned off the engine.

"I am not concerned about the distance, but am fascinated by the number of fossil fuel burning vehicles," he said.

"This is America, Spock." I reached in back for my sweatshirt and my father's old spring jacket for Spock. "This is what we do." I handed the jacket to him and he set it on the dashboard.

"I am not as affected by temperature fluctuations as you are," he said.

"Spock, just bring the damn coat!" My anger scared me, so I turned to look out my window for a moment to see a peaceful horizon. Instead, I saw a woman in the car next to mine, dancing in her seat as she put her car into park. Her lips moved with the words of a song and her eyelids fluttered shut. I thought for a moment of my brother singing along to his Bob Dylan's greatest hits tape as he drove us from the funeral, his voice cracking at the high notes and tears running down his face. I was in the passenger seat of my own car, letting him drive because the funeral director held the passenger door open for me, eyes down, with a hand out for assistance and I obeyed. We had just watched our parents in side-by-side coffins being lowered, by an air jack, into the ground. "Why didn't we get a limo?" I had asked my brother.

He stared ahead, but paused in his lyrical protest against capitalism, "They're gas guzzlers," he said. "Bad for the planet. Mom wouldn't want that."

As Spock and I walked up to the gate, I tied my sweatshirt around my waist. Since he didn't have any money, I purchased two orange tickets that said TICKET on them from a thin old man in a wooden kiosk. He flattened out two dirty dollar bills before handing them to me as change along with my halves of the tickets. "There's gonna be a raffle." His voice floated from the shadows behind the chicken wire. "So keep your stubs. It's good you got two tickets. Next."

When we walked through the gate, I was momentarily stunned by the flashing lights and mechanical music of the carnival rides. Children screamed as they slid along the seats of the Tiltawhirl, screamed at their parents for more rides, or screamed in frustration in front of the snow cone vender. I hadn't been around so much motion and noise since I worked the annual sixth grade field trip to the chocolate factory. I felt light-headed. "Perhaps you need some refreshment," Spock said and I realized my hand was pressed to my forehead.

"No," I tried to say, but his dark eyes stared back at me. "No, you couldn't buy me a soda anyway." I tried to laugh. "You don't have any money."

I staggered forward, down past the row of games where every challenge seemed to require hand-eye coordination and offered something fuzzy and supposedly soft as a reward, past the carousel and the kiddie rides. I tried to start a conversation with Spock to distract me from all the insane pings and whizzings, but my mouth dried up and my words got lost, until we reached the end of the carnival section and I paused to take a breath at the amphitheater entranceway. To cover my confusion, I asked Spock how things worked in the future with no money. He told me there were plenty of resources in the galaxy for all sentient life to share. When I questioned if all parts of the universe were so enlightened, Spock remarked that, unfortunately, many portions of the galaxy still engaged in monetary trade and other barbarisms.

"Oh jeez, Spock. Come on. I smell burning engines. The derby must have started." Although, I knew he didn't like to be touched, I pulled on his arm a little, but he didn't move and I could tell he was forming a question. We stood outside of the open-air amphitheater with people strolling past, while the smell of fried doughnuts blended with exhaust. Engines roared and tires screeched in the distance.

"Do you also engage in employment for monetary funding?" he asked.

"Spock," I said. "All the good seats in the bleachers will be taken."

"You have not answered my question."

"Yes, yes. I work." I kicked at the gravel. "I have some time off is all."

"I have not observed your employment and have been here approximately two of your weeks. Perhaps you could explain."

"Spock, I told you." I started walking so he would follow. "My parents died. School gave me time off. That was May, now it's June and I have summers off anyway."

His stride matched mine and he leaned in to talk. "You have not explained your situation in such detail."

I told him that I taught physical education to middle school students who didn't go to school in the summer. But I got the end of May off too because my parents died in a car crash and my principal thought I needed some space. I smiled and added, "Not like outer space, but time alone." I explained how my principal told me to take a leave of absence because she didn't think I was dealing with things very well—thought I was shell shocked or something, and I explained how I was surprised she used those very words: "shell shocked." Spock didn't seem to understand, but I didn't want to bother explaining, so I told him how she gave me this card for a psychiatrist, who asked what I thought other people thought of me. Can you imagine? I asked Spock, and he replied that no, he could not imagine. The psychiatrist wanted to know if I was worried about what was happening to my relationship with my best friend Joanie. I told the psychiatrist that a person who lost both parents shouldn't have to be worrying about other people. I never went back.

"Humans in my time engage in elaborate ceremonies to commiserate the death of a fellow being," Spock said. "Perhaps other people wanted to worry about you."

"Well, my brother came down from Oconomowoc, but he didn't stay. He's busy living in his yurt, being all organic and shit." And for a moment, I no longer saw Spock standing sedately in front of me. Instead, I imagined my brother as he would be at that moment, making red sauce from his early tomatoes, pushing his long hair out of his eyes with the back of his hand and not noticing when some dark, loose strands accidentally fell into the pot. His food always had something extra in it—a strand of hair clinging to the inside of a pasta bowl or yarn fuzz from one of his hand-knit sweaters floating in the soup. He couldn't see beyond the organic goodness of his food to observe rules of general hygiene, and when some of the sauce bubbled over onto the white enamel stove, he'd keep stirring. The sauce would bake onto the warm stove, harden, and he wouldn't even reach for a sponge. Then he'd look through his Plexiglas window, start humming a little ending tune, turn off the burner, and head out for some weeding before dark. He could sing while driving a car or hiking up hill, but he always hummed at the end of a project, not during it—make organic red sauce, hum, clean the bathroom with useless biodegradable soaps, hum, knit a sweater, hum. I could even hear him laying out a tune, as he grabbed his tools from his trunk and headed out into the garden that surrounded his round home—wading through his organic plants, shuffling past the remaining tomato clusters that leaned onto cornstalks, stepping between the soybean and zucchini plants, sticking his fingers deep into the earth to touch the hairy roots of forgotten potatoes, falling to his knees to let the tears come. He would be thinking of Mom in her garden and Dad mowing the lawn. Grieve, then hum. Weed, then hum. His garden didn't have clear demarcations, but his movement through time always did. I wondered if he was thinking of me.

Standing just inside the amphitheater, I turned to tell Spock, "My brother's weird. He can't live at our house because the lawn has pesticides, so he's up north in his year-round tent. You'd think he'd want to be with his sister after our parents died. You'd think he wouldn't want to be alone right now." I started walking as the summer sky began to fade into the white of early evening.

"The memories concerning your family had intrigued me," Spock said, and I stopped at the base of the wooden bleachers.

"You saw my family in the mind meld?" I was shocked. "So why ask?"

"I needed you to interpret your memories." His head tilted slightly and he grasped my father's old jacket in his left hand.

Before I could reply, I heard the announcer's voice blasting out of the metal speaker fifteen feet above our heads. "Ladies and gentlemen! You are about to witness the strength that has carried your children for years! Now, in early retirement, these school buses still yearn for the chance to prove their metal . . ."

"Let's go, Spock," I said, not wanting to interpret more memories for him or even demand he return them. "Let's go watch the derby, get some metal, then get off this stupid planet."

Spock followed me up the wooden steps and into the middle level of the bleachers, where we sat down. When I was young, my father took me to this derby every year. We quickly learned that if you sat near the top, you might have a better view, but clouds of exhaust congregated at that height, so the middle was best. My mother and brother came with us the first year, then stayed home after that—probably sitting in the garden contemplating the stars and possibilities of cosmic life. Without saying anything, I knew they enjoyed the quiet of the backyard more than the noise of Dad and me screaming and cheering for trucks, old vans, school buses, and anything that would crash over and over again. Me and Dad. We wanted action, burning oil, the sound of metal crushing metal.

Down in the oval arena, school buses circled, beeping and revving their engines, till there was equal space between them on the dirt-packed floor that had earlier been filled with jumping horses, prize pigs, and men tying themselves into harnesses to pull as many tractors as they could. Now it was school bus time. The fleet of school buses circled menacingly, then began slamming into each other. Sometimes five buses were in the ring at the same time and it became a tag team thing with two buses joining forces to topple another by both ramming its side. Other times, there seemed to be so many buses in the ring they couldn't drive forward without smashing into each other. At one point, after we'd been there for about half an hour, there were only two buses in the ring and they turned toward each other, increased their speed, and crashed engine to engine in the center. The metal folded and crunched with such a familiar thigh-buckling, bone-twisting sound that I was surprised to hear a sustained ringing afterwards, like a bell made out of school bus metal sounding deep and clear, till it wiped out my vision of Spock and the people cheering for their favorite buses. Suddenly, all I saw was my parents' car in the drainage ditch and the highway barrier bent where the other car crumpled into it. Then I heard the voice of the policeman who'd been standing next to me when I went to the morgue to identify the bodies. I heard him say the driver would be punished to the full extent of the law, so I didn't need to worry. Full extent of the law, and he added something about how we got to take care of these drunk drivers. I saw my parents under those white sheets—just strange lumpy bodies until the coroner on the other side of the glass pulled at the edges to show my father's face, purple and bent somehow, and then my mother's.

The smell of auto exhaust enveloped me, and for a moment I didn't know where I was. I heard someone say "daughter" in a calm voice. "Spock?" I said tentatively. "Dad?"

"Daughter." I recognized Spock's monotone voice. "I am concerned that these school buses will be completely destroyed." I focused again as two school buses drove away from each other. More people were crowding into the bleachers and they were cheering too loudly for me.

"Ladies and gentlemen," the announcer's voice started up again. "These two warrior school buses separate from the battle for a brief moment, returning to their corners of the ring, beaten and bruised, but not conquered!"

"Spock, there's a couple of rounds." I tried to remember what he had asked. "Plenty of school bus metal."

"Will they be completely damaged?" he asked me.

"No." I waved my hand at him and tried to take deep, diaphragm breaths. "The engines won't last that long. See," I pointed as two buses started toward each other from their corners of the ring and crashed head-on again. "They only go like fifteen miles per hour and mostly aim for the engines which give out before the rest of the body."

"Fascinating," he said as the buses squealed into reverse before hammering each other again. One bus slammed into the other's side so hard, it rocked back and forth and then fell over. The remaining bus started a victory lap around the ring that was cut short when its engine caught on fire. Both drivers scrambled out—one through his window—and ran for the protective shed at the far end, while three men dragged fire hoses into the ring and doused the fire. "See, they have some safety precautions here, and that one still standing has a good body."

By the time the minibuses were circling the arena, my hands were shaking again. I thought to hand Spock a five and ask him to go get us some sodas, but my mouth was too dry to ask, and I couldn't always see him there next to me, as if my peripheral vision were fading and I couldn't stop myself from staring straight ahead at crash after crash of yellow school buses. Finally I couldn't take it anymore, so I turned directly to Spock, and told him we needed to go, but the bleachers had become so crowded by then with cheering fans, that I wasn't even sure how to get to the aisle where the steps were. I didn't know if I could move forward, so I stood awkwardly on the wooden plank with my arms out for balance for some reason, till a guy behind me said loudly, "Are you going anywhere, miss? Maybe you could sit down."

"I can't . . ." I started to say and then remembered how Martin and I used to shimmy under the bleachers when we were young. I squatted down on the wooden plank, then slid under the seat and onto the complex set of bars before swinging to the dirt floor in the shadows beneath. I landed, knees bent to take the stress.

Spock landed next to me, pulled my arm, and said, "This way."

"No, Spock," I said. "No, I think the exit is that way. I need to get out of here."

"We need metal," he said and I had to agree with him. He started a cautious jog away from the exit, down the long row under the bleachers, bending his head down every ten feet at the cross beams. I stayed close behind him, feeling my heart pound. When we reached the far end of the bleachers, he surveyed the sheds and cement barns ahead of us, searching for the school buses.

"Spock, I think they bring them over there—behind the monster trucks." I pointed to where a tow truck was dragging a dented school bus past large 4×4's gearing up for their sprint into the ring. He scanned the area in front of us for anyone protecting the school buses, suddenly looking more dangerous than he did fiddling with wires in my basement, or peering over paper menus in confusion. Crouched there under the bleachers, looking for the battered school buses, he seemed almost animal-like, powerful, adept at espionage, hungry for school bus metal. I leaned in next to him to study the dusty spaces between cement barns being lit by orange fluorescent lights high above the ground that sputtered on automatically as the sky slid into darkness. His eyes searched for shadows, mentally mapping a dark path to the buses—cross to the overhang on the sheep barn, then twenty feet to the side of a truck parked to unload hay, then a sprint to hide behind the gas pumps near the crumpled buses, waiting for their last ride to the dump. Spock bent his knees, searched the ground at his feet, and grabbed a large stone. "What are you—" was all I got out before he hurled the stone an impossible distance to strike a lamppost. It exploded in a brief spurt of light and smoke before leaving the space in front of us in darkness.

"Now," was all he said before we ran, crouched and low, as one being across the dusty gravel surface. We stopped with our backs pressed to the cement barn and I realized his hand was on my arm, melting through my sweatshirt, leading me into the safety of the next shadow. He no longer had my father's jacket. We ran again.

The next morning, I woke with a dusty taste in my mouth and tried to hang onto a dream about school buses flying above the cornfield at the end of my street. My digital clock radio blinked at 7:02 AM, so I pulled the damp sheets away from my legs, stood up to search my bedroom floor for some clothes, and forced my legs into a pair of dirty jeans. Then I remembered I had left Spock working in the basement, the night before. He had already cut the school bus metal piece to fit into his communication machine and was fiddling with some circuits to make the thing work. He told me when it was operational, he would contact his ship, which had gotten stuck in some other time as it always seemed to do, and then his shipmates would come to this time, pick us up, and head into the future again. Spock just needed to amplify his transmitter to adapt for multiple time waves. It was interesting at night, but in the morning I felt dried out. My palms smelled like the metal bars below the bleachers and my eyes itched. I tucked my Packers nightshirt into my jeans, pulled my hair into a messy ponytail, then made a quick mental list of what I would bring with me into the future: the necklace my parents gave me for my bat mitzvah, the sweater Martin knitted even though it was too small, a ceramic bowl from Joanie, my basketball jersey. I wondered how much Spock would let me bring, so I walked down the hall to his room to see if he was up.

I knocked lightly on the hollow door. When there was no response I opened it slowly, saying, "Spock?" but he wasn't there. His daybed was pushed together and his clothes from the night before were folded in perfect squares and sitting on a corner at the end of the bed. The green Packers hat lay on top with its emblem glaring up at me.

"Spock?" I said again to the empty room, thinking that he too had left without letting me say goodbye.

I felt a few hot tears streak down my face. I repeated his name one more time, then ran down the hall, slammed open the basement door, and padded down the cold, cement steps. On the last step, I realized the light was already on and Spock was hunched over his communication machine on the folding table next to the dryer. I stopped at the last step and he turned. "I have already contacted my ship and am waiting for them to adjust the transporters."

"Oh, Spock." Looking at him there in his uniform, without my father's hat, made me feel more lonely, like I was prepared to miss him.

"My captain has been informed that you will be joining us."

Suddenly, the machine crackled and buzzed. The yellow metal piece Spock cut from the side of the bus rattled against a metal clip attached to my old hard drive and a spark flashed, bright and hot, then was gone. "Spock," a strange voice came through clearly. "We've got the transporters set and are locking down your coordinates. Are you and the young lady ready?"

"Are you prepared to leave?" Spock asked me, but I couldn't respond, so he pressed a button and spoke at his machine. "Mr. Scott, we require a few minutes."

"Right. Scott out" came back. My knees felt weak. I leaned on the wall and slid down to sit on the last, cold step.

"Are you unwell?" Spock asked but all I could do was shake my head. "You are crying."

"Spock, I thought you'd left without me."

"I agreed to take you with me."

"I know, but I was afraid." A sob came up through my chest and made a sucking noise as I tried to stop it.

"I am preparing for us to transport together as we agreed. I would not leave you alone."

"I know," I said, feeling guilty that I had doubted him. "I know, but . . ."

Although he waited attentively for me to finish my sentence, all I could do was stare at the floor and then at him. "Do you remember what I have explained concerning the transporter device?" he asked.

"Yes," I said obediently.

"You will not be harmed, although the sensation may feel odd to you." I nodded. "Are you prepared to leave?" he asked.

"No," I said feeling my hands begin to shake. "I can't go." The machine buzzed again.

"Do you require more time to prepare?"

"No, Spock. That's not it. I don't know . . . I can't go into space."

"Then I must leave without you," Spock said.

The voice from the machine interrupted us. "Mr. Spock, are ye ready for transport?" Spock looked at me for permission.

"You can go now, Spock." He raised a hand with his middle fingers separated, which I recognized, from his memories, as his planet's special greeting. I raised my hand too. "Live long," I said.

"Next year in Jerusalem," he said. Then he pressed a button on his communication machine and turned slowly into floating diamonds that sparkled and hummed in my basement before fading completely into silence.

By the end of July, I started jogging again on the high school track. Joanie must have seen me from her window, because she came over with vegetables from her father's stand and made me eat salad. When I said I really wanted to see Martin, she told me to drive up there. I should have driven up there weeks ago, but I started crying and told her I didn't want to drive. I was afraid. So she dumped her tape collection straight from her passenger seat to the driveway, shoved me in her car, and drove me up to Martin's place herself. He was so happy to see me, he started plucking vegetables the minute we pulled in the driveway and almost had a meal planned by the time we stopped the car. We sat in his garden a while before we went inside to cook vegetarian style, and then Joanie drove me home. The next weekend she drove me up again and after that, I could drive myself.

I also started reviewing the new health curriculum for school and called my principal to let her know I was ready to come back in the fall. I told her I was doing well, but I didn't tell her that sometimes memories rush out of nowhere and take over my mind. It's not a bad experience, but it's not something I'd tell my principal. If I sit on the front steps shucking corn, I sometimes see my father out on the gravel next to the road, trying to get the mower to start, or I hear my mother pulling the car into the garage, shouting for help with the groceries as soon as she opens the door. I can't explain how much I miss them. Other times, I shut my eyes and visions flood back from places I have never been—satellites, strange space-ships, rooms filled with odd equipment, but then the memories swirl around and I see the Vulcan desert, stretching out into the horizon. In the distance, Spock walks towards me in robes that flap in the dusty wind, and it's always a relief to see him.

Under the Roof

Kate Wheeler

Moist, lead-lemon Bangkok dawn: Miss Bi Chin's Chinese alarm clock goes off, a harsh metallic sound, like tiny villagers beating pans to frighten the dragon of sleep. She opens her eyes and sees a big fire ant crawling up her yellow mosquito net; feels how the black earth's chill has penetrated her hipbones. At first she does not know where she is.

Tuk-tuks, taxis and motorbikes already roar behind the high garden wall; but the air is still sweet, yesterday's fumes brought down by the dew. She has slept outside, behind her house, under the sal tree. All around her lie pink, fleshy blossoms, fallen during the night.

She lies still on her side, allowing last night's trip to Dom Muang airport to bloom in her mind, seeing the American monk stalk from the barrier, his brown robe formally wrapped to form a collar and tight scroll down his right arm. Straight out of Burma. It delights her to remember his keen, uncertain look as he scanned the crowd for her unfamiliar face. Then she waved, and he smiled. On the way home, the taxi driver charged them only half price.

She heaves up to sitting; the monk, who is standing now at her screened upstairs window, sees her hips' awkward sideways roll, her hands pressing the small of her back. Both of them have the same thought: the body is a heap of suffering! The monk steps back quickly, lest Miss Bi Chin catch him gazing out the window—worrying about what will become of him out here in the world. As he moves into the shadow, he suddenly realizes that the worry itself is the world's first invasion, and again he is struck with gratitude for his robes. Having to be an example for others protects me, too, he thinks. It works from the outside in, the way forcing yourself to smile can make you feel happy.

Miss Bi Chin rolls up her straw sleeping mat and hurries into the house with it under her arm. Her bones ache, but she takes joy in that. Why should she rent a hotel room when she can sleep for free in her own back yard? It's not the rainy season. She will earn great merit for helping the monk to sleep as the rules require, under a roof where there is no woman. By now he must have completed his morning meditation.

In her mind she sees the Thai monks going for alms food right now all over the city: hundreds of them in bright orange robes, bare feet stepping over broken glass and black street garbage. They shave their heads only on full moon day, they have TVs and they seduce American tourists. They don't care if the tourists are women or men. Thai people crave too much for sense pleasures. Miss Bi Chin would not donate so much as an orange to Thai monks; she saves her generosity for the good, clean monks trained in Burma.

As she lights the gas under the huge aluminum teakettle, the old man comes shuffling into the dark kitchen. He pulls the light cord, searing the room with jerks of blue fluorescence. "Why do you cook in the dark, Chinese sow," he says in Malay. He is her mother's second husband's brother and lived off the family for years in Penang. Now he has come here to torture her and make her life miserable.

"Shh," she says, motioning with her head. The American monk sits cross-legged at a low table in the next room. His eyes are downcast and a small smile curves his lips. Beautifully white, he resembles the marble Buddhas they sell in Rangoon.

"So what? He doesn't understand me," the old man says. "Why don't you bring in a real man for a change? You'd be a lot less religious if you were satisfied." And I'd be happier living here, he thinks, if she were a normal woman, not lost in pious dreams.

His words roll off her mind like dew from the petals of a white lotus. "You will go to all the hells," she predicts. "First the hot and then the cold."

The old man laughs. "I am Muslim. Will I go to the same hell as you and your rag-wrapped *farang*? I am waiting for my breakfast." He walks in and shows all his teeth to the American monk. "Goo mornin sah!"

"Hey," the monk says. "Thanks for the bed. I slept great."

The old man can only nod. He doesn't understand English. Miss Bi Chin bites her tongue, deciding it is better for the monk's peace of mind not to know it was her bed that he slept in. Of course, she moved it into the sewing room.

This American monk is the favorite of the Rangoon abbot, Miss Bi Chin has heard. He's been in intensive meditation for three years, completing two levels of insight practice and the concentrations of the four heavenly abodes. But the monastery's friend in the Department of Religious Affairs lost his position in November, and the monk's last visa renewal application was rejected. He has come to Thailand to apply for re-entry into Burma; approval will take at least three months, if it comes at all. Conditions in Burma are unstable; the government has had to be very strict to maintain order, and it does not want too many foreign witnesses to its methods. Recently, they changed the country's name to Myanmar, as if this would solve its problems.

If the monk cannot return, the abbot may send him back to America to found a monastery. The monk has not been told. The streams of defilements are strong in the West: all the American monks that the abbot has known disrobe soon after they go home, so they can enjoy sense pleasures. Ideally, the monk should stay in Burma a few more years; but the abbot hasn't worn robes all his life to forget that the world is not ideal. This monk is addicted to pondering, a common Western vice, but he has a devoted heart, and his practice has been good. Pork should fry in its own fat; the American devotees cry out for a monastery. This monk may be the perfect candidate.

The abbot sees no reason to make a decision yet. He's asked Miss Bi Chin, the monastery's great supporter, to report on the monk's behavior: whether living unsupervised in capitalist Bangkok becomes his downfall.

Seeing him wait for his food, so still, Miss Bi Chin has no worries. She's studied his face, too, according to Chinese physiognomy. A broad forehead means calm, the deep lines at each side of the mouth mean kindness.

"Breakfast for you." She kneels at the monk's side, offering the dishes from a cubit's distance, as the Buddha prescribed. The monk touches each plate and she sets it on the table. Wheaties, instant Nescafé with condensed milk, sliced mango, lemon cookies from England, and a bowl of instant ramen noodles.

He hasn't seen such food in three years. He smiles in gratitude at Miss Bi Chin and begins eating.

Miss Bi Chin sits on one side with her feet tucked behind her and her hands in the respectful position. Rapture arises in her mind. She has helped Western monks before, and she knows they do not do well on the diet in Rangoon—too much oil and hot pepper. This monk is bony, his skin rough. She will buy chicken extract, milk powder, and vitamins for him, she will take early lunch hours to come and cook his lunch: monks eat no solid food between noon and dawn.

She stops her ears against the sound of the old man, slurping in the kitchen like a hungry ghost.

The monk wipes his mouth. He has finished everything except the noodles, which remind him too much of Burmese food. Miss Bi Chin notices. She'll reheat them for herself with fish paste; the monk's future breakfasts will be entirely Western.

Because the monk is American, he sometimes feels unworthy of being bowed to and, living on donations, guilty about the extent to which he has learned to enjoy such treatment. Miss Bi Chin, for example, is not rich. She works as a secretary at American Express, and says she refused promotion twice so that she can feel free to neglect her job when monks need help. He'd like to thank her for the food, for everything she is going to do for him, but this is not allowed.

If he were still a carpenter, he'd build her a kitchen countertop; as a monk, example and guidance are the only returns he can offer—they're what she expects, he reminds himself, slipping again into the Asian part of his mind. Her donations bring her merit. She supports what I represent, the possibility of enlightenment: not me specifically.

He clears his throat. "Where did you learn such good English?"

"Oh! My mother sent me to a British school in Penang."

"And you speak Burmese, Thai, and what else?"

"Malay, Cantonese, a little Mandarin."

The monk shakes his head. "Amazing. You're one smart lady."

Miss Bi Chin laughs in embarrassment. "I am Chinese, but my family moved to Malaysia, and we had to learn all the languages on the way. If you had my same *kamma*, you would know them, too."

"Listen." The monk laughs. "The abbot did his best to teach me Burmese." It's hard for him to imagine that this woman is also a foreigner here.

"Better for you," Miss Bi Chin says promptly. "For a monk it is most important to maintain virtue and concentration. Learning languages is only worldly knowledge. The Burmese won't let you alone if they know you can speak. When I go to meditate at Pingyan Monastery, I have to hide in my room." She laughs.

The monk smiles, charmed. Faith makes Miss Bi Chin glow like a smooth golden cat; yet her black eyes sparkle wickedly. He will have to be careful to see her as his older sister, or even as a future corpse.

He'd be surprised to know that Miss Bi Chin thinks of herself as ugly. As a child, her mother would tweak her arm hairs and say, "No one will marry you, Black Dog. Better learn English so you can feed yourself." True, no Asian men want Miss Bi Chin, but the reason may not be her skin—there are plenty of married women as dark. No, she is too well educated, too sharp-tongued, and most of all too religious. From her own side, the only Asian men she is interested in are celibate, monks. She had a long relationship with an American, Douglas, the heir to a toy fortune who does business in Bangkok and Singapore. He smokes Dunhills in a holder, and sponsors the publication of Buddhist texts. Younger than she, he left her a year ago for a glamorous twenty-year-old Thai. She still sees him sometimes at Buddhist meetings, drawling his reactionary opinions. How she ever was involved with him is a mystery to her.

Now she cries, "What is there in this world worth talking about? Everything is only blah, blah, blah. I must go to work now and type meaningless reports so that I can sustain my life and yours. I will come back to cook your lunch. Please use my house as you wish. I have many Buddhist books in English. The old man will not bother you."

She shuffles toward the monk on her knees, to remove the plates. Not to introduce the old man as her uncle is one of her secret acts of revenge.

How terrible my life would be without monks, she thinks.

The monk paces slowly up and down Miss Bi Chin's unfurnished living room. His body feels soft and chaotic among the sharp corners, the too shiny parquet, the plastic flowers under a tinted portrait of his abbot, the most famous teacher in Burma. This photograph shows the abbot's terrifying side, when his eyes, hard and sharp, pierce into each person's heart to lay bare its secret flaws. The monk prefers his tenderness, eyes that make you want to fall over sideways.

This is the first day in three years the monk has not been surrounded by other monks, living the life called "pure and clean as a polished shell": its ten precepts, 227 rules, daily alms round, chanting at dusk. The monastery wall was like a mirror facing inward; beyond it was another barrier, the national boundary of Burma. He often used to speculate on what disasters could be happening in the outside world without his knowing. Meanwhile, cocooned within the walls, the discipline of the robes, and the fierce certainties of his teacher, the monk's mind grew dextrous, plunged into nothingnesses too subtle to remember. He was merely left with a yearning to go back to them; now ordinary happiness feels harsh and coarse.

Outside, traffic roars like storm surf. What a city! He was a different man when he passed through on the way to Rangoon, drank a Singha beer at the airport bar, defiantly toasting his future as a renunciate. Even then he'd been shocked by Bangkok—everything for sale: plastic buckets, counterfeit Rolexes, bootleg software; and of course the women, dressed as primly as third-grade teachers, hoping a client will choose to marry them.

Burma may attack your health, he thinks, but Bangkok will suck you to your doom.

What if his visa is denied?

Will he disrobe? His civilian clothes are even now in a suitcase in the monastery's strong room: they must be eaten up by mildew. He's not ready to go back home as a shaven-headed, toga-wearing freak. No way would the abbot let him stay and practice under a Thai, not down here where they've got monks running around claiming to be reincarnations of Gotama the Buddha. There's a Burmese center in Penang, which Miss Bi Chin supported before she moved up to Bangkok; but she said last night it's near a huge highway and so is unsuitable for the absorption practices; plus, she added confidentially, the head monk in Penang hates Westerners. She ought to know: he's her cousin. If I get sent to Penang, the monk thinks, I'll be able to practice patience for about two weeks and then I'll be out of the robes. I was never a lifer, anyway. Or was I?

I know this is only a form.

For sure, he isn't ready just yet to lose the peace, the certainty of being a monk; nor to be separated from the abbot, his teacher: the only man on earth, he's often told himself, he truly, deeply respects. And loves.

He catches himself planning to sneak across the border at Chiang Rai and run up to Rangoon through the forest with help from Karen insurgents. Bowing three times at the abbot's feet. Here I am. In his mind the abbot laughs at him and says, Peace is not in Burma or in Bangkok. Peace comes from dropping one's preferences. That is why we beg for our food, we take what is given.

The monk stops in front of the abbot's portrait and makes the gesture of respect, palms together.

He feels the world stretching out around him. I'm here, he thinks; suddenly he's in his body again, feeling its heaviness and insubstantiality.

He can even feel the strengthening effect of the milk in the Wheaties he just ate. Conditions in Thailand are good for healing the old bod; he can make it a project. In the States he ran and did yoga fairly regularly; in Burma he never exercised. He was never alone, and people would gossip if they saw him in an undignified posture.

Carefully he spreads his sitting cloth, a maroon-and-orange patchwork square, on the straw mat where he ate breakfast; now he lies flat on it, easing the bunched muscles of his shoulders. Slowly he raises his legs to vertical, letting the small of his back flatten against the cool straw. His sacrum releases with a loud pop.

He tucks the skirt of his robe between his knees and raises his buttocks off the ground, until he is in full shoulder stand, the queen of poses, the great redistributor of psychic energy. His mind flies, faster than light, to Vermont.

He's lived as if he'll never go back to where people know him as Tom Perkins, a carpenter and the more or less unreliable lover of Mary Rose Cassidy, who still lives in Brattleboro, where she's a partner in a cooperative restaurant. She's known he would ordain ever since they came East together in seventy-three. They were both moved by the calm faces of monks they saw; but only he had that realization at the great dome of Borobudur in Java. Tapped it, and said, "Empty. That's it! There's nothing inside." Mary Rose saw in his face that it was a deep moment for him. After coming home, they learned to meditate together at a center in western Mass. She kept saying the tradition was sexist and stifled your *joie de vivre;* Tom wondered if she did it only to keep him from getting too far away.

And she didn't expect him to be gone this long. He's written her four letters saying: my practice is getting deep, it's fascinating, I want to renew my visa.

He should've broken up with her. A year ago he knew: but it seemed cruel to cut her off by mail, and more appropriate as a monk to be vaguely affectionate, vaguely disconnected, than to delve into his past and make a big mess. He halfway hoped she'd lose patience and break up with him herself; but she says she's had no other lover since he left, and she sends a hundred dollars every other month to the monastery treasurer for his support. It's more than enough.

She would have stopped sending money. He would've had to be supported entirely by the Burmese. God knows they have little enough to spare. Think what his plane ticket to Bangkok would have cost in kyat. Four months' salary for the average worker, even at the official rate; at the black market rate, the real value of Burmese money: three years' salary.

He lowers his legs as slowly as he can, feeling unfamiliar pulls in his belly and chest.

He turns to look out the large front window—the old man is staring in at him. He's been sweeping dead leaves off the cement courtyard. He wears ancient blue rubber thongs and a checked sarong; his fine-skinned purplish breasts sag over his ribs. His gaze is clouded and fierce, an old man's rage. The monk has assumed that he is some sort of servant, a trusted retainer of Miss Bi Chin's; he didn't quite take the old man into consideration. Now, this stare rips away all barriers between them.

Lying on the floor, his robes in disarray, he's Tom again, for the first time since he ordained.

With as much dignity as he can muster, he gets to his feet and goes out the back door, into the tiny walled garden where Miss Bi Chin slept. The old man has swept the pink sal flowers into a pile. The fresh ones look like parts of Mary Rose; the decaying ones, black and slimy, remind him of things the abbot says about sensuous desire. He watches one blossom fall, faster than he'd expect. It's heavy, the petals thick as blotting paper. He picks it up, rubs one petal into bruised transparency.

I should call Mary Rose while I've got the Thai phone system, he thinks. I need to tell the truth.

Now he wishes he'd studied the rules, for he doesn't know if using the phone would break the precept against taking what is not given. It's a subtle thing, but how impeccable does he have to be? Miss Bi Chin offered her house, but then steered him into her library. She surely expects to do all his telephoning. Surprising Mary Rose with an overseas collect charge isn't too monkly, except that she still considers him her lover. The irony of this is not lost on him.

Well, it's ten P.M. in Brattleboro. If he waits until Miss Bi Chin comes home it'll be too late, and what's more, she'll overhear everything: the phone is in the kitchen where she'll be cooking lunch. He walks around the corner of the house and asks the old man's permission to use the phone.

The old man waggles his head as if his neck had lost its bones. He says in Malay, "I don't understand you, and you don't understand me!"

The monk decides that this weird movement contains some element of affirmation. In any case, his mind is made up.

As he watches his hand travel toward the phone, he remembers the abbot talking about the gradations of defilement. Desire shakes the mind. The body moves, touches the object, touches it, causing the object to move. When he touches the receiver, he picks it up quickly and dials.

"Tom?" The satellite transmission is so clear, Mary Rose sounds like she's in the next room. "Oh, it's fantastic to hear your voice!"

When he hangs up, an hour later, he feels sick—he can't help imagining her expression when she gets the phone bill. Yet he has to admit, he's intensely alive, too, as if he'd stuck his fingers in a socket, as if someone had handed him a sword.

He thinks: Maybe this will create a vacuum that my visa will rush into.

He goes up to Miss Bi Chin's sewing room and closes the door. Cross-legged on his sitting cloth, he tries to cut off all thoughts of Mary Rose so he can send loving-kindness to the abbot, his benefactor. At first tears come, his body feels bludgeoned by emotion; but then his loving feeling strengthens, the abbot's presence hardens in his mind. Suddenly he and the abbot are welded together, a bond tighter than Krazy Glue. The monk's lips curve up: here there is no grief.

Miss Bi Chin and the old man are eating dinner, chicken and Chinese cabbage in ginger sauce; the monk is upstairs reading a list of the Twenty-Four Mental States Called Beautiful.

"Your monk talked on the phone for two hours," the old man says slyly. "He put his feet above his head and then pointed them at the portrait of Pingyan Sayadaw."

It is not true that the monk pointed his feet at the portrait, but as soon as the old man says so, he begins to believe himself. He's tired of having monks in the house, tired of the prissy, superior way his step-niece behaves when these eunuchs are about. What good do they do? They live off other people, beg for their food, they raise no children. The old man has no children either, but he can call himself a man. He was a policeman for six years in Malaysia, until a bullet lodged near his spine.

Miss Bi Chin pretends he does not exist, but he pinches her bicep, hard.

"Ow!" she cries, and jerks her arm away. "I *told* him he could use the house as he pleased." Too late, she realizes she shouldn't have descended to arguing: it causes the old man to continue.

"Well, he did that. He only waited for you to leave before changing his behavior. I think he's a very loose monk. He wandered up the stairs, down the stairs, examining this and that. Out into the garden to stare at the sky and pick up flowers. Then he got on the phone. He'll be poking in the refrigerator tomorrow, getting his own food."

"You just hate monks."

"Wait and see," the old man says lightly. "Have you noticed his lower lip? Full of lust and weakness."

Miss Bi Chin lowers her face until all she can see is her bowl of soupy cabbage. The old man is her curse for some evil deed in the past. How he abuses her, how he tries to poison her mind! She tells herself that the old man's evil speech is a sign of his own suffering, yet he seems to cause her more pain than he feels himself. Sometimes she enjoys doing battle with him—and she has developed great strength by learning to seal off her mental state so that he cannot infiltrate. This strength she uses on different occasions: on a crowded bus when an open sore is thrust beneath her nose, or when her boss at American Express overloads her with work. At other times the old man defeats her, causes her defilements to arise. Hatred. Fear. A strange sadness, like homesickness, when she thinks of him helpless in the grip of his obsessions.

She could never kick him out. Crippled, too old to learn Thai or get a job, how would he survive in Bangkok? And he does make himself useful, he tends the garden and cleans the floors and bathrooms. Even more important, without him as witness, she and her monks would not be allowed to be in the same house together. The Buddha knew human nature very well when he made those rules, she thinks.

Washing up, she hears that the old man has turned on his TV and is watching his favorite talk show, whose host gained fame after a jealous wife cut off his penis, and he had it sewn on again.

"Why do you have to watch that!" she scolds at his fat, unresponsive back.

She goes up to the sewing room in a fury, which dissipates into shame as soon as she sees the monk reading. The light from the window lies flat and weak on the side of his shaven head. His pallor makes him look as if he has just been peeled; her ex-lover Douglas had a similar look, and it gives her a shiver. She turns on the yellow electric lamp so he will not ruin his eyes and leaves the door wide open, as is necessary when a monk and a woman are together in a room.

"Hello, sister," he says. The edges of his eyelids feel burnt by tears; Miss Bi Chin notices redness, but thinks it is from ill health.

She begins to speak even before she has finished her three bows. "Please instruct me, sir, I am so hateful. I should practice meditation for many years, like you, so I can attain the *anagami* stage where anger is uprooted forever. But I am tied to my six sense doors, I cannot become a nun, I must live in this world full of low people. I think also, if I quit my job, who will support you monks when you come to Bangkok?"

As she speaks he takes the formal posture, and unconsciously sets his mouth in the same line as the abbot's in the portrait downstairs. Usually when someone bows to him, the beauty of the ancient hierarchy springs up like cool water inside him. Today he'd like to run from this woman, bunched up on the floor, getting ready to spill out her hot, messy life.

But he has to serve her, or else why give up Mary Rose?

"I'm not *anagami*. I'm just an American monk." He waggles his head from side to side, trying to look cheerful, maybe even throw her off track.

"You are so humble!" she says, looking up at him with eyes tormented and devoted as a dog's.

Oh my God, he thinks. Mary Rose. He forces himself to go on. "I understand your wish to renounce the world. Look at me, I left behind a very good woman to do this. I don't regret it," he adds quickly.

She thinks, he should not be talking about his woman; and then: who was she? He must have loved her, to look so regretful even after three years.

"Of course not. Monks enjoy a higher happiness," she says.

"But you don't need to be a nun to purify your mind. Greed, hatred, and delusion are the same whether you are in robes or not. Don't be hard on yourself. We all get angry."

"I am hard because hatred is hard." She says something in Pali, the scriptural language. But he can tell she's relieved, she's heard something that has helped her. She goes on more softly, "Sometimes I want to strike out against one person."

Miss Bi Chin feels a great relief as she confesses this, as if a rusty pin had been removed from her flesh.

"You'll also hurt yourself." The monk regrets his occasional cruelties to Mary Rose. Once, feeling perverse, he called her a cow, only because he knew she was sensitive about her big breasts. The word, the moment, the look on her face, have come back to his mind hundreds of times. And today she said that he wasted three years of her life, that he is a coward, that he insulted her by not speaking sooner.

"I know! I know!" Miss Bi Chin falls silent.

The monk tries for a better topic. "Who's the old man you have living with you? He gave me quite a look through the window."

He has the psychic powers, Miss Bi Chin thinks. "You've guessed my enemy. My step-uncle. My mother sent him to me. I cannot get rid of him." She picks like a schoolgirl at the hem of her dress, hearing the old man's mocking voice: "If you don't have the guts to throw me out, you deserve whatever you get."

The monk sees her face go deep red. That horrible old man! He sees him staring in the window again, his rheumy, cruel eyes. I'd better be careful though. Maybe they've slept together. You never know, when two people live in the same house.

"Every personal relationship brings suffering," he says cautiously.

"Better to live alone if one wants to free the mind," Miss Bi Chin quotes from the admonitions of the abbot. "Should I ask Uncle to leave?"

"Um, any reason why you can't?"

"Why not!" She giggles. She is not so much planning to kick out the old man as letting herself fall just a little in love with this monk. He is so breezy and American, like a hero in the movies; yet he has much wisdom. "Well, he has to stay here until you get your visa, because you and I would not be able to be in the house alone."

The monk smiles uncertainly. "I may not get a visa."

"Of course you will. You have good *kamma* from practice."

"Yet we never know when our *kamma* will ripen, do we. Good or bad."

They both nod slowly, looking into each other's eyes.

"What will you do if you can't go back?" She really wants to know; and it gives her a thrill to talk about this, knowing that the monk is ignorant of the abbot's intentions. Perhaps she'll report the answer to Rangoon.

"I'll try to remain in equanimity."

"That's a good answer for the abbot, she thinks, but it's not enough for me. She extends herself: "Would you like to go back to your country and begin a monastery?"

"Oh, no," he says lightly.

"Why?"

"I have no interest in making others follow rules. I'm not a cop, basically."

"Don't you miss your home?"

"Yes, but . . ."

"I should have offered you to use the phone. Maybe you want to call your parents."

"I've already used it. I hope that's all right."

A shock runs down Miss Bi Chin's back. So it's true what the old man says. "You used the phone?"

"It was sort of urgent. I had to make a call. I did it collect, there'll be no charge to you. Maybe I should call Penang and confess?"

"Oh, no, no, no," she says. "I offered you to use my house as you wished. Who did you talk to?"

"Well, my old girlfriend from the States," and he finds himself describing the whole situation to Miss Bi Chin, confessing. Recklessly, he even says he might have postponed breaking up because he was afraid to lose a supporter. Because Miss Bi Chin is a stranger—and because she knows so much more about being a monk than he does—he feels compelled to expose his worst motivations. If forgiving words come out of these quietly smiling lips, he'll be exonerated. If her face turns from gold to brass and she casts him out, that will be right also.

As he speaks, Miss Bi Chin feels she is walking through a huge house, where rooms open up unexpectedly one after another. When she was in the British school, she had to read a poem about the East being East and the West being West, and never the twain shall meet. This is not true: she knows she can follow this monk far into his labyrinth, and maybe get lost. For him it is the simplest thing to say: the old man is bad, ask him to leave. But for himself, it is so complicated. In one room of his mind he is a monk, and using the phone was an error; in another room calling was the right thing to do. First he is too strict with himself, then he lets go of the rules altogether.

Should she tell the abbot? What would there be to tell? That the monk used the telephone after she had already given permission? That he was impatient to perform a wholesome act?

Miss Bi Chin has a water heart: it flows in uncontrollable sympathy toward the monk. She knows he was afraid to be forgotten when he went so far from home. That is the true reason he did not cut off this girlfriend, but he is a man and cannot admit such kind of fears.

She interrupts. "If I were Mary Rose," she tells him, "if Mary Rose were Burmese, or even Thai, as soon as you ordained, her reason for sending money would change. She would donate to earn merit for herself. You would then feel grateful but not indebted. You would feel to strive hard in meditation, to make her sacrifice worthwhile. And I think that your mind is very pure and you are trying to perform your discipline perfectly, but because you were in intensive practice you do not know in precise way what monks should do and not do when they are in ordinary life. Therefore I think you should spend your time here studying the texts in my library and learning what you did not learn."

At the end of this speech she is breathless, shocked to hear herself admonishing a monk.

"Thank you," he says. "That's great." His face is broken up by emotion; he looks as if he might weep.

Now, she thinks, should I tell the abbot that his monk is falling apart?

Not yet. It's only his first day.

Within a week it is obvious to the old man that Miss Bi Chin and the monk are in love. "I should call Rangoon," he teases Miss Bi Chin. They both know he will never do so, if only because he will not know how to introduce the topic to a person he has never met. But the threat gives him power over her. Miss Bi Chin now ignores it when he fails to sweep or clean the bathrooms. The monk sometimes sweeps away the blossoms under the sal tree; the old man stands at the window of the sewing room, enjoying this spectacle. Miss Bi Chin made loud remarks about the toilet but ended up cleaning it herself. She also serves the old man his meals before going in and prattling with the monk. The old man has never felt so satisfied since he moved in here two years ago.

Miss Bi Chin, too, is happy. These days she feels a strange new kind of freedom. She and the monk are so often in the same room—he sits in the kitchen while she cooks, and otherwise they go to the sewing room and study or meditate—that the old man has fewer opportunities to pinch or slap. In the past she even feared that the old man might kill her, but he seems calmed by the monk's purity of mind.

The monk actually wants to know what she thinks about this and that. When she comes home from work, he asks respectfully how her day was, and they discuss her problems. He sees so clearly people's motivation! Then they go to the texts and try to look behind the surface to see what is the effect on the mind of each instruction, always asking, what did the Buddha intend? When they disagree with each other, they don't let each other off the hook: sometimes their arguments are fierce, exciting.

"Why do Burmese and Thais call each other lax?" he asks one night. "The Thais accuse the Burmese because Burmese monks will take stuff straight out of a woman's hand. Then the Burmese turn around and say Thais drink milk after noon. Can't they see it's all relative?"

"You don't know Thai monks," she replies hotly. "Won't take a pencil from a woman's hand but you don't know what they take from her other parts."

"Yeah, but not all Thai monks are bad. What about those old Ajahns up north? They live under trees."

"Insects also live under trees! Burmese get good results in their meditation, in the city or in the forest. You better listen to your own teacher to know what is right. No one reaches enlightenment by saying 'it is all relative.'"

His lips go tight, but then he nods. "You're right. Pingyan Sayadaw says Western skepticism makes people sour inside. You stay at the crossroads and never go anywhere. 'I don't believe this path, I don't believe that path.' Look at the power of mind he has."

"Such a strong monk," she says joyously.

No man has ever yielded to her thinking; it fills her heart with cold, delicious fire.

"Incredible," the monk replies, his pale eyes shining.

Then they meditate together, and her mind becomes so fresh. She feels she is living in the time of the Buddha with this monk. When the old man accuses her of being in love, she retorts that she's always been in love with the truth.

The monk is getting healthy, eating Wheaties and doing yoga every day. Miss Bi Chin often asks if there's anything he needs, so he can say "A bottle of vitamin C" or "A new pair of rubber thongs" without feeling strange. He feels pleasantly glutted with conversation. In Burma, he never sifted through his thoughts, the idea was simply to take in as much as he could. At Miss Bi Chin's, he can sort, digest, refine. She helps direct his studies, she's almost as good as a monk; and in turn he's helping her figure out how to deal with daily life.

A perfect marriage would be like this, he thinks, except sex would screw it up with expectations. At times his feelings for Miss Bi Chin do grow warm, and he tosses on her bed at night; but there's no question in his mind about these feelings. They'll go away at the third stage of enlightenment. Having left Mary Rose, he feels more like a monk than ever. It's good exercise for him to see Miss Bi Chin's loveliness with detachment, as if she were a flower or a painting in a museum. When she exclaims that she's ugly and dark, he corrects her, saying, "All self-judgment reinforces the ego."

He writes the abbot every week. "Living in the world is not as difficult as I feared, but maybe this is because Miss Bi Chin's house is like a monastery. I am studying in her library. Her support is generous and her behavior is impeccable. She sleeps outside, under a tree. One night it rained and she went straight out to a hotel."

The monk has only two fears during this period. One is that the embassy of Myanmar will not approve his visa. The other is that it will. When he thinks of Pingyan Monastery, he remembers its discomforts: diarrhea in the Rains, in April prickly heat.

I have my head in the sand, he thinks; or, I am asleep between my mother's breasts.

Miss Bi Chin is showing the monk a large bruise on her upper arm. It is the blue-black of an eggplant and has ugly spider's legs spreading in all directions around it. If he were not a monk, he'd touch it gently with his finger.

"I can't believe he does this to you," he says. "Don't you want him to leave? I'll be there when you say it. I'll stand over him while he packs."

"If he left, you'd have to go also. Where? He'd come back the next day. He was in the narcotics squad in Malaysia. I don't know what he would do. I think something. He has his old gun in a sack. It is broken but he could fix it."

Hearing about the gun makes the monk's stomach light with horror. Human beings, what they'll do to each other. Imagine a rapist's mind, a murderer's. Delusion, darkness, separation. How has Miss Bi Chin let this evil being stay in the house? How has she been able to live under the roof with such fear?

"He's got to go. If I'm still here he'd be less likely to bother you," the monk says. "I'm an American, after all. He'd get into big trouble if he pulled anything. Now that I can use the phone"—he laughs a little—"I can get on the horn to the embassy."

"But he is my step-uncle," Miss Bi Chin says weakly. She doesn't really want the monk to be proposing this. He sounds not like a monk, but like any other American boasting about his country's power.

"Look," the monk says. "I'll sleep outside. I'll eat outside. I'll stay outside all day. We can leave the gate open so people in the street can see us. I think this thing with the old man is more serious than you think. We can work out the monk part. The Patimokkha only talks about sleeping under the same roof and sharing a secluded seat, and in the second case a woman follower has to accuse me of seducing you."

"Okay. I'll get you a tent," Miss Bi Chin says.

"No way. You didn't have one," the monk retorts. "Why don't you find him a job instead?"

The old man knows something is wrong: when he comes back from the soda shop at six, the two of them are sitting in the patio chairs side by side, facing the gate, like judges.

"You must leave this house tomorrow," Miss Bi Chin says. The monk's face bears a look the old man knows is dangerous: determination mixed with terror, the look of a young boy about to pull a trigger. In a flash he calculates his chances. The monk is not healthy and probably knows no dirty fighting tricks, but is thirty years younger and much larger. He must have been a laborer once, his arms and chest show signs of former strength; and he's been exercising every day.

The old man makes his hands into claws. "Heugh!" he cries, and fakes a pounce: only six inches forward. Of course, the monk leaps to his feet. The old man laughs. This kind of thing brings vigor in old age.

"So you lovebirds want privacy?" he says. "Watch out I don't take the kitchen knife to you tonight. I'm old but I'm still a man."

"I got you a job guarding the Chinese market," Miss Bi Chin says. "They'll give you a room in back." She was surprised how easy this solution was, once the monk opened her mind to it. Now she owes the monk her happiness. Her house suddenly seems vast; her nostrils fill with the sweet scent of sal flowers, as if the old man were a fire emitting sharp smoke which had been put out.

The next morning she calls a taxi. All of the old man's clothes fit into a vinyl sports bag, but his TV is too big to carry on the bus.

Watching him go, old and crooked, out the gate, Miss Bi Chin feels bad. Her mother will not understand. Loyalty is important in a family. She's been living in this house with the American monk, who tells her about the youth revolution when everyone decided their parents were wrong. This was the beginning of meditation in America; even the monk got interested in spiritual things at first because of drugs.

Now the monk meets her in the garden. He's smiling softly. "Remember the test of loving-kindness?" he asks her. "You're sitting under a tree with a neutral person, a friend, and an enemy, and a robber comes and says you have to choose who he'll kill?"

"I remember," she says dully. "I refuse the decision."

The abbot's letter has taken a month to arrive. He writes through an interpreter: "My son in robes: I hope you get a visa soon. I am glad you keep good morality. Miss Bi Chin says you are suitable to be a teacher and your speeches are refined. I praise her for sleeping outside, but maybe it is your turn. Be careful of desire and pride, and do not think too much."

Miss Bi Chin has sent several glowing reports by aerogram. Now she is not so sure. She hates sleeping in the bed, she feels she has lost her power in some obscure way. She and the monk are trying hard to keep the rules. They avoid being in the house together, but there are too many robbers in Bangkok to leave the street gate open, so they rely on the fact that they're always visible from the second floor of the elementary school across the street. They joke about their debt to one small, distracted boy who's always staring out the window; but this is almost like a lovers' joke. Miss Bi Chin feels disturbed by the monk's presence now. When he looks at her with soft eyes she feels nothing but fear. Perhaps he is in love with her. Perhaps he thinks of her at night. She dreads his quick buzz of the doorbell, announcing he's coming in to use the bathroom.

One morning at work she types an aerogram to the abbot. It makes her happy to see the clarity of the Selectric type on the thin, blue paper. "I worry about the American monk. We're alone together in my compound ever since he asked my uncle to leave my house. We try to keep his precepts, but I want your opinion. He spoke about his personal life. There was a woman in love with him at home. He said the precepts are relative, what is most important is the effect on the mind."

She tosses this in her Out box and watches the office boy take it away with her boss's letters to America. For some reason, she thinks of the gun lying in the bottom of the old man's sports bag as he walked off down the street.

"Don't you want to go home and teach your own people?" Miss Bi Chin asks again.

She's brought up this subject many times, and the monk always says no. But today his answer surprises both of them. With the old man gone, things have fallen into place. He likes sleeping under the sal tree, the same kind of tree under which the Buddha was born and died. Monks did this in ancient times, dwelt at the roots of trees. He loves its glossy green leaves and pink flowers; he imagines it is the tradition, and at night his roots go down with its roots, deep into the black soil. "Maybe I'm in a special position," he says. "Americans are hungry for truth. Our society is so materialistic."

"You don't want to be an abbot though," Miss Bi Chin says. "It is too tiring."

"I don't know," he says. "If my teacher asked me to I guess I'd have to go."

"Well, an abbot wouldn't be staying here alone with me, I can tell you that much," Miss Bi Chin bursts out.

That night he lies awake under the sal tree. Why didn't she tell him sooner, if it wasn't proper for him to stay? Is she in love with him? Or is she teaching him step by step?

He remembers the rules he's studied. Miss Bi Chin herself could be the woman follower who accuses him of seduction. Even though they haven't shared a seat, it's possible that if she brings a charge against him, there'd be no power in his denial, since they've been rather secluded together in her compound.

He understands something new: a monk's life has to be absolutely clearcut. These rules were made for a reason. Ambiguous situations mean murky feelings, subterranean defilements. Again he can thank Miss Bi Chin for showing him how to go.

Whether he gets his visa or not is unimportant. He must go to Penang and live with other monks and prepare for the responsibilities of the future. If the Penang abbot hates Westerners, it's probably because he's never met one who appreciates the robes. If it's difficult to be there, it will develop his mental strength.

He imagines himself a monk in old age. The stubble on his head will grow out white, he'll laugh at the world like his teacher. Old Burmese monks are so very much alive, he thinks.

Their bodies are light, their skin emits a glow. If you can feel free amid restrictions you truly are free.

In the morning he is quiet as Miss Bi Chin serves his breakfast on the front patio.

He is red now, not white: his blood is healthy. He keeps his eyes down as she hands him the plates. Wheaties, mango, cookies, Nescafé. Talk to me, she cries inside herself. She stares at his mouth, seeing its weakness and lust. It shows the part of him she loves, the human part.

She hasn't slept all night, and her mind is wild as an untamed elephant. Maybe the abbot will get her aerogram and make the monk disrobe. He'll stay in her house and live a lay life; they can make love after having their conversations. I could call the embassy and withdraw his visa application, she thinks. What is the worst that could happen? That I am reborn as a nun who'll be seduced by a foreigner?

At last she understands the old man, who said once he didn't care if *kamma* punished him in a future life, as long as he got to do what he wanted to in this life. How can we know who we'll be, or who we were? We can only try to be happy.

Frightened by her thoughts, she watches the monk bite a U shape out of his toast. He's being careful, moving stiffly as a wooden puppet; and he must have shaved his head this morning, it is shiny, hairless, there is a small bloody nick over his ear.

She knows she won't be able to cancel his visa application; and that her aerogram will result, not in the monk's disrobing, but in his being sent to Penang and forbidden to stay with her again. She hasn't accused him of downfall offenses, or disgusting offenses. So he'll go on with his practice and maybe become an abbot, or a fully liberated arhat. At least I was full of wholesome moral dread when I wrote that aerogram, she thinks. When the benefits come, I can enjoy them without guilt. Such as they'll be. Someone will give me a new Buddha image, I'll be offered another promotion and refuse it. She laughs under her breath. Is this what I was looking for when, as a young girl, I began running from temple to temple and lost all my friends?

"What are you laughing about," the monk says,

"I was thinking of something."

"I have to go to Penang," he says. His voice is low and hollow, so neither of them is sure he's actually spoken.

"I am sorry my house is unsuitable for you to stay."

"No, it's been wonderful to be here. But I need to be around other monks. I feel like we've been playing with the rules a little bit. We're in a gray area."

He smiles at her coaxingly, but she refuses the bait. "I'll buy you a ticket to Penang this afternoon."

How can she be so cold suddenly? She's pulling him out, compelling him to make the contact. "I'll miss you. Don't tell the abbot, okay?"

"If there is no lust, a monk may say he will miss."

"I want this to stay between us," he says. "You've been like my sister. And teacher. I'm sorry I have to go."

"Every personal relationship brings suffering," she says, but she's smiling at him, finally, a tiny complicated smile he'd never believe could appear on her golden face. Suddenly he sees her eyes are full of tears, and he knows he'll be lonely in Penang, not only for Miss Bi Chin but for Mary Rose, who also fixed things so he could ask for whatever he wanted.

Nothing changes, the old man thinks. There they are, sitting in the front courtyard, talking about nothing. He's standing at the jalousied window of the third-grade classroom, during the children's first morning recess. He knew this was the time. Bi Chin doesn't go to work until nine-thirty.

He woke up in a rage that drove him to the bus stop, still not knowing what he would do—something: he has his pistol in the sports bag. He had it fixed, and late at night he practices shooting at bottles floating in the *khlong* past the Chinese market. His aim isn't what it was. The pistol is heavier than he remembered, his eyes are bad, his arm shakes.

He knew an idea would come when he was actually standing at the window, and it has. He sees one thing he can succeed at. He can at least hit that plate glass window, shatter it behind their heads. He sees it clearly, bursting, shower of light. They run inside and slam the door. Miss Bi Chin in her terror grabs the monk. Ha! They find themselves embracing. That'll be a good one, if he doesn't miss and blow one of their heads off.

Happy with this solution, the old man begins to hum as he unzips the sports bag. The gun's cold oil smell reaches his nostrils, making him sharp and powerful. He's always wanted to break that window, he doesn't know why. Just to see it smash. I'm an evil old man, he thinks. Good thing I became a cop.

Selected Bibliography

Allen, Roberta. 2002. *The Playful Way to Serious Fiction.* New York: Houghton Mifflin Company.

Atchity, Kenneth. 1986. *A Writer's Time.* New York: W. W. Norton.

Bauer, Douglas. 2000. *The Stuff of Fiction: Advice on Craft.* Ann Arbor: The University of Michigan Press.

Booth, Wayne C. 1961. *The Rhetoric of Fiction.* Chicago: University of Chicago Press.

Borges, Jorge Luis. 1973. *Borges on Writing.* Ed. Norman Thomas di Giovanni, Daniel Halpern, and Frank MacShane. New York: E. P. Dutton.

Boswell, Robert. *The Half-Known World: On Writing Fiction.* 2008. Saint Paul, Minnesota, Graywolf Press.

Bowen, Elizabeth. 1950. *Collected Impressions.* New York: Alfred A. Knopf.

Brande, Dorothea. 1981. *On Becoming a Writer.* Los Angeles: Jeremy Tarcher.

Burroway, Janet. 1992. *Writing Fiction,* 3rd ed. New York: HarperCollins.

Carlson, Ron. *Ron Carlson Writes a Story,* 2008. Saint Paul, Minnesota, Graywolf Press.

Dillard, Annie. 1989. *The Writing Life.* New York: Harper and Row.

Fitzgerald, F. Scott. 1978. *The Notebooks of F. Scott Fitzgerald.* Ed. Matthew J. Bruccoli. New York: Harcourt Brace Jovanovich.

Forster, E. M. 1954. *Aspects of the Novel.* New York: Harcourt Brace & World.

Gardner, John. 1984. *The Art of Fiction.* New York: Alfred A. Knopf.

Hall, Donald. 1979. *Writing Well.* Boston: Little, Brown.

Hemingway, Ernest. 1984. *Ernest Hemingway on Writing.* Ed. Larry W. Phillips. New York: Charles Scribner's and Sons.

Hills, Rust. 1987. *Writing in General and the Short Story in Particular.* Boston: Houghton Mifflin.

Hughes, Elaine Farris. 1990. *Writing from the Inner Self.* New York: HarperCollins.

Hugo, Richard. 1979. *The Triggering Town.* New York: W. W. Norton.

James, Henry. 1947. *The Art of the Novel.* Oxford: Oxford University Press.

————. 1947. *The Notebooks of Henry James.* Oxford: Oxford University Press.

————. 1948. *The Art of Fiction.* New York: Charles Scribner's and Sons.

Kennedy, Thomas E. 2002. *Realism and Other Illusions: Essays on the Craft of Fiction.* La Grande, OR: Wordcraft of Oregon.

Koch, Steven. 2003. *The Modern Library Writer's Workshop.* New York: Random House.

Lodge, David. 1992. *The Art of Fiction.* New York: Penguin Books.

Macauley, Robie, and George Lanning. 1987. *Technique in Fiction,* 2nd ed. New York: St. Martin's Press.

Madden, David. 1988. *Revising Fiction: A Handbook for Fiction Writers.* New York: New American Library.

Minot, Stephen. 1988. *Three Genres,* 4th ed. Englewood Cliffs, NJ: Prentice-Hall.

O'Connor, Flannery. 1969. *Mystery and Manners.* New York: Farrar, Straus & Giroux.

O'Connor, Frank. 1963. *The Lonely Voice: A Study of the Short Story.* Cleveland: World Publishing.

Pack, Robert and Jay Parini, eds. 1991. *Writers on Writing.* Hanover, New Hampshire: University Press of New England.

Plimpton, George. 1953–1989. *Writers at Work: The Paris Review Interviews*, 8 vols. New York: Viking Penguin.

———. 1989. *The Writer's Chapbook*. New York: Viking.

Reed, Kit. 1982. *Story First: The Writer as Insider*. Englewood Cliffs, NJ: Prentice-Hall.

Shelnutt, Eve. 1989. *The Writing Room*. Atlanta, Georgia: Longstreet Press.

Stern, Jerome. 1991. *Making Shapely Fiction*. New York: W. W. Norton.

Strunk, William C., and E. B. White. 1979. *The Elements of Style*, 3rd ed. New York: Macmillan.

Times Books. *Writers on Writing: Collected Essays from the New York Times*. 2001. New York: Henry Holt and Co.

Welty, Eudora. 1977. *The Eye of the Story*. New York: Random House.

West, Paul. 2001. *Master Class: Scenes from a Fiction Workshop*. New York: Harcourt.

About the Contributors
of Exercises

DOUGLAS BAUER has written three novels, *Dexterity*, *The Very Air*, and *The Famous Book of Iowans*, and two works of nonfiction, *Prairie City, Iowa*, and *The Stuff of Fiction: Advice on Craft*. His most recent book is a memoir, *Prairie City, Iowa: Three Seasons at Home*. His stories and essays have appeared in *The New York Times*, *Esquire*, *Agni*, *Epoch*, *Harper's*, and many others. He teaches in the low residency MFA program at Bennington College.

JORDAN DANN is the Education Programs Coordinator for the Aspen Writers' Foundation, and creator of "Story Swap," a program she created in a collaboration with the Anderson Ranch Arts Center.

RON CARLSON is the author of eight books of fiction, most recently *A Kind of Flying* (selected stories) from W.W. Norton, and the young adult novel *The Speed of Light* (Harper-Collins). Carlson won the 1993 Ploughshares Cohen Award. He teaches writing at University of California, Irvine.

LAURENCE DAVIES edits the collected letters of Joseph Conrad. His stories have appeared in *New England Review*, *Natural Bridge*, *Mystic River Review*, *StoryQuarterly*, and *The Diagram*. He is finishing a novel, *The Cup of the Dead*, and putting together a collection of his microfictions.

Until his recent death, GEORGE GARRETT was the Henry Hoyns Professor of Creative Writing at the University of Virginia and the author of twenty-five books. His most recent were: *The Sorrows of Fat City*, *Whistling in the Dark*, and *My Silk Purse and Yours*. In 1989 he received the T. S. Eliot Award, and more recently won the PEN/Faulkner Bernard Malamud Award for Short Fiction.

A founder of *Ploughshares*, DeWITT HENRY is the author of *The Marriage of Anne Mae Potts*, *The Other Side of Silence*, *Fatherings: Reflections by Men*, and *Safe Suicide*. He teaches writing at Emerson College.

HESTER KAPLAN is the author of a collection of stories, *The Edge of Marriage*, which received the Flannery O'Connor Award for Short Fiction, and a novel, *Kinship Theory*. Her fiction has been widely published and twice included in *The Best American Short Stories*. She received a Grant from the National Endowment for the Arts in 2007. She is on the faculty of the MFA program at Lesley Univerisity and the author of the forthcoming novel, *The Tell*.

CHRISTOPHER KEANE's most recent novel is *Christmas Babies*. He is also a screenwriter and the author of *Hot Property: Screenwriting in the New Hollywood*. He teaches a graduate workshop at Emerson College in Boston.

WILLIAM MELVIN KELLEY has published four novels, including the recently reissued *A Different Drummer*, a book of stories entitled *Dancers on the Shore*, and the nonfiction book, *The Huntress*. He teaches at Sarah Lawrence.

ROD KESSLER is the author of *Off in Zimbabwe*, a collection of stories and a collection of his book reviews, *Guided Tours of Hell*. He teaches writing at Salem State College, where he is also editor of *The Sextant* and an alternating director of the Eastern Writers' Conference.

WILLIAM KITTREDGE is the author of *The Nature of Generosity,* as well as an autobiographical book titled *Hole in the Sky* and two previous books, *Owning It All* and *We Are Not in This Together.* He teaches at the University of Montana.

MARGOT LIVESEY is the award-winning author of a story collection, *Learning by Heart,* and the novels *Homework, Criminals,* and *The Missing World.* Her most recent novel is *The House on Fortune Street.* Born in Scotland, she currently lives in the Boston area and teaches at Emerson College in Boston.

ROBIE MACAULEY is the author of two novels, a collection of short stories, and two nonfiction books. His *Technique in Fiction* (with George Lanning) has been reissued by St. Martin's Press.

CAROL-LYNN MARRAZZO is a teacher and writer who lives in New Hampshire. She received an MFA from Vermont College in Montpelier and is currently completing a collection of stories titled *Closing Time.*

CHRISTOPHER NOËL is the author of the novel *Hazard and the Five Delights,* the memoir *In the Unlikely Event of a Water Landing,* and a collection of short stories titled *A Frail House.* He also adapted the children's story *Rumplestilskin.* Noël teaches in the Vermont College MFA program.

Poet and memoirist DAVID RAY's twenty-first book is *When,* a collection of poems. He is the author of, among others, *Not Far from the River* and *The Maharani's New Wall and Other Poems. Sam's Book* won the Maurice English Poetry Award in 1988. Ray is a professor of English at the University of Missouri–Kansas City, where he teaches both fiction and poetry workshops.

FREDERICK REIKEN's first novel, *The Odd Sea,* won the Hackney Literary Award and was selected by *Booklist* and *Library Journal* as one of the best first novels of 1998. His second novel, *The Lost Legends of New Jersey,* was a *New York Times* "Notable Book of 2000" and *Los Angeles Times* "Best Book of the Year." His short fiction has been published in *The New Yorker.* He teaches at Emerson College in Boston.

KEN RIVARD recently finished a screenplay about a mother and son coping with the son's learning disability and is currently working on a collection of stories and a novel. He teaches a fiction workshop in the Harvard Extension Program.

THALIA SELZ has contributed fiction to many magazines, including *Partisan Review, Antaeus, Chicago,* and *New Letters.* Her stories have been anthologized in *Best American Short Stories* and *O. Henry Prize Stories.* She has won twenty-three literary prizes and fellowships. She teaches at Trinity College in Hartford, Connecticut.

JAMES THOMAS is the author of *Pictures, Moving,* a collection of stories, and the coeditor of *Sudden Fiction, Sudden Fiction International,* and *Flash Fiction.* He teaches fiction writing at Wright State University, where he also codirects a summer writing program for public school teachers.

MELANIE RAE THON's most recent novel is *Sweet Hearts.* She is also the author of the novels *Meteors in August* and *Iona Moon,* and the story collections *First, Body: Stories* and *The Girls in the Grass.* She teaches at the University of Utah.

Credits

Index